Building Model-based Enterprise Architecture

Implementing model-based enterprise architecture with Sparx EA, MDG, and the TOGAF Standard

Mudar Bahri

bpb

www.bpbonline.com

First Edition 2026

Copyright © BPB Publications, India

ISBN: 978-93-65897-166

LIMITS OF LIABILITY AND DISCLAIMER OF WARRANTY

To View Complete
BPB Publications Catalogue
Scan the QR Code:

Dedicated to

The soul of my mom,
who left our world,
a couple of months before this book was published

About the Author

Mudar Bahri is an independent mentor and consultant specializing in enterprise architecture. He assists architects in establishing, acquiring, and refining practical EA skills to provide decision-makers with valuable artifacts that support their decisions regarding changes to the enterprise. He advocates for enterprise architecture as a tool to bridge gaps rather than creating ones; thus, it must be straightforward, practical, and accessible to all stakeholders.

As a certified TOGAF Enterprise Architect and an expert user of Sparx Systems Enterprise Architect, he created comprehensive repositories to assist businesses in documenting their enterprise contents using interconnected artifacts, each showing a different perspective and addressing various stakeholders' needs. This includes end-to-end solution architectures, strategy maps, digital transformation strategies, cloud migration plans, application and integration architectures, Business Capability models, and business process models.

About the Reviewers

❖ **Abder** is an accomplished technology leader with global enterprise architecture and service delivery for multibillion-dollar companies. Known for his ability to engage with key client decision makers, Abder excels at eliciting key insights into business and technology challenges, pain points, and opportunities. He is an accomplished technology leader with more than twenty years of experience leading global enterprise architecture and service delivery for multibillion-dollar companies. Known for his ability to engage with key client decision makers, Abder excels at eliciting key insights into business and technology challenges, pain points, and opportunities.

He worked for firms ranging from small start-ups (such as Ten Dots) to large multinational companies (HPE, SONY, TOYOTA).

Abder earned an MBA from Keller Graduate School of Management, as well as a PhD in physics and an M.Sc. in computer science from the Free University of Brussels, Belgium.

❖ **Mark Morgan**, a 30-year submarine Navy veteran, is working for a 3rd defense contractor as a lead systems and MBSE engineer. During his Navy time, he was involved in integrated product teams for afloat platforms at various stages of their lifecycle. Mark's past and current work involves system design, architecture, and **digital engineering** (**DE**) as an output of systems engineering. His practitioner work and technical leadership in leveraging multiple DE tools and techniques continue to move engineering disciplines to the DE domain. Mark has over 10 years of teaching and curriculum development experience in electronics, program management, and systems engineering for the Navy and two universities. Along with various certifications and formal training, Mark holds a B.S. in electronics engineering, M.S. in systems engineering, and is a doctoral candidate in applied systems engineering, focusing on test and evaluation. Mark is an INCOSE CSEP member, private pilot, and amateur radio operator.

Acknowledgement

First and foremost, I want to express my deepest gratitude to my children. Your patience and understanding have been invaluable throughout this journey. Thank you for giving me the time and space to write, and for always being my source of inspiration and joy.

Thank you to all the readers for your trust in this book and its content. I wrote this book for my past self, someone who struggled to find the right resources to improve my EA practice. I hope you find it useful.

I would also like to extend my heartfelt thanks to BPB Publications. Your belief in my work and the opportunity to be part of your esteemed family have been a tremendous honor. Your support and guidance have been instrumental in bringing this book to life.

Finally, I am profoundly grateful to every person I have worked with over the past 30 years. Your contributions to my knowledge and growth have been immeasurable. Your collaboration, insights, and encouragement have shaped my career and enriched my life in countless ways.

Preface

Theoretically, an **enterprise architecture (EA)** practice does not require a tool, and it can be performed using documents, presentation slides, and spreadsheets. Practically, a successful EA practice requires a tool that combines all the produced artifacts in one place, where users can easily access and use them. The users of the EA repository are stakeholders from the various parts of the enterprise; each is interested in specific sets of artifacts to use to support their decisions. Since everything in the enterprise is connected, a change to a component can result in changes to multiple other components, which themselves can result in changes to other components. Without having all enterprise elements in a single repository, identifying the dependencies among the affected elements will not be possible. This is why EA is important as a practice, and this is why the EA repository is essential for its success.

The EA repository is a database of interconnected artifacts. It requires software to create and contain the artifacts, and it requires a framework to guide and govern the lifecycle of these artifacts, from creation to decommissioning. This book uses **Sparx Systems Enterprise Architect (Sparx EA)** as the software and uses TOGAF 10 as the framework. Sparx EA does not support TOGAF by default, necessitating the use of **Model Driven Generation (MDG)** to embed TOGAF within Sparx EA. Learning Sparx EA in general, and mastering MDG specifically, are two major achievements that you will gain by completing this book.

On the other hand, TOGAF is usually not familiar to everyone in the enterprise, which can make communicating its terminologies using plain language a bit challenging and can result in uninterested users. The effectiveness of an EA practice can be assessed by the level of users' acceptance and trust in its content. To achieve that, reference models need to be set and established, so users can visualize the results instead of imagining them. Describing what a capability map is using a capability map diagram, which depicts how a Business Capability, such as the enterprise architecture Business Capability, is easier than describing a capability map using words and definitions. Understanding TOGAF's content metamodel and setting a reference architecture using practical examples is another major achievement that you will gain by the end of this book.

Chapter 1: Introduction to Enterprise Architecture Repositories - **Enterprise architecture (EA)** involves defining and categorizing enterprise elements and their relationships to support decisions. The practice of EA has documentation as a big part of it, producing artifacts like diagrams, catalogs, and matrices that describe various views of the enterprise. As the practice of EA matures and gets more attention from stakeholders in the enterprise, the number of

EA artifacts will increase, which requires an efficient repository to maintain these artifacts and to easily access them when needed. This chapter discusses the importance of EA and the efficiency of using a repository.

Chapter 2: Sparx EA Crash Course - Creating diagrams is essential in business and IT alike as they simplify complex descriptions. Many models in the market can be used to create an EA repository. This chapter introduces Sparx EA, the chosen tool for this book, and guides you through its basics, user interface components, and creating your first diagram, making it an ideal starting point for Sparx EA beginners as well as experts.

Chapter 3: Introducing Model Driven Generation - The **Model Driven Generation** (MDG) allows Sparx EA to be extended to include frameworks that are not provided as part of the software. Users will be required to create custom MDGs to accommodate the frameworks that are not included, like TOGAF. This chapter introduces the essentials of MDGs while building example components from the TOGAF content metamodel.

Chapter 4: Advanced Model Driven Generation - This chapter introduces additional MDG techniques like shape scripts, special attributes, Tagged Values, standard connectors, and customizing diagram types, to enhance the MDG that was started in the previous chapter, and allows additional EA artifacts to be created using it.

Chapter 5: Structuring the Repository - The main purpose of the project browser is to provide a hierarchical view of the repository elements, so users can easily find what they need. The number of artifacts in a mature EA environment can contain thousands of elements and diagrams. Proper structuring is crucial to maintain users' trust and ensure the repository remains a reliable source of information. In this chapter, we will build the structure of an EA repository using the guidelines from TOGAF.

Chapter 6: Modeling Business Capabilities - Business Capabilities are crucial in enterprise architecture. For any enterprise that plans to practice enterprise architecture, the enterprise architecture Business Capability needs to be established first. This chapter will guide you in modeling the Business Capability of a typical EA practice with understandable examples.

Chapter 7: Modeling Projects - Projects are integral elements to the enterprise, linking to other elements through relationships. This chapter focuses on updating the MDG created in previous chapters to support creating project artifacts, then using the updated MDG to create the artifacts that enrich the repository.

Chapter 8: Modeling Applications - Application architecture is crucial in modern enterprises due to the dependency of businesses on technology. A reliable EA repository should include sufficient description and documentation for all the applications within the enterprise. TOGAF offers three components for modeling different abstraction levels of application architecture. This chapter will modify the MDG to enable it to create application architecture artifacts at the three levels of abstraction.

Chapter 9: Modeling Application Integrations - Data integration is crucial for meaningful business use, requiring documentation of data flows, data structures, and data transformations. This chapter will cover modeling data architecture artifacts at three levels: conceptual, logical, and physical, ensuring the repository meets the needs of all enterprise consumers.

Chapter 10: Modeling Cloud Environments - Cloud environments are considered technology environments, and modeling them should be like modeling any on-premises environment. Architects must be aware of the different definitions between the cloud industry and EA, particularly regarding services, logical components, and physical components. This chapter focuses on updating the MDG to include necessary stereotypes for technology architecture artifacts, providing sample references, and using the image library to enhance the appearance of cloud artifacts.

Chapter 11: Modeling Business Services - For a business to exist, it must provide services to consumers. Consumers are interested in the services provided, not how they are internally performed. Functions and Processes, on the other hand, describe how the business organization performs internally. This chapter will explore the similarities and differences between business services, Functions, and Processes, their interactions, and how different actors engage with them, using practical examples.

Chapter 12: Modeling Organizations and Strategies - Organization charts are commonly used to model the hierarchy of Organization Units. Organization Units, along with strategy elements, are part of the business architecture layer in TOGAF. This chapter will teach you how to model business architecture artifacts, such as organization structure, and artifacts showing the associated strategy elements to the identified Organization Units.

Chapter 13: Repository Management Processes - Maintaining a repository is an ongoing task that requires regular updates to ensure stakeholders are satisfied and trusting the quality and accuracy of the artifacts. This requires housekeeping tasks like deleting unneeded elements, changing element types, and merging duplicates. In this chapter, we will learn how to perform these maintenance Processes in Sparx EA using models built using the MDG that was developed in the previous chapters.

Chapter 14: Publishing EA Artifacts - A successful enterprise repository should be accessible to the entire organization, not just Sparx EA users. While copying diagrams to documents offers flexibility in formatting, it requires manual updates, which is inefficient for large enterprises. This chapter will teach you how to automatically generate and publish Sparx EA content using

Coloured Images

Please follow the link to download the
Coloured Images of the book:

https://rebrand.ly/d29ca6

We have code bundles from our rich catalogue of books and videos available at https://github.com/bpbpublications. Check them out!

Errata

We take immense pride in our work at BPB Publications and follow best practices to ensure the accuracy of our content to provide with an indulging reading experience to our subscribers. Our readers are our mirrors, and we use their inputs to reflect and improve upon human errors, if any, that may have occurred during the publishing processes involved. To let us maintain the quality and help us reach out to any readers who might be having difficulties due to any unforeseen errors, please write to us at :

errata@bpbonline.com

Your support, suggestions and feedbacks are highly appreciated by the BPB Publications' Family.

Piracy

If you come across any illegal copies of our works in any form on the internet, we would be grateful if you would provide us with the location address or website name. Please contact us at business@bpbonline.com with a link to the material.

If you are interested in becoming an author

If there is a topic that you have expertise in, and you are interested in either writing or contributing to a book, please visit www.bpbonline.com. We have worked with thousands of developers and tech professionals, just like you, to help them share their insights with the global tech community. You can make a general application, apply for a specific hot topic that we are recruiting an author for, or submit your own idea.

Reviews

Please leave a review. Once you have read and used this book, why not leave a review on the site that you purchased it from? Potential readers can then see and use your unbiased opinion to make purchase decisions. We at BPB can understand what you think about our products, and our authors can see your feedback on their book. Thank you!

For more information about BPB, please visit www.bpbonline.com.

Join our Discord space

Join our Discord workspace for latest updates, offers, tech happenings around the world, new releases, and sessions with the authors:

https://discord.bpbonline.com

Table of Contents

CHAPTER 1

Introduction to Enterprise Architecture Repositories

Introduction

Enterprise architecture (**EA**) is a discipline that many organizations have adopted or have been motivated to adopt over the past two decades for the purpose of guiding effective change and generating value for the organization. EA is the art of defining and categorizing the elements that compose an enterprise and defining the relationships among these elements, to get useful information that supports making strategic and tactical decisions. The EA practice is all about documentation because this is what architecture in general is. Architecture is nothing but documenting designs, whether they will be used to build houses, cars, roads, software, or an enterprise. The opposite of proper documentation in the business world is the unknown, and no successful business can be based on unknowns. This is where EA becomes a very important practice.

The EA practice produces artifacts, which are diagrams, catalogs, and matrices that document the identified EA elements and the relationships between them. Each artifact describes a specific view of the enterprise, so as your EA practice matures and grows, the number of produced artifacts will increase too. This number of artifacts requires having an efficient way of maintaining them and maintaining the relationships between them. An efficient way is to have an enterprise architecture repository, a database that contains all the EA artifacts in one place.

In this chapter, we will talk about the importance of EA as a practice for any type of business, and then we will talk about the importance of making the EA practice efficient by using a repository and the approach that this book provides for building it.

Structure

This chapter contains the following topics:

- Importance of EA as a practice
- Approach for building the EA repository

Objectives

The objective of this chapter is to refresh your memory on some important topics in EA, such as why it is important, what an EA capability is, what architecture governance is, and the importance of having an EA repository. The second objective will introduce our tested approach for building EA repositories using **The Open Group Architecture Framework (TOGAF)** Standard, **Unified Modeling Language** (**UML**) notation, and **Sparx Systems Enterprise Architect** (**Sparx EA**) software tool.

Keep in mind that this chapter is not meant to teach you everything about these topics. The entire book requires that you are already familiar with the EA concept in general, the EA frameworks, especially TOGAF Standard, modeling in general, especially in UML, and some familiarity with modeling tools such as Sparx EA.

Importance of EA as a practice

EA can be used to solve small and big organizational challenges alike. The scope of the enterprise, and the detailed description of elements and relationships, will vary based on the size and the maturity of the organization and the EA team, but the concepts remain the same. EA must describe the future state, also known as the **To-Be state**, and the current state, also known as the **As-Is state**, of the enterprise. The description of the future state enables the right people to understand what must be done to meet the goals and objectives within the operating context of the enterprise. The gaps between the current state and the future state highlight what must be changed.

Changes to the enterprise can include any alteration to any element in the enterprise or to any relationship between its elements. This, for example, can include changing an application component, a technology service, or a data element. It can also include making enhancements to a business process, establishing a new role, merging two business units, introducing a new business service, responding to an external opportunity or threat, migrating to a cloud environment, upsizing, or downsizing the business, and these are only some examples. Some of these changes are minor, while some can be classified as major, but the common factor among all of them is that decision makers need to be aware of them when they occur, and they need to plan for their impact accordingly. Even a minor change can result in major impacts if not planned properly.

EA can be used for multiple purposes and for different scopes. It can be used to support decisions at strategy, portfolio, projects, or solution levels:

- When EA is used to **support strategy**, it is used to identify change initiatives and to support portfolios and programs.

- When EA is used **to support portfolios**, it supports cross-functional, multi-phase, and multi-project programs and initiatives. The architecture scope will typically include a single portfolio and will be used to identify projects, set their terms of reference, align their approaches, identify synergies, and govern their projects' execution.

- When EA is used to **support projects**, it will typically include a single project and is used to clarify the purpose and value of the project, identify requirements to address synergy and future dependency, assure compliance with architecture governance, and support integration and alignment between projects.

- When EA is used to **support solution delivery**, it will typically cover a single project or a project phase and is used to define how the change will be designed and delivered, identify constraints, controls, requirements, and finally act as a framework for governing change.

Knowing that EA can be used to cover different scopes sets our expectations for the deliverables that we can get as an outcome of the architecture work. There is a common misunderstanding among EA practitioners that EA deliverables should remain at high levels only, which is not true based on the different scopes that the EA capability covers.

EA capability

An EA capability is defined as having the ability to develop and maintain the architecture of a particular enterprise and use the architecture to govern changes. EA capability is a management concept that facilitates planning improvements in the ability to practice and deliver effective architecture. Just like any other Business Capability within the enterprise, an EA capability needs to be used by a business unit, delivered by business functions, influenced by Course of Actions, enables Value Streams, uses Business Information, and is operationalized by Processes. We will talk in more detail about EA capabilities specifically, and about modeling Business Capabilities in general, in *Chapter 6, Modeling Business Capabilities*, but until then, keep in mind that the EA capability is no different than any other enterprise Business Capability.

The role that enterprise architects play within organizations, and the type of artifacts they produce, vary based on many factors such as the size of the organization, the size of the team, the EA maturity, and the experience levels of both. Above all, it depends on the scope of the architecture development project as mentioned earlier in this chapter. At all levels, the enterprise architect can play an essential primary role in enabling cross-team communication and can ensure that the risks are clearly identified and communicated so that decisions can be made with an appropriate understanding of potential problems and difficulties. These communications are documented as architectural artifacts stored in an EA repository, so let us learn what an architecture repository is.

Defining the EA repository

As mentioned in the previous section, EA defines the elements of an enterprise and their relationships that comprise the scope of the EA landscape. These elements and relationships need to be described in the form of **architectural artifacts**. These artifacts describe multiple and different aspects of the current and target architecture, and they take the form of diagrams, catalogs, and matrices. Diagrams, also known as models, are graphical representations of elements and relationships. Catalogs are lists of elements that are usually of the same type. Matrices represent relationships between different types of elements in a tabular format.

Note: **The terms diagram and model will be used interchangeably within the context of this book.**

A single artifact is best when created to represent a single view of a specific part of the enterprise. It is usually difficult to fit the entire enterprise into one model. It will be either very complicated or difficult to read and understand, and the result in both cases is a useless diagram. Trying to tell everybody about everything is usually a bad modeling strategy because the primary purpose of modeling is to describe a complex point of view in a simple visual way. Therefore, architects should use multiple artifacts to describe aspects of the enterprise from different points of view. These discreet artifacts will have a loose or no linkage among them if they were developed separately, by different people, using different tools, and stored in different locations. Just imagine a large enterprise with about 50 architects, each following a standard and using a tool of their own convenience, and the result will be far from a useful EA repository.

For example, application architects may develop a set of models describing the application components and how they integrate. They will also develop some models describing the technology and infrastructure services that are required for the solution. At the same time, a technology architect may have developed a set of models and artifacts describing the components in a specific data center or a cloud environment, and the applications that these components will support. Each of these architects provides their view of the story. If they both use a different modeling tool or store their artifacts in separate file locations, the possibility of having a clear linkage between the application components and the technology components will be unlikely to happen. This voids the main purpose of EA, which is to describe the elements of the enterprise and the relationships between them, to know the impact of changes, and to plan to respond to them.

A unified EA repository not only serves the purpose of linking artifacts, but it also serves the reusability of the enterprise elements. It is inefficient to redescribe the enterprise every time artifacts are developed. In our previous example, the application architect and the technology architect may both end up modeling multiple elements more than once if they are working separately, because neither of them sees what the other is developing. In a large enterprise, with a large team of architects, each is responsible for modeling a specific part of the enterprise landscape; the number of redundant models and elements can be tremendous. Redundancy is always translated to inefficiency, higher cost, inaccuracy, and slower progress, which is obviously not a business success recipe.

Every produced artifact has an associated price and effort, and all approaches to modeling require trade-offs. The effort must not exceed the value gained, or else the result will be impeding the enterprise from performing effective change. Architects must trade-off between effort and value and should ensure that they are optimizing for the entire EA team, rather than personal preference. It is the architecture governance board's responsibility to tell what the desired level of details is, and what trade-offs must be made to maintain the effort vs value balance.

In a large enterprise, determining the starting point for the EA practice can be quite challenging. A traditional waterfall approach, with its sequential phases, may prove to be time-consuming. Therefore, adopting an agile approach to EA becomes essential.

Agile EA

Agile enterprise architecture is a way of building EA artifacts that involves the principles and values of an agile methodology. Agile EA aims to deliver value to stakeholders faster, respond to changing needs in the environment, and collaborate across different stakeholders and teams. Agile EA is not a specific framework or method, but rather a mindset and a set of practices that can be applied to any enterprise architecture approach. Being agile simply means being adaptive to the continuous changes to the requirements within your enterprise and being responsive with the right amount of information, at the right time, and to the right people.

Note: We are not following the Open Agile Architecture from The Open Group (https://pubs.opengroup.org/architecture/o-aa-standard/index.html), but we advise you to take a look at it.

Stakeholders within an enterprise expect the EA practice to support their decisions everywhere in the enterprise. They need you to provide them with facts and evidence, not with lectures that are full of unknown terminologies and acronyms. Product owners want their products to be out on the market as soon as possible. EA for them must help to achieve that goal and speed up that process. They will not feel comfortable adding tasks to their scope of work that they do not believe are needed just because the EA framework says so. They will not be happy if you ask them to hold their progress and wait until the EA office finishes tailoring the framework, defining Value Streams, and defining the governance model. Defining, or even just refining, all these components can keep you and the rest of the team busy for months, if not years, and stakeholders will soon perceive you as an obstacle and a risk to the project. It is a fact that you need to respect if you want to have a successful EA practice that cooperates with the rest of the enterprise.

Agile EA focuses on delivering the most essential and valuable aspects of the architecture and eliminating waste and unnecessary complexity. Having an agile culture and using agile delivery methods does not necessarily lead to products with agile characteristics. Agile delivery must balance the business value of early delivery of EA artifacts to the consuming stakeholders, and connecting to other components in the ecosystem that would add value to the produced artifacts. The key to being more practical than theoretical is setting up the scope and prioritizing your tasks to deliver useful artifacts within the available time.

After a quick refresher on EA and its importance as a practice, the next section will show you the approach that this book will provide to build an EA that works.

Approach for building the EA repository

Having an EA repository that contains up-to-date artifacts supports your mission to succeed in your EA practice and endeavor, but to establish a solid and reliable repository, you need to follow an approach, and that approach should be built on industry's best standards to take away the efforts of defining what has already been defined by experts around the globe. Building an EA repository requires having the following:

- **A methodology**: To use as a reference for the EA practice.
- **A modeling notation**: To unify the look and feel of your models across the different EA layers, and among the different team members.
- **A modeling tool**: The actual software that will be used to build the repository.

In our approach for building an EA repository, we will use TOGAF as the methodology, UML as the modeling notation, and Sparx EA as the modeling tool. This approach is based on years of practice and many successful developments of EA capabilities within organizations of different sizes, a variety of business models, different maturity levels, and distant geographical locations. There is no one right way to do EA, but this way has been tested for being practical and able to deliver results. Let us explore the rationale behind selecting TOGAF as our methodology, rather than opting for an alternative EA methodology or framework.

Using the TOGAF Standard as the methodology

When The Open Group released version 9.0 of its famous framework in early 2009, TOGAF became the most widely accepted EA framework. TOGAF provided enterprise architecture practitioners with rich content, a metamodel, a Process method, and dozens of guides and techniques to support the development journeys and to make implementing EA achievable.

TOGAF also helps in establishing an enterprise architecture capability that drives operational excellence in the management of digital products. It helps organizations manage, mature digital products, and deliver operational excellence by simplifying complexity in the digital ecosystem.

EA practitioners chose to use the TOGAF Standard as the framework to follow for many reasons. We will look at each one of them individually in the following subsections and see why more than 135,417 practitioners chose to use it and be certified in it (according to **https://togaf9-cert.opengroup.org/certified-individuals** on the date of writing this chapter).

The Open Group has provided all TOGAF versions online for free. This makes it possible for people at all levels of experience to explore, read, and learn the framework at their own pace without feeling constrained by costly subscriptions or time-limited trials. Some frameworks require paid memberships, but this is not the case with TOGAF. EA practitioners also find it very convenient to have the material online and accessible anytime, anywhere, and on any device.

Note: **Having the TOGAF Standard's online content bookmarked in your browser makes it easy to reach it whenever you need it. Here is the URL if you want to do that https://pubs.opengroup.org/togaf-standard/index.html.**

The TOGAF Standard comprises several components that constitute the framework. This discussion will begin with an introduction to three key components, starting with the content framework.

Introducing the TOGAF content framework

The TOGAF content metamodel serves as the central element of the TOGAF content framework. It offers architects a foundational structure, detailing the components of the enterprise and their interrelationships. The TOGAF metamodel, coupled with its taxonomy, provides architects with an enhanced comprehension of these elements and their connectivity.

TOGAF offers a comprehensive set of definitions for key terminology used by architects, facilitating a unified language among professionals and enhancing their communication and documentation processes. While individuals from diverse backgrounds may interpret these definitions differently, the presence of a standardized taxonomy significantly minimizes the potential for misunderstandings and disputes.

The TOGAF content metamodel is available online at: **https://pubs.opengroup.org/togaf-standard/architecture-content/chap02.html**. This resource presents the metamodel diagram, illustrating the connections between various elements. It also provides definitions for each metamodel entity depicted in the diagram. Additionally, it includes tables that suggest optional attributes for these entities and lists all possible relationships with other elements. This resource is essential for every TOGAF practitioner and will be referenced frequently throughout this book. *Figure 1.1* displays a UML representation of the TOGAF metamodel:

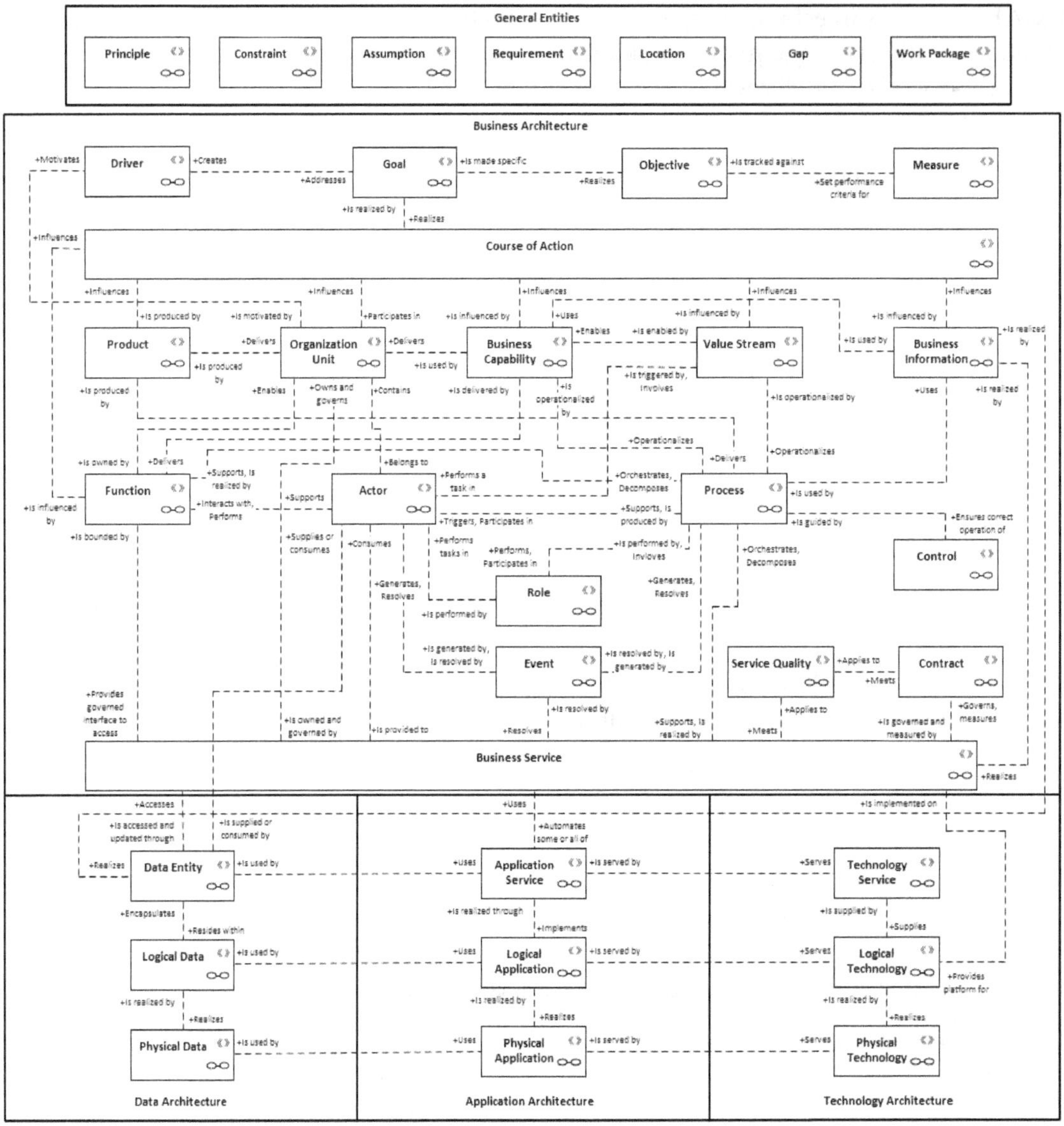

Figure 1.1: UML representation of the TOGAF metamodel

Given the size and complexity of the metamodel figure, it may be challenging to read directly from the book. Therefore, we have provided a link to the online resources for easier access. Additionally, each chapter will include small sections of the metamodel, focusing on one element at a time in a diagram, referred to as the focused-metamodels. For instance, *Chapter 6, Modeling Business Capabilities*, will present a focused-metamodel emphasizing the Business Capability element and its possible connections. Similarly, *Chapter 8, Modeling Applications*, will feature three distinct focused-metamodels, corresponding to the application service, logical application component, and physical application component elements.

Note: **Identifying, classifying, and relating the elements of the enterprise is the heart and soul of EA.**

The second key component of TOGAF is the architecture development method, or the ADM for short.

Introducing the Architecture Development Method

The **Architecture Development Method (ADM)** is a series of development phases, each with a defined set of inputs, steps, and outputs. *Figure 1.2* represents the ADM cycle in UML notation, as defined by the TOGAF standard:

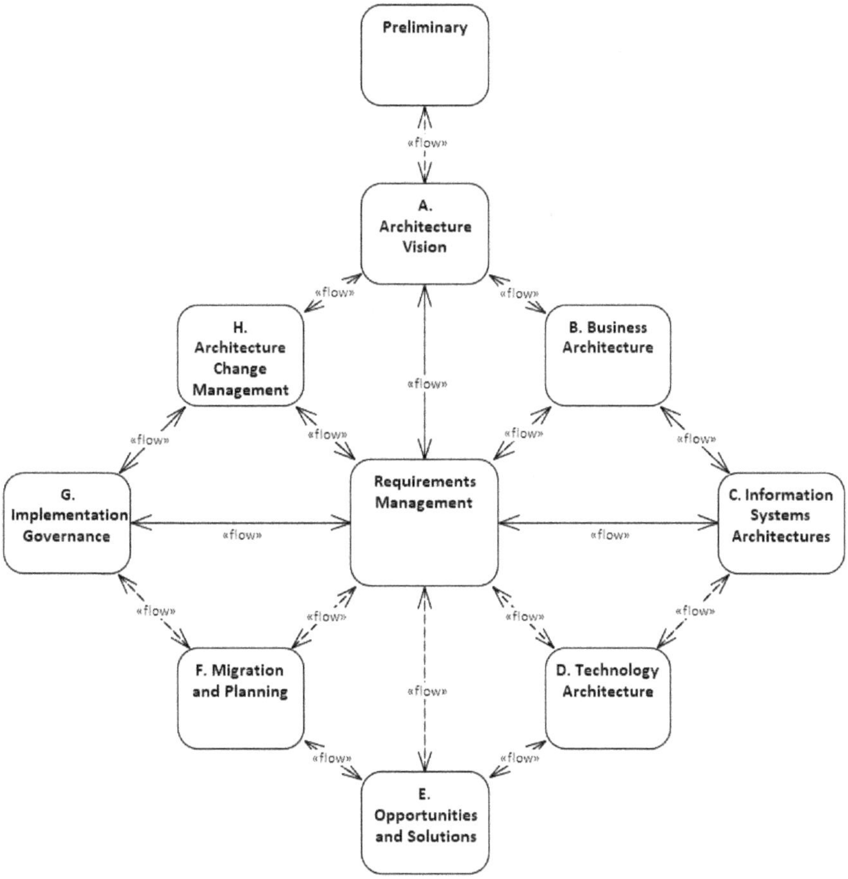

Figure 1.2: A UML representation of the TOGAF Architecture Development Method

Architects find it easy to develop architecture content by following a sequence of steps. The ADM suggests doing the architecture work in phases, and each phase has a list of inputs, steps, and outputs, so there is less confusion about what to do and where to start. The TOGAF ADM should not be misinterpreted as a linear waterfall Process model. It is a logical method that places key activity steps together for the purpose of understanding the relationship between activities and clarifying information flow. If your concern is in developing a transitioning roadmap, for example, you can jump directly to phase E, Opportunities and Solutions. The EA practitioner needs to consume the mandatory inputs and produce the mandatory outputs, and this applies to all ADM phases.

Architects coming from different backgrounds and having different experiences can all find something useful in the TOGAF Standard that they can use in their area of expertise. Architects with application development backgrounds will use the TOGAF Standard in conjunction with the software development methods they have practiced for years. Architects with management and business administration backgrounds can use the TOGAF Standard in conjunction with business process management, strategy crafting, performance and quality management, and other domains that all fit perfectly within the TOGAF content framework.

In this book, we will not incorporate the ADM into our artifact development process. Instead, we will employ the agile, demand-driven approach mentioned earlier in this chapter. It is crucial, however, to be familiar with the phases of the ADM, as they may prove useful in the future when the enterprise reaches a sufficient level of maturity to adopt them.

The third core element of the TOGAF Standard is its extensive collection of reference models, which address a variety of business and technology scenarios and offer diverse solutions for different challenges.

Introducing the TOGAF reference models

The TOGAF Standard targets to address all the issues that enterprise architects may encounter during their implementation engagements. It provides a set of reference models and methods to help architects solve common problems. These reference models and methods are as follows:

- **Architecture maturity models**: They provide techniques for evaluating and quantifying an organization's maturity in EA.

- **Architecture project management**: It is intended for people responsible for planning and managing architecture projects.

- **Architecture skills framework**: It provides a set of roles, skills, and experience norms for staff undertaking EA work.

- **Digital Business Reference Model (DBRM)**: It guides the adoption of relevant aspects of The Open Group TOGAF Standard and other related standards.

- **Government Reference Model (GRM)**: It is used to categorize and segment operational departments to operate an effective architecture function.

- **Microservices Architecture (MSA)**: It provides guidance on how the architect can use the TOGAF Standard to develop, manage, and govern MSA or any architecture where MSA is part of the scope.

These reference models can be modeled as shown in *Figure 1.3*. This figure can be considered as an EA artifact within your EA repository to guide the architects to external resources. You will learn more about this topic and how to create similar diagrams in *Chapter 13, Repository Management Processes*:

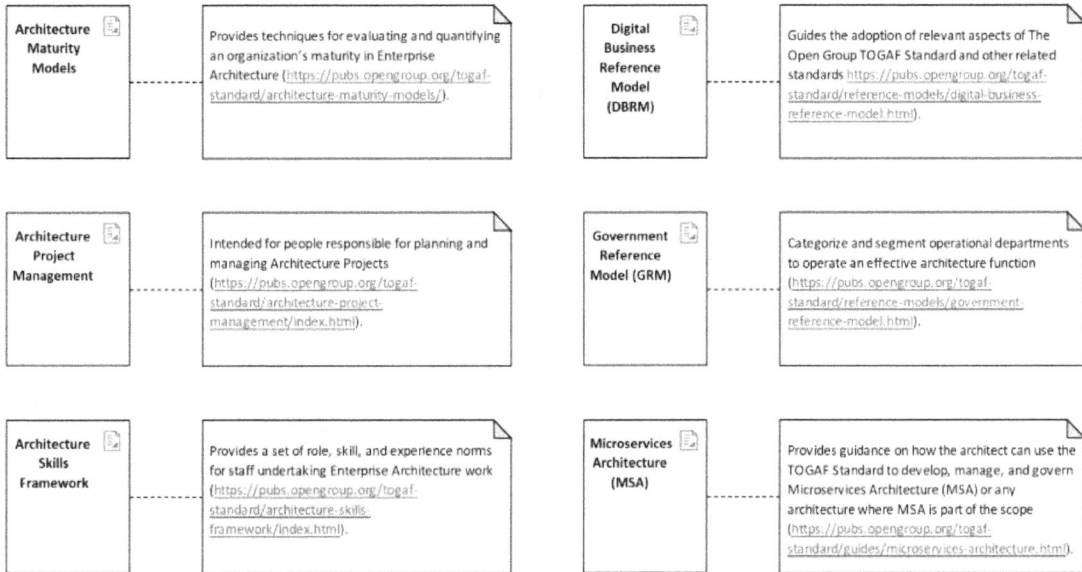

Architecture Maturity Models	Provides techniques for evaluating and quantifying an organization's maturity in Enterprise Architecture (https://pubs.opengroup.org/togaf-standard/architecture-maturity-models/).	Digital Business Reference Model (DBRM)	Guides the adoption of relevant aspects of The Open Group TOGAF Standard and other related standards https://pubs.opengroup.org/togaf-standard/reference-models/digital-business-reference-model.html).
Architecture Project Management	Intended for people responsible for planning and managing Architecture Projects (https://pubs.opengroup.org/togaf-standard/architecture-project-management/index.html).	Government Reference Model (GRM)	Categorize and segment operational departments to operate an effective architecture function (https://pubs.opengroup.org/togaf-standard/reference-models/government-reference-model.html).
Architecture Skills Framework	Provides a set of role, skill, and experience norms for staff undertaking Enterprise Architecture work (https://pubs.opengroup.org/togaf-standard/architecture-skills-framework/index.html).	Microservices Architecture (MSA)	Provides guidance on how the architect can use the TOGAF Standard to develop, manage, and govern Microservices Architecture (MSA) or any architecture where MSA is part of the scope (https://pubs.opengroup.org/togaf-standard/guides/microservices-architecture.html).

Figure 1.3: *A model showing the TOGAF Standard reference models and methods*

With more people showing interest in The TOGAF Standard, The Open Group wanted to encourage practitioners to be distinguished by becoming certified in the framework. With the increasing demand for experienced enterprise architects, becoming TOGAF certified is a desire and sometimes a requirement by employers when hiring or contracting enterprise architects. Refer to the TOGAF certification portfolio if you are interested in learning more about the certification programs (**https://www.opengroup.org/certifications/togaf-certification-portfolio**).

Having provided the rationale behind selecting TOGAF for our approach, we shall now elucidate the reasons for choosing UML as the modeling notation.

Using UML as the modeling notation

The UML was introduced for the first time in 1995 by *The Three Amigos, Grady Booch, Ivar Jacobson,* and *James Rumbaugh*. The purpose of inventing it was to unify the way that solutions are documented by providing the developers with a set of elements to use on a recommended set of diagrams. To model a specific flow of actions within an application, for example, you can use **activities** and **activity diagrams** to show the steps, the inputs, and the outputs. To model the sequence of calls between multiple application components and what data is sent and received to and from each of them, you can use **sequence diagrams**.

Note: **UML has gone through multiple rounds of revisions and enhancements, and it is currently at version 2.5.1. UML is managed and supported by the Object Management Group (OMG), which also manages several other standards like BPM and SysML. The complete UML specification can be accessed and downloaded from https://www.omg.org/spec/UML.**

It is essential to understand that UML will not be applied as-is for our EA artifacts. We intend to extend and customize UML so that we can retain the necessary aspects, such as the appearance of the elements, also known as the notation, while omitting unnecessary components for us, like UML rules and constraints. These will be substituted with rules and constraints derived from the TOGAF Standard. The next topic will provide further insights into extending UML.

Extending UML

UML was not originally created to model EA artifacts; however, UML has a very powerful feature that allows it to be extended to any new standard through **stereotypes**. This is what will be explained in detail in *Chapter 3, Introducing Model Driven Generation*, and *Chapter 4, Advanced Model Driven Generation*. The **Model Driven Generation** (**MDG**) is the way to build a metamodel into Sparx EA. These chapters explain in step-by-step instructions how to extend the standard UML elements and relationships to include the TOGAF Standard elements. Having the standard embedded within the tool that your team of architects uses will allow them to build EA artifacts in a consistent manner, governed by the EA framework of your choice, which is TOGAF in our case.

Your goals should target extending all the elements and the relationships that are defined in the TOGAF content metamodel. However, we will take it in an agile, not a waterfall approach, meaning that we will build the MDG starting with the most needed elements, then we will add more elements as we progress. If we need elements to model business processes, for example, we had better start by building the MDG starting from the Process element and the elements that are related to it, then we can expand as needed from there.

The extended elements will use the UML notation but will not enforce the UML rules and constraints. We will only use the notation or the shapes from UML, but not the entire standard. The TOGAF metamodel's rules and constraints will be built in our MDG instead. This means that if we have an element in our MDG that looks like a UML activity, it does not mean that the rules that govern it will enforce UML rules and constraints, but the rules that we will build within the MDG to enforce the TOGAF Standard.

Figure 1.4 shows how we have extended the standard UML component element into physical application component and logical application component elements from the TOGAF content metamodel, and how we extended the UML activity into application service. We have also extended the standard UML realizes relationship into the TOGAF Implements relationship.

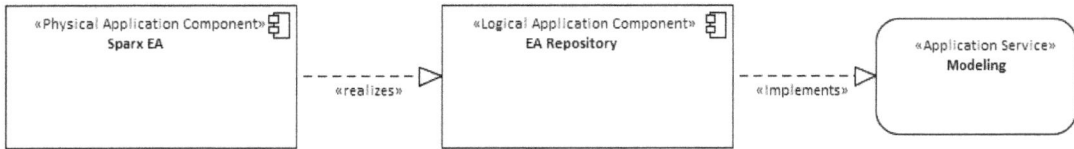

Figure 1.4: *Using extended UML elements to model EA artifacts*

We could have chosen any UML element to extend the physical application component element and not necessarily the UML component element, but it makes more sense to find the most similar matching element to reduce the learning curve for the diagrams' audience. UML elements are categorized into structural and behavioral elements. The next subsection will provide more information about these categories.

Understanding structural and behavioral elements

UML has two main groups of elements and diagrams: structural and behavioral. **Structural elements** are the components, relationships, and organization that define the static structure of an enterprise. Examples of structural elements are classes, objects, actors, and components. They are represented by a set of structural diagrams such as class diagrams, object diagrams, component diagrams, and composite structure diagrams. The relationships between elements, such as generalization, aggregation, composition, and dependency, are also considered as structural elements.

Behavioral elements, on the other hand, are the actions, interactions, and processes that describe the dynamic behavior of an enterprise. Examples of behavioral elements are activities, actions, and use cases. They are represented by a set of behavior diagrams, such as use case diagrams, activity diagrams, state machine diagrams, sequence diagrams, communication diagrams, and timing diagrams.

When we build our MDG, we better extend TOGAF structural elements from UML structural elements and extend TOGAF behavioral elements from UML behavioral elements. Although this is not required, it makes more sense to maintain the same concept of elements classification between the standard that we extend from and the standard that we are extending to. *Chapter 3, Introducing Model Driven Generation,* and *Chapter 4, Advanced Model Driven Generation,* will elaborate more in detail on building the MDG, but this was an introduction to the approach.

Another notation, such as ArchiMate, could have been used instead of UML notation. The following subsection provides reasons for choosing UML over ArchiMate.

ArchiMate vs. UML

The Open Group has created ArchiMate, a modeling language that is specialized to model EA artifacts. The reason for choosing UML over ArchiMate in this book is that UML is more common, especially among non-technical people. UML was invented in 1995, while ArchiMate was adopted by The Open Group and officially introduced in 2009. ArchiMate's notation includes a large list of shapes, with different meanings to each. The service, for example, takes the shape of a round rectangle, the function looks like a chevron, and the role is like a horizontal cylinder. ArchiMate users need to learn the meanings of many new symbols that are not widely used to be able to understand the diagrams that use ArchiMate's notation. You must keep in mind that for many enterprise users, learning something new, as large as ArchiMate's notation, is not something that they will be interested in, which makes the diagrams useless for them.

Sometimes, it is easier for us to change than to ask others to do. The resistance to EA artifacts that are modeled with UML notation could be less than for those that are modeled with ArchiMate notation. The main reason for using UML is that it has a limited set of shapes and employs stereotypes to describe different types of shapes. In UML, elements like business services, functions, and roles have stereotype labels indicating what they are in text format. This results in a lower learning curve for users to understand diagrams using UML notation, which is why it is chosen for this book. The concepts in this book will remain applicable if you opt for ArchiMate notation or another notation, but the appearance of your diagrams will differ accordingly.

After stating the reason for selecting UML as the modeling notation in our practical EA approach, we will explain why Sparx EA was selected as the tool.

Using Sparx EA as the tool

Using an EA tool is not mandatory to establish an EA practice, but it makes things easier, more efficient, and better governed when you have one. If you or your organization is not using an EA tool, it is highly advised to do so unless you are still in the very early discovery phases. There are dozens of options out in the market, and each tool has advantages and disadvantages over the others, but finding the best tool (or software in general) for your needs is an exercise that you need to do before procuring any software. This book will help you if you choose to use Sparx EA; it does not contain any comparisons with other tools. However, you can find many comparisons on the internet, which we highly encourage you to read about.

Sparx EA, is a modeling tool that has evolved over the years from being just for UML modeling in the early 2000s to a tool that can model almost everything today such as mind maps, cloud environments including **Amazon Web Services (AWS)** and Microsoft Azure, wireframes and user interfaces, projects, strategies, application components, Kanban workflows, and many others, but most importantly it supports the ability to build enterprise architecture repositories. Sparx EA also supports many of the known industry standards in addition to UML, such as **Business Process Modeling Notation (BPMN)**, **System Modeling Language (SysML)**, **National Information Exchange Model (NIEM)**, ArchiMate, and many more.

Note: **The number of supported standards varies based on the selected Sparx EA license. Please refer to the comparison between the different licenses (https://sparxsystems.com/products/ea/compare-editions.html) and decide your needs accordingly.**

Check Sparx Systems' website for an up-to-date price list and to learn more about the different licenses they offer (**https://sparxsystems.com/products/ea/shop/index.html**). For the record, we are using the **corporate license** for this book, so every diagram and every instruction provided in it is doable with this license, plus many other diagram types that exceed the scope of this book. You can download a trial copy now and get familiar with the different components of the UI, as well as get used to the way of creating diagrams. Sparx Systems has a huge library of resources that can help you learn about the product and become an expert in it. It will be extremely helpful to explore the fundamental materials provided at this location (**https://sparxsystems.com/resources/index.html**), so you know where to find additional help when needed.

If you have not used Sparx EA before, the next chapter, *Sparx EA Crash Course*, will give the essentials to work with it. It is also important to mention that this book is not sponsored by Sparx Systems and is not affiliated with any of their partners. We have chosen Sparx EA mainly for the following reasons:

- **Low cost of ownership**: Sparx EA is a tool that anyone can purchase without massively hurting their pockets. If you are learning and practicing at your own cost, you can get Sparx EA up and running for a few hundred dollars. Most other EA tools cost an average of $10,000 per user, so you can see how huge the difference is. If you work for an organization that does not want to put a big investment in an EA tool, either due to budget constraints or to lower the risk involved with building the EA capability, then Sparx EA is an excellent tool to start with. Once the maturity of your organization's EA capability increases, you may choose to migrate to a more sophisticated and more expensive tool if needed.

- **Direct download and free trial**: If you want to explore Sparx EA, you do not have to go through a long procurement process where you submit online forms and wait for the marketing team to call you back, ask you for more questions, schedule a demo, and make a purchase order before even putting your hands on the tool. With Sparx EA, all you need to do is register with your email address, and you will be provided with a link to download a fully functional, 30-day trial copy. If you like it, pay for the license online, enter the provided license key, and your trial version will become a licensed version.

- **Widely known**: Sparx EA is a very well-known tool in the market, and almost every architect has used it at some point or at least heard of it.

Keep in mind that a product that is affordable and available for all does not necessarily mean a low-quality product. The quality of any product in general is measured by its ability to realize your needs and requirements within the product's capabilities and yours. If you need to nail a nail, then the screwdriver is a low-quality product to do it. It is essential to make sure what your requirements are, be sure of what the product is capable of, and finally, be sure that you have sufficient knowledge and skills to use it for the stated purpose. Only then can you judge its quality.

Conclusion

In this chapter, we talked about the importance of EA and how it can help to support organizations' decisions by controlling the changes and determining their impact. We also learned why having an EA repository is very important for a successful EA practice because it provides the required linkage between the many models that will cover different perspectives of the enterprise. Then we introduced our approach for building the repository, which includes three main components: the methodology, the modeling notation, and the software tool, and we will use TOGAF, UML, and Sparx EA, respectively.

In the next chapter, we will start using Sparx EA by building some sample diagrams and providing step-by-step instructions.

Points to remember

- EA can be used for multiple purposes and for different scopes.

- EA is about documentation, and documentation is what the keyword architecture implies.

- The more you document your enterprise, the more you know about it, and the better you can respond to changes.

- Changes in the enterprise include every possible alteration to its current state, either due to internal or external factors or requirements.

- Knowing how much is good enough to document is a key success factor in an EA practice. Too much documentation can overwhelm, while too little can be useless. There is no precise way to decide what is good enough, as it differs from one enterprise to another, one project to another, or one team to another.

- An EA capability is just like any other Business Capability, so it requires business processes, applications, information, technologies, and, most importantly, capable people, to successfully operate it.

- Following an agile approach in EA means that you are not required to go through the architecture development lifecycle from the beginning to the end. Instead, you can go directly to any ADM phase in response to business needs.

- The practice of EA produces artifacts, and diagrams are the most common form of artifacts as they represent information graphically.

- Having an EA repository is not mandated by TOGAF for an EA practice, but it is an essential part of its success; therefore, it is highly recommended to have one.

- Connected artifacts within a repository help to understand bigger pictures, which help decision makers make better decisions.

- Using TOGAF as the methodology, UML as the modeling notation, and Sparx EA as the tool is the approach that this book is following, but it is not the only way.

Key terms

- **Enterprise architecture**: The art of defining and categorizing the elements that compose an enterprise and defining the relationships among these elements, to get useful information that supports making strategic and tactical decisions.

- **EA capability**: The ability to develop and maintain the architecture of a particular enterprise and use it to govern changes.

- **Enterprise architecture repository**: A database that contains all the EA artifacts in one place.

- **Agile enterprise architecture**: A way of building EA artifacts that involves the principles and values of an agile methodology.

- **Structural elements**: The components, relationships, and organization that define the static structure of an enterprise.

- **Behavioral elements**: The actions, interactions, and processes that describe the dynamic behavior of an enterprise.

Join our Discord space

Join our Discord workspace for latest updates, offers, tech happenings around the world, new releases, and sessions with the authors:

https://discord.bpbonline.com

CHAPTER 2
Sparx EA
Crash Course

Introduction

Whether you are a new or experienced practitioner in any IT or business domain, we can confidently say that you should have developed several diagrams on many occasions during your life. Diagrams simplify the description of things around us, as per the adage, *A picture is worth a thousand words*. Financial charts, organization charts, flow charts, data flow diagrams, entity relationships diagrams, network topology diagrams, city maps, and strategy maps are all forms of diagrams, and the list is very long for sure. In the world of EA, diagrams are a very common type of EA artifact, so you need to master the art of developing them to master EA.

After we talked about the importance of EA as a practice in the previous chapter and understanding the importance of having an EA repository to contain all the architecture work, it is time now to put our hands on Sparx EA, our tool of choice for this book, and start practicing. For the best benefits, we will start by learning the basics of using the tool, and this is the main objective of this chapter. We will explain in detail how to start using Sparx EA, what the components of its user interface are, and how you can use these components while creating your first diagram. If you have not used Sparx EA before, this chapter is the right place to start.

Structure

This chapter will include the following topics:

- Starting Sparx EA
- Sparx EA user interface
- Creating your first diagram

Objectives

The primary objective of this chapter is to get you ready to use Sparx EA. Even if you have used it before, it is still a good idea to go through the content of this chapter in case there is something that you need to be aware of. It contains step-by-step instructions to perform the basics, which will be useful when we reach advanced topics.

Starting Sparx EA

Developing diagrams requires software for sure, and many users are familiar with Microsoft Visio, and more recently, Lucidchart is gaining popularity. If these are the only modeling tools that you have used before, then you need to read this chapter very carefully, as Sparx EA has some fundamental differences with them. The most important difference that confuses users is that elements that are placed on diagrams in Sparx EA create repository occurrences too, while elements that are placed on Visio or Lucid diagrams do not act that way and remain as visual elements on the diagrams. Even though this feature can be confusing for many but without it, you cannot use the tool as a repository. Remember that our goal of having a repository is not just to build diagrams, but to build multiple interdependent diagrams, each showing a different aspect of the enterprise, without losing the traceability among them.

If you have not installed Sparx EA yet, then it is time to do it. A free, fully functional 30-day trial version can be downloaded from **https://sparxsystems.com/products/ea/trial/request. html**. Installation is straightforward; once you launch the software, the **License Management** pops up a screen, as shown in *Figure 2.1:*

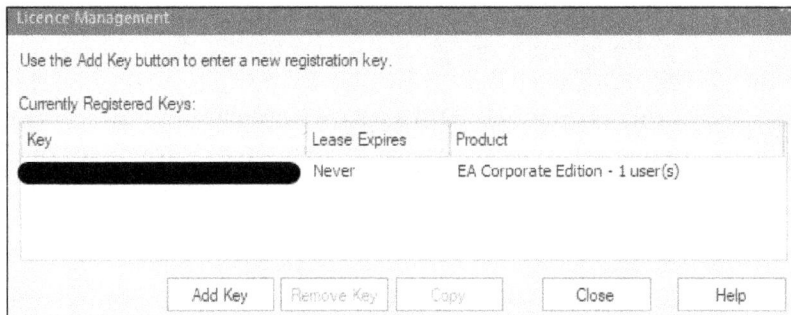

Figure 2.1: *License Management popup*

It will ask for a key, which is what you will obtain from Sparx Systems when you purchase the software. If you leave the key blank, Sparx EA will start the 30-day trial timer, but will give you full access to all the features with an unlimited number of diagrams. If you are using Sparx EA on a corporate computer and network, you will need to contact the technical support for instructions on how to install and run the software, and more importantly, how to obtain the license key. Many corporations use floating licenses when they have many contributors to the EA content instead of dedicated licenses. Floating licenses require connecting to a license server that acts as a storage location to save license keys and distribute them to users when they need them. We will not spend a lot of time explaining the installation instructions, as they can be obtained from Sparx Systems' online documentation or from your tech support. Administering Sparx EA and its licenses is not within the scope of this book, and we recommend the user guides that can be found at **https://sparxsystems.com/resources/user-guides/17.1/**. If everything is working and Sparx EA is up and running, let us have a look at the main components of its user interface in the next section.

Sparx EA user interface

Once you launch Sparx EA, you will see a screen like the one in *Figure 2.2*. The main components of Sparx EA user interface are surrounded with dashed lines to help you identify with ease:

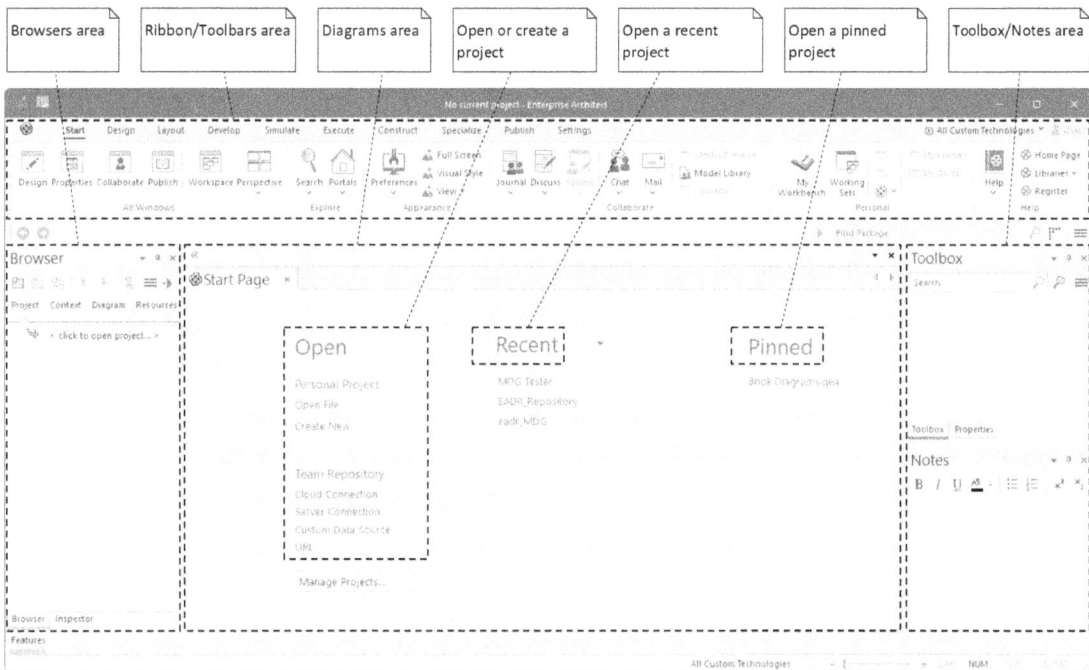

Figure 2.2: *Main components of Sparx EA's user interface*

Note: **Some figures contain screenshots of the entire screen, and that makes the fonts too small and hard to read, but the purpose of these figures is to provide overall views, not to tell what each UI text is. It is highly recommended that you explore the screens from the Sparx EA user interface while looking at these figures.**

Take a moment exploring each area while you read the description in the following subsections. You may see a slightly different view from the one in the preceding figure, such as seeing the **Toolbox** to the left instead of the right, and that is fine. Most windows can be repositioned, some can be docked to the screen's edges, and some can be docked together to form tabbed windows. Try to move things around and experience how docking and undocking windows work. The four main components of Sparx EA are the diagrams area, the browsers area, the ribbon and toolbars area, and the toolboxes and notes area. We will take a closer look at each in order, starting with the diagrams area.

Diagrams area

The largest section of the Sparx EA user interface is the **Diagrams area**, and it is where the EA artifacts are created and updated. In other words, this area is where the actual work gets done. When Sparx EA starts, it shows the **Start Page** by default. The **Start Page** is a tabbed diagram document in the diagrams area. When you create more diagrams, they will all get tabbed in the diagrams area next to the start page in the order they were opened in. The **Start Page** contains three sections: **Open**, **Recent**, and **Pinned**. For a brand new Sparx EA installation, the **Recent** and **Pinned** sections will be empty, but once you create new projects, the most recent ones will appear under the **Recent** section. The **Pinned** section is where you maintain a list of the projects that you want to keep accessible regardless of their recency.

To create a new project or open a project that is not listed under **Recent** or **Pinned**, you will need to use the **Open File** and **Create New** options under the **Open** section.

Note: **The EA repository that we are planning to create is considered a project from Sparx EA's point of view. In other words, within the context of Sparx EA, a project is a generalized form of a repository.**

The following format will be used when providing instructions to use a specific action on the screen: **Area** ❘ **Section** ❘ **Subsection** ❘ **Action**. For example, to create a new project, the instruction will be: Click on **Start Page** ❘ **Open** ❘ **Personal Projects** ❘ **Create New**, to create a new project.

Follow these steps to create a new repository project:

1. Click on **Start Page** ❘ **Open** ❘ **Personal Projects** ❘ **Create New**.
2. Select the file location where you want to store the repository.
3. Give your repository a meaningful name, such as **CompanyName_EA_Repository**, or any other name of your choice.
4. Leave the default file type as it is, **Enterprise Architect Project (*.qea)**.

Now you have an empty repository, and you can see its name listed under **Recent**. If you right-click on the project name, a context menu will appear containing an option to **Pin Connection**. Select that, and your project will always appear under **Pinned** until you decide to unpin it.

To open an existing project, you can either click on **Start Page | Open | Personal Projects | Open File**, and the standard Windows open file dialog box will pop up. Select the desired file and click **Open**. Another way to open a project file is to find it using the **Windows File Explorer** and double-click on it, which will launch a new instance of Sparx EA with the selected file opened in it.

Note: **Sparx EA allows opening many instances at the same time, each containing a different project file.**

We will add more content to this project as we progress throughout this book, but before that, let us finish exploring the remaining components of the user interface, and the next one is the **Browser** area.

Browser area

The **Browser** is a view that shows the elements in the repository in a hierarchical, nested tree. Think of it like Windows Explorer, but instead of files, we have diagrams and elements, and instead of folders, we have packages. *Chapter 5, Structuring the Repository,* will show you multiple ways to build complex yet easy-to-navigate repository structures with elements and diagrams grouped into packages, to serve the demands of your enterprise users.

The **Browser** area contains four tabs: **Project**, **Context**, **Diagram**, and **Resources**. Each gives you a different scope to look at, but the most common tab is the **Project Browser**, and this is the one that we will be talking about in this chapter. The **Context Browser** shows a hierarchy that has the selected package as the root node. If you are selecting an element or a diagram, the root node will be the containing package of that element or diagram. For example, if you have an element that contains other elements, the top-level node in the context browser will be the package that contains the selected element, and all child elements will be listed in the hierarchy. The **Diagram Browser** is very similar to the context browser, but the root node for the browser's tree is the selected diagram itself, and the diagram's elements and relationships will be listed as well. The **Resources Browser** provides a different perspective as it lists packages containing templates of different categories, as we as the custom metamodels that you build. We will learn more about the custom metamodels in *Chapter 3, Introducing Model Driven Generation.*

Since the **Project Browser** is the primary browser used in this book, it will be discussed in more detail next.

Project Browser

The first thing to pay attention to in the **Project Browser** is that there is currently a single element in the hierarchy known as the **Model** package. Model packages are root packages in any repository hierarchy. You can have multiple model packages in a project, but you cannot nest models within other models. Think of model packages like the **C:** and **D:** drives on your computer. You can have as many drives, but you cannot have the **C:** drive as a parent to the **D:** drive. The child packages and elements in one model package can be moved to packages under other model packages without constraints if they are within the same project file. You can also have diagrams in a model package that contain elements under another model package.

Let us take a moment before we get lost in detail while talking about structuring packages, as this will be covered in *Chapter 5, Structuring the Repository*. For now, we need to keep exploring the **Project Browser** window, which you can see in *Figure 2.3*:

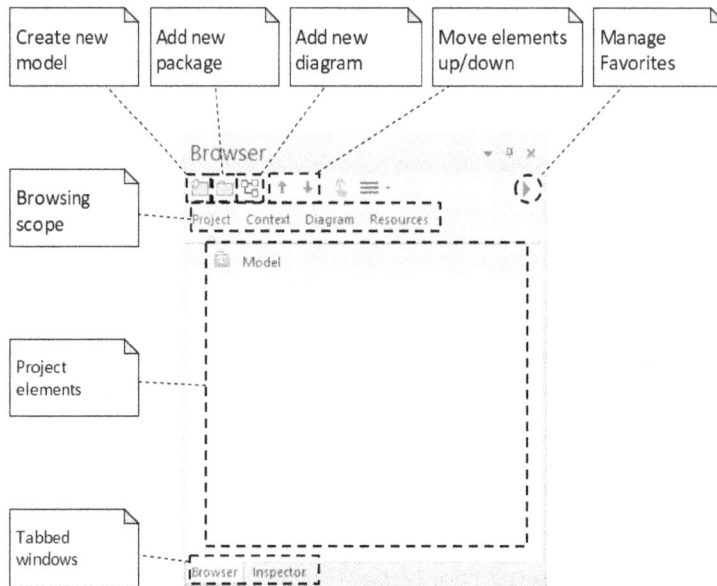

Figure 2.3: Project Browser window

At the top of the **Project Browser** window, there are buttons to create a new model package, add new package to an existing model, add new diagram to a package, or move elements up and down within a package. To the right of these buttons, there is a menu with additional options like **Open Project**, **Reload Project**, **Model Builder**, **New Package**, **New Diagram**, **New Element**, and a few other options. Some menu options already have separate buttons to perform the same actions, and this is how Sparx EA is designed. It usually provides many ways to do the same thing from different locations. People who like keyboard shortcuts find it more convenient to use shortcuts while modeling, because one hand will be free most of the time while the other one is holding the mouse. You will be introduced to these shortcuts when we encounter them in the book, and you can always learn about them by looking at the menu text and the tooltips.

At the bottom of the window, you can notice that there are two tabs: **Browser** and **Inspector**. The Browser is the active tab, which we have introduced already, while the other tab is to give you context information about a specific element. If you click on an element on a diagram, the **Inspector** window will show you some contextual information about this element, such as the other elements that are linked to it. An important thing to remember is that the **Browser** and the **Inspector** are both tabbed windows, which means they can be undocked from their position, get docked on other sides of the screen, or even be left floating on top of other windows. You can also close the tabs that you do not use frequently, and dock new tabbed windows as needed. The user interface of Sparx EA is very flexible and customizable, and this is one of its important strengths.

Renaming the model node

Before we move to a different UI component, let us do a small exercise to rename the default name of **Model** to **Sandboxes**, and create a Sandbox for yourself in it. Let us look at the following steps:

1. Click on the **Model** in the **Project Browser**.
2. Press *F2* on the keyboard to rename the model.
3. Type **Sandboxes**, then press **Enter**.
4. Click on the **New Package** button. A dialog box like the one in *Figure 2.4* will appear.

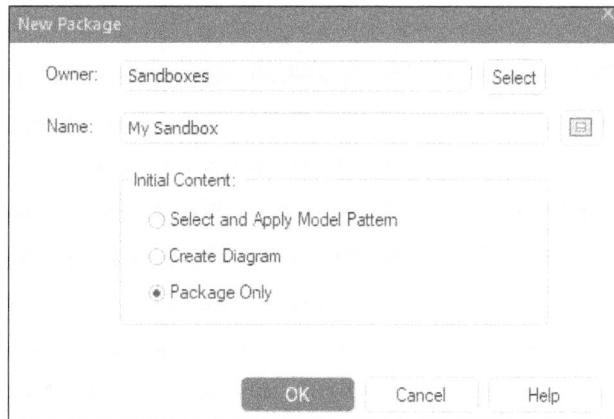

Figure 2.4: *New Package dialog*

5. Provide a **Name** for your Sandbox. You can use your first name, last name, full name, or any naming convention of your choice.
6. Select **Package Only** from the option buttons.
7. Click **OK**.

Now you have your own space to do experiments on anything new you learn about modeling, without affecting other elements in the repository. We will add more diagrams and elements in this workspace, but let us continue exploring the UI elements.

Ribbon and toolbars area

At the top of the screen, and just like many Windows-based applications, you will find a ribbon containing a set of toolbars, each is divided into toolbar sections, and each section contains a set of buttons. We cannot afford to explain each toolbar and its buttons, as this can be learned from online help, and while you use Sparx EA more. We will look at the first toolbar in some detail and will learn about the other ones as we progress. *Figure 2.5* shows the **Start** toolbar, which is the first toolbar in the ribbon from the left. As you can see, it contains sections that are divided with a thin gray line, and these sections are: **All Windows**, **Explore**, **Appearance**, **Collaborate**, **Personal**, and **Help** from left to right.

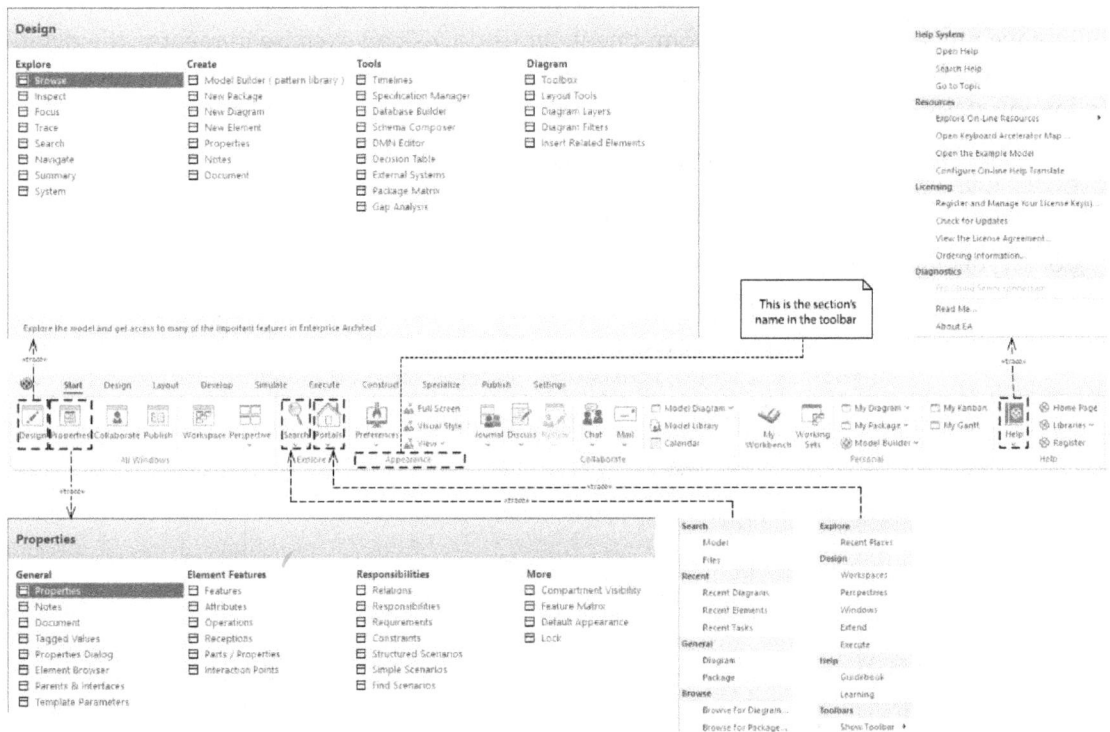

Figure 2.5: Start toolbar highlighting some of the actions

The first section in the **Start** toolbar is the **All Windows** section, which allows showing and hiding different types of windows like the **Toolbox**, and the **Notes**, in addition to the ability creating new diagrams, packages, and elements. For example, if you accidentally close the **Browser** window and want to open it again, click **Start | All Windows | Design | Explore | Browse**.

The **Explore** section, includes **Search** and **Portals** options, and each has a list of different sub-options. **Search** provides you with different ways to find content in the repository. When your repository grows to contain hundreds and even thousands of elements, you will need an efficient way to search and find them. The **Portals** button allows you to change and customize the user interface to the way that suits your work style. Remember when we mentioned earlier that Sparx EA allows many ways to do the same thing? Another way to show the **Browser** window if closed is to:

1. Click **Start | Explore | Portals | Design | Windows**. This will show the **Portals** sidebar that contains a list of options.

2. In **Portals** side bar, click on **Explore | Project Browser** to show the **Browser** window again.

Another thing to notice about the toolbar buttons is that some of them contain a small down arrow, which indicates that clicking on the arrow will open a drop-down menu with multiple options to choose from. *Figure 2.6* shows the **Preferences** popup dialog box that will appear after clicking on **Start | Appearance | Preferences**:

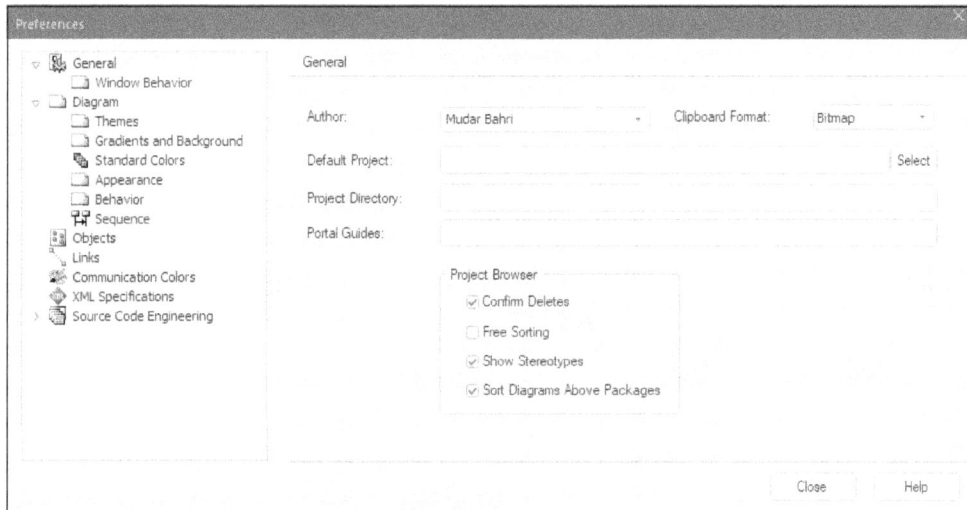

Figure 2.6: *Preferences dialog box*

Make sure that your name is written correctly in the **Author** field as this is the value that will be used for every diagram or element you create. Take some time exploring the remaining toolbars and their options, and do not hesitate to use help if you struggle to understand any of them. Pay special attention to the **Design** and **Layout** toolbars, as these two, along with the **Start,** are the ones that we will use the most in this book. Now, let us have a look at the last component of Sparx EA's UI.

Toolbox and Notes area

The fourth area on Sparx EA's user interface is a collection of windows that includes by default the **Toolbox**, **Properties**, and **Notes** windows. You can add or remove windows as desired. You can dock them to a side, keep them floating, pin them, or set them to auto-hide. The interface is very flexible and customizable as mentioned earlier. The **Toolbox** contains elements that compose your diagrams, and each type of diagram is associated by default to a toolbox. For example, in a UML components diagram, the toolbox will contain the elements that are usually placed on a components diagram, such as a component, a packaging component, an interface, etc. The **Properties** window allows you to set the properties of the diagram elements such as name, stereotype, alias, keyword, and others. Each element and diagram have properties that are different. The content of the properties window will change as you click on different elements and diagrams. The **Notes** window allows entering any free-text note to elements for better documentation. Each element and diagram have its own notes section.

Creating your first diagram

Let us create a diagram together and learn a few more things about the user interface items and how to effectively use them.

Choosing the diagram type

Refer to the following steps to create a diagram that contains two UML structural component elements:

1. Click on the Sandboxes model package and expand its contents by clicking on the small > symbol next to the package name.

2. Right-click on the child Sandbox package that you created earlier, which should be having your name, and select **Add Diagram…** from the context menu.

3. The **Model Builder** dialog box will pop up like the one in *Figure 2.7*:

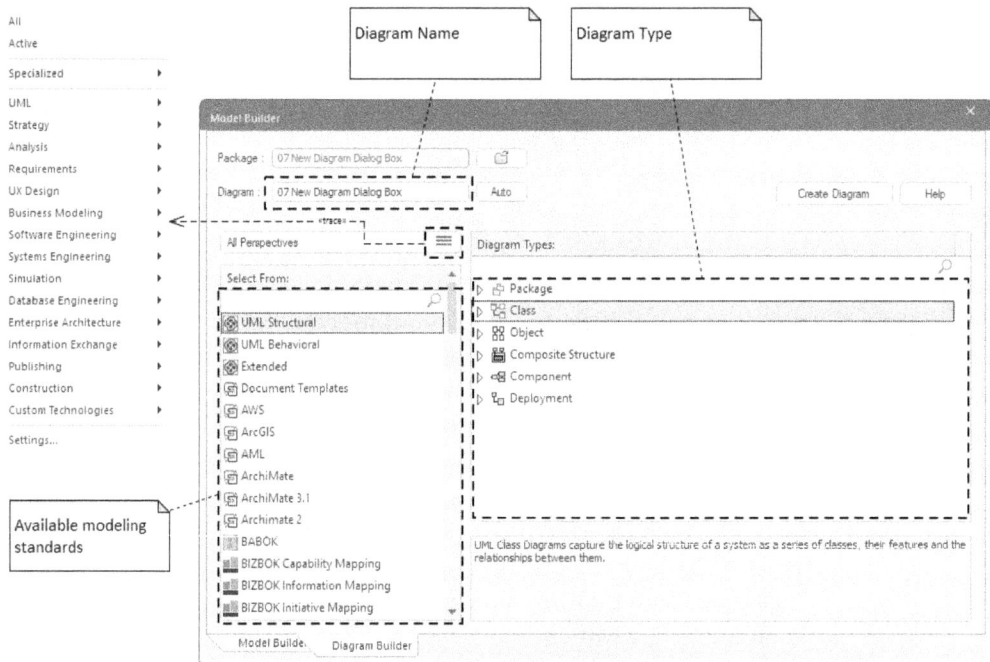

Figure 2.7: New Diagram dialog box

4. Give a meaningful name for the diagram. In this example, we are planning to create an applications catalog diagram, so enter `Applications Catalog` in the **Diagram** field.

5. Select **UML Structural** from the list of available modeling standards and select **Diagram Types | Component**. If you see an empty list of model methodologies, simply click on the three horizontal lines menu, informally known as the hamburger menu, and select **All.**

6. Click the **Create Diagram** button to create a new diagram using the settings that were provided in the dialog box.

The **Select From** list contains the standards that are supported by your Sparx EA license, so the standards that you see in your version may vary from the ones that are in the previous figure. Clicking on a specific item in the available modeling standards list will show all diagram types that are provided under the selected standard, on the right side of the screen. Take a moment and explore the supported methodologies and the provided diagram types. You do not have to test and understand each one of them, but only remember that this is the process to follow to create new diagrams, and it will be the same process to follow for creating the custom diagram types that we will build throughout this book. Let us learn how to add elements to the new diagram that we just created.

Adding elements to the diagram

After the dialog box closes, a new diagram with the name **Applications Catalog** will be created in your Sandbox and will open by default in the diagrams area right next to the **Start Page**. The **Toolbox** will be set by default to the **UML components** toolbox, which means it will contain the elements that are allowed to be used in this type of diagram. Explore the elements that are included in the **Toolbox** and see how they are categorized into groups. To perform an action from a toolbox, we will use: **Toolbox | Group | Element**. Continue with the following steps to complete this example diagram:

1. Click on **Toolbox | Component | Component,** then click on the diagram area to create a new element of type component.

2. Name the new element **CRM System**. To rename an element, click on it, then press *F2* on your keyboard to enable renaming it. There are other ways to do that too, and we will mention some of them in different examples.

3. Repeat the same steps to create another component and name it **Sales System**.

Figure 2.8 shows the diagram after placing the two components on it:

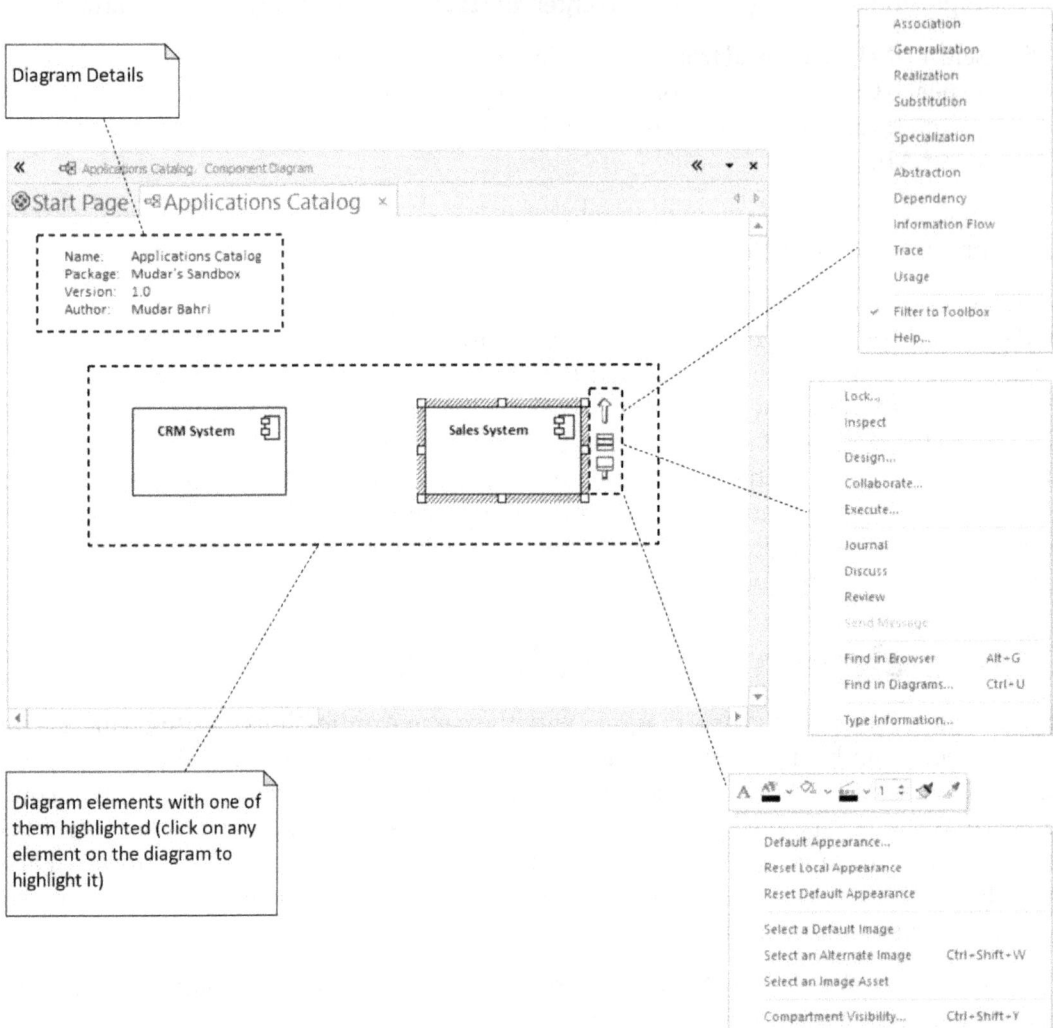

Figure 2.8: The diagrams area

As you can see, there are the two component elements that you have placed. Click on any of them and it will be surrounded with a rectangle with handles on each edge and corner to resize the element. You will also see three icons to the right side of the highlighted element, and each of these icons provide a set of actions that can be performed on the selected element. Pay special attention to the arrow shape icon, which we will use the most, and it helps in creating relationships between the elements on the same diagram.

At the top left edge of the diagram, there is an area that contains the diagram's name, package name, diagram version, and the author's name. This area is known as **diagram details**, and you can turn it on or off by right-clicking on the diagram then selecting **Properties ...** from the context menu. A dialog box will pop up with a list of options at the left and a set of attributes in each options tab as you can see in *Figure 2.9*:

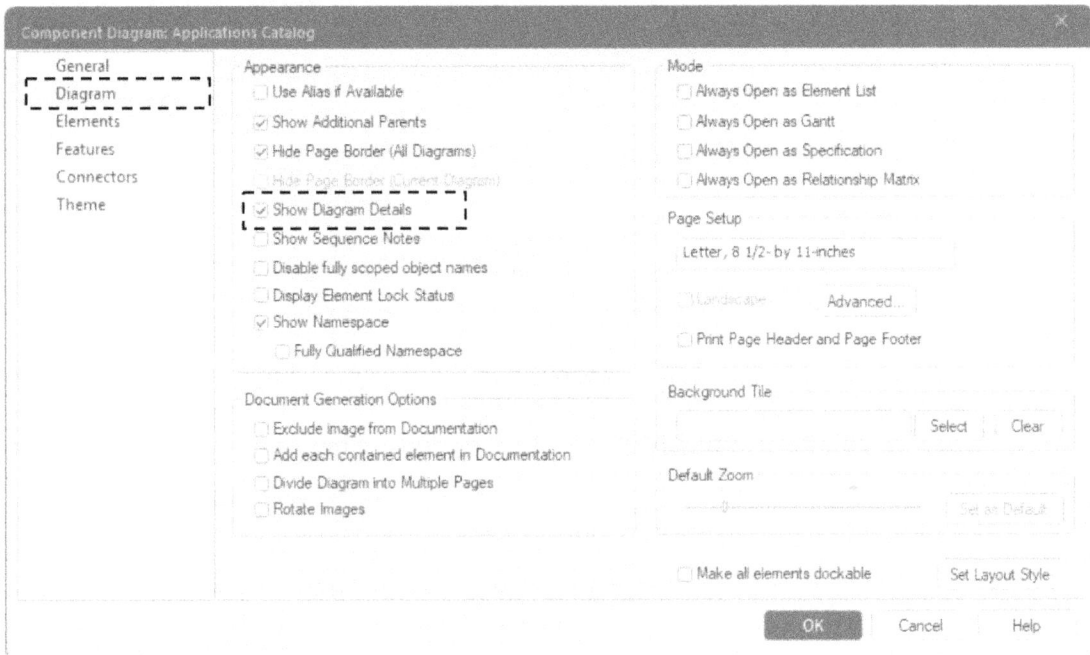

Figure 2.9: *Diagram properties dialog box*

Check the **Diagram | Appearance | Show Diagram Details** checkbox to show diagram details and uncheck it to hide them. Now we need to indicate a flow of information between the two components, so we will create a flow relationship, and this is how we do that.

Creating relationships

We will continue with the same example to create a **Flow** relationship between the two application components that we added to the diagram, by following the given steps:

1. Click on the **CRM System** component. Click and hold the arrow icon that appears at the top-right corner of the component, drag it, and release it on the **Sales System**.

2. A context menu will appear with a list of options. These options are the valid relationships that can be created between two components as per the UML's specification. Select **Information Flow**.

3. A dialog box like the one in *Figure 2.10* will pop up asking to specify what data will flow from the source component to the target.

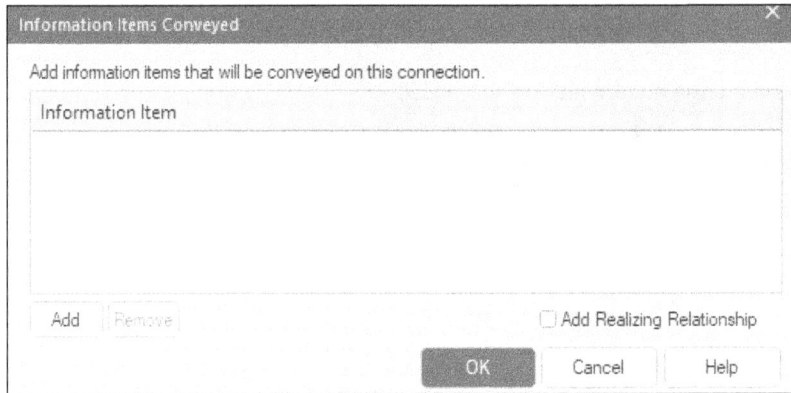

Figure 2.10: Information Items Conveyed dialog box

We will skip adding data on this **Information Flow** relationship to avoid complicating our first exercise and will keep it just as a general flow. We will see examples in later chapters of this book utilizing the feature of conveying data on information flow relationships.

4. Click **Cancel** to return to the diagram.

    You should see an arrow shaped connector with a dotted line body, and a label showing the word ‹‹**flow**›› located under the line like the one in *Figure 2.11*:

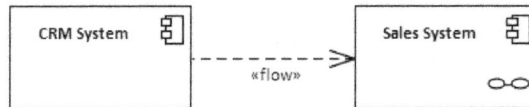

Figure 2.11: The information flow relationship

The diagram indicates a flow of information from the **CRM System** to the **Sales System**. Next, we will learn how to delete this relationship from one diagram but not entirely from the repository, which is also known as hiding the relationship, or how to delete it completely from the repository.

Hiding and deleting relationships

Continue the same exercise using the diagram that we have created, and follow these steps to hide the relationship between the two components:

1. Right-click on the body of the relationship and select **Delete Connector** from the context menu. Alternatively, you can left-click on the connector and press the **Delete** button on the keyboard.

2. The **Remove Connector** dialog box will ask you if you want to hide the connector or delete the connector from the model completely, so select **Hide the connector**.

3. Keep the **Don't ask again** checkbox unchecked. It is recommended to keep this checkbox unchecked whenever you see this dialog box, because you will always need to choose between the two options.

> Note: **If you accidentally checked the Hide the connector box and want to get the dialog box back, go to the Start menu and select Start | Appearance | Preferences | Links and check the Prompt on connector deletes checkbox.**

4. Click **OK** to close the dialog and return to the diagram.

It is time now to add more details to one of the application components by creating a home page that opens when you double-click on the element.

Creating composite child diagrams

A **composite diagram** is a child diagram that is associated with a specific element. The biggest benefit of composite diagrams is that they act as the home page of the elements, and from that home page, you can add more diagrams describing the element from different views, such as the application composition. You can have only one composite diagram per element. You can have as many child diagrams per element as needed, but only one of them can be selected as the composite diagram, which will respond to the double-click action. There are many tricks in this book to show you how to create useful home pages with multiple views in them.

Let us continue with our example and create a composite diagram for the **Sales System** to show its subcomponents. Refer to the following steps:

1. Right-click on the **Sales System** component and select **New Child Diagram | Add Diagram**.

2. A dialog box like the one in *Figure 2.7* will pop up.

3. The name of the diagram will default to the name of the parent component, so let us keep the value in the **Diagram** text field as it is, **Sales System**.

4. Click **Select From | All** from the available modeling standards to list all the available standards.

5. Select **UML Structural** from the list of methodologies and select **Diagram Types | Component** from the list of available UML structural diagrams.

6. Click **OK,** and a new empty diagram will open in a new tab.

7. Close the tab by clicking on the small **x** symbol. You should see the **Applications Catalog** diagram that we created earlier.

8. Right-click on the **Sales System** once again and select **New Child Diagram | Composite Structure Diagram**. A chain symbol appears now on the bottom-right corner of the component. This is an indicator that this component has a composite child diagram linked to it.

9. Double-click on the **Sales System** component, and this will open the empty child diagram in the same tab that the parent component was in to show the child diagram. Also, notice that the tab is showing a small back arrow instead of the **x** symbol, so by clicking on it, you can go back to the previous diagram.

10. Click once on the **Component** element in the **Toolbox**, then click on the diagram area to create a new component and name it **Customers**. Repeat this step to create two more components and name them **Orders** and **Billing**. If you look at the **Project Browser,** you will see that the three newly created components are children of the **Sales System** component, because we created them on its composite child diagram.

11. Now from the **Project Browser** window, drag the **Sales System** component and drop it onto the diagram.

12. A dialog box will pop up with options. Select **Drop as | Link**, keep all the other options without change, then click **OK**.

13. Click on the **Customers** component, click and hold the arrow connector, drag it, and release it on the **Sales System**. Select **Association** from the context menu.

14. Repeat the last step for the **Orders** and **Billing** components.

15. Press *Ctrl+S* to save your work.

Note: **Use the Toolbox to create new elements and use the Project Browser to reuse existing elements.**

Being able to reuse elements on many diagrams is a main differentiator between modeling tools that maintain repositories like Sparx EA, and the modeling tools that do not maintain repositories like Visio and Lucid. The repository is your database, and its elements are the data. The diagrams are like user interfaces where you can use the same set of data on many different UI screens. To get a list of all the diagrams that a specific element has been used in, right-click on the element and select **Find | Find in all Diagrams,** and a dialog box will pop up with an element usage list. Try it on the Sales System component, and you should get a dialog box like *Figure 2.12*:

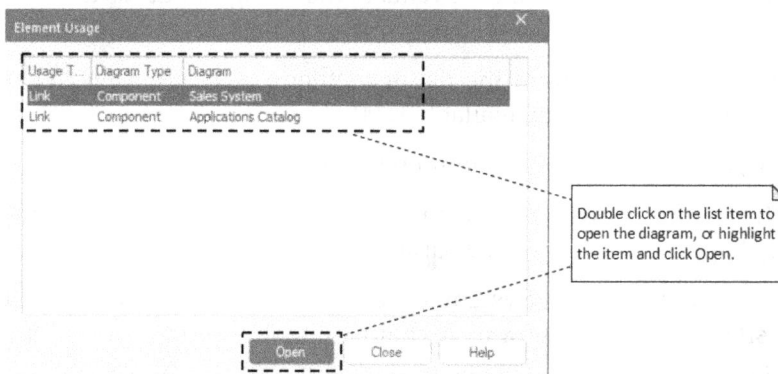

Figure 2.12: Element usage dialog

If you have followed the example properly, your diagram should look like the following:

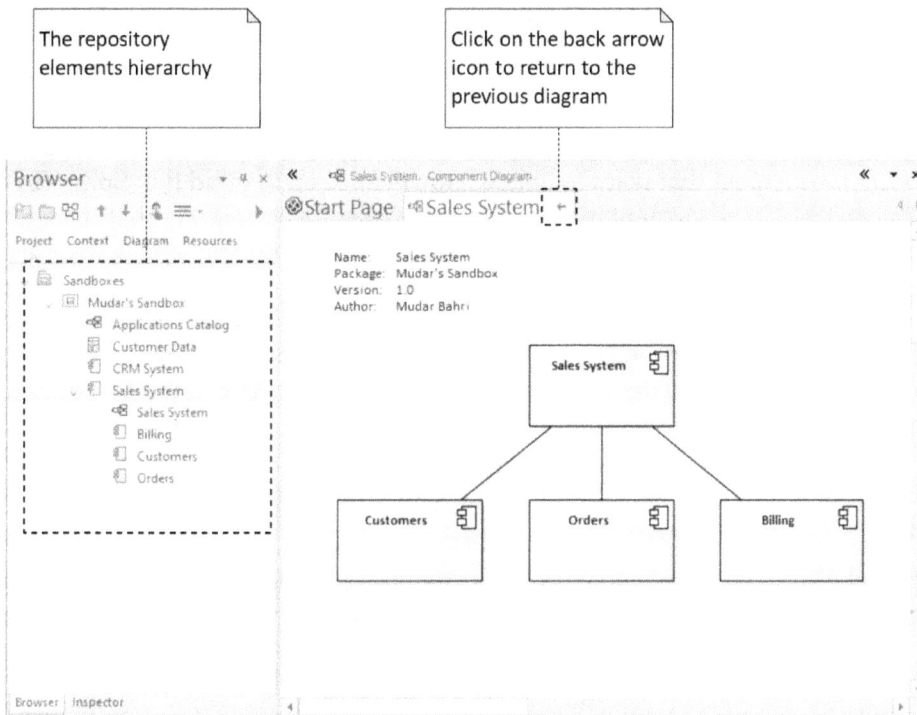

Figure 2.13: *A composite child diagram*

When elements are no longer required, they can be removed from an individual diagram that uses them or deleted entirely from the repository. The next subsection will explain the difference between these two actions and when each should be applied.

Deleting elements

To delete an element from a diagram, right-click on the element on the diagram and select **Delete** from the menu. Another way is to click on the element and press the delete button on your keyboard. This will remove the element from the selected diagram only but will keep it in the repository. In other words, the element in question will persist within the repository, remains available for use in other diagrams, and may already be present in some existing ones. If you need to completely delete an element from the repository, you need to right-click on it in the **Project Browser** and select **Delete**. A message box will pop up to confirm the deletion stating that **Any child elements will be removed as well**. If you confirm with a **Yes**, the element and all its child elements and diagrams will be deleted permanently, and there is no way to undo this action.

There are three steps that are highly recommended to take before deleting any element permanently from the repository. They are as follows:

1. Make sure that you are deleting the right element.
2. Make sure that it is not used in other diagrams.
3. Make sure that it is not linked to other elements.

Step 1 is to make sure that you are deleting the element that you want to delete. This sounds simple in our practice example as we only have a couple of elements so far, and you can easily identify the element that want to delete. However, keep in mind that Sparx EA does not automatically highlight an element in the **Project Browser** if you select it on the diagram. With a repository of hundreds and even thousands of elements in it, you may have several elements that have the same name, or you may have a complex nested structure that hides your target element inside a deep hierarchy. As a result, you may accidentally delete the wrong element. If that wrong element has been used in, say, 50 other diagrams, then deleting it permanently will result in a big loss of valuable information. More importantly, you cannot undo that action. So, to make sure that you are deleting the right element, you need to right-click on it on the diagram and select **Find | In Project Browser** and now you are sure that the highlighted element in the browser is the same highlighted element on the diagram, and this is what you want to delete.

Step 2 is to make sure that the element is not being used in other diagrams. An element in the repository can be used on many diagrams, as we learned. If you are working in a working environment with multiple contributors to the repository, an element that you create will be used by others. So, counting on your memory that you have not used the element in many places is not safe enough. So right-click on the element in the **Project Browser**, then select **Find in all Diagrams** to see the element usage. If the list is empty, or it contains diagrams that you are aware of, and you are still fine to delete the element from all of them, then you can consider this step as completed.

Step 3 is to make sure that the element is not linked to any other elements in the repository. In our example, the **Customers** component is linked to the **Sales System** component. Removing the Customers' component from the diagram does not remove the link that exists to the **Sales System**. This scenario can happen very frequently, where you may delete an element from all diagrams, but you still want to keep it in the repository, either for future use or to maintain the relationships that already exist with other elements. Deleting an element without checking for possible links to other elements will result in a loss of valuable information, because remember that relationships are as important as elements.

To check for existing relationships, you can right-click on the element in the **Project Browser** or on the diagram and select **Properties | Properties …,** and the element's properties dialog box will pop up. Select the **Links** tab from the left, and a list of existing **Relationships** will be listed on the right, showing what are the related elements, what are their types, what type of connection (relationship) between them, and stereotypes if available. *Figure 2.14* shows the **Links** tab in the properties dialog box of a component:

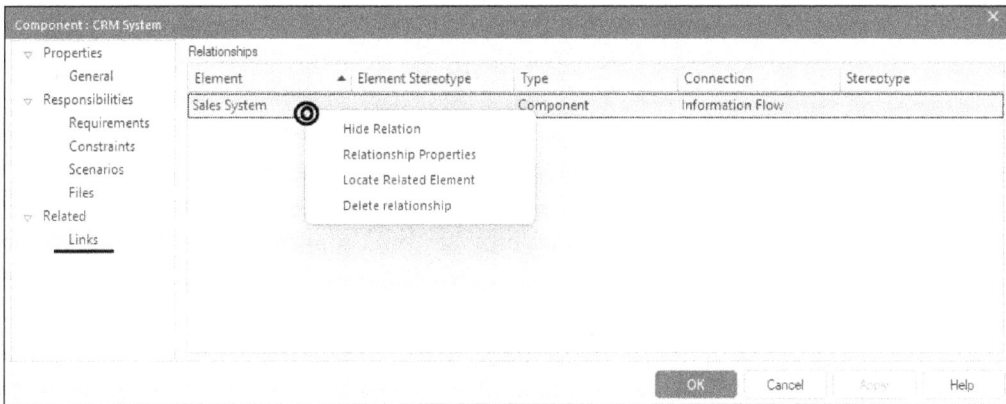

Figure 2.14: Element's properties dialog box

Right-clicking on any listed relationship will bring up a context menu with options that can be performed on the selected relationship, such as hiding it, showing more information about it in a separate dialog box, locating the related element in the **Project Browser**, or deleting the relationship. Whatever your choice is, just make sure that you are aware of what is connected to an element before committing to deleting it permanently.

So far, we have learned how to create diagrams, elements, and packages, and we have also learned how to reuse them, relate them, and delete them when they are no longer needed.

Conclusion

This concludes our example for this crash course. The intent was to get you ready for modeling real-world examples by showing you the essential steps that will be followed in the remaining chapters and examples. Building an EA repository is as simple as creating diagrams, creating elements, creating diagrams, and reusing elements. To make the repository useful, it must be well structured, the models must be meaningful and understandable, and the elements must be properly organized, so that repository users can easily reach where they want to and understand it. The exercise that we did in this chapter was made with simple UML elements and connectors, but to build EA artifacts that are based on TOGAF, we need to extend the standard UML toolboxes and diagrams and create new TOGAF toolboxes and diagrams, and this is what we will start to learn in the next chapter.

Points to remember

- Sparx EA allows us to open many instances at the same time, each containing a different project file.

- Model packages are the root nodes. You can have many model packages for many hierarchies in the same repository, but you cannot nest model packages inside other model packages. The root must stay as a root.

- When creating a new diagram, the type of the diagram must be specified.

- A default toolbox will be associated with each type of diagram, and it will contain the elements that are frequently used on that type of diagram.

- Placing an element from a toolbox on a diagram creates a new element in the repository and adds it visually to the diagram.

- Placing an element from the project browser on a diagram allows you to reuse the element on the diagram.

- You can reuse the same elements on any number of diagrams as needed.

- Keyboard shortcuts are very handy, and they can speed up the modeling process.

- Every element has properties, including diagrams and connectors.

- You can either hide a relationship connector from a diagram but keep it in the repository or delete the connector permanently.

- Composite child diagrams can act as the home page for repository elements.

- An element can have only one composite child diagram, but it can have many child diagrams.

- To permanently delete an element, you must delete it from the **Project Browser**. Deleting an element from a diagram removes it visually but keeps it in the repository.

- Before permanently deleting an element, make sure that you are selecting the right element in the repository and that it is not used on any diagram. Also, ensure that it is not linked to any other element.

Key terms

- **Sparx EA project**: A generalized keyword describing the type of files that Sparx EA creates. An EA repository is a Sparx EA project.

- **Model package**: The root node (package) in any repository hierarchy.

- **Package**: An element in the project hierarchy that acts as a container for other packages, elements, and diagrams.

- **Catalog**: A diagram showing a list of elements that are of the same type.

- **Composite diagram**: A child diagram that is associated with an element to open when the element is double-clicked on.

CHAPTER 3

Introducing Model Driven Generation

Introduction

The **Model Driven Generation** (**MDG**) is the way that Sparx EA allows users to extend its built-in frameworks. In enterprise architecture words, this is where you define the metamodel of the framework that you chose for the EA practice within your organization. If your organization is following a domain-specific framework that is not built in Sparx EA, you will have no choice but to build your own MDG that extends the framework into the tool. We will build parts of the **TOGAF enterprise metamodel** into Sparx EA because it is the framework that we chose for this book, but the concept is the same if you want to build any framework in Sparx EA.

Although building MDGs is an essential skill for customizing and extending Sparx EA, it is one of the most poorly documented topics, which makes it harder to learn. The online MDG documentation (**https://sparxsystems.com/resources/user-guides/17.1/modeling/mdg-technologies.pdf**) can easily cause your head to spin within minutes, and there are very few clear examples on the internet that can guide the reader in step-by-step processes.

Building a customized metamodel within any EA tool is an advanced topic. You need to be familiar with the tool itself, and you need to be familiar with the framework that you are implementing and how to read and understand its metamodel. In *Chapter 2, Sparx EA Crash Course*, we provided you with the essentials to use Sparx EA. We started building an EA repository, and we learned what the components of the Sparx EA user interface are, how to build a simple package structure, how to make a diagram, how to add elements to it, how to connect the elements, and how to safely delete them if they are no longer needed. In this chapter, we will advance your skills by showing how to build the TOGAF metamodel into Sparx EA. We advise you to practice while reading for the best benefit because it is a long chapter that is full of instructions.

Structure

This chapter is structured in two sections:

- MDG development lifecycle
- Building the MDG

Objectives

The objective of this chapter is to learn how to plan for changes to the MDG, to ensure that they are well documented, approved, tested, and implemented like any change to software products. We will learn then how to execute the MDG development plan to build a small but working custom metamodel in Sparx EA using elements from the TOGAF enterprise metamodels.

MDG development lifecycle

Just like any other software, whether it is simple or complex, building the MDG requires following a lifecycle to be done properly. You will start by identifying the elements and the relationships that need to be built, incorporating them into the new version of the MDG, publishing the MDG (generating the MDG file), testing it, and then using it in an architecture repository to build artifacts. *Figure 3.1* shows the MDG development lifecycle modeled using a standard UML activity diagram. This lifecycle is not part of the TOGAF Standard, but it is a development process suggested by us that is based on the traditional **system development lifecycle (SDLC)**:

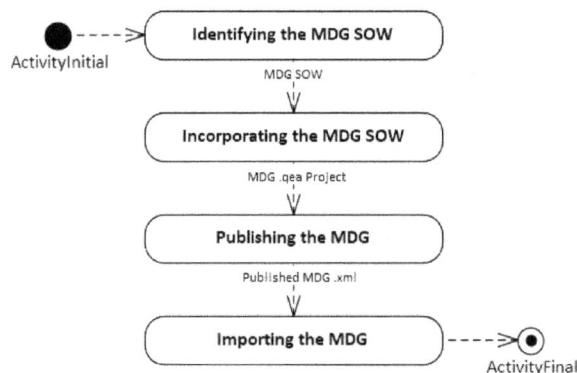

Figure 3.1: MDG development lifecycle

Do not get confused by the number of Sparx EA project files that we will create and use. We will be using three different projects throughout this book, and here is a quick description of each:

- The main **repository project** can be considered as the life or production repository of our EA artifacts. This is the project that we started in *Chapter 2, Sparx EA Crash Course*, and we will continue to enrich it with more artifacts as we progress. We will always refer to it as the *EA repository project*.

- The **MDG project** contains our custom metamodel. We will start working on this project in the next section of this chapter, *Building the MDG*, and we will continue to enrich it with metamodel elements and relationships as we progress in this book.

- The third project file is the **MDG testing project**, which we will use to test the MDG changes before we import them to the EA repository. This project is of less importance than the other two, so it is up to you to keep it or discard it after every test as it should not contain any valuable artifacts in it. Some architects like to keep their testing results for historical purposes, but it is a personal preference.

Note: **The MDG project file is as important as the EA repository project file, so make sure to keep both project files secured and backed up.**

To better understand the phases of the MDG development lifecycle, we will look at them in more detail.

Identifying the MDG SOW

The TOGAF metamodel includes about three dozen elements and more than one hundred possible relationships between them. Building an MDG that contains the entire TOGAF metamodel will require a large investment of time and effort, which can be critical and hard to secure. Thinking with an agile mindset, you should start with a **minimum viable product** (**MVP**) for the MDG, which only includes what you need to start with. You only need the parts of the metamodel that will support the artifacts that you are about to create. When new artifacts require additional metamodel elements, you can always go back and incorporate them within the MDG. It is an iterative approach that allows you to start creating useful artifacts in a shorter time.

The TOGAF Standard has been chosen to be the reference framework for this book. The TOGAF enterprise metamodel (**https://pubs.opengroup.org/togaf-standard/architecture-content/Figures/34_contentfwk8.png**) will be our guide for building the MDG. Open this diagram in a separate tab in your internet browser and bookmark it or print it and keep the paper in reach while reading this book, as we will refer to it in this chapter and in many other chapters to come.

Metamodels are often described as *models about models* or diagrams that guide us in creating other diagrams. EA involves defining and categorizing an enterprise's elements and their relationships. To do this, we need a reference to identify the potential elements and their connections. An experienced EA practitioner, particularly one familiar with TOGAF, can map enterprise elements to the metamodel. For instance, an EA expert would recognize a department as an **Organization Unit**.

Find the Organization Unit in the TOGAF metamodel diagram. Once you do, you will see that it is connected to several other elements through a set of relationships. Each relationship has two labels that tell how to read the relationship from both directions. Take, for example, the relationship between the Organization Unit and the driver element. The labels on the connector tell the two possible ways to read the relationship. The first way is to read it starting from the Organization Unit, so the relationship will be read as: an Organization Unit is motivated by a driver. The other way to read it is to start with the driver, so the relationship will be read as: a driver motivates an Organization Unit.

Note: We will discuss the elements and their definitions when we use them later, but to keep it simple for now, we only need to know how to use the TOGAF metamodel.

Each iteration to update the MDG should include a list of all the elements and the relationships that will be created or updated in the iteration. This list is the **scope of work** (**SOW**) of the desired iteration in the MDG development lifecycle. If our short-term target is to build artifacts based on the Organization Unit element, for example, then the MDG SOW should be a simple list that contains all the elements and the connectors that will be covered in that iteration only. Once the SOW is defined, the next step will be to incorporate it into the MDG project file.

Incorporating the MDG SOW

The MDG project is a Sparx EA project that contains diagrams, elements, and relationships. Like all Sparx EA projects, it is persisted in a file with **.qea** file extension. It defines how the custom metamodel that we are building works. The goal of using MDG is to extend the capabilities of Sparx EA to allow us to easily and consistently create EA artifacts that are not built into the product using toolboxes and special diagram types. For example, we want Sparx EA to provide us with a diagram of type **organization decomposition diagram,** which is not built into Sparx EA, and we want to have a toolbox that contains an element of type Organization Unit, and to have all the relationships that we need and can use in this model.

A typical MDG project contains the following three packages:

- **Profile package**: Contains all the customized stereotypes of the elements and the relationships.

- **Diagram profile package**: Contains the customized diagram types that we will use to build the EA artifacts.

- **Toolbox profiles**: These can be one or more customized toolboxes that will be associated with the diagram profiles.

In the section, *Building the MDG*, we will create a new MDG project and learn more about these packages in more detail. In the later chapters, we will resume the same MDG project and add a new MDG SOW to it as we progress.

In all cases, the MDG project file cannot be used in its **.qea** format and must be **published** before being imported and used in EA repository projects.

Publishing the MDG

Making changes to software requires the code to be rebuilt, and making changes to a website requires republishing it before users can start seeing the changes. Making changes to an MDG project also requires publishing it for changes to take place. Publishing the MDG does not produce a binary file but an XML file. The XML file is simply a translation of all the packages and the diagrams that are in an MDG project into a set of XML tags, attributes, and values. When the XML file is imported into another project, Sparx EA understands the elements, relationships, diagrams, and toolboxes that have been extended and thus will include them in its user interface so architects can use them to build EA artifacts.

The publishing process is simple, but it involves multiple steps. If we can suggest enhancements to Sparx Systems for future enhancements to Sparx EA, then being able to publish the MDG in a single step will be at the top of the list of these suggestions. Publishing an MDG can be confusing to new MDG developers, but it involves the following steps:

1. **Publishing the profile package**: This occurs at the package level and converts all its content into a single profile XML file.

2. **Publishing the diagram profile package**: Also works at the package level and produces a single diagrams XML file.

3. **Publishing the toolbox diagrams**: This step works at the diagram level and produces a single XML file for each toolbox diagram defined.

4. **Generating the MDG**: This step combines all the above XML files into a single XML file, which is the MDG file that can be imported into other Sparx EA projects.

Publishing errors will be displayed only if there is a fundamental problem that the MDG publisher cannot understand. Still, in many cases, the generator will display a message indicating the successful publishing of the MDG. This, however, does not mean that everything will be guaranteed to work as expected, which unfortunately can consume a lot of time to find and fix. If you have used a programming language with no compilers, like JavaScript, you know how difficult it can be to find issues in the code. This is why it is highly advisable to create a copy of the last working MDG project before making any changes to it, so you can roll back to the point in time before the changes are made.

To see how the MDG works, it must be imported into a different project, either to test it or to use it, and the process in both cases is the same.

Importing the MDG

Like any other software product, the MDG must be tested before it is imported to the main repository project. The main reason for testing an MDG is to ensure that the metamodel that is being built and developed contains the right elements and relationships and applies the desired constraints when connecting elements. No fatal errors will occur if the MDG is incorrect, and Sparx EA will not crash from an incorrect MDG, but if your metamodel has incorrect elements or relationships, it will result in incorrect artifacts. Incorrect artifacts mean wasted time and effort, which is something that no one wants to have.

A separate Sparx EA project will be needed just for testing. Using traditional testing techniques, such as test cases, can be helpful. If you are testing your own work, you must switch hats from being the MDG developer to being the MDG tester, and it is even better to have the MDG tested by a specialized testing team, especially in larger organizations. To test an MDG, the published XML file must be imported into the testing project. This will make all the MDG elements, relationships, diagram types, and toolboxes available for use in the testing project.

Sparx EA will give basic errors if the XML file is corrupted or not found, but will not give useful errors if there is something logically wrong in the MDG. Therefore, make sure that the testing scenarios cover every possible aspect that an architect can go through. Once everything works and behaves as desired, then it is time to import the MDG to the EA repository.

Importing the MDG to the main EA repository project is exactly like importing it to the testing project. Keep in mind that some of the diagrams that you may have created using older versions of the MDG will be automatically updated when you import a new version of the MDG, but some diagrams will not and must be updated manually. If, for example, you have defined a usage relationship between elements A and B in an older MDG version, then you change that relationship to dependency in a later MDG version, all the diagrams that have been created with the older version will be updated to reflect the new relationship type. However, if you delete the stereotype of element A from the MDG, Sparx EA will not automatically delete all the occurrences of this element.

We will take examples to clarify both cases as we progress. After you have been introduced to the theory of the MDG development lifecycle, it is time to practice it to understand it better. It is important to keep in mind that the exercise that we are about to start is not a sample exercise for illustration purposes only; it is a cornerstone in building an actual MDG that we will use throughout this book, which you can also use in your enterprise. So, make sure that you understand this chapter very well and do not give up easily.

Building the MDG

For a practical learning example, our MDG will start with the elements and the relationships that will be needed in *Chapter 6, Modeling Business Capabilities*. Then, at the beginning of each upcoming chapter, we will identify what needs to be added to it and create an SOW for that iteration. With this agile iterative approach, we can deliver value in less time, which is a key success factor for a successful enterprise architecture practice.

In the previous section, *MDG development lifecycle*, we introduced the methodology for building an MDG. In this section, we will follow it and build a small but functional MDG, so the first thing to do is to identify the MDG SOW.

Identifying the MDG SOW

To know what is in the scope of work for the current MDG development iteration, we must ask what we are planning to achieve. Our short-term goal is to have an MDG that contains what we need to build EA artifacts in *Chapter 6, Modeling Business Capabilities*. Therefore, we will use the TOGAF metamodel, starting with the **Business Capability** element, and identify how it is connected to the elements around it. The list of elements and relationships that we identify will be the SOW of this iteration of the MDG development.

Follow these steps to define the MDG SOW:

1. Find the Business Capability element on the TOGAF metamodel diagram. It is in the business architecture layer, located almost in the middle of the diagram.

2. Trace the relationships from the Business Capability element to the elements that are connected to it.

3. Write down how the Business Capability element is related to the other elements. Also, write down how the other elements are related to the Business Capability element.

The resulting list will contain the following:

- Business Capability is influenced by the **Course of Action**. Course of Action influences Business Capability.

- Business Capability enables a **Value Stream**. Value Stream is enabled by Business Capability.

- Business Capability is used by an **Organization Unit**. The Organization Unit delivers Business Capability.

- Business Capability is delivered by **Function**. Function delivers Business Capability.

- Business Capability uses **Business Information**. Business Information is used by Business Capability.

- Business Capability is operationalized by **Process**. Process operationalizes Business Capability.

As you can see, the list contains six new elements in addition to the Business Capability element, which makes them seven. The list also contains relationships that can be read in two directions. The first direction is from the Business Capability to the elements, and it tells how the Business Capability is related to them. The second direction is read from the elements to the Business Capability, and it tells how they are related to it.

In most cases, reading a relationship from one direction to the other can have the same meaning, but it depends on whether we are reading it forward or backward. In a few other cases, a single connector can have a completely different meaning if the labels are read forward or backward. In a case like this, we will have two relationships even if the TOGAF metamodel is showing them as one. A good example is the connector between the Business Capability and the Organization Unit. The Delivers and Is used by relationships are very different relationships. Therefore, we will consider them as two; so we will use two statements regarding the Organization Unit in the SOW instead of one:

- Organization Unit uses Business Capability. Business Capability is used by Organization Unit.

- Organization Unit delivers Business Capability. Business Capability is delivered by Organization Unit.

Note: **We will delay the definitions of all the identified elements and relationships to later chapters. We will keep our focus in this chapter on creating the MDG, not the definitions and meanings.**

Our MDG SOW is what we have in the following list:

- **Create the following elements**: Business Capability, Organization Unit, Course of Action, Value Stream, Function, Process, and Business Information.

- **Create the following relationships**: Influences, enables, operationalizes, uses, and delivers.

- Relate the elements to each other as defined in the TOGAF metamodel.

- Create a new toolbox to contain the new Business Capability elements and relationships.

- Create a new Business Capability diagram type and associate the toolbox with it.

The next step is to incorporate the MDG SOW into an MDG project.

Incorporating the MDG SOW

Building an MDG follows the same concept of creating diagrams, placing elements on them, connecting the elements, and deleting them when they are no longer needed. This is where the name MDG came from because the development is model-driven, meaning it is based on models, and as we know, the name model is another name for the name diagram. The only thing to keep in mind is that MDG development uses special elements and connectors that are different from those in standard UML.

Since this is our first MDG development iteration, we will create a new project for building the MDG, starting from the first step, which is initiating a new MDG project.

Initiating a new MDG project

Sparx EA allows opening many sessions at the same time. We will use this feature to have the MDG developed in its own project. If having multiple sessions of Sparx EA open at the same time confuses you and causes you to make mistakes, you do not have to. You can close a project and open another as desired if you find working on a single session at a time easier. It is preferable to pin all three projects on the start page to be able to switch between them quickly. Whatever your preference is, let us follow these steps to create a new MDG project:

1. Start Sparx EA. In the new empty project, the **Start Page** will be opened by default in the diagrams area.

2. Click on **Create New** to create a new project file and provide a file name for the project.

3. Provide a file name of your choice following the same naming convention that you use for Sparx EA project files, if you have one. A suggested naming can be a combination of the abbreviated company name that you work for, underscore, and a name indicating the purpose of the file, such as `abc_mdg_TOGAF10.qea`.

4. Once the file is created in the specified location, the **Project Browser** will contain a single new **Model** element listed.

5. From the toolbar, click on **Start | Design | Create | Model Builder (pattern library)**. The **Model Builder** in *Figure 3.2* will open:

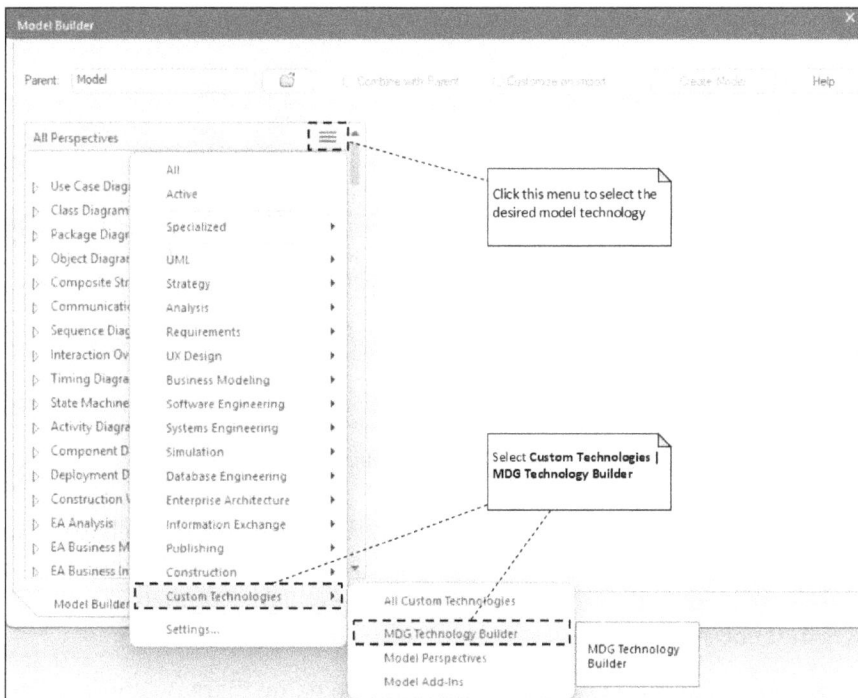

Figure 3.2: Creating a new MDG project from a pattern

6. Click **Custom Technologies | MDG Technology Builder** to narrow the list of available patterns to MDG technology builder only.

7. Expand the **MDG Technology Builder** item to see the list of MDG patterns, which includes two elements: **Starter Template**, and **Basic Template**.

8. Select **Basic Template**. Leave all the other settings unchanged and click the **Create Model** button on the top right side of the screen, as indicated in *Figure 3.3*:

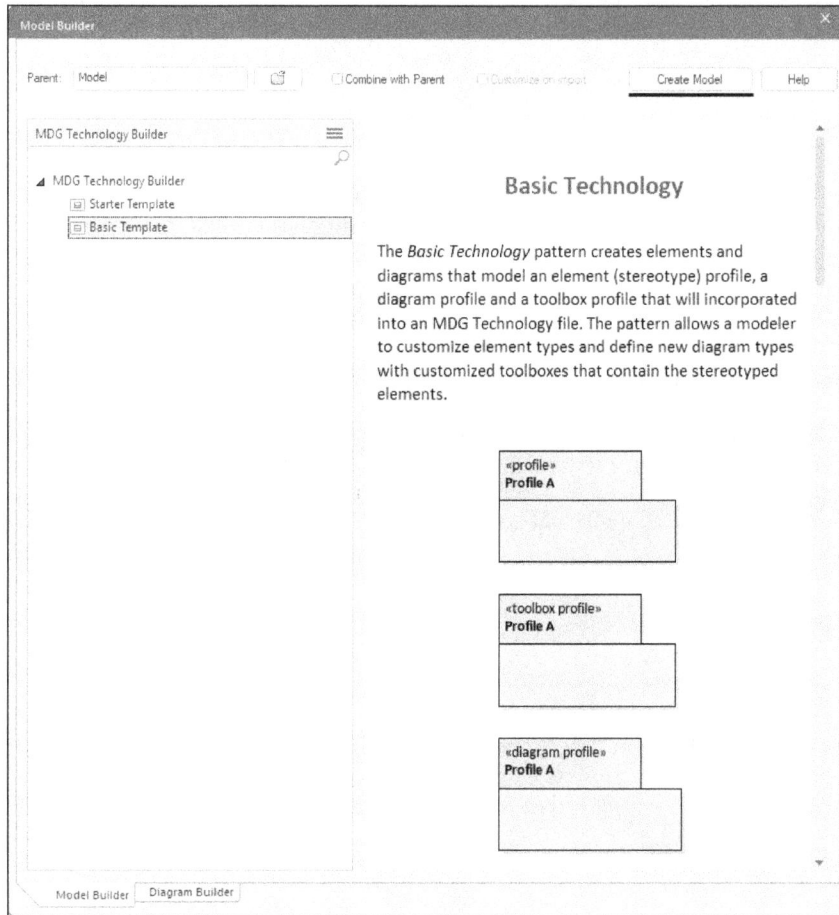

Figure 3.3: Selecting basic technology template

9. A popup will prompt you to name the MDG. Enter any name you like but make it self-descriptive such as `TOGAF10_MDG`. This name does not have to be the same name as the project file that you entered in *Step 3*. This name will differentiate the MDG from other MDGs that you may have.

A new package with the name **TOGAF10_MDG** (or the name that you chose in *Step 8*) will be created under the **Model** element in the **Project Browser** as you can see in *Figure 3.4*:

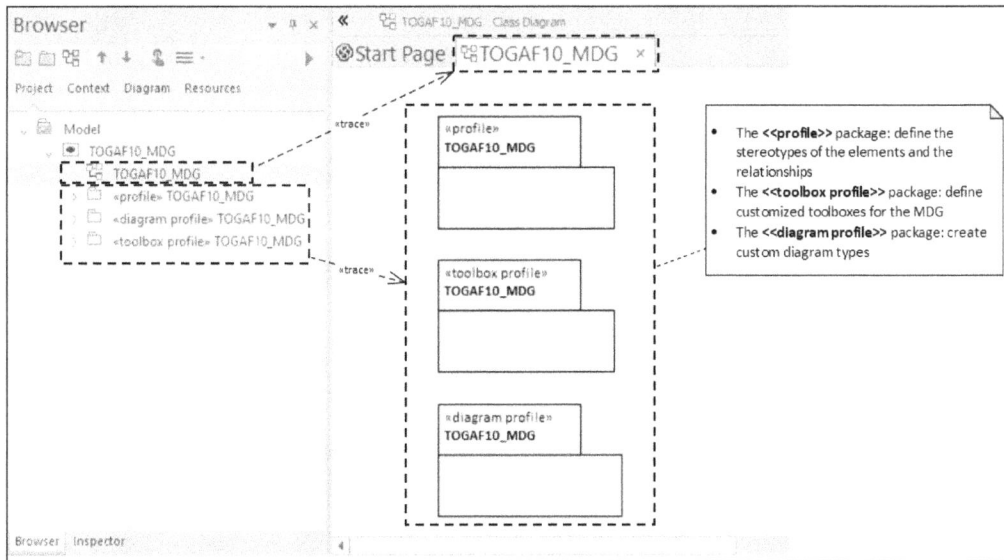

Figure 3.4: *MDG package structure*

Note: **The ‹‹trace›› relationship between any two elements indicates that both elements are the same but with two different representations.**

Let us explore the created packages and diagrams before going into detail. The **TOGAF10_MDG** package will contain a diagram and three packages, and they all have the same name but with different stereotypes. The **TOGAF10_MDG** diagram will open by default in the diagrams area, showing the three **TOGAF10_MDG** child packages. The packages have the following three different purposes:

- **The package with the ‹‹profile›› stereotype**: The package that will contain the metamodel's stereotypes of the elements and relationships. Since Sparx EA does not contain a Business Capability element, for example, we must extend a standard UML element, such as the activity. The new element will look like a UML activity element but with the ‹‹**Business Capability**›› stereotype. We will do the same thing for relationships. We will extend a standard UML relationship such as the **Association** into a TOGAF relationship like ‹‹**Influences**››. We will see in detail how to do this in the *Extending elements* and *Extending connectors* subsections.

- **The package with the ‹‹toolbox profile›› stereotype**: The toolboxes contain the elements and connectors that we can use on customized diagram types. Since we are creating new elements and connectors for the MDG, we need to create new toolboxes to contain them, so they can be used on the diagrams. We will learn more about this in the *Building custom toolboxes* subsection.

- **The package with the ‹‹diagram profile›› stereotype**: The package that will contain new customized diagram types that are not in Sparx EA by default. The diagram types that will be created in this package will be linked to the toolboxes from the ‹‹**toolbox profile**›› package, so Sparx EA can provide us with the right toolboxes for the selected types of diagrams. We will learn more about it in the *Extending diagrams* subsection.

Let us first start with extending the elements.

Extending elements

Extending elements basically means stereotyping base UML elements with new stereotypes, which by UML nature makes them different elements. They will look like the base elements, but they will be recognized differently in the repository. A stereotype is an extension to a base element or connector, so to create new element types that are not in Sparx EA by default, we must stereotype base UML elements. With the MDG SOW in hand, the first stereotype that we need to create is the Business Capability element. Follow these steps to see how:

1. Double-click on the profile package. This will open a diagram showing the contents of the package, which will be empty.

2. Look at the **Toolbox** and notice how it contains the elements that we can use in MDG profile diagrams. The **Toolbox** is divided into sections and elements are categorized in it.

3. The **Profile** section in the **Toolbox** is expanded by default. The **Profile Helper** section below is not, so click on it to expand it. You may use the helpers to simplify or speed up the MDG creation process, but you can also do it without using them.

4. Click **Add Stereotype** helper, then click on the diagram, which will open the **Add Stereotype** dialog.

   We must set some important values in this popup dialog to create the Business Capability stereotype.

5. Enter the value `Business Capability` in the **Name** field.

6. Keep **Type | Element Extension** selected.

7. Click the **Add Metaclass** button to tell Sparx EA what the metaclass is that we need to extend.

   Meta classes are the base UML classes that we will extend through stereotyping. We can use any metaclass we want, but if the target stereotype represents a structural element, then we had better use a UML structural metaclass. If the stereotype represents a behavioral element, then we had better use a UML behavioral metaclass. Since the Business Capability element is considered a behavioral element, we had better use a UML behavioral element as its metaclass.

   Stereotypes will inherit all the properties of their metaclasses in addition to their appearance. If the metaclass has a property called Status, for example, the stereotype will also have that same property. If the metaclass appears as an oval shape, so will the stereotype. This is why it is helpful to familiarize yourself with the properties and appearance of the meta classes to find the proper one to extend.

8. Check out the list and see which UML element has the best visual representation of the Business Capability element. We will choose **Activity** as it seems to be the nearest match we could think of, but you can choose a different metaclass if you prefer a different appearance.

9. Select **Activity,** then click **OK**.

10. Click on **Extensions | Activity** in the list. Now you see two sets of attributes, one on the left for the new **Stereotype**, and the other set on the right is for the base **Metaclass**. You can either add values in these attributes to override their default values, or you can leave them with their defaults.

11. Leave all the attributes without changing their values. We will come back and change some of these attributes when we need to, but let us keep it simple for now.

The **Add Stereotype** popup should look like the one in *Figure 3.5*:

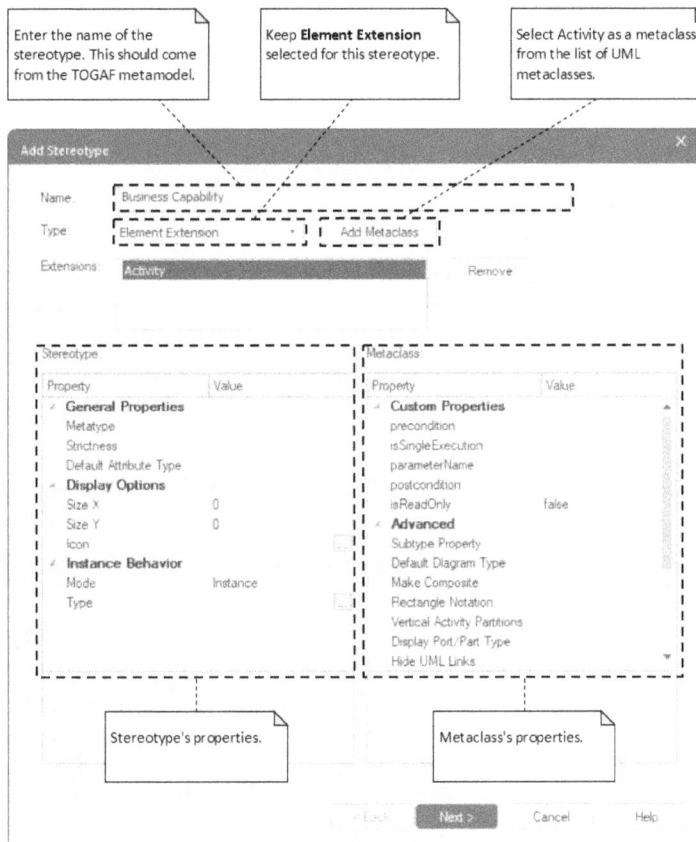

Figure 3.5: Add stereotype dialog

12. Click **Next** to accept the settings on this screen and move to the next one. The **Define Tagged Values** popup will ask if you want to create new Tagged Values. We will skip this for now and will revisit it later in *Chapter 4, Advanced Model Driven Generation*.

13. Click **Next** to open the **Define Shape Script** popup, which we will also skip for now and save for the same chapter.

14. Click **Finish**.

The helper finishes, and it will create two elements on the diagram and in the **Project Browser** connected by the extension relationship, which is represented by a solid line with a solid triangular arrowhead. This can be read as: the Business Capability stereotype extending the activity metaclass. Organize these two elements in a nice way, as you can see in *Figure 3.6* and explore what is on the diagram and what is in the **Project Browser**.

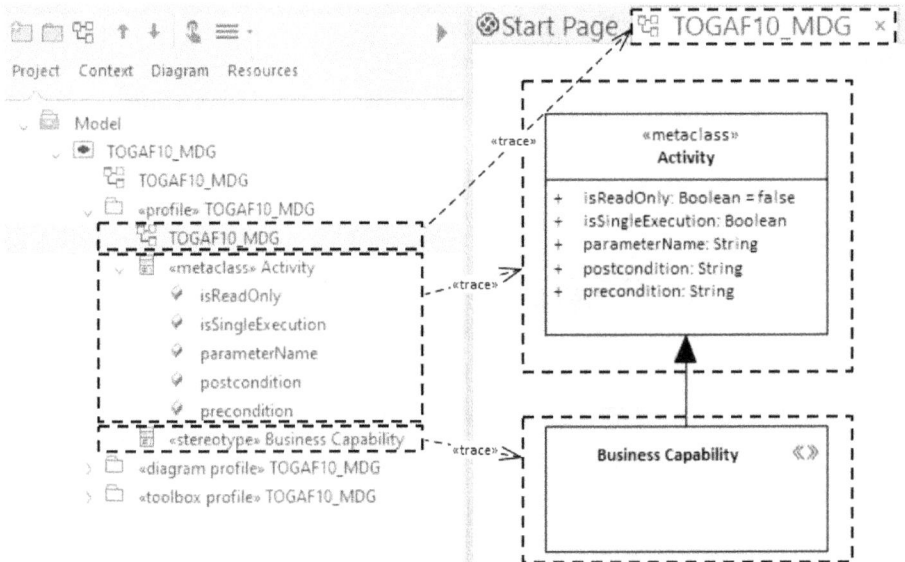

Figure 3.6: Business Capability stereotype

The first element is the base ‹‹**metaclass**›› that we chose to extend, and in this case, it is the **Activity** metaclass. Notice how expanding the ‹‹**metaclass**›› in the **Project Browser** to the left shows its attributes that you can also see on the right. These are default properties that we have not adjusted their values, but Sparx EA lists them by default. We can safely delete them and remember that we can add them back if needed, so we will delete them from the **Project Browser** either one by one or by selecting all of them and deleting them together. If other properties from *Figure 3.5* were overridden, they will appear on this diagram too.

We have six more stereotypes to create and add to the MDG, so repeat the same steps to create the Process stereotype:

1. Click on **Add Stereotype** helper, and then click on the diagram.

2. Enter the value **Process** in the **Name** field.

3. Keep **Type | Element Extension** selected.

4. Click the **Add Metaclass** button. The Process is considered a behavioral element, so the best UML match is the **Activity**.

5. Select **Activity** then click **OK**.

6. Click **Next**, click **Next**, then click **Finish**.

Repeat the same steps for the **Function, Value Stream**, and **Course of Action** stereotypes. *Figure 3.7* shows the five new stereotypes, all extending the activity metaclass:

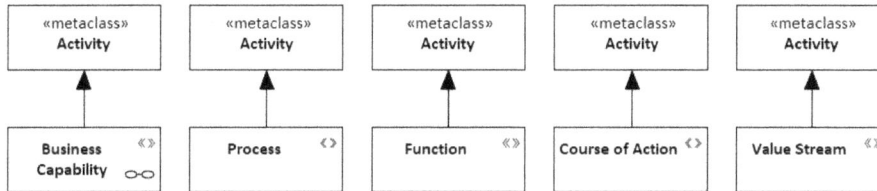

Figure 3.7: *Newly created behavioral stereotypes*

You may wonder, if all the elements extend the same metaclass, then why did we not extend all of them from the same metaclass? The answer is yes; it is possible, as we can see in *Figure 3.8*:

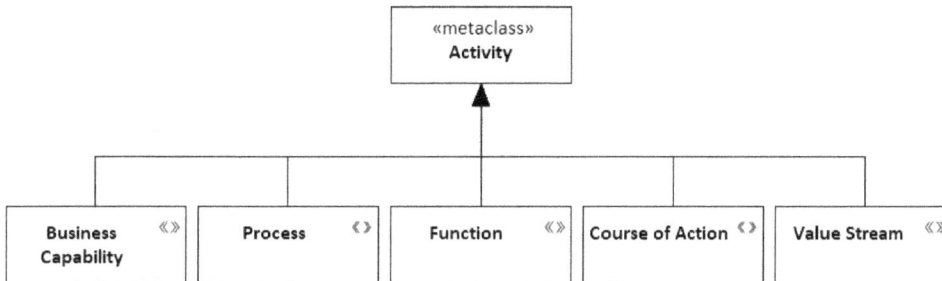

Figure 3.8: *Extending from the same metaclass*

Following this approach is possible but will create a scalability constraint to the MDG. Any change that we make in the future to the metaclass's attributes will affect all the extended stereotypes, which is a double-edged sword. On the one hand, we will make the change only once. On the other hand, we may not like all stereotypes to have the same change. For example, setting the default diagram type to a specific diagram type will affect all the stereotypes, which is something that we do not want to happen because each stereotype would have a different default diagram type. Therefore, we will keep following the first approach in *Figure 3.7* as it gives us more scalability.

There are still two more elements from the MDG SOW that have not been added yet, and these are the Business Information and the Organization Unit. Both elements are structural elements, so we better use a structural UML metaclass to extend from. Technically, and as we mentioned earlier, we can still extend the activity metaclass, but to have a more professional look at our MDG elements, it is better to extend structural UML elements such as the Class for structural stereotypes. Follow the same steps for extending the two remaining stereotypes:

1. Click on **Add Stereotype** helper then click on the diagram.

2. Enter the value `Organization Unit` in the **Name** field.

3. Keep **Type | Element Extension** selected.

4. Click the **Add Metaclass** button.

5. Select **Class** then click **OK**.

6. Click **Next**, click **Next**, then click **Finish**.

Notice that the attributes of the **Class** metaclass are a bit different from those for Activity, which is expected since one metaclass is behavioral and the other metaclass is structural. Repeat the same steps for the Business Information stereotype, delete all the unneeded properties from all the metaclasses, and the result should now look like *Figure 3.9*:

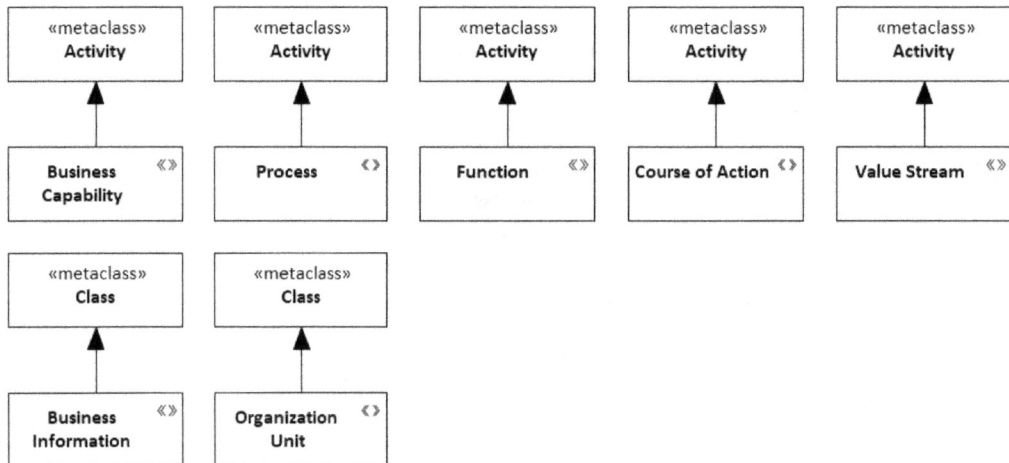

Figure 3.9: Extended stereotypes and their metaclasses

All elements on this figure are well aligned and perfectly spaced. This is a highly advisable practice to follow in any diagram you make. Always make your diagrams outstanding, even if no one else will see them but you. Even if they are for temporary use or are just drafts. A diagram is an artifact that carries your signature, so make sure it reflects your true image as a skilled architect. Paying attention to the fine details is a huge factor for making your diagrams outstanding.

Now we have added the elements that we have in the MDG SOW, the next step is to add the relationship connectors.

Extending connectors

The steps for extending connectors are very similar to those for extending elements. UML relationships are very simple, and they are: association, generalization, realization, dependency, aggregation, and composition. Since we are only concerned about extending them with stereotypes at this time, we should not spend time trying to understand what they mean. What is more important is how they look because the extended stereotypes will inherit their shapes. *Figure 3.10* lists the standard UML relationships.

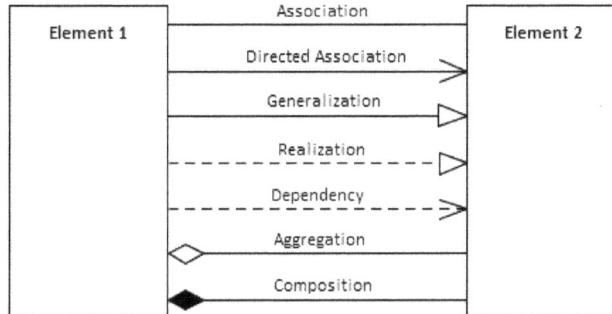

Figure 3.10: *UML standard relationships*

Notice how there are two shapes for the association relationship, one with an arrowhead and one without. Having an arrowhead helps in better understanding how to read the relationship by knowing where to start the reading and where to end, in other words, what is the source and the destination of the relationship.

Follow these steps to create the influences connector stereotype. We will use the same stereotype helper that we used in the previous subsection, but some selections and properties need to be adjusted to work for the connectors:

1. Click on **Add Stereotype** helper from the **Toolbox**, then click on the diagram. The **Add Stereotype** dialog will pop up.

2. Type **Influences** in the **Name** field. This is the label that will appear on the connector to differentiate this stereotype from other stereotypes.

3. Select **Connector Extension** from the **Type**.

4. Click on **Add Metaclass**, select **Association** or any other connector metaclass from the list, then click **OK.**

5. Click on **Association** in the **Extensions** list box.

6. Find the **Direction** property in the list of **Metaclass** properties and set its value to **Source -> Destination**. If you do not set this value, the MDG will still work, but the connector will look like a line with no arrowhead, and understanding it will be harder.

7. In **Metaclass | Connector Options | Meaning Forwards**, enter **Influences**.

8. In **Metaclass** | **Connector Options** | **Meaning Backwards**, enter `Is influenced by`.

9. Click **Next**, click **Next**, then click **Finish**.

You should see the new influences relationship on the diagram, and it will look like the other stereotypes but with a different metaclass. The metaclass shows that it has three overridden properties: the **direction, _MeaningBackwards,** and the **_MeaningForwards**. These properties will appear on the diagram as class attributes because we have altered their default values.

Repeat the same steps and create the enables, delivers, and operationalizes by providing the values `Enables`, `Delivers`, and `Operationalizes` in the **Name** field, respectively. You also need to set the **_MeaningBackwards** and **_MeaningForwards** attributes accordingly. The last relationship is the uses, and we will do the same steps, but we will use the **Dependency** metaclass instead of the association. We can use the association, of course, but using the *uses* stereotype on a dependency relationship is more aligned with the industry. The outcome should look like *Figure 3.11*:

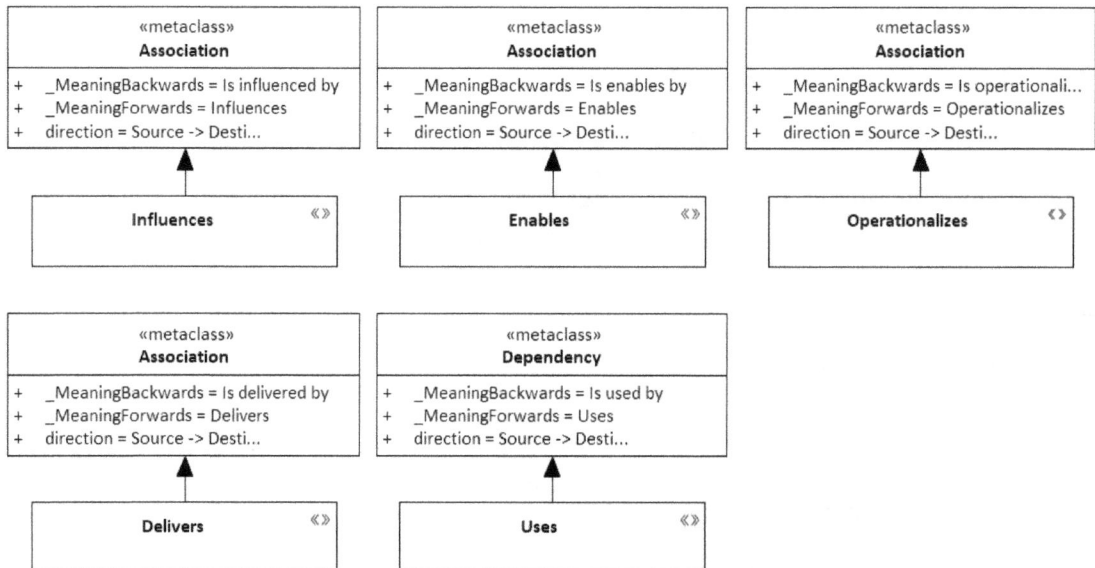

Figure 3.11: The connectors' stereotypes

We have the elements and the connectors' stereotypes, and what we need to do next is to define the relationships between them.

Defining relationships

At this point, we have the stereotypes that we need. What is still missing is to define how stereotyped elements can be related to each other through stereotyped connectors. We need to restrict the possible relationships to what we have in the MDG SOW. Follow these steps to do that:

1. Right-click on the Business Capability stereotype and select **New Child Diagram** | **Composite Structure Diagram**. This will create a composite child diagram in which we will define the details of the relationships. This way, we keep the details of each stereotype composed in a separate diagram, or else we will end up with hundreds of crossing lines on the profiles diagram.

2. Double-click on the Business Capability stereotype to open its composite child diagram.

3. From the **Project Browser**, drag the Business Capability stereotype element and drop it onto the empty diagram.

4. The dialog box in *Figure 3.12* will pop up asking you to choose how you want to drop the Business Capability on the diagram.

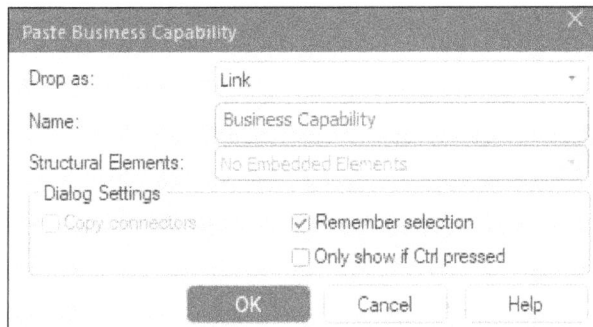

Figure 3.12: Paste Business Capability dialog

5. Select **Drop as** | **Link** and leave all the other options unchanged.

6. Optionally, check the **Remember selection** checkbox so that Sparx EA remembers your choices and makes them the default for next time.

7. Drag the Business Information, Course of Action, Function, Process, Organization Unit, and Value Stream stereotypes and drop them onto the diagram as links too.

8. Click the **OK** button.

Place the Business Capability element in the center of the diagram and organize the elements around it in a nice way. Refer to the MDG SOW to remember what the identified relationships are, and start with the relationship between the Business Capability and the Value Stream, which is *Enables* and *Is enabled by*:

1. From the **Toolbox**, expand the **Metamodel** group if it is not already expanded, and click on **Stereotyped Relationship**. The mouse icon will change into a hand shape.

2. Click and hold down the mouse button on the Business Capability stereotype on the diagram.

3. Move the mouse above the Value Stream stereotype and release it. A new connector with a ‹‹**stereotyped relationship**›› label will be created, going from the Business Capability

stereotype to the Value Stream stereotype. This indicates that this relationship is not a standard UML relationship but a stereotyped one. Therefore, we must provide the name of the connector's stereotype to use.

4. Double-click on the ‹‹**stereotyped relationship**›› connector (on the dashed line itself) to open the connector's properties dialog box.

5. Click on the **Tags** tab and enter the value **Enables** in the **stereotype** tag, as you can see in *Figure 3.13*, then click the **OK** button.

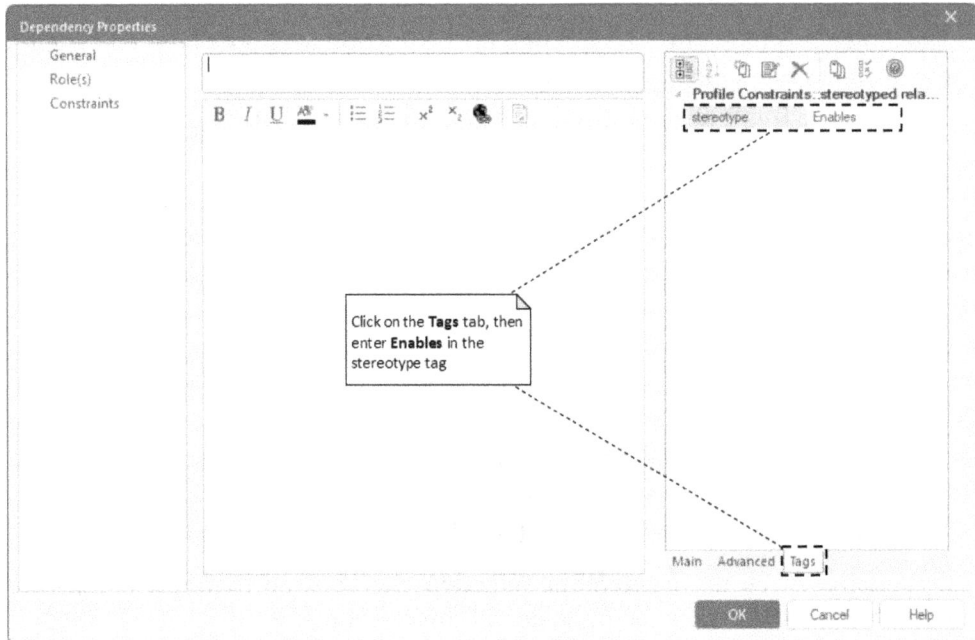

Figure 3.13: Connector's properties dialog box

Note: Make sure that you provide the name of the stereotype exactly as it is defined, including the case of letters.

You can now see an additional description added to the connector's label identifying the name of the stereotype that this connector represents, as you can see in *Figure 3.14*.

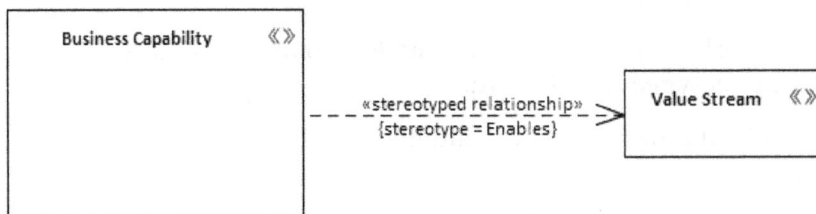

Figure 3.14: A stereotyped relationship

Entering the name of the stereotype in the Tagged Value was a free text, manual entry, not a selection from the list of extended relationships that have been created. This is another area that future versions of Sparx EA need to consider enhancing. No warning will be displayed when entering invalid values. Making mistakes like this can easily happen and it usually results in people spending hours trying to find what is wrong without getting any helpful error messages. Unfortunately, developing MDGs is not as easy as it should be, but at the same time, once you practice it multiple times, you will know better how to deal with it.

Repeat *Steps 1* to *5* to add the remaining relationships between the Business Capability stereotype and the other stereotypes. This means that we will create:

- A stereotyped relationship with **stereotype** tag value = **Uses**, going from the Business Capability to the Business Information.

- A stereotyped relationship with **stereotype** tag value = **Influences**, going from the Course of Action to the Business Capability.

- A stereotyped relationship with **stereotype** tag value = **Delivers**, going from the Function to the Business Capability.

- A stereotyped relationship with **stereotype** tag value = **Operationalizes**, going from the Process to the Business Capability.

- A stereotyped relationship with **stereotype** tag value = **Delivers**, going from the Organization Unit to the Business Capability.

- A stereotyped relationship with **stereotype** tag value = **Uses**, going from the Organization Unit to the Business Capability.

Your final diagram should look like the one in *Figure 3.15*. This artifact is called the **Business Capability focused-metamodel**. Focused-metamodels are partial views taken from the entire metamodel, showing and focusing on one element at a time.

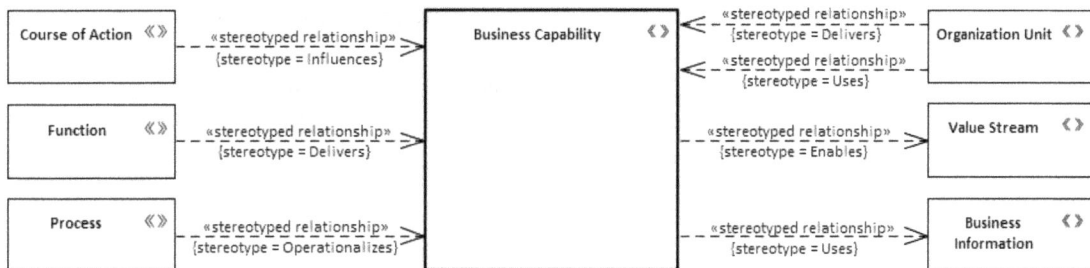

Figure 3.15: Business Capability focused metamodel

Now we need to perform a cleanup exercise before leaving this topic to another which is the visibility of the connectors on other diagrams. To know what we are targeting to clean up, look at the TOGAF10_MDG diagram which contains the stereotypes that we have defined earlier. The diagram will look like the one in *Figure 3.16*:

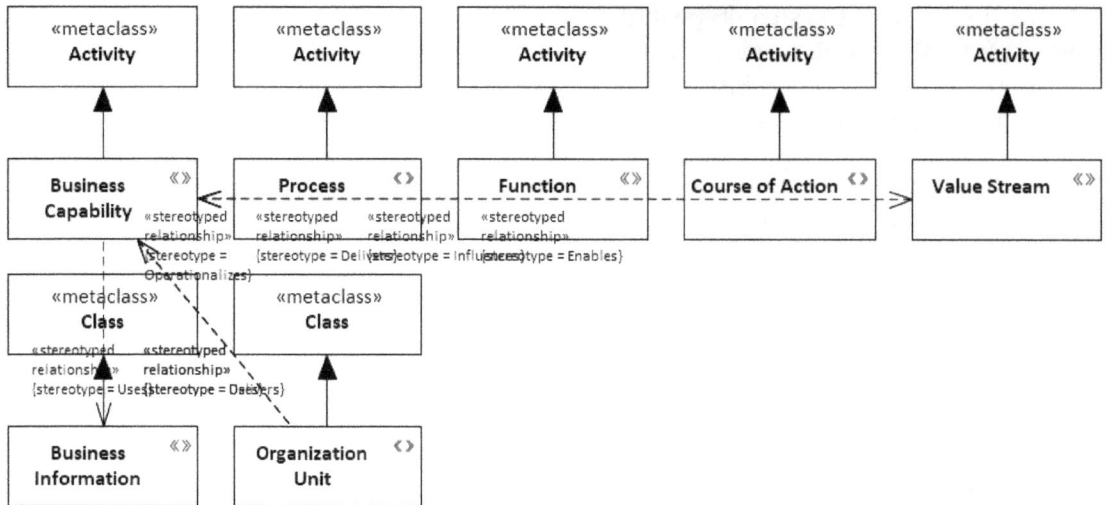

Figure 3.16: Unsuppressed relationships appearing on every other diagram

When we add a relationship between any two elements on a diagram, Sparx EA automatically adds the same relationship to every other diagram that contains these two elements, even if this is not what we want to happen. Sparx EA cannot tell whether we want the relationship to appear or not, so it displays it by default. Therefore, we must manually ask it to hide the relationship from appearing in other existing diagrams, because the relationship might be irrelevant to the context of those diagrams. Perform the following steps to clean up the other diagrams from the irrelevant relationships:

1. Open the Business Capability focused metamodel diagram.

2. Right-click on the dashed line of one of the connectors—not on its label—and select **Visibility | Hide Connector in Other Diagrams**. A dialog box like the one in *Figure 3.17* will pop up showing you a list of all other diagrams that this connector has been added to:

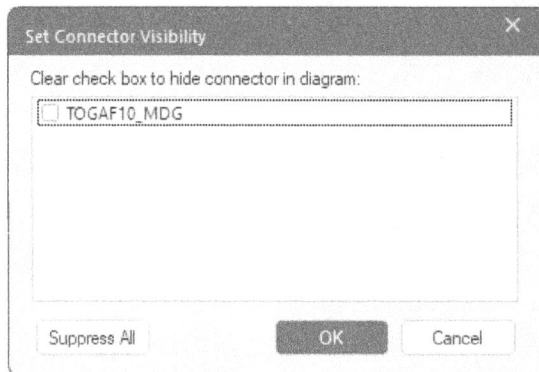

Figure 3.17: Set connector visibility dialog

3. Since we do not want this connector to appear on any other diagrams, including the **TOGAF10_MDG**, you must uncheck the box that is next to the diagram names in the list. You can uncheck all the boxes by clicking on the **Suppress All** button if the list has many items.

4. Click **OK** to close the dialog.

To avoid having your diagrams miss every time you add a new relationship, always check using **Visibility | Hide Connector in Other Diagrams** and hide it when it is not needed. Forgetting to do this is common, but you can always hide the unwanted relationships on any diagram by clicking on the relationship, pressing the *Delete* key on the keyboard, and choosing **Hide** the connector.

Now that we have created the stereotyped elements and the connectors that we need, let us put them in a toolbox so we can use them.

Building custom toolboxes

We all know what the toolboxes are and what they are used for. We have already introduced toolboxes in *Chapter 2, Sparx EA Crash Course*, and we have used them in multiple examples so far. Toolboxes in Sparx EA can usually contain multiple sections, also known as **toolbox groups**. They combine similar or related elements into sections, so using the toolboxes and navigating through their content can be easier.

In this section, we will create a new toolbox, and it will contain the newly created elements and connectors' stereotypes so they can be used on diagrams to create specialized EA artifacts. Follow these steps to create the Business Capability toolbox:

1. Make sure that the **TOGAF10_MDG** diagram that is in *Figure 3.4* is open and active. We already worked on ‹‹**profile**›› **TOGAF10_MDG** to create the stereotypes, and now we will work on the ‹‹**toolbox profile**›› **TOGAF10_MDG**.

2. Double-click on the ‹‹**toolbox profile**›› **TOGAF10_MDG** package. This will open an empty diagram showing the package's contents.

3. From the toolbox, click on **Create Custom Toolbox**, then click on the diagram.

4. A dialog box will pop up prompting you to specify the location of the toolbox profile package. Select the ‹‹**toolbox profile**›› **TOGAF10_MDG** package, then click **OK**.

5. Another dialog box will ask you to provide a name for the new toolbox. Enter `Business Capability Toolbox` in the **Toolbox Name** field. Optionally provide a **Description** and click **OK**.

6. A new diagram representing the Business Capability toolbox will be opened, with a new element on it having the ‹‹**metaclass**›› **ToolboxPage** name and stereotype. Sparx EA will automatically adjust the diagram's name to **TOGAF10_MDG_Business_Capability_Toolbox** by adding the MDG name as a prefix and separating the words with underscores instead of spaces.

7. Move the ‹‹**metaclass**›› **ToolboxPage** element from the corner of the diagram and place it around the center for better visibility. Do not rename this element or else Sparx EA will stop recognizing the diagram as a toolbox.

8. From the toolbox, click on **Profile Helpers | Add Toolbox Page**, then click on the diagram. The **Add Toolbox Page** dialog will pop up.

9. Provide a name such as **Elements** and optionally enter text in the **Tool Tip** field.

10. Click on the **Add** button (click on the button itself, not the arrow symbol next to it).

11. A dialog box will ask you to select the elements to be added to the toolbox page. Expand the ‹‹**profile**›› **TOGAF10_MDG** and select the **Business Capability**, **Business Information**, **Course of Action**, **Function**, **Organization Unit**, **Process**, and **Value Stream** stereotypes, then click **OK**. Remember that holding down the **Ctrl** key while selecting allows the selection of multiple elements.

12. The **Toolbox Items** section will now contain all the selected stereotypes. Provide an **Alias** for each element in the list, and they should be **Business Capability**, **Business Information**, **Course of Action**, **Function**, **Organization Unit**, **Process**, and **Value Stream**, respectively, as you can see in *Figure 3.18*. The aliases that you provide here are the elements' labels that will appear in the toolbox.

13. Click **OK** to accept and close.

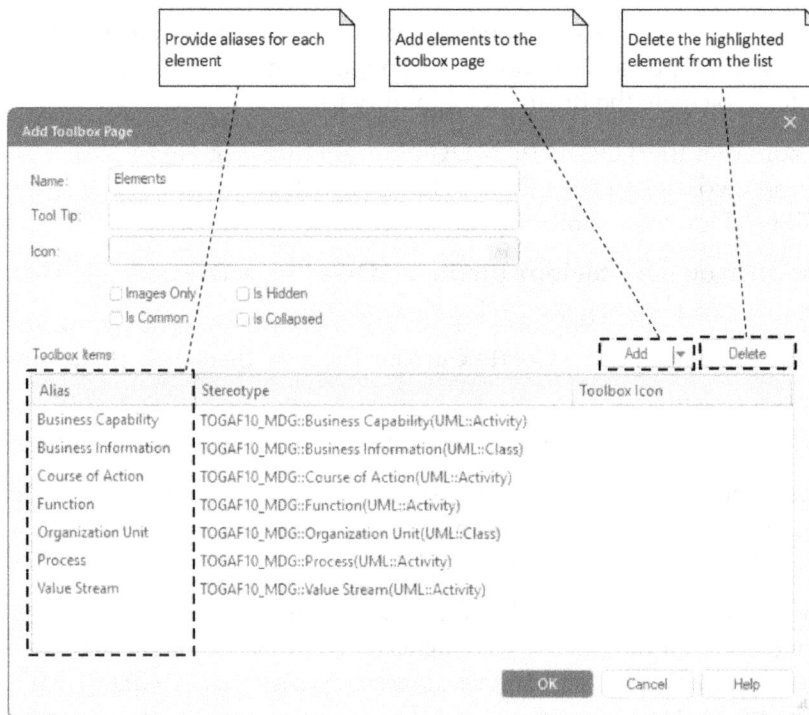

Figure 3.18: Add toolbox page dialog box

Once the dialog box is closed, you will see a new element extending the ‹‹**metaclass**›› **ToolboxPage**. The metaclass contains seven attributes representing the seven stereotype elements that we selected to include. Next, we need to add another toolbox page for the connectors, so continue with these steps.

14. Click **Profile Helpers | Add Toolbox Page** and click anywhere on the diagram.

15. Provide value in the **Name** field, such as `Connectors`.

16. Click the **Add** button, select the ‹‹**profile**›› **TOGAF10_MDG,** and add the **Delivers**, **Enables**, **Influences**, **Operationalizes**, and **Uses** stereotypes.

17. Provide aliases for all the connectors, which should be `Delivers`, `Enables`, `Influences`, `Operationalizes`, and `Uses,` respectively, then click **OK**.

Another element extending the **ToolboxPage** metaclass will be placed on the **TOGAF10_MDG_Business_Capability_Toolbox** diagram. Adjust the size of the elements and align them properly to look nice and clean, as depicted in *Figure 3.19*:

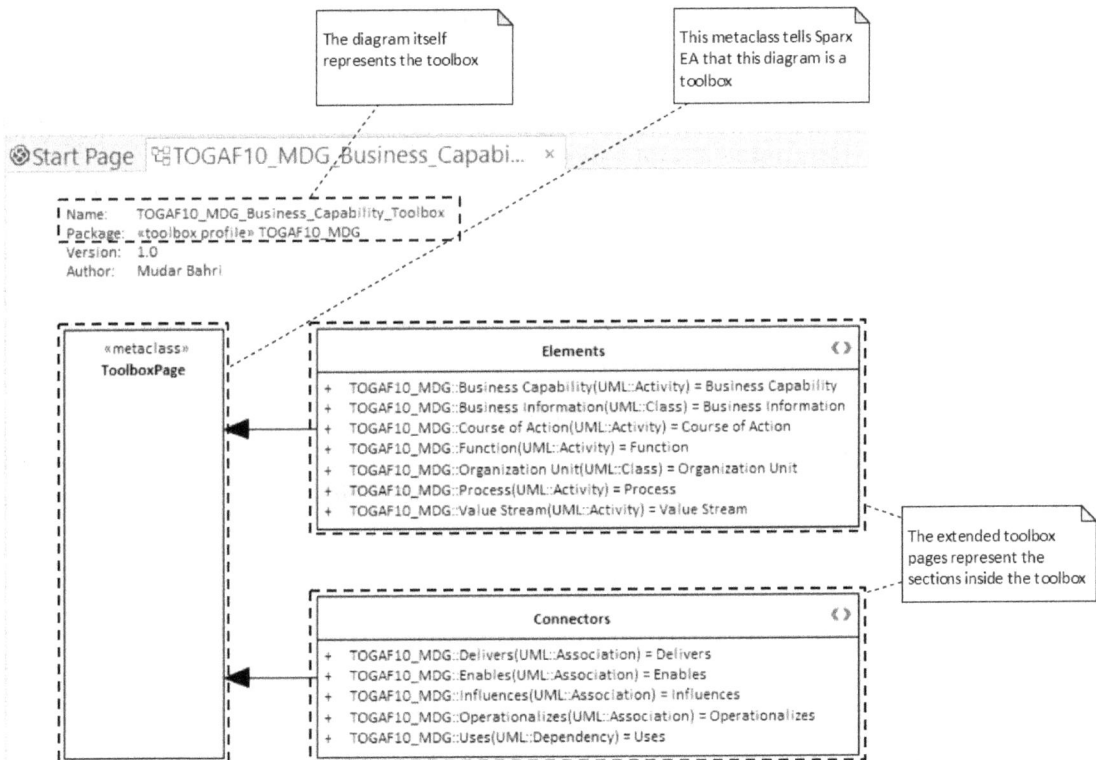

Figure 3.19: A toolbox with two toolbox pages

You can create as many toolboxes as needed. Each toolbox will be in its own diagram, and each can contain as many toolbox pages as needed. You can then associate these toolboxes to active by default with specific types of diagrams. To see how that works, we need to learn how to extend diagrams.

Extending diagrams

As you have experienced while creating diagrams in Sparx EA, whenever you create a new diagram, Sparx EA asks what the diagram type is, then it provides the proper toolbox associated with it by default. A diagram of type UML activity will have the UML activity toolbox associated with it while a diagram of type UML component will have the UML component toolbox associated with it. However, if we need to have a diagram of the type of *Business Capability Map,* we must tell Sparx EA to associate it to the Business Capability toolbox, or else it will only come with a toolbox that has the common elements and common relationships.

In this subsection, we will learn how to create a diagram of a type Business Capability map which we can use to create Business Capability map artifacts. Follow these steps to learn how:

1. Double-click on the ‹‹**diagram profile**›› **TOGAF10_MDG** package to open it.

2. From the **Toolbox**, click on **Profile Helpers | Add Diagram Extension**, then click on the diagram. The **Add Diagram Extension** dialog box will pop up.

3. Enter **Business Capability Map** in the **Name** field.

4. Select the extension type from the dropdown list. A diagram extension type represents the metaclass diagram that you want to extend. You can select any type you prefer but let us select **Activity** since we extended the Business Capability from the UML activity metaclass.

5. Optionally enter a value in the **Description**.

6. In the **Properties** section, find the **Toolbox Profile** property then select **TOGAF10_MDG_Business_Capability_Toolbox**. This is the toolbox that we created in the previous subsection.

7. Leave the remaining properties unchanged as shown in *Figure 3.20*, and click **OK**.

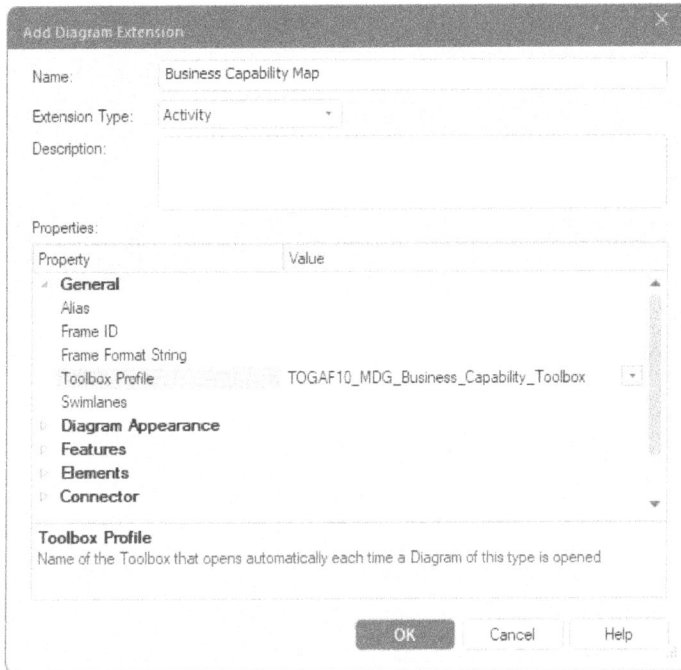

Figure 3.20: *Add diagram extension dialog box*

The diagram will contain a **Business Capability Map** stereotype extending the **Diagram_Activity** metaclass. Check out *Figure 3.21* for reference:

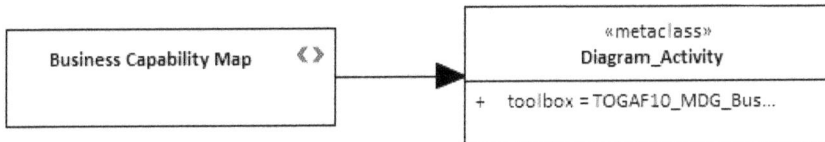

Figure 3.21: *Business Capability map diagram type*

Extending the diagram type was the last step in incorporating the MDG SOW phase of the MDG development lifecycle. You must be excited by now to see your MDG in action, and to do that you must publish it first, so let us learn how.

Publishing the MDG

Publishing the MDG basically means translating all the diagrams that we have created into a common markup language, which is XML. Publishing an MDG takes several steps. Here is an overview to help you understand them before we talk about them in more detail:

1. Publish the profile package, and the result is one XML file.
2. Publish the diagram package, and the result is another XML file.

3. Publish each toolbox diagram separately, which results in an XML file for each toolbox diagram.

4. Generate the MDG technology, which is also an XML file that combines all the previous XML files into one, and it is the target file that can be imported to be used in other repositories.

These steps are better performed in order, especially for the MDG technology step, which must always be the last step. If changes are made to elements in the profile package only and nothing else has been changed in other packages, we only need to republish the profile package and regenerate the MDG technology. The MDG technology wizard will reuse the previously published, unchanged XML files in the new MDG version. We will start by publishing the profile package, followed by the diagram package, the toolboxes, and finally the MDG technology, so let us learn how.

Publishing the profile package

Follow these steps to publish the profile package:

1. In the **Project Browser**, click on the ‹‹**profile**›› **TOGAF10_MDG** package. Make sure that you are highlighting the package not a diagram or an element inside it.

2. From the ribbon bar, click **Specialize | Technologies | Publish Technology | Publish Package as UML Profile** as indicated in *Figure 3.22*:

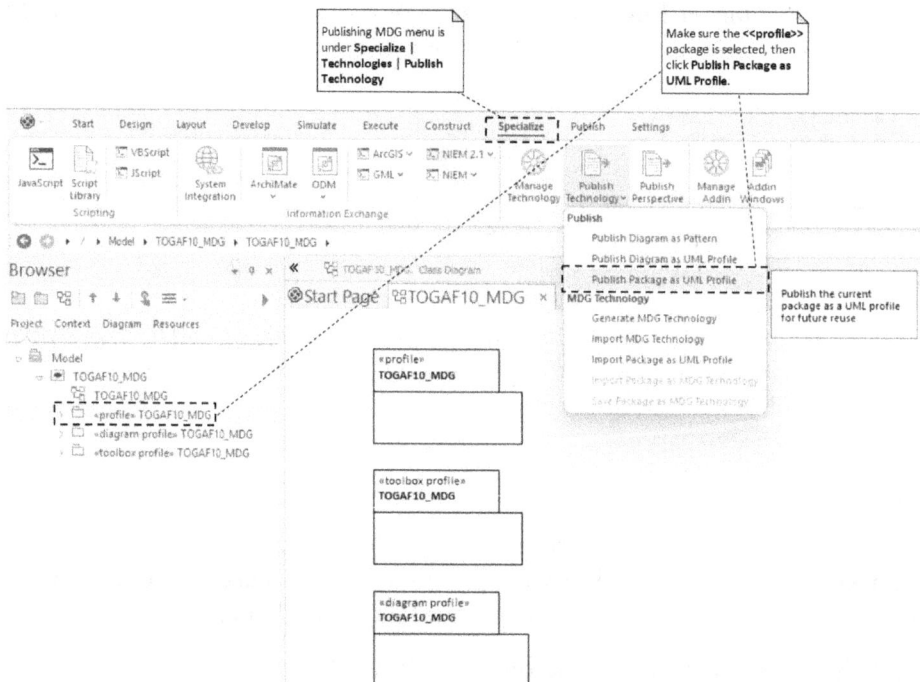

Figure 3.22: Publishing the profile package

5. Browse to find the same location where you stored the profile and the diagram profile XML files. Provide a descriptive name for the file such as `Business_Capability_Toolbox.xml` and click **Save**.

6. Click **Yes** if Sparx EA asks to overwrite an older version of the file or not.

7. Leave all the other options unchanged and click **Save**.

We have published all the XML files that we need for the MDG, and the last step is to generate the MDG technology.

Generating the MDG technology

The MDG technology file is another XML file that combines all the previously published XML files into one, with some additional tags, of course, to let Sparx EA understand what it is. The MDG Technology Creation Wizard is a software wizard that collects information in several sequential screens, such as where the XML files are, what to include, and what not to include to generate the technology. Because generating and regenerating MDG Technology files can be very repetitive, saving this information in a file will help speed up the process. For this reason, the wizard provides you with the ability to save this information in what is called the **MDG Technology Selections** (**MTS**) file. It is up to you to use it or not, but because it saves time, we will use it in the following steps, which will show how to generate the MDG Technology file:

1. From the ribbon bar, select **Specialize** | **Technologies** | **Publish Technology** | **Generate MDG Technology**. It does not matter what element is selected in the **Project Browser**.

2. This will launch the **MDG Technology Creation Wizard**. The first screen is just introducing the technology so skip it by clicking **Next**.

3. The second screen provides several selections regarding using an MTS file. You can either choose not to use one, create a new one, or use one that has already been created.

4. Since it is useful to use one, select **Create a new MTS file** and click **Next**.

5. In the third screen, provide the name and path for the MTS file, then click **Next**.

6. The wizard will ask for information about the MDG itself, such as its name, filename, ID, version, and other values. Enter `TOGAF10_MDG` in the **Technology** fields, provide a name and location for the MDG's XML file, provide a unique ID, and enter a text describing what the MDG is for in the **Notes** field, as depicted in *Figure 3.25*:

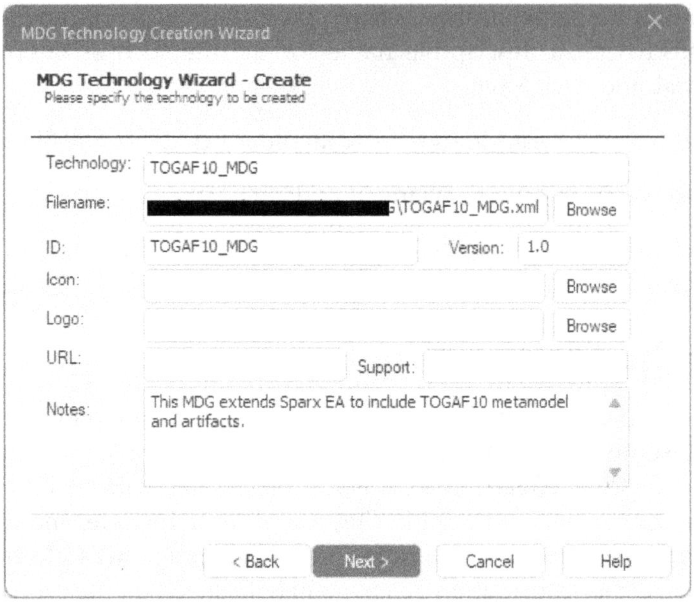

Figure 3.25: MDG Technology information

7. The rest of the fields are optional and can be left blank for now, so click **Next**.

> Note: **The ID value must be unique, as you cannot import two MDGs with the same ID into one repository.**

8. The next screen asks you what you want to include in the MDG. There are many options that we have not used yet, so we will only check the relevant boxes.

9. In the **Metamodel** group, check **Profiles**, **Diagram Types**, and **Toolboxes**.

10. Leave all the other boxes unchecked and click **Next**.

11. The wizard will start asking you about the XML files one by one, and it starts by asking you about the profiles file. Click on the *ellipsis* button to browse for the folder that contains the file. Select it and click **OK**.

12. A list of all the XML files that were found in that location will be listed to the left. From the list of **Available Files**, highlight the `TOGAF10_Profiles.xml` (or any other name that you chose), and click on the **->** button to move it under the **Selected Files** list as explained in *Figure 3.26*, then click **Next**.

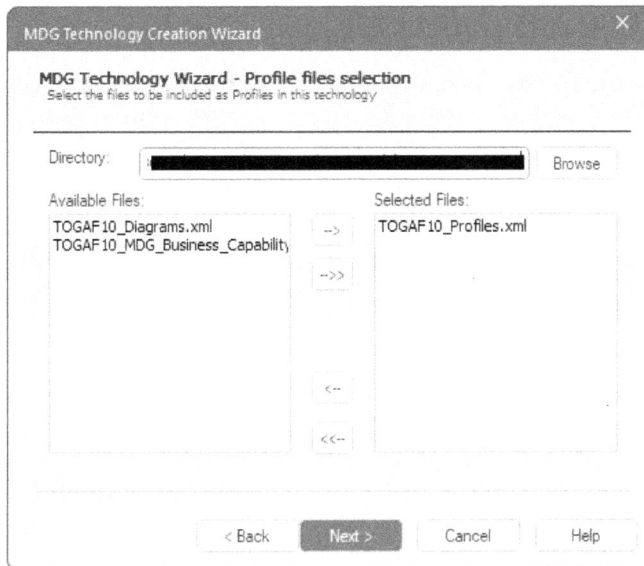

Figure 3.26: Selecting the published profiles file

13. The next screen will ask for the published diagrams file, so do the same by browsing for the folder, selecting **TOGAF10_Diagrams.xml**, moving it to the list of selected files, and clicking **Next**.

14. Do the same for the toolbox files. Keep in mind that there might be many toolbox files in the future. Select **TOGAF10_MDG_Business_Capability_Toolbox.xml**, then click **Next**.

15. The last wizard screen shows a summary and a checkbox to **Save to MTS**. Keep this box checked and click **Finish**.

If everything was done right, you should get a message saying that the **MDG Technology is successfully created** in the location that you defined. It is the message that everyone hopes to see after all these steps and screens, and the best reward that we hope to have is an MDG that works, so let us test it out.

Importing the MDG

If you built software before, you know for sure how it feels to see it being used by users. The same is true for MDGs. Seeing other architects using your product to create EA artifacts is a great reward for the effort that you made to build it. But before you deploy it to be used in the main repository, you need to test it, and even better, have someone test it after you do. In this subsection, we will import the MDG that we built into a new empty project that will be dedicated just for testing, so let us do that.

Creating the testing project

Creating the MDG testing project is not different from creating any project, but here is a quick reminder on how to do that. If you struggle with any of the following steps, refer to *Chapter 2, Sparx EA Crash Course,* to refresh your memory:

1. Start a new session of Sparx EA.

2. Click on **Create New** on the **Start Page** to create a new project file and provide a file name for the project, such as `Testing_TOGAF10_MDG`.

3. The **Project Browser** will contain the new **Model** element.

4. To import the MDG, use the ribbon bar and click **Specialize | Technologies | Publish Technology | Import MDG Technology**.

5. The **Import MDG Technology** dialog box will pop up. Use the ellipsis button to browse and find the `TOGAF10_MDG.xml` file. This is why it was important to give meaningful file names when publishing them.

6. Select the desired file and click **Open**. The dialog will display some read-only information about the MDG, such as its name, version, and notes.

7. Keep **Import To Model** selected and click **OK**. Unfortunately, there is nothing that indicates what happened, so we must manually check if the MDG was imported successfully or not.

8. In the **Browser** window, click on the **Resources** tab, which will show a list of resource packages.

9. Near the middle of the list, there is a package named **MDG Technologies**. Expand it, then expand its child package, **Model Technologies**. If the import was successful, you must see a package named **TOGAF10_MDG**.

10. Expand the **TOGAF10_MDG** package and all its subpackages. A successful MDG import will look like what you can see in *Figure 3.27*:

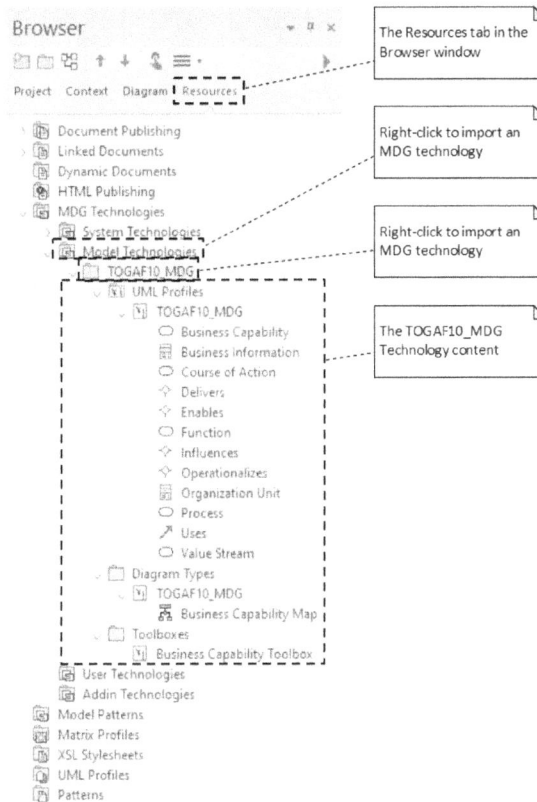

Figure 3.27: *MDG technology as a resource*

If you see all the listed resources under the **TOGAF10_MDG**, then it is a good indicator that the publishing and importing steps were successful. Right-clicking on **Model Technologies** gives you the ability to import an MDG from here as an alternative way to import it using the toolbar option. Also, right-clicking the **TOGAF10_MDG** gives you the ability to delete the MDG technology from the project. Next, let us create some test diagrams using the newly created MDG.

Creating the first testing diagram

The steps for creating testing diagrams are the same as those for creating other diagrams. To start testing the MDG, perform the following:

1. Create a new view package under the model node and provide a name for it.

2. Select **Create Diagram** from the **Initial Content** options list and click **OK**.

3. The **New Diagram** dialog box will ask you to select the type of diagram.

4. Click on the hamburger menu under **Type** and select **All,** which is at the top of the list.

5. A list of all the available diagram types will be provided. Scroll down all the way to the end, and the **TOGAF10_MDG** should be there.

6. Alternatively, you could select **Specialized | Model Technologies** to get a shorter list that has custom MDGs only.

7. Click on it, and the **Business Capability Map** diagram type will be listed under **Diagram Types** as you can see in *Figure 3.28*, then click **Create Diagram** to create the diagram.

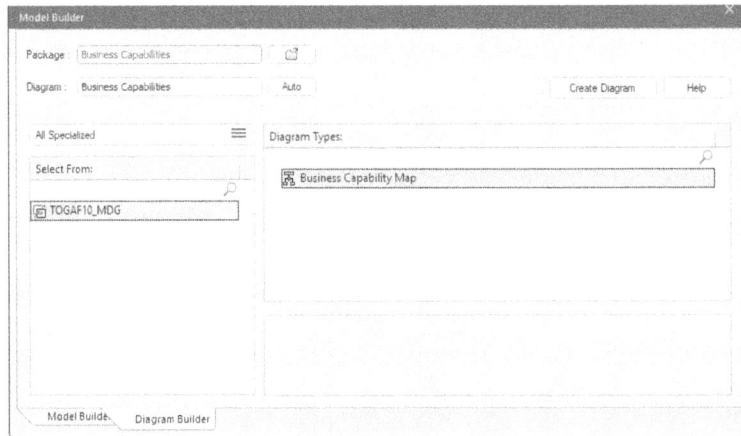

Figure 3.28: Business Capability Map diagram type

A new package containing the new diagram will be created. Open the diagram which should be empty, and check the **Toolbox**. The **Toolbox** should contain the elements and the connectors, grouped into two toolbox groups, as we wanted them to be, as depicted in *Figure 3.29*:

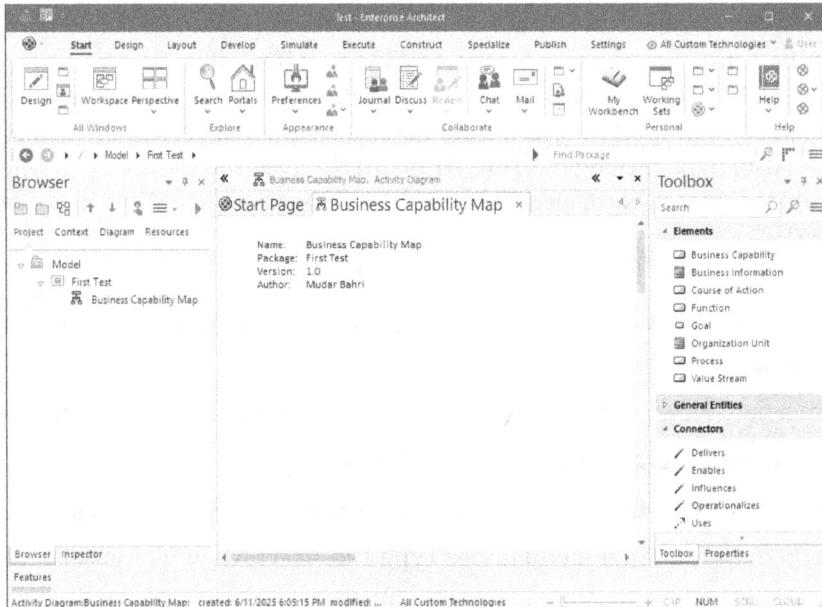

Figure 3.29: The Business Capability toolbox associated with the diagram

There are toolbox groups that Sparx EA included such as the common elements and the common relationships. They are included by default in every toolbox, and they contain elements and relationships that are common to any diagram type. The Note, Text, and Boundary elements are examples of common elements. Dependency, Realize, Trace, and Note Link are examples of common relationships. We will show how to use the common elements and relationships when we need them.

Start testing the MDG by placing elements on the diagram and connecting them to each other. Try connecting elements by using the relationships that are defined in the toolbox or by drag-dropping the connector's handle that appears near the top right corner of elements when they are clicked. Test the MDG by creating diagrams that model Business Capabilities from your real-world work environment. This means you will be testing the MDG while learning more about your enterprise by practicing modeling it at the same time. Note down any incorrect or unexpected behavior from the MDG, go back to the MDG to fix it, go through the publishing, generating, and importing cycle again for the new changes to take effect, and then do your tests again. *Figure 3.30* shows an example of a Business Capability map. More real-life examples will be provided in the later chapters.

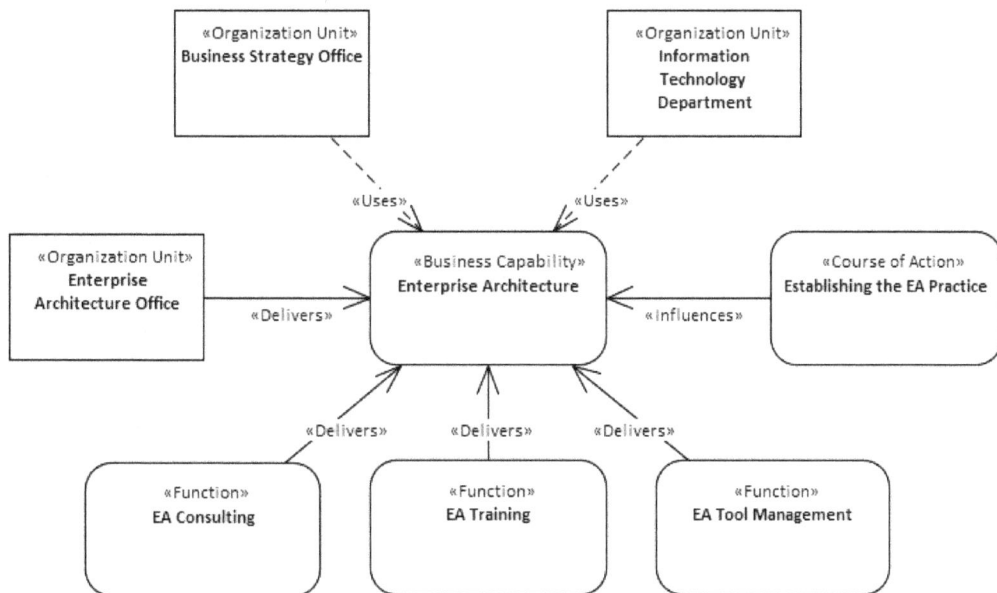

Figure 3.30: *Sample artifact created using the MDG*

Additionally, while using the connectors handle to connect elements, the context menu will contain additional relationships other than the ones that have been defined, as depicted in *Figure 3.31*. These relationships are standard UML relationships that are included by default. They can be suppressed by adjusting a property of the metaclass as we will see in *Chapter 4, Advanced Model Driven Generation*. Remember that the goal of this chapter was to introduce MDG and keep it as simple as possible.

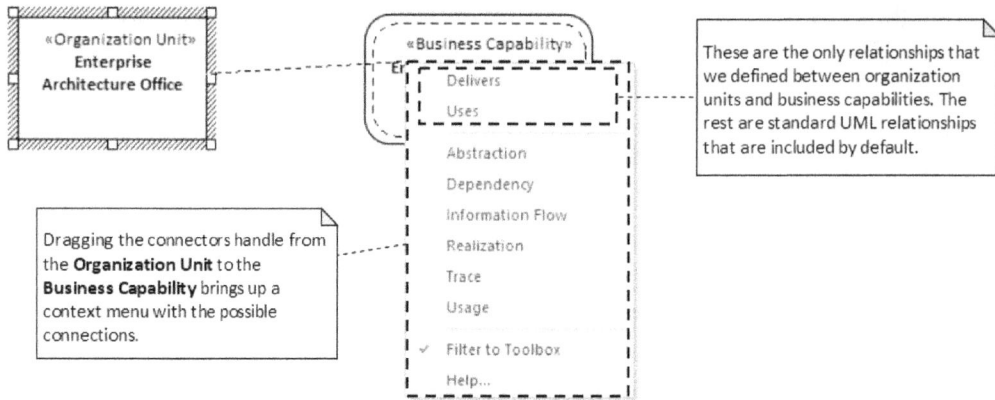

Figure 3.31: Connectors handle context menu

Once you finish testing the MDG using the testing project, it is time to roll it out into the production repository.

Importing the MDG to the production repository

Importing the MDG to the production repository is not different at all from importing it to the testing repository. The steps are the same, but here are a few things to remember:

- Before importing an MDG, you had better remove the older version from the resources before importing the newer version. To remove the MDG from the project, open the **Resources** tab in the **Browser** window and find **MDG Technologies | Model Technologies**, right-click on **TOGAF10_MDG**, and select **Remove Technology**.

- Removing an MDG technology from the resources will not damage the diagrams that have already been created.

- You do not need to restart Sparx EA after importing a new MDG version.

Spend sufficient time understanding all the sections in the chapter before moving to the next one.

Conclusion

MDG is a challenging topic, but mastering it is an essential milestone towards mastering Sparx EA, not only to create TOGAF artifacts but to extend it to any desired framework.

In the later chapters, we will create more real-life diagrams using the custom-made MDG, but before that, we will tweak and refine the MDG in *Chapter 4, Advanced Model Driven Generation*, to make it more suitable for the scenarios that we are planning to introduce. You already have most of the core concepts in this chapter, and the advanced topics in the next chapter are refinements and adjustments to what you learned here.

Points to remember

- Developing an MDG follows a similar approach to the traditional system development lifecycle.

- MDG is required when working on frameworks that are not supported in Sparx EA as out-of-the-box.

- MDG development can be in an agile way, where development is focused only on the elements and relationships that are required the most soon. Other elements and relationships can be added later when there is demand.

- MDG development takes place in a separate Sparx EA project file.

- A properly built MDG contains stereotypes of elements and relationships as well as specialized diagram types and toolboxes.

- A relationship that is created between two elements will automatically appear between them on all the diagrams that contain the same two elements unless you suppress its visibility.

Key terms

- **MDG**: Stands for Model Driven Generation, which is a visual way of defining a customized metamodel in Sparx EA.

- **Metamodel**: This is a model provided by the framework to guide what the elements of the enterprise are, and what the possible relationships between them are.

- **Focused-metamodel**: A smaller portion of the whole metamodel that focuses on elements, each at a time.

- **Metaclass**: This is a base class of a standard UML element, relationship, or diagram type that we can extend to create new ones.

- **Stereotype**: This is a way that indicates an extended or altered functionality from the original element.

- **MTS**: Stands for MDG Technology Selections, which is a file that saves the values of the MDG technology creation wizard.

Join our Discord space

Join our Discord workspace for latest updates, offers, tech happenings around the world, new releases, and sessions with the authors:

https://discord.bpbonline.com

CHAPTER 4
Advanced Model Driven Generation

Introduction

In the previous chapter, we introduced the MDG and how it is an essential capability that an EA practice requires if Sparx EA is the tool they use. Without MDG, different architects within the enterprise will start accommodating the standard UML elements and relationships in different ways. An architect may decide to represent processes as extended UML activities, while another may decide to extend or use a different element instead. Having a mature MDG that extends your entire metamodel is very important to enforce compliance when producing different artifacts by different architects. The artifacts may still have differences when it comes to the appearance of the diagrams, but an MDG will enforce that the elements and relationships will be used in a consistent and compliant way.

Building MDGs is naturally an advanced topic; therefore, when we introduced it in the previous chapter, it was intended to simplify the example as much as we could. We skipped some pages from the MDG creation wizard and left some properties unchanged because our target was to deliver a minimum viable product of the MDG. It works for testing purposes, but it may not be ready yet to be used for real-world examples. This chapter will introduce additional MDG techniques that can help you to increase the maturity of your MDG, thus enabling you and your team to deliver higher-quality artifacts and a more reliable repository that can be trusted as the source of useful information. You do not have to use all these techniques, but it is important to know what you can do. In this chapter, we will learn how to use shape scripts and how to use the special attributes. We will then learn how to add Tagged Values and how to add standard connectors to a custom toolbox. Later, we will understand and learn how to customize diagram types.

Structure

In this chapter, we will discuss the following topics:

- Using shape scripts
- Using special attributes
- Adding Tagged Values
- Adding standard connectors to a custom toolbox
- Customizing diagram types

Objectives

By the end of this chapter, you will learn additional MDG techniques that will make your custom-made MDG look and behave like a professionally developed add-on to Sparx EA. The MDG should become like a product produced and maintained by the entity responsible for the enterprise architecture practice, which you probably belong to. Learning techniques such as changing the shapes of the elements and connectors, changing the default behavior of stereotypes or their metaclasses, adding custom attributes to elements, and customizing the behavior of the new diagram types are all important topics that you need to be aware of because, sooner or later, you will need them.

Using shape scripts

The TOGAF architecture metamodel does not have a specific visual representation for its elements, and they all appear as solid white rectangles. Some other frameworks use specific shapes to represent different elements. **ArchiMate,** for example, despite being argued if it can be categorized as a framework or not, uses different symbols for different element types. A function in ArchiMate has a different visual appearance than a process. UML also uses different visual representations of different elements. Some architects like to use colors to differentiate elements from different architecture layers, so elements from the business architecture layer appear in a different color than those from the application architecture or the technology architecture layers. Finally, there might be a business or regulation requirement to follow a specific notation of specific elements or to follow a specific coloring theme that you need to enforce across the entire repository. For cases like these, you may find that there is a need to override the default shapes that are inherited from the UML metaclasses, and this is what we will learn in this section.

Opening the shape editor

The shape editor provides the ability to define a specific shape for the selected element over the default metaclass shape using a simple scripting language. This language is known as **EAShapeScript**, and currently, it is in version 1.0. It looks like JavaScript, and any programmer can learn it in no time. Let us get familiar with EAShapeScript and change the appearance of the Process element.

To open the shape editor and edit the shape of the Process element, perform the following steps:

1. Open the MDG project in Sparx EA.

2. Open the profiles diagram from ‹‹**profile**›› **TOGAF10_MDG**.

3. Right-click on the **Process** element on the diagram and select **Edit with Profile Helper** from the context menu.

4. The **Stereotype Properties** dialog will pop up. Select **Shape Script** from the left tab.

5. Click the **Edit** button.

6. The **Shape Editor** dialog box will pop up with a single empty **main** function.

Figure 4.1 shows what the shape editor dialog box looks like:

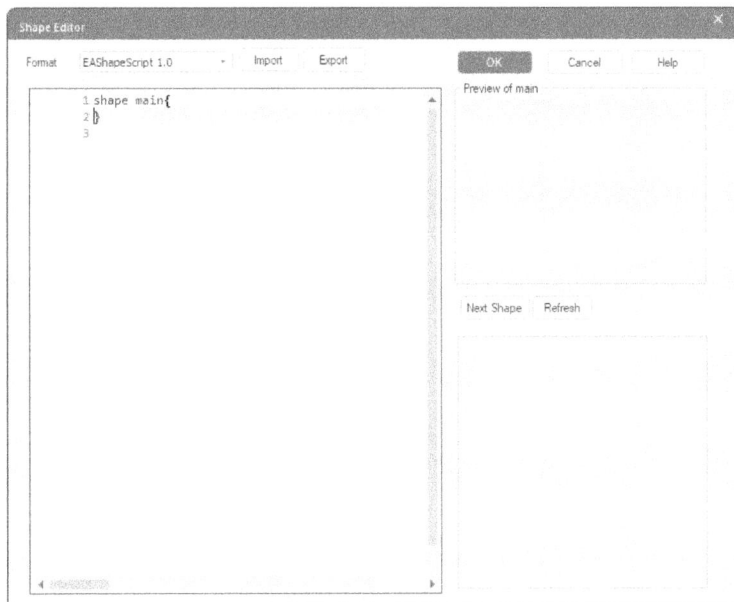

Figure 4.1: *Shape editor dialog box*

To customize the shape's appearance of the Process element, we need to provide instructions in *Drawing Methods*, so let us see how.

Customizing the shape's appearance

The complete guide to the drawing methods is available online at **https://sparxsystems.com/ enterprise_architect_user_guide/17.1/modeling_frameworks/drawing_methods.html**. We will explore some of them as we practice, and you can always refer to the online documentation for more.

To use the round rectangle shape and make the Process element have a round rectangular element, follow these steps:

1. In the script editor, enter a new line after the **shape main{**.

2. Enter the command **RoundRect(0, 0, 100, 100, 30, 30);**.

3. Click on the **Refresh** button.

The **RoundRect** method takes six parameters, and they are all required. These parameters are left, top, right, bottom, corner width, and corner height. The area that is labeled **Preview of main** in the shape editor dialog will show how the shape will look after executing the script. This is how the element will look on diagrams, and you can adjust the provided values as needed. If you want the corners to be more rounded, for example, increasing the values of the last two parameters will do that.

If the preview shows an empty (gray) area without a drawing in it, it means that your script has an error and could not be executed. Check *Figure 4.2* to see what the shape editor dialog box should look like:

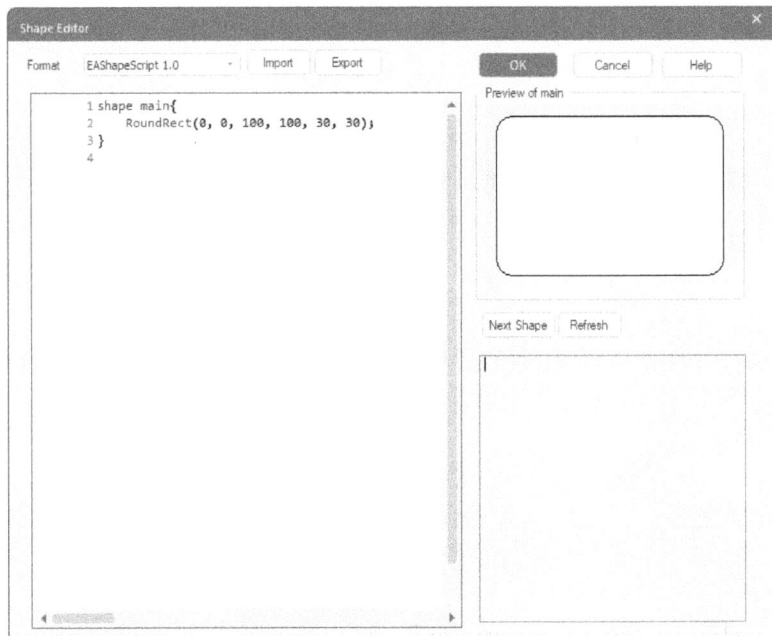

Figure 4.2: Drawing the round rectangle shape

You can get very creative in designing your shapes, as it all depends on how much time is available and how important it is to customize them. *Figure 4.3* shows another example of how the Process element can look if you write the script that is provided in the script area:

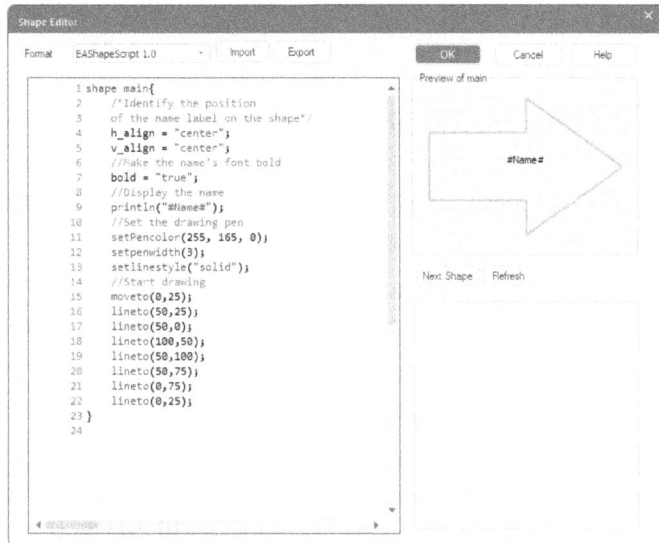

Figure 4.3: A more customized shape of an element

Notice how we started this shape with three attributes to set values like the horizontal and vertical alignment, and the font style of the element's name. These attributes are known as **Shape Attributes**, and they *must* be set before starting the drawing methods. In most cases, you will need to use both the shape attributes and the drawing methods for more sophisticated shapes. The complete list of shape attributes is available at **https://sparxsystems.com/ enterprise_architect_user_guide/17.1/modeling_frameworks/shape_attributes.html**.

Note: **It is highly advisable to create a folder in the bookmarks bar in the internet browser to save all the resources that we are providing in this book for quick access when you need them.**

Keep in mind that you can also edit and customize the shapes of the relationships as well and not only the elements. In the MDG example that we are working on, all the relationships are extending the UML associate relationship with a direction pointing from source to target. You can use the shape editor to customize how each connector looks like using the applicable shape attributes and drawing methods. After finishing all the needed customizations, you must test the MDG again.

Testing the shape

To test the new shape, you must re-publish all the profiles that have been affected by the changes, then re-generate the MDG. Please refer to *Publishing the MDG* and *Testing the MDG* sections in *Chapter 3, Introducing Model Driven Generation* and follow the same instructions. We need to keep in mind that re-publishing all profiles is not required, but only the profiles that have been changed. Since we have not changed anything in the toolboxes and diagram type profiles, there is no need to republish them. Publishing unchanged profiles does not hurt but can waste time, especially when you have dozens of toolboxes. This is what you need to do to test the recent changes to the MDG:

1. Publish the ‹‹**profile**›› **TOGAF10_MDG package**. Answer by **Yes** when asked to overwrite the existing file.

2. Generate the MDG technology. Use the previously generated MTS file to get all the saved settings in the creation wizard.

3. All the wizard's settings should remain unchanged, so keep clicking **Next** until the end, make sure that **Save to MTS** is checked to keep the wizard up to date, then click **Finish**.

4. If the MDG is successfully generated, open the testing project in Sparx EA, preferably in a separate session.

5. Go to the resources browser by clicking on **Browser | Resources | MDG Technologies | Model Technologies**. You should see the **TOGAF10_MDG** that we imported in the previous chapter listed.

6. Right-click on the **Model Technologies** package again and select **Import Technology**, select the MDG file, then click **OK**. This will update the MDG technology with the newer version.

7. Create a new diagram and place a new Process element on it from the **Toolbox** and explore how it looks.

Customizing how the elements and the relationships look can be fun, and in some cases, it can be important for the quality of the artifacts, but it can also be time-consuming, so always value the need for doing it. There is still more that you can learn about shape scripts, which you can use the online references for. The purpose of this section was mainly to introduce the shape script feature, but it is up to you to decide how far you want to go with it.

Note: **We will revert to the default shape in the MDG used in this book. Further examples will not show the customized but the default appearance of the elements.**

Let us look at another topic in customizing the MDG and it is about adjusting the properties of the stereotypes and their metaclasses using the special attributes.

Using special attributes

In *Figure 3.5* in *Chapter 3, Introducing Model Driven Generation*, there were two lists of properties, one on the left to set the stereotype's properties and another on the right to set the metaclass's properties. We intentionally did not change any of them earlier to simplify the example.

Now that you are more familiar with the MDG building process, we can explore some of the available properties so that we can give a more professional look to the elements and the connectors in the MDG.

Note: **The words attribute and property are used interchangeably in Sparx EA's documentation for the same meaning, and we are following that too.**

We have used the profile helper to extend the elements and set some of the connectors' properties. Unfortunately, not all the properties that you can extend are provided through the profile helper dialog box, so we need to learn how to set the properties without using the profile helper. The complete list of the special attributes is available at **https://sparxsystems. com/enterprise_architect_user_guide/17.1/modeling_frameworks/supportedattributes_2. html**. Take a quick look to familiarize yourself with them, then bookmark the page. As you can see, the page contains two sets of attributes. The upper set is for stereotypes' attributes, and the lower set is for metaclass attributes. Let us start with the stereotypes' attributes.

Using the stereotypes' attributes

When a stereotype extends a metaclass, the stereotype inherits all the attributes of its parent metaclass, just like in **object oriented programming (OOP)**. However, there are many attributes that can be added to the stereotype to differentiate its appearance or behavior from its parent metaclass. In this subsection, we will explore three of these attributes, and you can follow the same approach for any other attribute in the list. We will see how to change the stereotype's default shape size, how to hide the metaclass's name, and how to change the default toolbox icons of the stereotypes, and we will start with changing the default shape size.

Changing the default shape size

While testing the MDG in the testing project, you may have noticed that when placing elements on a diagram, they appear in their default size. If you place multiple elements of the same type on the diagram, they all appear with the same width and height. The default size of the Business Capability elements, for example, is 135 pixels in width and 75 pixels in height. You can read the size and the position of any element on a diagram by clicking on it, and checking the status bar at the bottom left side of Sparx EA's window. Click on the **Enterprise Architecture** Business Capability on the diagram that we created in the MDG testing project, and the status bar should read from left to right: **Activity: Enterprise Architecture Left: 341 x Top: 230 – Width: 135 x Height: 75**. See *Figure 4.4* for reference:

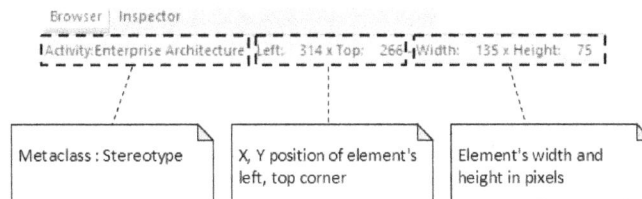

Figure 4.4: *Status bar element's information*

The **Left** and **Top** values may differ in your case because you could have placed the Business Capability element in a different location on the diagram. If you move the element to a new location, these two values will change accordingly. The **Width** and **Height** should have the same values as our example because these values are inherited from the UML activity metaclass. All the other elements that extended the same metaclass, such as the Function, Course of Action, Value Stream, and Process, have the same width and height. To make the Business Capability element appear in a different size, you will need to set the Size X and Size Y attributes as explained in the following steps:

1. Make sure that the MDG project is open.

2. Open the **TOGAF10_MDG** diagram from the ‹‹**profile**›› **TOGAF10_MDG** package.

3. Right-click on the **Business Capability** stereotype on the diagram and select **Features | Attributes**.

4. The **Features** window will open, and the **Attributes** tab will be activated. The attributes tab contains a grid that will be used to define the attributes that we want to override.

5. Enter the value **_sizeX** in the **Name** column and set the **Initial Value** to **150**. The remaining columns can be left blank.

6. On a new line, enter **_sizeY**, and give it an **Initial Value** of **50**.

Note: **Attribute names are case sensitive. Sparx EA will not give an error if you enter an invalid attribute name, but the MDG will not behave as expected.**

With the previous steps, we have overridden the default width and height of the Business Capability stereotype with different values. *Figure 4.5* shows how the two attributes should appear in Sparx EA:

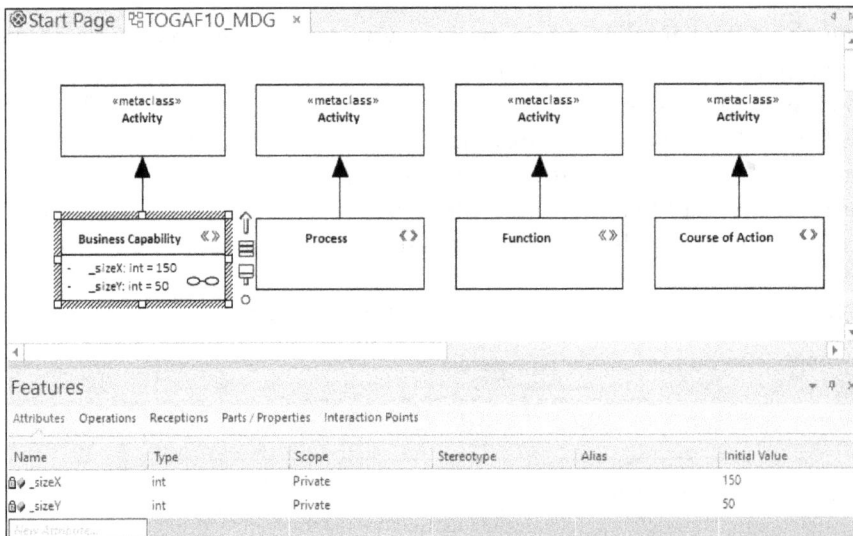

Figure 4.5: Setting stereotypes' attributes

Note: **The Type and Scope columns in the Features | Attributes window have no effect in this context, so it is the same if you set them all to blank or leave them with the default values. In general, we prefer to delete the attributes that we do not use.**

Publish the MDG profile, regenerate the MDG technology, and test it in the MDG testing project. If you place a new Business Capability element on the diagram, it should appear in the new size that we have set. If it does not, then you might have done something incorrectly, so redo the steps again and make sure that you are matching the cases for attribute names.

Another professional adjustment that you can make to the MDG extended elements is hiding their metaclass name from being viewed by MDG users. Let us see why you would do that and how.

Hiding metaclass name

In *Figure 4.4*, the leftmost part of the status bar shows the name of the selected element, preceded by its metaclass name. The new stereotype Business Capability we created is not displayed in the status bar. It makes more sense if the status bar displays the stereotype's name instead of the metaclass's name. To learn how to do it, follow these steps:

1. In the MDG project, click on the Business Capability element and open the **Features | Attributes** window if it is not already opened.

2. Enter the new attribute **_metatype**, and type **Business Capability** in the **Initial Value**.

Republish the MDG profile, regenerate the MDG technology, and import it to the testing project. Click on the Business Capability element on the diagram, and the status bar should show the stereotype's name instead of the metaclass name, as explained in *Figure 4.6*:

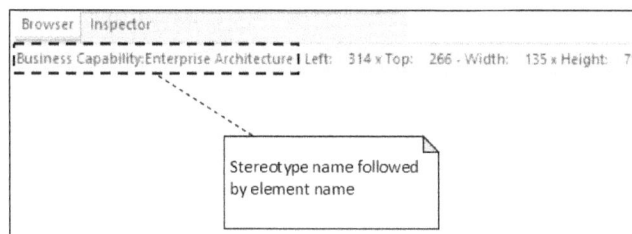

Figure 4.6: Displaying stereotype's name

The next technique is changing the stereotype's icon that appears in the **Toolbox** and in the **Project Browser**.

Changing stereotypes' icons

Every toolbox element has an icon to visually represent it beside its name. Elements are also represented with icons in the **Project Browser**. Stereotypes inherit the icons of their parent metaclasses. In our MDG, the Business Capability stereotype appears exactly like the Function, Course of Action, Value Stream, and Process, and they all look like their parent, the Activity metaclass. This is okay, and it does not affect the quality of the artifacts that will be created with these stereotypes; however, if you want your MDG to look more professional by providing a different icon for each element, we will explain how to do it.

The internet has thousands of icons that can be purchased or used for free, and you can draw your own icons. The only condition is that icons must be 16x16 pixels in bitmap format. Follow these steps to change the icon of the Business Capability element:

1. Download an icon to your local drive.

2. Copy the full file path and name of the downloaded icon to the clipboard.

3. In the MDG project, click on the Business Capability element and open the **Features | Attributes** window.

4. Enter the new attribute **icon** and paste the file path from the clipboard into the **Initial Value**.

5. Republish the MDG profile, regenerate the MDG technology, and import it to the testing project.

The **Project Browser** and the **Toolbox** must now show the new Business Capability element icon, as indicated in *Figure 4.7*:

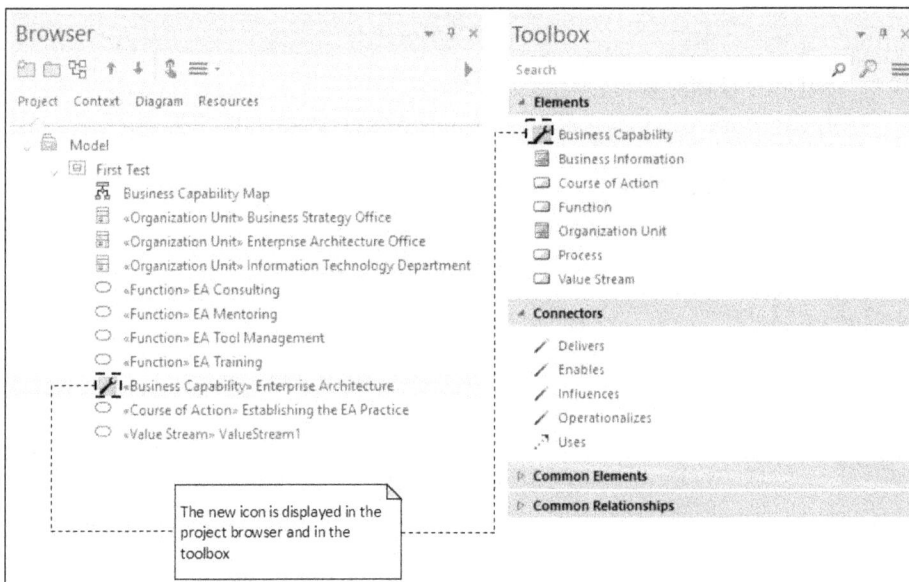

Figure 4.7: The new icon for the Business Capability element

The new icon will be associated with the Business Capability stereotype in the **Project Browser** and the **Toolbox**. Think about the amount of time and effort that you will need for finding and assigning a unique icon to each element and connector stereotype. If it is a cosmetic step, then it could be better done when there is time for it.

There are more attributes that we can apply to custom MDG stereotypes, but you are now familiar of where to find them and how to use them, so we had better leave the remaining attributes for your exploration exercises that we always recommend. Let us look at a similar topic, but this time, we will apply special attributes to the metaclasses.

Using the metaclasses' attributes

Metaclasses have a different set of attributes than those for stereotypes, but they are both adjusted in the same way. Metaclasses' attributes also differ based on each metaclass type. The attributes that are available for the activity metaclass, for example, are different from those that are available for the component, class, or association metaclasses. In *Chapter 3, Introducing Model Driven Generation*, we experienced assigning values to the **_MeaningForwards** and **_MeaningBackwards** attributes that are available for the association metaclass but not for the activity or the class. We used the profile helper dialog box for that, but we could have done it by typing the attribute names and setting their initial values. We will explore two more attributes in this subsection, so let us have a look at the first one.

Hiding UML links

When using the quick linker handle (the arrow-shaped handle) to connect two elements, you may have noticed that the context menu contains not only the relationships that we defined, but also additional UML relationships that are included by default, as indicated in *Figure 4.8*:

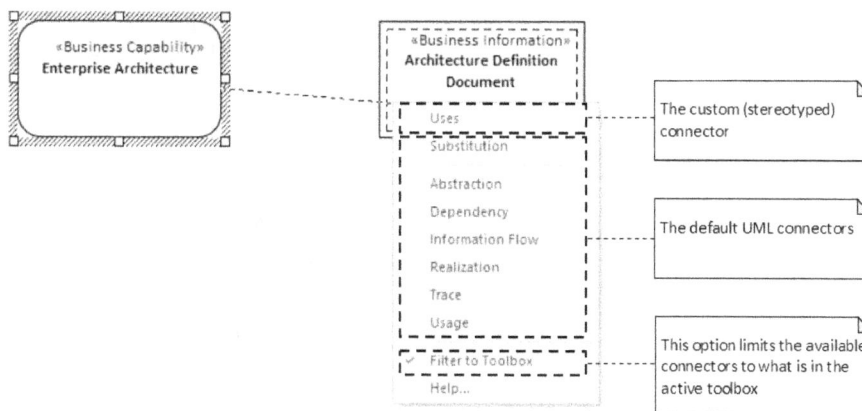

Figure 4.8: Quick linker menu

If you uncheck the **Filter to Toolbox** menu item, the quick linker menu will contain even additional UML relationships that are irrelevant to the context. To prevent the users of the MDG from creating artifacts that contain incorrect or unwanted relationships, we have to hide the default UML relationships. To apply this limitation, follow these steps:

1. In the MDG project, click on the **Activity** metaclass that the Business Capability stereotype extends, and open its **Features | Attributes** window.

2. Enter the new attribute **_HideUmlLinks** and enter **True** in the **Initial Value**.

3. Republish the MDG profile, regenerate the MDG technology, and import it to the testing project.

4. In the MDG testing project, use the quick linker to connect from the **Enterprise Architecture** Business Capability to any other element on the diagram.

The menu should now contain the extended relationships only, and all the default UML relationships should be hidden, as illustrated in *Figure 4.9*:

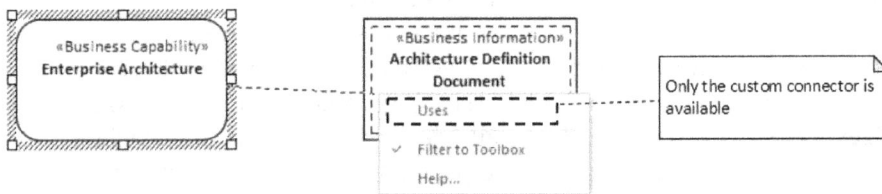

Figure 4.9: *Quick linker menu without the UML relationships*

Even unchecking the **Filter to Toolbox** option does not bring up the irrelevant UML connectors anymore.

Note: **This change applies currently to the Business Capability stereotype only, because we changed the attribute only in its metaclass. We must do the same for all the other metaclasses to have the same limitation on their menus.**

The next attribute that we will look at is setting the composite child diagram of stereotypes to a specific diagram type.

Setting composite child diagram type

Composite child diagrams have been covered in *Chapter 2, Sparx EA Crash Course*, but as a reminder, a composite child diagram is the default or the home page diagram of an element. An element that has a composite child diagram will be distinguished by a small chain symbol on it, and the element will respond to double-clicking it by opening its composite child diagram. To create one for an element, right-click on it and select **New Child Diagram | Composite Structure Diagram** from the menu. To delete it, right-click on the element and uncheck the **New Child Diagram | Composite** option, then delete the diagram from the **Project Browser**.

In the MDG test project, if you create a composite child diagram for the enterprise architecture Business Capability element, the child diagram will be set to UML activity diagram type by default, and the UML activity toolbox will be displayed. This is not what we want the child diagram of an element of type Business Capability to behave like, so we need to set what the composite child diagram type should be and override the default. For a Business Capability element, we will set its composite child diagram type to **Business Capability Map**, and that diagram type is already associated with the Business Capability toolbox that we need. Follow these steps to learn how to do it:

1. In the MDG project, click on the **Activity** metaclass that the Business Capability stereotype extends, and open its **Features | Attributes** window.

2. Enter the new attribute `_defaultDiagramType` and enter `TOGAF10_MDG::Business Capability Map` in the **Initial Value**.

3. Republish the MDG profile, regenerate the MDG technology, and import it to the testing project after removing the older version.

Notice that in *step 2*, the diagram type name must be provided in the format *Profile::Diagram Type*. If you do not provide the profile name, Sparx EA will not give any errors, but again, the MDG will not function as desired, and it can take a lot of time just to figure out why.

Another attribute that is relevant to composite child diagrams and can be overridden is the `_makeComposite` attribute, which is false by default, but when it is set to true, it creates a composite child diagram by default every time you create a new element. You can try it out as an exercise and experience the results.

You can discover the remaining attributes at your convenience since you know how it works. We will also cover some attributes in future chapters when there is a need for them, but now we need to cover another important topic, which is the use of Tagged Values.

Adding Tagged Values

In real-life models, we will always find a need to store information about the elements that we model. Take, for example, the Business Capability element. It will be of great value to have properties that are specially made to store Business Capability values, such as the maturity level, and the name and email address of the person who is responsible for managing it. The current properties dialog box is standard for all the elements, and it contains standard properties like **Name**, **Stereotype**, **Alias**, **Keywords**, **Notes**, and others. To extend these properties and include the custom ones, we need to add Tagged Values to the stereotype in the MDG, so let us start with adding the simple ones.

Adding simple Tagged Values

Before we start with the steps of adding Tagged Values, let us make sure that we are on the same page of understanding and that we are referring to the same thing when we talk about Tagged Values. When right-clicking on any element, either on a diagram or in the **Project Browser**, a context menu will appear. Selecting **Properties | Properties** from the menu will open the properties dialog box. In the right section of the dialog box, there are three tabs: **Main**, **Advanced**, and **Tags**. A fourth tab having the name of the MDG will be added when we have Tagged Values defined within the MDG.

Note: A keyboard shortcut to open the properties dialog box of any element is selecting it, then pressing Alt + Enter.

Let us add two custom attributes to the Business Capability stereotype:

1. Open the MDG project and open the profiles diagram.

2. Right-click on the **Business Capability** stereotype element and select **Edit with Profile Helper** from the context menu.

3. From the tabs on the left side of the dialog box, select **Tagged Values**. If you defined Tagged Values earlier, they will all be listed as **Property** and **Default Value** pairs.

4. Right-click anywhere on the empty area on the grid, and a context menu will provide you with four options: **Add Tagged Value**, **Add Specialized Tagged Value**, **Create Tag Group**, and **Delete,** as shown in *Figure 4.10*:

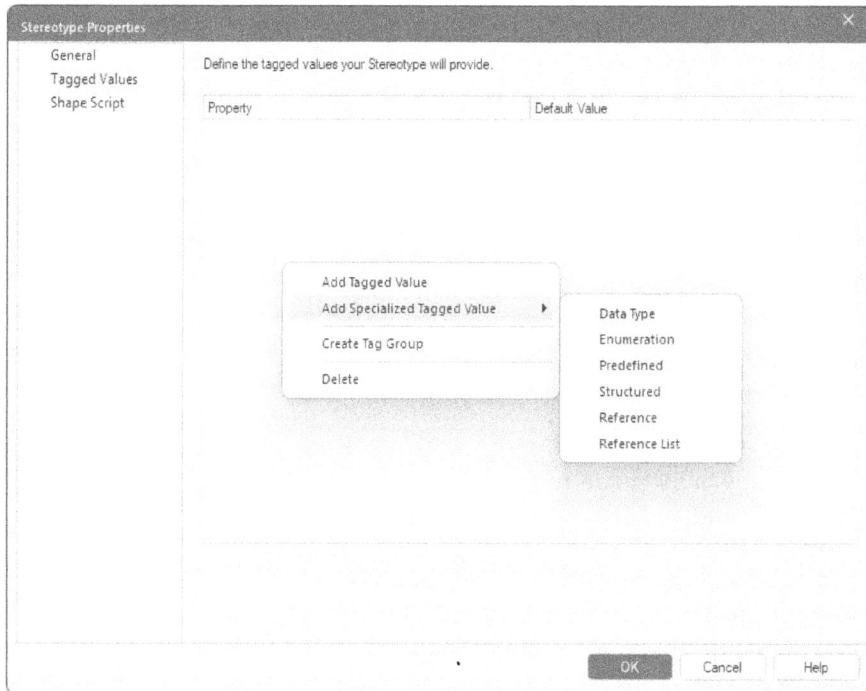

Figure 4.10: Tagged Values context menu

5. Select **Add Tagged Values** from the menu.

6. A small dialog box will appear. Enter `Owner Name` in the **Name** field and click **OK**.

7. Repeat *Steps 5* and *6* to add another Tagged Value and give it the name `Owner Email`.

8. You can optionally set a default value for any of the new properties.

9. Regenerate the MDG technology and import it to the testing project.

10. Create a new diagram of type Business Capability map and place a new Business Capability element on it. It must be a new element from the **Toolbox**.

11. Right-click on the new Business Capability and select **Properties | Properties** from the context menu.

12. The new **TOGAF10_MDG** tab should be available now. Open it, and the two new custom properties should be listed.

13. To set values to the custom properties, click in front of the name and type in the desired value. *Figure 4.11* shows how the new custom properties will look:

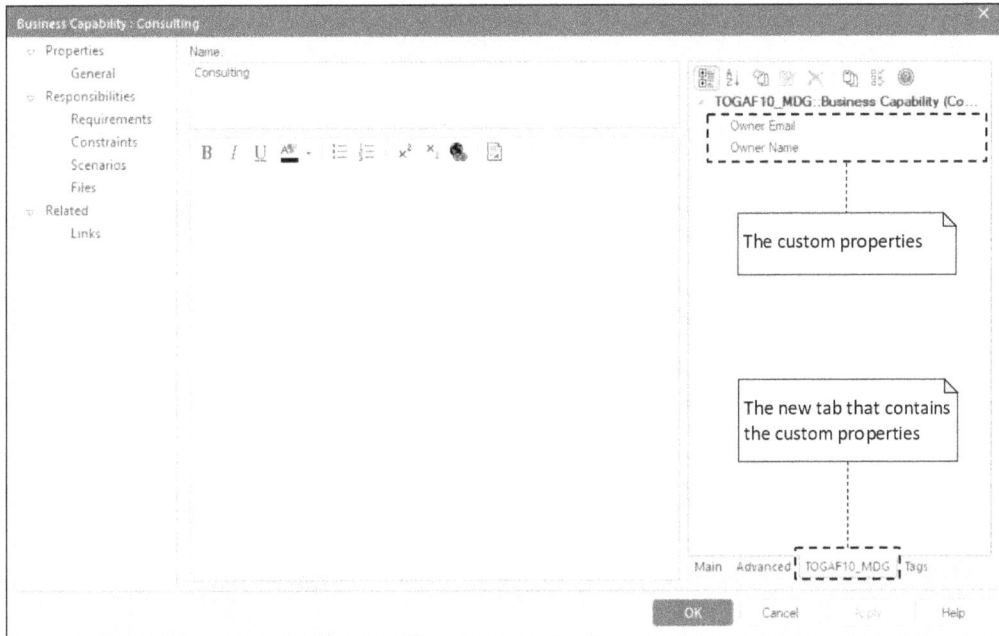

Figure 4.11: New custom properties

Now right-click on the **Enterprise Architecture** Business Capability, which has been created using an older version of the MDG and select **Properties | Properties**. Notice that the Tagged Values tab is not available even though we are using the newest MDG version. That is because the new Tagged Values must be synchronized, and to do so, you need to do the following:

1. From the **Resources** window, open **MDG Technologies | Model Technologies | TOGAF10_MDG | UML Profiles | TOGAF_MDG | Business Capability**, and right-click on it.

2. Select **Synch Tagged Values and Constraints** from the context menu. The **Synch Profiles Elements** dialog box will pop up.

3. Click **OK**, and a list of new un-synched Tagged Values will be displayed. See *Figure 4.12* for reference.

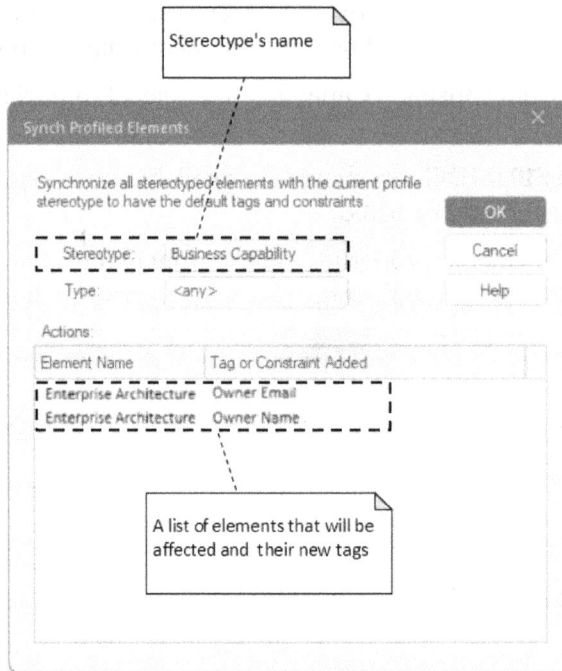

Figure 4.12: Synch profile elements dialog box

4. Select the Tagged Values that you want to sync by clicking on them. You can multi-select by holding the *Ctrl* key on the keyboard while clicking, just like any other Windows application.

5. Click **OK** again, then close the dialog box by clicking **Cancel** or on the **X** symbol.

After synching the new Tagged Values, check the properties of the enterprise architecture Business Capability, and you should be able to see the two new Tagged Values.

If you want to control what values can be entered in a Tagged Value, such as forcing selection from a drop-down list or a date picker, then you need to add a specialized Tagged Value instead, and this is what we will learn next.

Adding specialized Tagged Values

Simple Tagged Values are efficient and very useful, but there are some situations where you want to have more control over the values that Tagged Values can accept. In this subsection, we will learn two ways of controlling that through specialized Tagged Values, and the first one is by using enumerations.

Adding enumerated Tagged Values

To add a Tagged Value that provides a list of values to choose from, you need to create an enumeration and then link it to the Tagged Value to get its values from. To learn how to do it, perform the following steps:

1. In the MDG project, open the profile diagram.

2. From the **Toolbox**, click on the **Enumeration** element, then click on the diagram to create a new enumeration.

3. Give the enumeration a descriptive name such as `Maturity Levels`.

4. Right-click on the **Maturity Levels** enumeration, then select **Features | Attributes**.

5. In the attributes list, and under the **Name** column, enter `CMM1`. Repeat four more new lines and enter the values `CMM2`, `CMM3`, `CMM4`, and `CMM5`.

6. Right-click on the Business Capability stereotype on the diagram and select **Edit with Profile Helper** from the context menu.

7. Select **Tagged Values** from the list on the left side of the dialog box.

8. Right-click on the empty area of the list of properties and select **Add Specialized Tagged Values | Enumeration**.

9. When the **Add Enumeration Tagged Value** dialog box pops up, enter `Maturity Level` in the **Name** field, then click **OK**.

10. A dialog box will prompt you to select an enumeration element. Locate the **Maturity Levels** enumeration in the profile package, select it, and click **OK**.

11. Click **OK** to close the **Stereotype Properties** dialog box.

12. Regenerate the MDG technology and import it to the testing project.

13. Synch the Tagged Values as explained in the subsection, *Adding simple Tagged Values*.

14. Open the properties dialog of the **Enterprise Architecture** Business Capability and go to the Tagged Values tab.

15. The new attribute **Maturity Level** should be available as a new Tagged Value. Click on the drop-down list, and you should see the maturity levels in the list as indicated in *Figure 4.13*:

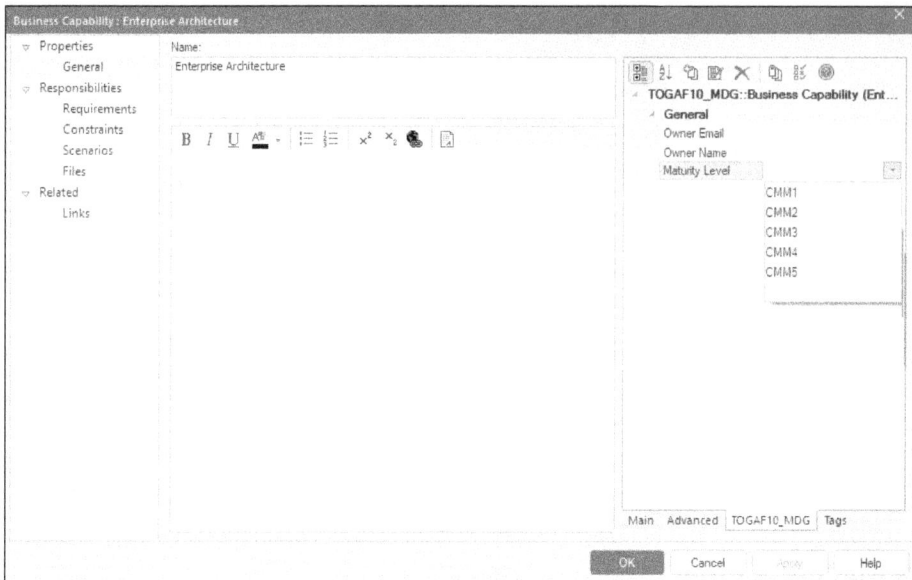

Figure 4.13: *Enumerated Tagged Values*

Note: There is an empty item in the list that is added by default to the list in case you want to set the value back to empty.

The maturity level is a property that is mainly associated with Business Capabilities, so it is unlikely that you will use it with other elements. However, when you need to create a Tagged Value that can be reused within many other stereotypes, such as the element's initiation date, it is better to use predefined Tagged Values, as we will see next.

Adding predefined Tagged Values

To use predefined Tagged Values in stereotypes, we must first define them, as their name implies. Sparx EA has a place to define the project-level Tagged Values that can be reused by multiple elements within the project. Properties like initiation date and deprecation date are applicable to almost every element, so defining them at the project level can be of value. To learn how to predefine Tagged Values, follow these steps:

1. In the MDG project, in the ribbon bar at the top, click on **Settings | Reference Data | UML Types**. This will open the **UML Types** dialog box.

2. Click on **Tagged Value Types** on the left side of the dialog.

3. Click on the **New** button, then in the **Tag Name** field type `Initiated On`.

4. Optionally provide a **Description,** such as `Inititation date of the element`.

5. In the **Detail** field, you need to provide a Tagged Value Type, and this field is what identifies how the Tagged Value behaves.

6. The complete list of the Tagged Value Types is available at **https://sparxsystems. com/enterprise_architect_user_guide/17.1/modeling_frameworks/ predefinedtaggedvaluetypes.html**. Search through the list until you find the **Date** Tagged Value Type.

7. Copy the value that is provided in the **Format** column, which is `Type=Date;` exactly the way it is written, including the semicolon.

8. Paste this value in the **Detail** field in the **UML Types** dialog box.

9. Click the **Save** button, and the new Tagged Value will appear in the **Defined Tag Types** list at the bottom.

10. Repeat the same steps to add the `Deprecated On` tag name and enter `Type=Date;` in the **Detail** field. Do not forget to click the **New** button before adding a new value to the list, or else you will overwrite the previous tag name's values.

11. Repeat the same steps to add `Owner Name` and `Owner Email` tag names, and enter value `Type=String;` in the **Detail** field. It makes more sense to have these two properties at the global level.

12. Compare your screen to *Figure 4.14* then click **Close** if everything looks fine.

Notice how clicking on an element in the **Defined Tag Types** list shows its Tagged Value Type in the **Detail** field. You can change this value whenever needed, so if you decide to change this property to be of type string, paste this value `Type=String;` in the **Detail** field and click **Save**.

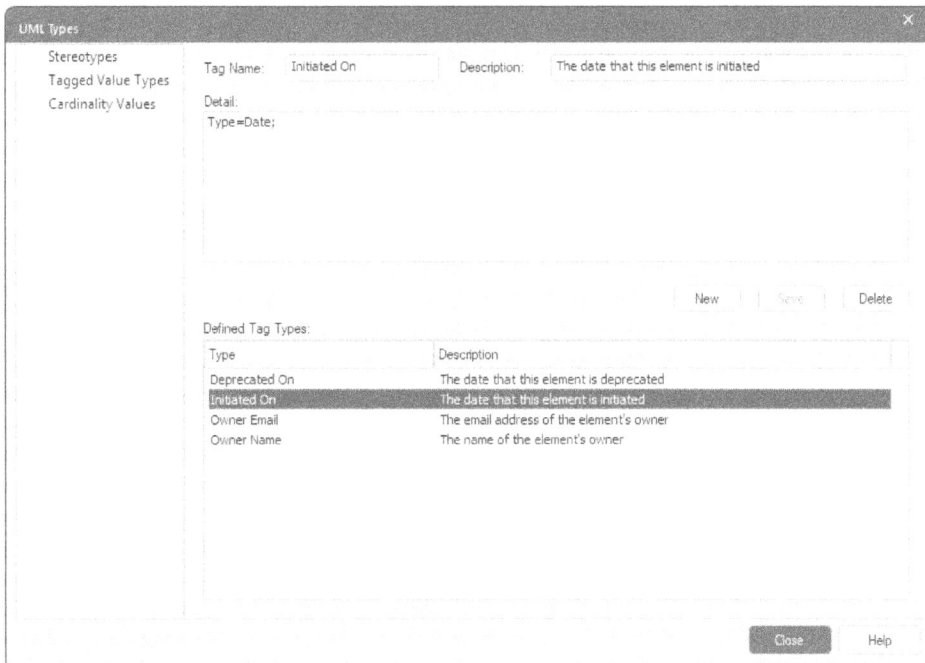

Figure 4.14: *UML types dialog box*

Since we have the Tagged Values defined, we can now use them to stereotypes, so follow these steps to add them to the Business Capability stereotype:

1. In the MDG project, open the profiles diagram.

2. Right-click on the **Business Capability** stereotype and select **Edit with Profile Helper**.

3. Select the **Tagged Values** tab on the left.

4. Right-click on the **Owner Name** and select **Delete**. Do the same for **Owner Email**.

5. Right-click on the empty area in the list.

6. Select **Add Specialized Tagged Value | Predefined**. The **Add Predefined Tagged Value** dialog will open with a list of all the predefined Tagged Values.

7. Select the **Initiated On** property and click **OK**.

8. Do the same, add the **Deprecated On**, **Owner Name**, and **Owner Email** properties.

9. Click **OK** to close the **Stereotype Properties** dialog box.

10. Republish the profile and regenerate the MDG.

11. There is an extra step that you need to take while generating any MDG that uses Tagged Value Types, which is to include them during the MDG generation.

12. When you reach the step that prompts **Select the information to be included in your technology**, you must check the **Tagged Value Types** box as indicated in *Figure 4.15*:

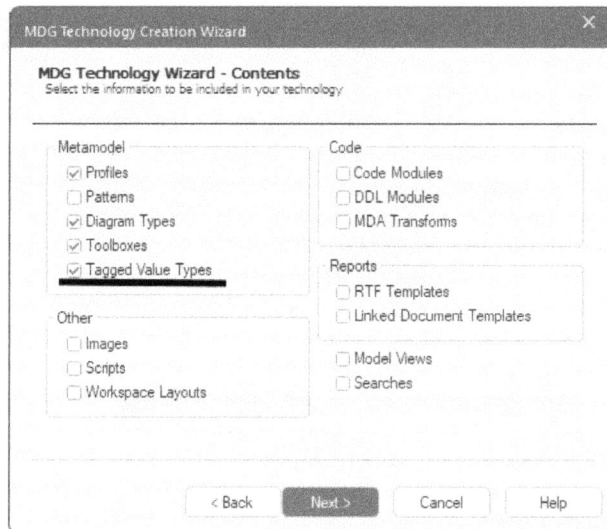

Figure 4.15: Include Tagged Value Types

13. If the **Tagged Value Types** box is checked, the **MDG Technology Creation Wizard** will add an additional step asking you to select the Tagged Value Types that you need to include from the list of all Tagged Value Types defined in Sparx EA.

14. Select all the Tagged Values that are listed under **Available Tagged Values** and continue as usual. Once the MDG generation is completed, import it to the MDG testing project, synch the Tagged Values, and test them. There should be a small down arrow that, when clicked, will open the date picker control for the field of type date.

Note: **The Tagged Value Types are defined at the project level not at Sparx EA level, which means they are not available between different projects.**

The list of Tagged Value Types that Sparx EA provides is rich and can provide MDG users with the flexibility they need to define custom properties that fit every need. There is a Tagged Value Type to provide up and down spins for properties that can be increased or decreased by clicking on the spin buttons, there is one to lookup files on the computer, one to create a progress bar, one to open the color chooser, and many others that we cannot cover all of them, but basically, they all follow the same steps except for the value.

When the number of custom properties (Tagged Values) increases, you may find that it is easier and more organized to have them grouped into tag groups, which we will learn next.

Creating tag groups

Tag groups are custom-defined groups to combine similar Tagged Values (the custom properties) together for better organization. In our example, we can have a general group to contain the general Tagged Values that are applicable to every element and a specialized group for the Tagged Values that are applied to specific elements, such as the Business Capability. The following steps show how to do that:

1. In the MDG project, open the profiles diagram.

2. Right-click on the **Business Capability** stereotype and select **Edit with Profile Helper**.

3. Select **Tagged Values** from the choices on the left, and right-click on the empty area in the list.

4. Select **Create Tag Group** from the list, enter `General` in the **Group Name** field, and click **OK**. You should see the new tag group created.

5. Right-click on the **Owner Name** attribute and select **Move Tag to Group**. A dialog box will list all the available tag groups. Select **General** and click **OK**. The selected property will be moved inside the general group.

6. Repeat the same steps for **Owner Email, Initiated On**, and **Deprecated On**.

7. Create a new tag group, name it `Specialized`, and move the **Maturity Level** Tagged Value into it.

8. The Tagged Values are now organized into the two tag groups that have been created. You may regenerate the MDG and test it to see the results.

As you can see, the ability to add custom properties through Tagged Values is a very powerful feature to properly extend stereotypes and form a custom metamodel. It may look hard to learn at the beginning, but once you practice several examples, you will find how flexible and easy it is.

The TOGAF Standard recommended a list of attributes for each metamodel element, as well as a set of general attributes that apply to all elements. The list is available at **https://pubs. opengroup.org/togaf-standard/architecture-content/chap02.html#tag_02_05.** Use the list as a reference for the following exercise:

1. Add the ID, source, and category as predefined Tagged Values. To give you a hint, enter `Type=String; Default=;` in the **Detail** field, as they are all of type string and no default value is needed for any of them.

2. Add the new predefined Tagged Values to the Business Capability stereotype under the **General** tag group.

3. Regenerate the MDG and test it to see how the added properties look and behave.

Feel free to add any additional custom property that your business requires, but keep in mind one important condition: do not add properties that can be represented using elements and relationships. For example, you should never have a property called delivering organization unit to contain the name of the Organization Unit that delivers the specific Business Capability. Instead, you should have an element of type Organization Unit and a relationship of type delivers linking to the Business Capability. The Organization Unit must be modeled as an element by itself, not as a property of another element. So, before adding any new custom property, check the metamodel, and if there is an element for it, then you should not create it as a property.

The next section will take us to a different topic to learn when and how we will need to add the standard UML connector to a custom toolbox.

Adding standard connectors to a custom toolbox

In *Chapter 3, Introducing Model Driven Generation*, we created new connectors to allow the creation of the TOGAF Standard relationships that have no equivalents in UML, such as delivers, influences, and enables. However, in many cases, we will find a need to use the standard UML relationships such as *Composition*.

Even though composition is not defined in TOGAF, to be able to break elements down into smaller elements of the same type, we must have the composition relationship as part of the MDG because every element should have the ability to be modeled as a composition of smaller elements of its type. An application component, for example, can be composed of smaller application components. The same is true for all the elements in the metamodel, like Process, Function, data entity, goal, Organization Unit, and so on.

To define a standard connector in the MDG profile, there are two things that need to be done. The first is to define the standard connector in the stereotype to tell the Business Capability stereotype that it can have a composition relationship to another Business Capability. The second thing is to use a standard connector to add it to the toolbox. It does not matter which one you do first, but we will start by adding the standard connector to the stereotype first. To do this in a metamodel, you create a composition relationship to itself and identify the metaclass of the connector as depicted in the following steps:

1. Open the ‹‹**profile**›› package and open the **TOGAF10_MDG** diagram.

2. Double-click on the **Business Capability** stereotype on the diagram to open its composite child diagram.

3. From the **Toolbox**, expand the **Metamodel** group if it is not expanded, click on the **Meta-Relationship**, then click once on the **Business Capability** stereotype on the diagram and release. So it is a single click on the Business Capability stereotype without holding the mouse button.

4. A new connector that has a ‹‹**metarelationship**›› stereotype will be created from the Business Capability to itself.

5. Right-click on the connector and select **Visibility | Hide Connector in Other Diagrams**, click the **Suppress All** button to unselect all the diagrams, then click **OK**. This will keep the connector visible on this diagram only and will hide it in all the other diagrams.

6. Double-click on the new connector to open the **Dependency Properties** dialog box. Alternatively, you can right-click the connector and select **Properties** from the context menu.

7. On the right side of the dialog box, click on the **Tags** tab to open it.

8. Enter **Composition** in the **metaclass** property, then click **OK**.

Now we need to add the composition connector to the toolbox to be able to use it on diagrams. Without having the connector in the toolbox, there will be no way to use it, so follow these steps to add it:

1. Make sure that the MDG project is open.

2. Open the ‹‹**toolbox profile**›› package and open the **TOGAF10_MDG_Business_ Capability_Toolbox**.

3. Right-click on the **Connectors** stereotype and select **Edit with Profile Helper**.

4. Click on the small down arrow next to the **Add** button and select **Add Built-In Type | Connector**.

5. Type the word **Composes** in the **Alias** field and click **OK**.

6. A dialog box will ask you to select **Metaclass**. Select **Composition** and click **OK**.

Regenerate the MDG and make sure to republish the profile and the toolbox profile. Test the new changes to the MDG in the testing project by placing two Business Capabilities on a diagram and connecting them using the quick linker. The menu must contain two new options: **Composition to Whole** and **Composition to Part**, as depicted in *Figure 4.16*:

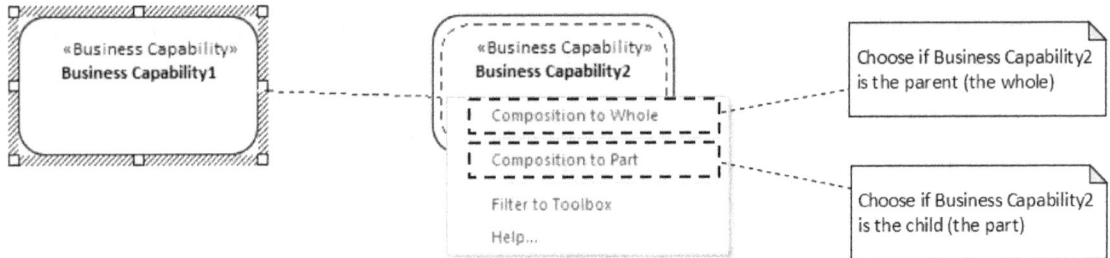

Figure 4.16: Composition relationship

The next section will discuss an important topic that allows you to create sub-diagram types; each of them can be specialized in creating a specific EA artifact.

Customizing diagram types

Part of building an MDG is extending diagram types, and we learned in *Chapter 3, Introducing Model Driven Generation*, how to create new diagram types. The ability to extend diagram types helps us to define diagram types that represent artifacts from the TOGAF metamodel. Additionally, creating new diagram types helps in maintaining consistency among the EA artifacts, especially when having many contributors to the content. It is also useful to have the right MDG toolbox assigned to the right diagram types. In this section, we will be more specific and create more specialized diagram types through what the MDG calls view specifications, so let us learn how.

Creating view specifications

View specification is another name for the diagram subtype. If we want to create a diagram subtype for the Business Capability map type that we currently have in the MDG, we need to create a view specification. Follow these steps to learn how:

1. In the MDG project, right-click on the ‹‹**profile**›› package and select **Add Diagram** from the menu.

2. Provide a descriptive name in the **Diagram** field, such as `Business Capability View Specifications`.

3. The **New Diagram** dialog box will open. From the **Type**, select **Management | MDG Technology Builder**, select **UML Structural**, select **Class**, then click **OK**.

4. From the ‹‹**diagram profile**›› package, drag the **Business Capability Map** element and drop it as a link on the new **Business Capability View Specifications** diagram that we just created in the ‹‹**profile**›› package.

5. From the **Toolbox**, expand the **Metamodel** group, click on **View Specification**, and then click on the diagram to create the new view specification. Rename it to `Business Capabilities Catalog`.

6. Use the quick linker to create **Extension** relationship from the **Business Capabilities Catalog** to the **Business Capability Map**.

7. Resize, align, and organize the elements to get something like *Figure 4.17*:

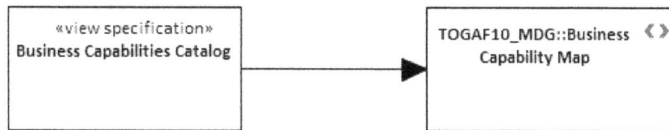

Figure 4.17: *A view specification extending a diagram type*

> Note: **The view specification elements must be created in the ‹‹profile›› package, not in the ‹‹diagram profile›› package, even though they are subtypes of diagrams.**

If we know that a specific sub-diagram type will use a limited set of stereotypes and connectors, it is a good idea to limit the toolbox of the new sub-diagram type to show only the relevant elements in it. A Business Capabilities catalog will only show a list of Business Capabilities and perhaps show how some Business Capabilities can be composed of smaller Business Capabilities. Therefore, the toolbox does not need to contain more than the Business Capability stereotype and the composition connector. You can add more elements, stereotypes, or connectors when needed, but this is how to create a toolbox that contains only the Business Capability stereotype and the composition connector. Make sure that the Business Capability view specifications diagram is still open.

8. From the **Project Browser** window, find the **Business Capability** stereotype, drag it, and drop it as a link on the diagram next to the view specification.

9. From the **Toolbox**, drag the **Metaclass** element and drop it on the diagram next to the view specification.

10. The **Extend Metaclass** dialog box will open. Select **Core Connectors** from the left tabs, check on **Composition** from the list of metaclasses on the right, and click **OK**. A new **Composition** metaclass will be created.

11. Use the quick linker to create an **Exposes** relationship from the view specification to the Business Capability stereotype.

12. Create another exposes relationship from the view specification to the composition metaclass.

This means that we are only exposing the two identified elements in this sub-diagram's toolbox. The final diagram should look like *Figure 4.18*:

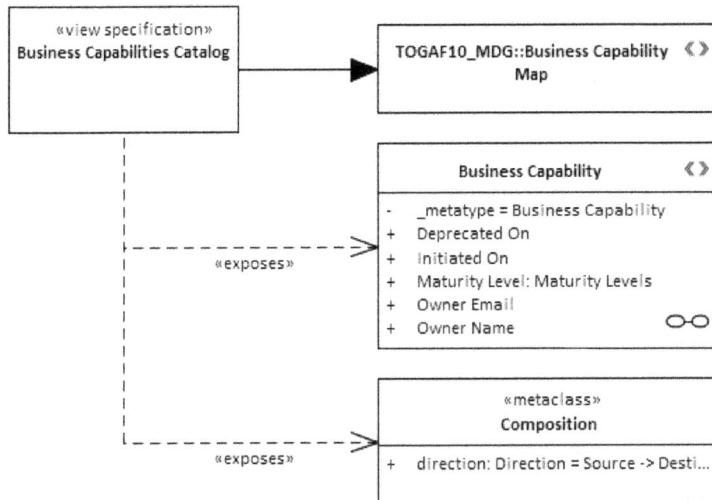

Figure 4.18: *Business Capabilities view specification*

The best way to test if it works or not is to regenerate the MDG and import it to the test project. Try to add a new diagram to a package, and the diagram types will show the newly created subtypes in addition to the default diagram type, as depicted in *Figure 4.19*:

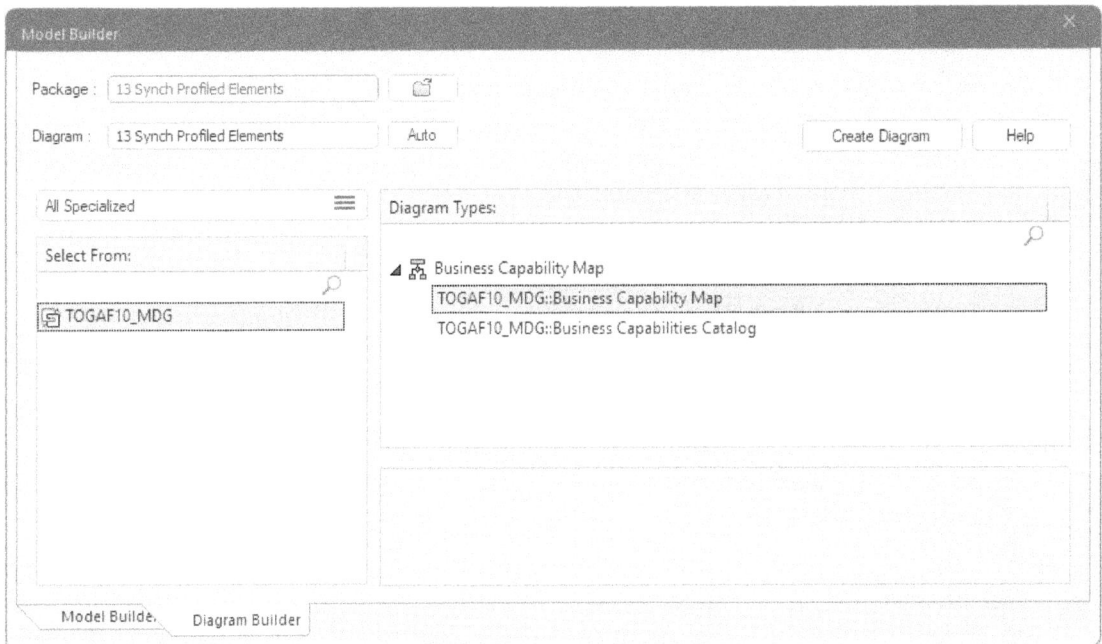

Figure 4.19: *New diagram subtypes*

Try out what elements and connectors will be in the **Toolbox** if you select the different subtypes. You can always change what is exposed in toolboxes when needed. The next subsection is about pre-setting the diagram properties for a more consistent appearance.

Pre-setting diagram type properties

If you open any diagram, right-click on any empty space, and select **Properties** from the context menu, a dialog box will be opened and will show the properties of the diagram. On the left side of the dialog box, there are tabs, and each one contains groups of options to customize how the diagram looks. For example, checking **Diagram | Appearance | Use Alias if Available** will tell the elements on the diagram to show the value that is in their **Alias** property if available instead of showing their names. Another example would be checking **Elements | Element Appearance | Hand Drawn,** which makes the elements on the diagram appear as if they are drawn by hand. Explaining all the options in all the tabs is not within the scope of this book, as all this information can be learned from the help. What we will learn in this section is how to use the diagram type properties to set some of these options so that each diagram that we create using this diagram type will be set by default to these values. To learn how to do that, follow these steps:

1. In the MDG project, open the diagram in the diagram profile package.

2. Right-click on the **Business Capability Map** stereotype and select **Edit with Profile Helper** from the context menu.

3. The **Edit Diagram Extension** dialog box will pop up, which we used in *Chapter 3, Introducing Model Driven Generation,* to set the default toolbox through the **Toolbox Profile** property.

   Notice how there are five property groups: the first one, opened by default, is the **General**, and there are four collapsed groups underneath it. These collapsed groups correspond to the tabs displayed when you open the diagram properties dialog box. *Figure 4.20* explains how the two dialog boxes are related:

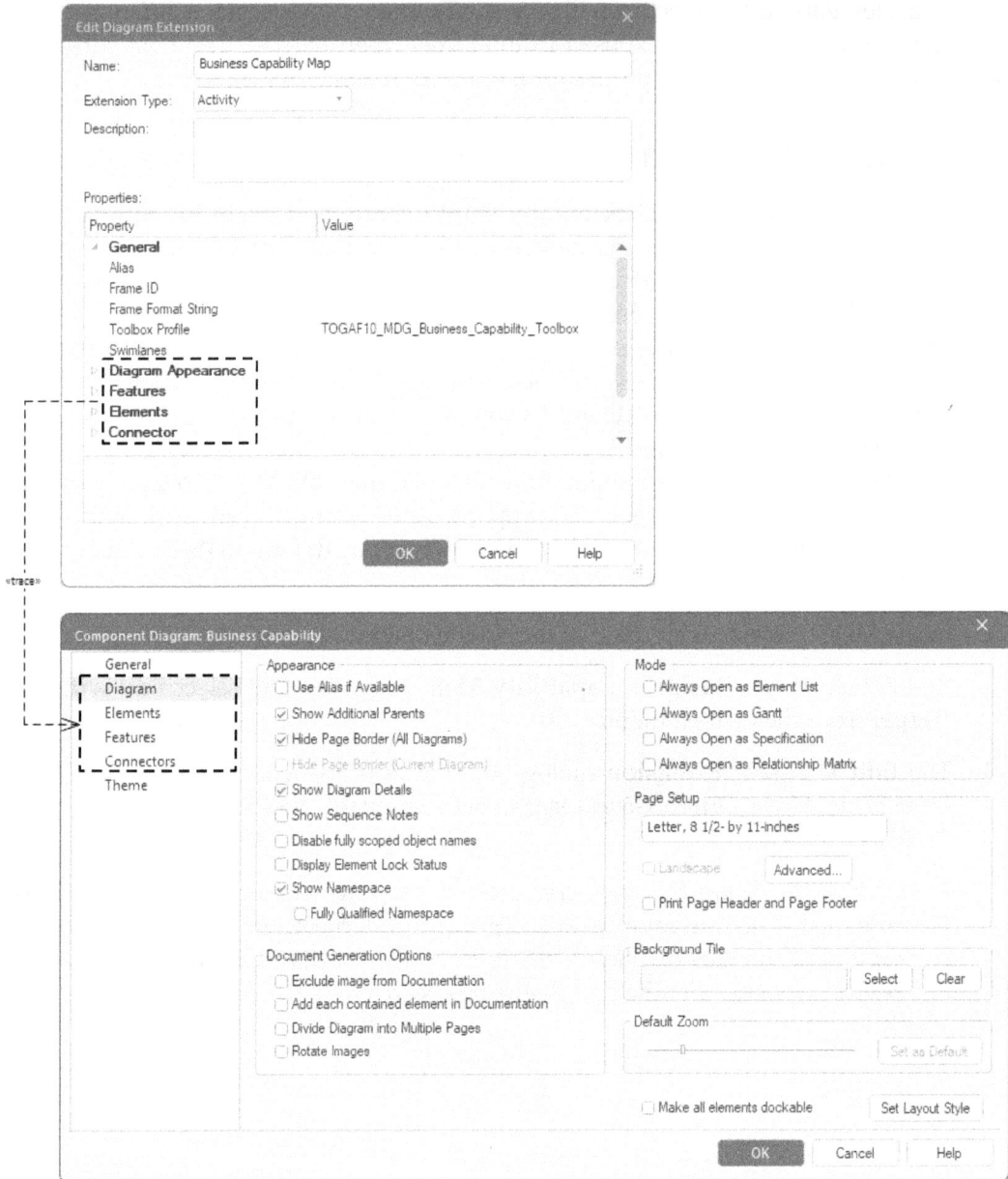

Figure 4.20: *Mapping diagram properties to MDG diagram extension dialogs*

Keep in mind that not all the options from the diagram's properties dialog box have equivalents from the **Edit Diagram Extension** dialog. Also, keep in mind that some options from the **Elements** tab in the diagram properties are placed in the **Diagram Appearance** group in the **Edit Diagram Extension** dialog, but this is how Sparx EA is built, and we have no control over it. Continuing with the example:

4. In the **Edit Diagram Extension** dialog, expand the **Diagram Appearance** group.

5. Set **Use Alias if Available** to **True**.

6. Set **Hand Drawn** to **True**.

7. Click **OK**.

8. Generate the MDG and import it into the testing project.

9. Create a new diagram of type **Business Capability Map**.

10. Place any element on the new diagram and see what it looks like.

11. Add any value in the **Alias** property of any element on the diagram, and the alias value will be displayed instead of the name.

You can always set and unset these settings from the diagram's properties dialog box. The idea was to introduce a way to change the default settings of the diagrams. With this last technique, we have reached the end of this chapter.

Conclusion

Mastering the MDG is mastering Sparx EA. Without knowing how to build a custom framework into the tool, you will always be limited to what is available in it out-of-the box, which may not suffice your business needs in many cases. Learning how to build an MDG is a process that starts with small steps that keep getting larger as you use it and explore it further. Learning does not end at this page, as there are still a lot more techniques that you can use for a more professional-looking repository and EA artifacts.

In the next chapter, we will provide different approaches for structuring the repository, but before we get there, let us remember some points from this chapter.

Points to remember

- Extended elements or stereotypes take the shape of their meta classes by default.

- You can change how the extended elements look by writing a script that gives you control over their appearance.

- You can differentiate an extended stereotype from its parent metaclass by overriding two sets of attributes, one for the stereotype itself and the other for its metaclass.

- You can hide the meta class's name from appearing in the status bar and in other places by making your stereotype a metatype.

- You can hide or keep the default UML relationships from the quick linker's menu.

- For each stereotype, you can define what diagram type its composite child diagram is.

- Tagged Values are the way that you can use to define properties for extended stereotypes.

- Tagged Values can be defined to accept text, date, time, color, file name, URL, enumeration, and many other types to control what can be entered in them.

- Remember not to add Tagged Values that can be represented using other elements and relationships.

- Extended toolboxes can contain standard UML connectors, such as composition, in addition to the extended stereotype connectors.

- Diagram types can be specialized into subtypes, each having only the relevant elements and connectors in its toolbox.

Key terms

- **Shape editor**: An editor that specializes in editing the shape script of a specific stereotype.

- **EAShapeScript**: The scripting language that is used to edit stereotypes' shapes.

- **Shape attributes**: A set of attributes that define the overall look of the shape, and they must be defined before the drawing methods.

- **Drawing methods**: A set of methods that are part of EAShapeScript language, to programmatically identify how a shape looks.

- **Tagged Values**: These are what MDG calls for stereotypes' custom properties.

- **Specialized Tagged Values**: These are Tagged Values that accept data in a specific or formatted way, such as dropdown lists, date pickers, color pickers, etc.

- **Tag groups**: These are the groups that combine a set of similar tags together.

- **View specification:** This is what Sparx EA calls the diagram subtypes in MDG.

Join our Discord space

Join our Discord workspace for latest updates, offers, tech happenings around the world, new releases, and sessions with the authors:

https://discord.bpbonline.com

CHAPTER 5
Structuring the Repository

Introduction

The main purpose of the **Project Browser** is to provide a hierarchical view of the repository and its elements so that users can easily find what they are looking for. In the real-world, our repository will contain a couple of thousands and maybe hundreds of thousands of elements and diagrams, because our goal as enterprise architects is to model the entire enterprise. Without properly structuring the repository and making it easier to navigate through, users will easily lose interest in using it as a trusted source of information and will find other sources to serve their needs. We must retain users' trust in the repository by providing them with a structure that makes sense to them.

A structure that makes sense to its users means they can easily learn how to navigate through it to reach the desired information. A good structure must be treated as a living and evolving structure because users' maturity increases, and their requirements change. There is no single structure that fits every enterprise, or else it would have been provided as part of the modeling tool itself. The TOGAF Standard provides a guideline for building an architecture repository and its main components. We will use it as a reference, and we will support it with solutions to make a practical example.

Structure

This chapter will include the following topics:

- Planning the structure
- Building the structure

Objectives

The objective of this chapter is to learn how to structure the EA repository to make navigating it easier and meaningful to its users. A good structure that is designed around users' needs and expectations will help retain their trust in the repository as their source of information, when they need it, and where they expect to find it.

Planning the structure

Building and changing the repository structure in Sparx EA is very simple, and it is like building the structure of a file system. Moving elements and diagrams from one package to another and moving packages from one parent package to another is as simple as dragging and dropping. In Sparx EA, moving elements from one package to another does not break their existing relationships with the other elements. For example, if you have a diagram showing element A and element B linked by a dependency relationship, and your diagram, element A, and element B are all located in the same package. Moving the diagram to a different package or moving any of the elements to a different package will still maintain your diagram's appearance with the two elements on it and will maintain the relationship between the elements, no matter where they are located.

You need to be confident that restructuring the repository will maintain the integrity of its elements, as well as maintain the appearance of most of the diagrams. The reason for saying most instead of saying all is that some diagrams will still require manual tweaks and slight adjustments, so you need to keep that in mind when you plan for changes. Since the repository is meant to be used by many users in the enterprise, it is highly recommended to involve the key users in the discussions and the decisions of structuring the repository. First, we need to know who the possible users of the repository are.

Identifying the repository users

The users of the EA repository can be divided into two main categories: contributors and consumers. The contributors are the users who will add content to the repository, and they are mainly architects with different specialties, such as business architects, data architects, application architects, technology architects, and solution architects. Contributors also include the business analysts, project managers, developers, testers, business process engineers, strategists, product owners, and, in some cases, contractors. Ideally, each contributor should contribute to their area of specialty instead of delegating that to the enterprise architecture business unit, because this can be a bottleneck in large enterprises. However, many EA practices start by being the only contributors to the repository, and then more contributors join the effort as their maturity level increases.

The second group of users is the consumers, who are mainly the managers, project sponsors, and product owners, or, in general, the business users. The repository for them is a source of information to help them make better decisions. They need read-only access to the repository and will rarely be interested in modifying its content. *Chapter 14, Publishing EA Artifacts,* will explain how to publish the content of the repository and make it available outside Sparx EA for those who do not have a license to use it, or who are not comfortable with that.

Both types of users need an easy way to navigate the content of the repository. If, for example, they like the way that the document management system is in use today, or the way that SharePoint is structured, you may consider building the repository in a similar fashion.

The targeted structure must be driven by users' interests and requirements and be guided by the EA framework. Involving the key users, both the contributors and the consumers, at the early stages of planning the repository structure is very important.

There are two ways that the hierarchy of the repository structure can be looked at. It is either a physical or a logical hierarchy. Let us understand the difference between the two.

Differentiating physical and logical hierarchies

Physical hierarchies represent the actual containment of children objects within a parent object. The physical hierarchy is the structure that makes up the Project Browser's tree. It is composed of root node packages, containing view packages, that can contain elements, diagrams, and packages.

There are three general types of objects in any Sparx EA repository: packages, elements, and diagrams. **Packages** are containers of other repository elements and can take the form of model packages, view packages, and regular packages. Model packages that are also known as the root nodes are the top-level packages of the hierarchy. A single repository can have more than one model package. They cannot contain elements or diagrams but only view packages. View packages are the packages that are directly contained within model packages. They can contain diagrams, elements, and other subpackages. A single model package can contain many view packages. The last form of packages is the regular packages, which include any package that has no specialized purpose. Packages can contain subpackages, diagrams, and elements, so packages can be nested inside other packages as deep as desired.

Elements are the atomic building blocks of the repository. They appear on diagrams and show relationships among them. They can be created from toolboxes, reused from the Project Browser, and they have a wide variety of types, stereotypes, shapes, and characteristics. Components, activities, use cases, processes, and data objects are only a few examples of elements. Elements can contain diagrams and other elements, but they cannot contain packages.

Diagrams are special types of elements that visually represent how elements are related, and they are the actual artifacts that are produced and consumed by users. Diagrams cannot contain elements, packages, or other diagrams. Elements that are placed on diagrams are linked internally by Sparx EA, so there is a hidden relation between the diagrams and the elements on them, but it does not form a hierarchical composition, neither physical nor logical.

Here are the main characteristics of the physical hierarchy:

- An element or a diagram can be physically contained in only one package at a time. Moving the element from its current containing package to another, changes the hierarchy physically.

- Moving a child package from its parent package to another moves all its contained children too.

- Deleting a package deletes all its content as well. Sparx EA will ask to confirm the delete action, and once it is confirmed, it is permanent and cannot be undone.

In a **logical hierarchy**, parent elements are related to their child elements using the composition relationship. When element A composes element B, for example, it has the exact same meaning as physically having element A containing element B. Composition is a standard UML relationship, and we talked about it briefly in *Chapter 4, Advanced Model Driven Generation*, in the *Adding standard connectors to a custom toolbox* section. It allows us to model the parent-child relationship without the need to physically relocate elements in the repository. Here are the characteristics of the logical hierarchy:

- An element can be logically contained or composed by any number of parent elements.

- A logical parent and its child elements can be in different packages; each package can be located in any physical location in the repository.

- Moving a logical parent physically from one package to another does not alter the physical location of its composed elements.

- Deleting a logical parent does not delete any of its composed elements.

Each type of hierarchy has its use, so we cannot say that physically structured hierarchies are better than logically structured ones. Physical hierarchies provide a stronger form of containment than logical hierarchies, while the logical hierarchy provides more flexibility to the structure. *Figure 5.1* shows a sample physical hierarchy in the Project Browser on the left, and a diagram showing the logical hierarchy between a parent element and its child elements, in which some are physically located in different packages:

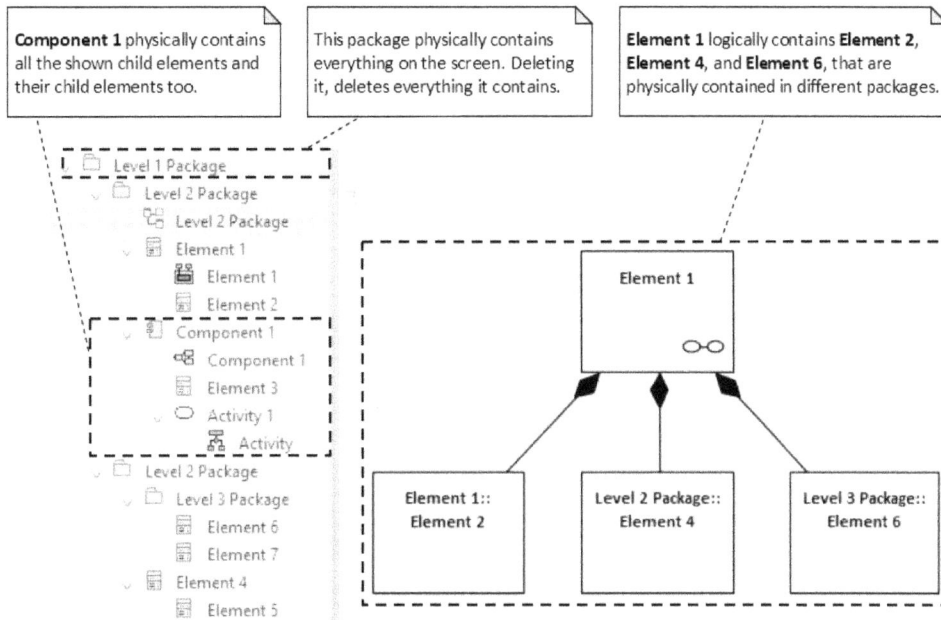

Figure 5.1: Physical vs. logical hierarchies

You can see that the top-level package is the **Level 1 Package,** and it contains all the other packages, elements, and diagrams. Deleting this package will delete everything that is physically located in it. Looking at the elements within the packages, **Element 2,** for example, can be moved to a different package by dragging it from where it is and dropping it where it should be. This will change its physical location, but if Element 2 was used on any number of diagrams, none of them will be affected. Looking at the right side of *Figure 5.1*, you can see that we have placed elements from different packages on the same diagram without changing their physical locations. **Element 1** is the logical parent of **Element 2**, **Element 4**, and **Element 6**, as per the diagram, because it is connected to them through a composition relationship. **Element 2** is a child of **Element 1**, both physically and logically.

Note: **Having a physical parent-to-child relationship between two elements does not automatically create the logical composition relationship between them. The composition relationship must be created manually if needed. Having the composition relationship between physical parent and its child elements adds better traceability to elements' hierarchy in larger repositories.**

The names of the child elements on the diagram are prefixed by the name of their physical containing package or element. This prefix can be shown or hidden by right-clicking on the diagram, selecting **Properties**, then checking **Diagrams | Appearance | Disable fully scoped object names**. It is useful sometimes to show the full object name, including the containing packages, and it is useful to hide it sometimes. This is why this is a diagram-level setting, as requirements can vary from one diagram to another.

In a nutshell, the physical structure is based on an actual containment of packages, diagrams, and elements inside packages. The logical structure is about using the composition relationship between elements on diagrams without altering their physical locations. Users of type contributors will be more interested in the physical structure because they need to know where to add, edit, or delete content. Users of type consumers will be more interested in the logical structure because they only interact with the repository content through diagrams.

A well-structured repository should take users from one diagram to another related diagram in a similar way that navigating a website works. Diagrams can contain links to other diagrams in different ways, and we will explore them with the proper examples when we encounter the need to do so.

Before we start constructing the repository structure, it is useful to use a standard to guide our approach. The TOGAF Standard is worth looking at and learning from.

Architecture repository reference model

To make the structure of the EA repository meaningful, the first thing that we should consider is to use a reference model to guide our development. TOGAF Standard provides that in the *Architecture Repository* chapter in its documentation, it is available online at **https://pubs.opengroup.org/togaf-standard/architecture-content/chap07.html**. It is highly recommended that you look at it and understand its components and definitions, because the main benefit of adopting an EA framework is to build on industry-standard foundations without re-inventing the wheel. It is important to use it as a reference rather than instructions that must be followed from A to Z. The TOGAF Standard's architecture repository reference model is a generic reference model that is supposed to work for all organizations at different maturity levels and of different sizes. If you are just starting an EA practice, then strictly forcing the standard can be overwhelming for you, your team, the users, and for the sponsors who want to see results.

To be practical, you need to understand the concepts of the standard and take what serves the current enterprise needs from it. You can always go back and add things as the architecture work evolves and new requirements are developed. Another thing to keep in mind is that the reference architecture can be implemented using multiple systems; therefore, we should not force everything to fit within Sparx EA. Managing calendars and decision logs, for example, are better handled using Outlook and SharePoint than using Sparx EA.

Note: **Avoid overthinking how to build the structure. Start with small artifacts and let the standard guide your way without forcing it.**

The bottom line is that you need to start somewhere, and if you overthink it, you may spend a lot of valuable time just trying to find the perfect structure that will most probably be changed as everyone's maturity increases, so let us learn how to build the structure.

Building the structure

When you start a new project in Sparx EA, all you get at the beginning is a single empty root package named **Model**. You can build an initial structure from the patterns that are provided by Sparx EA by right-clicking on the Model package and selecting **Add a Model using Wizard** from the context menu. This will launch a wizard-like process to help you, but these wizards can sometimes confuse and waste more time than they could potentially save. If you came from a programming background, you must have experienced that with several other tools that generate code, and Sparx EA is not an exception. Wizards are only helpful when you know how to properly modify their work and fit it within yours; therefore, we will build our structure without their help.

In *Chapter 2, Sparx EA Crash Course*, we started a project, and we used it to practice the examples in that chapter. In this chapter, we will continue from where we stopped there, at the Sandboxes package.

Sandboxes package

The Sandboxes package is useful for testing and practicing. They are not required to be in a repository, and they are not part of the TOGAF architecture repository, but they provide users with separate and designated packages where they can try new things.

Naming the Sandboxes can be anything you prefer, such as the user's first name, a combination of first name and last name separated by a period, or the user's first name followed by a space followed by the first letter of the last name. The only rule that you should enforce is consistency in naming Sandboxes.

In addition to personal Sandboxes, Sandboxes can also be created for projects where multiple team members can contribute to multiple artifacts that are related, each team member with their own specialty. This way, the project Sandbox will act as a development workspace before it is approved by the **Architecture Review Board** (**ARB**), and moved to the architecture content space. It is worth it to take notes from this paragraph, too, for additional important artifacts that you need to document in the repository, like the ARB structure and the architecture approval process. In *Chapter 6, Modeling Business Capabilities*, we will learn how to model similar artifacts and where to properly fit them. This is the approach of gradually building the repository as we contribute to its content, and while we do that, we adjust its structure to fit the right content in the right place. It is a more efficient approach than building a large and complex empty structure and then forcing your content to fit in it.

These are things to keep in mind when you use Sandboxes, especially when there are many contributors to the architecture content:

- **Sandboxes are not private**, so any user can see any other user's Sandboxes. Users can protect content in their Sandboxes from being modified or deleted by other users, but they cannot prevent them from viewing the content.

- **Sandboxes are not isolated from the other models in the repository**. This means that creating a relationship between an element in a Sandbox and another element in the architecture content package will be treated by Sparx EA the same way as a relationship between elements in the same Sandbox. Sparx EA does not treat the Sandboxes package any differently from other packages.

An alternative way to have a Sandbox package within the same project as the architecture content is to have the Sandboxes in a separate project. This keeps them completely isolated from the architecture content, but will require users to switch between repositories whenever they need to practice something, which can easily be resolved by pinning the different projects in use, so switching between them can be done quickly and easily.

Note: **To pin a project, go to the Start page, right-click on the project name that you want to pin, and select Pin Connection.**

Moving content between two separate projects can be done either by copying the structure from the source project to the clipboard and pasting it into the target project or by exporting the content from the source project as XML and importing it into the target project. Having the Sandboxes separated from the architecture content in two different projects provides more protection to the architecture content, while having them within the same project is more convenient. You can try one way and change to the other at any time, because it is more about how you and the other EA content contributors prefer to have it. Consuming users will be unlikely to interact with Sandboxes, so this practice is mainly for contributors.

We mentioned that Sandbox packages can act like a development workspace for testing and proposing new models. Now, it is time to build the most important package in the repository that will contain the actual architecture content.

Architecture content package

This package is a root package that is intended to contain the actual architecture work, which is the EA artifacts and their building blocks. This is the location that needs to reflect the needs of the contributors and the consumers alike, so it must be structured in a way that serves the needs of both. A good repository structure must look something like a good book in which information is provided in chapters, sections, subsections, and then text. Looking at the outline of a good book must tell what the book is about in general. Looking at the section headings gives more details and allows you to quickly find what you need. A good book must have a smooth flow of information, or else the reader will be lost and will stop reading it. The same is true when it comes to the architecture content.

The way to structure the architecture content varies based on different organizations' interests. In organizations where TOGAF is common to users, the structure may need to address the architecture layers and then drill down into the different elements in each layer. In a functional organization, the Organization Unit might be at the top level of the structure, followed by subunits, then the elements that are owned and controlled by the Organization Units. While in projectized organizations where projects are the heart of the business, the structure may look like a project management office dashboard where the top-level packages represent the projects, and lower-level packages represent phases, work packages, and tasks.

A good architecture that works best for your organization can be a combination of all the previous examples, and most properly, it will be that way. There is no one size that can fit all, so every architecture content is different, but let us explore the structure that follows the TOGAF content framework, and then we can talk about the possible ways to change it to fit your needs.

Structuring around the TOGAF content framework

Part of the TOGAF Standard is the **Architecture Content Framework**, which provides a guideline for how the content of an EA repository can be organized. The complete documentation can be found at **https://pubs.opengroup.org/togaf-standard/architecture-content/chap01.html**. It is a rich framework, and it is highly advisable to get yourself familiar with it. It groups the architecture content into three main groups:

- **Architecture principles, vision, and requirements** contain three subgroups: preliminary, architecture requirements, and architecture vision.

- **Architecture definition** contains four subgroups: motivation, business architecture, information systems architecture (data and application), and technology architecture.

- **Architecture realization** contains two subgroups: opportunities, solutions, and migration planning, and implementation governance.

Each of the subgroups contains groups of elements. The Technology Architecture subgroup, for example, contains the logical technology components, the physical technology components, and the technology services. Architecture content contributors who are familiar with the TOGAF Standard will find it easy to navigate in a structure like this, and it helps them find the information they need easily and quickly. Consuming users may prefer to have an easier way to navigate through the content, which will be through package diagrams. *Figure 5.2* shows on the left side how the TOGAF Architecture Content Framework can look in the **Project Browser**, where each group in the Architecture Content Framework is represented with a package element:

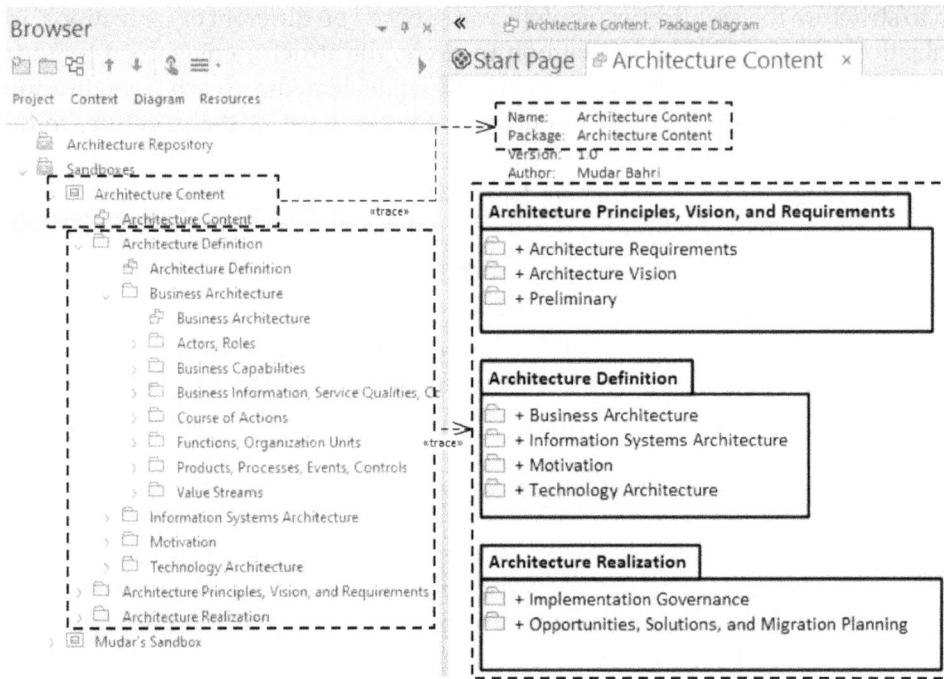

Figure 5.2: Structure using the TOGAF Architecture Content

On the right side, it shows what the package diagram will look like to users. Notice how packages are nested inside packages, and each package contains a diagram that shows the package content in a style like a file browser, which is a familiar style to almost every user.

Note: **Packages can be visually identified in the Project Browser by their single folder icon, while package diagrams can be identified by the smaller double folders icon.**

On the right side of *Figure 5.2*, there is one diagram named the **Architecture Content** diagram. It is the diagram that shows the content of the **Architecture Content** package, and it shows the three subpackages that the **Architecture Content** package contains. Double-clicking on any package of the three that are displayed on the diagram will drill down to their content and will open another diagram listing all the packages that they contain in the same nice way.

Figure 5.3 shows another example of a package diagram and its content. This will be the pattern that we will use for building the physical structure, and the entire repository will be structured this way. Users who are comfortable using the **Project Browser**'s tree navigation will use it. Users who are more comfortable navigating through diagrams will use them, and it will be like the experience of browsing the web or using a phone app.

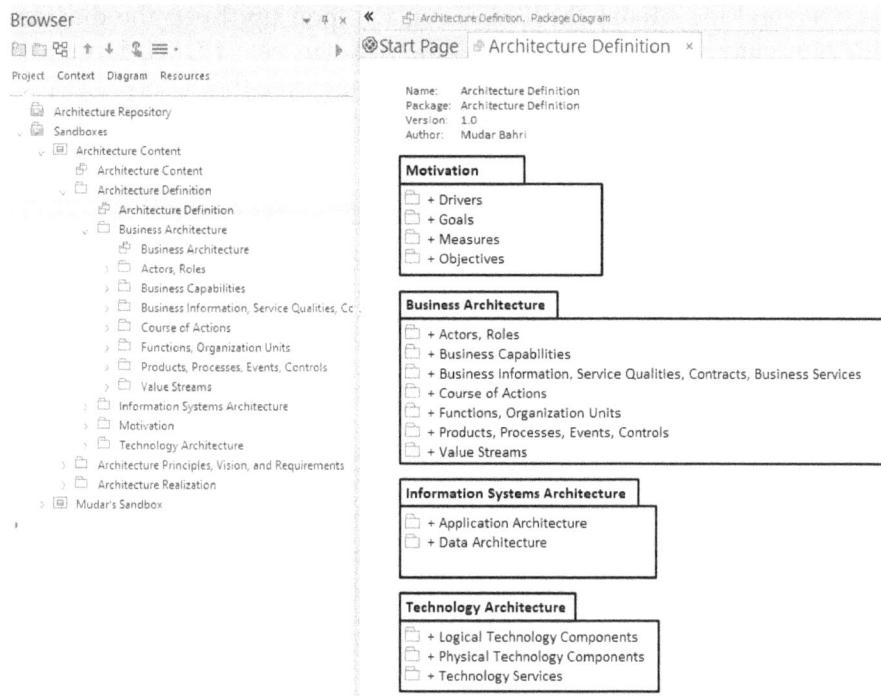

Figure 5.3: *Architecture definition package diagram*

Another thing to pay attention to in the two previous figures is that the structure was built in the **Sandboxes** package, not in the **Architecture Repository** package. This is the recommended approach for any proposed changes. Build the proof of concept in a Sandbox, propose it to the architecture review board, and once it is approved, move it to the right place in the **Architecture Repository** model package. We will learn more about the architecture approval process in *Chapter 6, Modeling Business Capabilities,* and *Chapter 13, Repository Management Processes.* One more thing to keep in mind is that consistency is a key success factor when it comes to building a repository. It is very important to consistently follow the same pattern across the entire repository structure.

In the next subsection, we will show you the steps for building the content framework proposed in *Figure 5.2* and *Figure 5.3* in Sparx EA.

Building the TOGAF content framework in steps

Follow these steps to create a repository structure that is based on TOGAF's content framework:

1. Open the **Sandboxes** model package, right-click on it, and select **Add View** to create a new view package.

2. When the **New Package** dialog pops up, enter `Architecture Content` in the **Name** field, and select **Create Diagram**.

3. Click **OK**, and the **Model Builder** dialog will pop up. Keep the diagram name as suggested which is the same name as the package, select **UML Structural** from the list of the available methodologies, select **Package** from the list of diagram types, then click **Create Diagram** to accept the choices and close the dialog. Use *Figure 5.4* for reference:

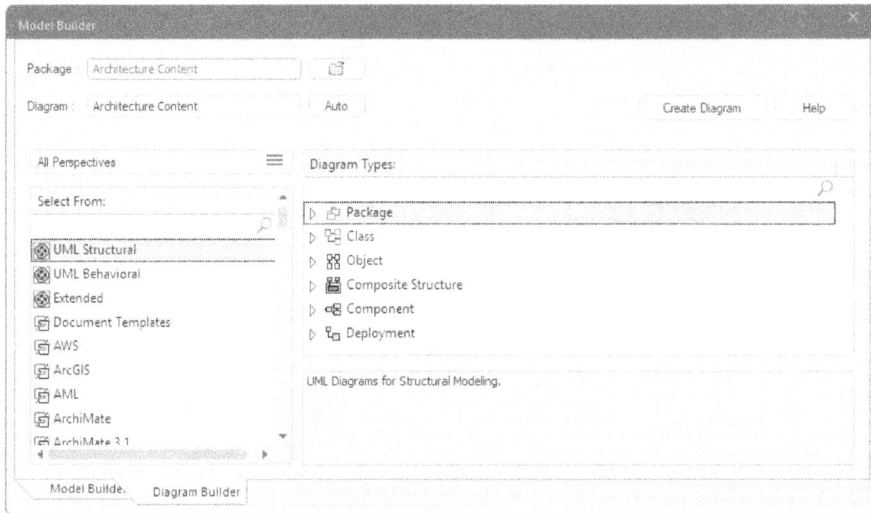

Figure 5.4: *Creating the architecture content package diagram*

4. You will have a new package, its name is **Architecture Content**, and it contains a single diagram that is currently empty.

5. From the **Toolbox**, click on the **Package** element, then click on the diagram.

6. The **New Package** dialog will pop up, so type `Architecture Definition` in the **Name** field, keep the **Create Diagram** option selected, then click **OK**.

7. Give the diagram the exact same name as the package, select **Package** from the list of available diagrams, then click **Create Diagram**, exactly like what we did in *step 3*.

8. Repeat *steps 5, 6,* and *7* to create two more packages under the **Architecture Content** package. Name the first `Architecture Principles, Vision, and Requirements`, and name the second `Architecture Realization`.

It is highly advisable to keep the names of the package diagrams matching the exact names of their containing packages to maintain smooth navigation and a better documented structure in the repository. If the package name is *XYZ*, name the package diagram *XYZ* as well. If you rename the package for any reason in the future, always remember to rename the package diagram to the same name, too.

Now, we have three packages inside the **Architecture Content** package. You can see them if you look at the **Project Browser** or if you look at the package diagram. You can either repeat *steps 5 through 8* to create all the remaining packages in the TOGAF content framework or create the package and subpackages on demand when you need to populate them with content. Remember that this is just the skeleton of the repository, which means there are no elements, diagrams, or artifacts of any type in it yet. The second half of this book is all about populating the skeleton with the proper artifacts.

The TOGAF content framework works for most types of enterprises, but some enterprise types may require customizing the content framework to fit their needs, and the next subsection will cover some of these different scenarios.

Considering different structuring scenarios

Since we all know that every enterprise is different, we must be ready to adjust the TOGAF content framework to better fit our needs. We will briefly look at possible requirements that can trigger the need to change the structure.

The structure can be created that reflects the states of the architecture, like the as-is and the to-be states. The entire structure can be duplicated into two packages: As-Is Architecture Content and To-Be Architecture Content packages. Another way to structure the architecture content around the states is to have one As-Is and many To-Be packages for a more specific strategic approach, like the 2025 Architecture Content, 2030 Architecture Content, and 2035 Architecture Content packages, for example. Elements can be used on diagrams across different physical packages, so you can still reuse elements from the 2025 package in the 2030 diagrams if these elements remain in use for a long time in the enterprise. Organization Units, for example, may remain in an organization under the same name for a very long time, so the same Organization Unit element can be reused across multiple states of the architecture.

You can apply the same architecture state concept on a more granular package level, which means that instead of having the separation of multiple states at the very top level package, you can have one architecture content package but at some package levels, say at the Business Capabilities package, you can have two or more packages representing the states or the strategies of the Business Capabilities such as the as-is Business Capabilities and the to-be Business Capabilities packages.

Another scenario is to group the structure by the Organization Units. This may sound like an anti-enterprise architecture pattern, but in many organizations, this could be the current (as-is) case. Whether we like it or not, there are still many organizations that operate in silos. There are organizations that have resulted from mergers and acquisitions, and some business units can be very independent from each other. Therefore, the possibility of structuring the repository around business units is there. In this case, you will have a package for each top-level Organization Unit, and each of them can have its own version of the content framework skeleton. You may also need to have a package for the shared enterprise components to contain the elements that are not explicitly owned by a specific Organization Unit. Your goal in a scenario like this, as an enterprise architect, can be to unify all these Organization Units into one structure, so your As-Is is built around the Organization Units, while the To-Be is more aligned with the TOGAF content framework.

A third scenario is to build the structure around projects in projectized organizations, where each project can have its own resources, applications, Organization Units, goals, and almost everything. In this case, the top-level packages under the architecture content will represent the project. Each replicates the entire architecture content structure. You can also have a separate package for the shared elements that are not explicitly owned by a specific project.

The scenarios and possibilities are endless, and you need to find the one that best fits your needs. It can be a mix of all the above, but this will be left for you to discover and decide. You can suggest all these scenarios by building empty skeletons in the Sandboxes, proposing them to the ARB, getting one of them approved, and then using it as a template.

We introduced the Sandboxes and architecture content model packages, and for more alignment with TOGAF's architecture repository reference model, you can add a third model package to the repository, which is the reference library package.

Reference library package

The reference library package is the package that contains references to the standards, framework, and global constraints and requirements that the organization follows or must adhere to. For example, take the TOGAF Standard. If it is the standard that your organization has chosen to use, you will need to keep the TOGAF references available and accessible for everyone. If you bookmark the TOGAF articles in your browser, they will be available only to you, while if you add these links to the reference library, they will be available for anyone who uses the repository. *Figure 1.2* from *Chapter 1, Introduction to Enterprise Architecture Repositories,* is an example of an artifact you can have in your reference library rather than having these reference models bookmarked in your browser just for you.

You can structure the reference library package in any way you want. You may decide to have a package for internal standards and another package for external. You can also have packages for legal constraints, regulations, recommended books on Amazon, and anything you need to keep a reference to. Remember, however, that Sparx EA is not SharePoint, and the whole point of having the reference library package is to provide quick and easy access to important resources. If there are hundreds or thousands of articles in it, people will find searching the internet easier and more convenient than looking in the reference library. So, you need to be selective about what to put in it.

Follow these steps to create a reference library package and two examples of the TOGAF and ArchiMate 3.2 references:

1. Right-click on the **Architecture Repository** model package or on the **Sandboxes** model package and select **Add Root Node** from the context menu.

2. Type `Reference Library` in the **Model Name** field and click **OK**. A new model package will be created with no content.

3. Right-click on the **Reference Library** package and select **Add View** from the context menu. The **New Package** dialog will appear.

4. Enter **External** in the **Name** field, select **Create Diagram**, then click **OK**.

5. Keep the diagram name as suggested, select the **Package** diagram type from **UML Structural** diagram types, then click **OK**.

6. From the **Toolbox**, click on **Package** and click on the diagram. The **New Package** dialog will open.

7. Type **Enterprise Architecture** in the **Name** field, select **Create Diagram**, then click **OK**.

8. The **New Diagram** dialog box will open. Keep the suggested name as is, select **Package** from the available **UML Structural** diagram types, and click **OK**.

9. A new **Enterprise Architecture** package will be created. Double-click on it to open its package diagram.

10. From the **Toolbox**, expand the **Common Elements** group, click on **Artifact**, then click on the package diagram to create a new artifact.

11. Select **Artifact** from the list of available artifact types.

12. Rename the artifact to **The TOGAF Standard**.

13. Double-click on the artifact to open its properties dialog. In the notes section, type some descriptive text like **A digital edition of the TOGAF Standard**.

14. Press the **Enter** key to start a new line. Click on the button that has a globe and a chain icon to add a URL to the TOGAF Standard on a new line.

15. Select **Web Site** from the **Type** list, type **https://pubs.opengroup.org/togaf-standard/** in the **Address** field, and click **OK**.

16. Click **OK** to close the properties dialog.

    The notes field of the artifact element now contains a link to the TOGAF Standard. The problem is that it is only visible if you click or double-click on the artifact. We want it to appear on the diagram so users can see it once they open the diagram. Continue with the following steps:

17. From **Common Elements** in the **Toolbox**, place a **Note** element on the diagram next to the artifact element.

18. Use the quick linker handle (the arrow-shaped handle) to create a relationship of type **Link** between the artifact and the note element.

19. Right-click on the connector and select **Link this Note to an Element feature**. A dialog box named **Link note to element feature** will open.

20. Select **Element Note** from the **Feature Type** options and click **OK**. You can see how the content of the artifact's notes section is now visible in the note element that is linked to it.

Repeat the same steps to create other artifacts in the reference library, as shown in *Figure 5.5*, which will allow the reference library to be rich with references that are available for everyone:

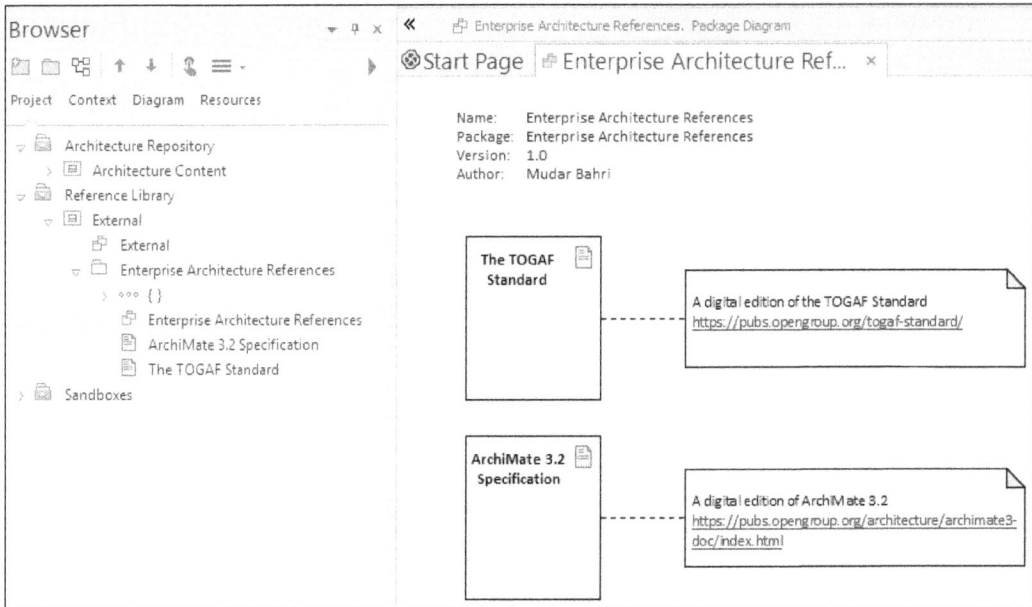

Figure 5.5: Example of reference library

Our repository is shaping up, as you can see, and it is ready to be populated with content. Part II of this book is full of different examples about the different artifacts that can be used to populate the repository, but let us recap this chapter before moving on.

Conclusion

An EA repository is the backbone of any EA practice, and without it, EA would never be efficient or useful. Investing in an EA practice without being coincident with investments in building a repository will most probably be a waste. A well-structured repository is a key to getting users' interest in it, so it must be in alignment with how the business operates, is structured, or is intended to be. Sparx EA allows us to restructure the repository early if we do not get the right structure from the first time, so do not overthink and plan to build the perfect structure right from the first time, because it will probably be adjusted multiple times before it gets stabilized. This is the natural evolution, and every stakeholder should expect it to happen this way. Let us keep moving and start populating the repository with artifacts. Since the best way to lead is to lead by example, we will start by modeling our EA practice; hence, the next chapter will be about modeling the Business Capabilities to encourage other Organization Units within the enterprise to do the same for the other Business Capabilities. We will learn how to make the EA capability an example to follow in modeling enterprise capabilities.

Points to remember

- The contributors are the users who will add content to the repository are mainly architects with different specialties.

- The consumers are the users who use the repository as a source of information to help them make decisions.

- Packages are the containers of other repository elements. They can contain packages, diagrams, and elements.

- Elements are the atomic building blocks of the repository. Elements can contain diagrams and other elements, but they cannot contain packages.

- Diagrams visually show how elements are related. They cannot contain elements, packages, or other diagrams.

- The physical structure is based on the actual containment of packages, diagrams, and elements inside packages.

- Moving elements physically from one package to another does not break their existing relationships with the other elements.

- The logical structure is about using the composition relationship between elements on diagrams without altering the elements' physical locations.

- Sandboxes provide users with separate and designated packages where they can try new things, but they are not required by the framework.

- The architecture content package will contain the actual architecture work, which is the EA artifacts and building blocks.

- The way to structure the architecture content varies based on different organization's interests.

- The reference library package is the package that contains references to the standards, framework, and global constraints and requirements that the organization follows or must adhere to.

Key terms

- **The Architecture Content Framework**: Provides a guideline to how the content of an architecture repository can be organized.

- **ARB**: The Architecture Review Board is a governance body that is responsible for reviewing and approving changes to the architecture.

Join our Discord space

Join our Discord workspace for latest updates, offers, tech happenings around the world, new releases, and sessions with the authors:

https://discord.bpbonline.com

CHAPTER 6
Modeling Business Capabilities

Introduction

Business Capabilities are a key aspect of enterprise architecture. Identifying and modeling Business Capabilities is an advanced topic that many EA practitioners address first, aiming for significant benefits and demonstrating high maturity. However, there are substantial risks associated with this approach, and your organization may not be ready to discuss it yet.

There is one Business Capability within the enterprise that you should be well-acquainted with and can start modeling with less effort: the enterprise architecture Business Capability. As the enterprise architect in your organization, you should be able to identify the elements related to the EA Business Capability or ask the pertinent questions to obtain specific answers. By modeling your findings and presenting them as EA artifacts, you accomplish two objectives simultaneously. The EA Business Capability will be modeled and documented, and the produced artifacts can serve as references to communicate better and explain what a Business Capability is to the rest of the enterprise. In this chapter, we will examine how to model the enterprise architecture Business Capability, what artifacts can be produced, and how to streamline the EA practice with examples that can be understood and accepted by the rest of the enterprise.

Structure

This chapter will include the following topics:

- Understanding Business Capabilities
- Building Business Capabilities artifacts

Objectives

The objective of this chapter is to learn how to model Business Capabilities in general, what artifacts to produce, and where to store them within the EA repository. We will use the enterprise architecture capability as an example to be followed, so the produced artifacts can be used as references to model the other Business Capabilities in the enterprise.

Understanding Business Capabilities

The TOGAF Standard defines Business Capability as a *particular ability that a business may possess or exchange to achieve a particular purpose* (**https://pubs.opengroup.org/togaf-standard/ architecture-content/chap02.html**). In simple words, Business Capability is the ability that makes an enterprise capable of doing what it is doing or planning to do. What makes a car manufacturer capable of building cars is the possession of certain capabilities that allow it to do that, like the knowledge (Business Information), the documented manufacturing steps (Processes and Functions), the required organizational resources (Organization Units) to deliver it, and to the strategic directions and initiatives by the organization (Course of Actions). If you apply the same definition to every type of business, such as shipping, banking, trading, training, farming, or catering, you will be able to start identifying what the true meaning of Business Capabilities is.

Business Capabilities can vary significantly from one business domain to another. A financial institution possesses different capabilities than a car manufacturing company or a software development company. This does not mean that every business has a unique set of Business Capabilities in all aspects. There are many capabilities that exist in most types of businesses, such as marketing, research and development, accounting, human resource management, project management, and information technology management. They may vary in the way they are conducted, but they share lots of similarities. The combination of all the Business Capabilities that an organization possesses is what differentiates one enterprise from the others.

Some Business Capability names may sound like the names of the Organization Units, some may sound like Function names, and some may sound like business services as well, which is true and very valid in the enterprise. Sometimes, the differentiator line is very thin between these, making them very hard to find or identify. In this chapter, we will provide as many guidelines and examples as we can to help you have a better understanding, and because the best way to learn is by practicing, we had better learn while contributing artifacts to the repository.

Building Business Capabilities artifacts

The TOGAF metamodel identifies all the possible elements within an enterprise and the possible relationships between them. All the models that we will build in the repository must adhere to the TOGAF metamodel, which means only the elements and the relationships that are defined in the metamodel will be used. For example, we cannot have a relationship between a Business Capability and a technology service because it is not in the metamodel. Also, we can only have a relationship of type used between Business Capability and Business Information because this is what the metamodel says. This is why we started building the MDG that enforces the TOGAF 10 metamodel, so we can be more confident that our artifacts are compliant with the industry standard.

We started building the MDG in *Chapter 3, Introducing Model Driven Generation,* and *Chapter 4, Advanced Model Driven Generation,* to provide us with what we need to build the artifacts in this chapter. It is far from being completed, but it is good enough for what we need to do now, so let us get started.

Importing the MDG

Before starting with the artifacts, we need to import the MDG into the main repository project. In case you forgot how to import an MDG, the following steps will remind you:

1. Open the MDG project that we last updated in *Chapter 4, Advanced Model Driven Generation,* and generate the MDG technology XML file. If you forgot how to generate the MDG file, please refer to the instructions in the *Publishing the MDG* section in *Chapter 3, Introducing Model Driven Generation.*

2. Open the main repository project that we used in *Chapter 5, Structuring the Repository.* It is recommended to make a backup copy of that file before starting to make changes to it.

3. Import the MDG XML file into the main repository project. If you forgot how, please refer to *Importing the MDG* section in *Chapter 3, Introducing Model Driven Generation.*

Now, we are ready to start modeling, so let us start with the simplest artifacts, the Business Capabilities catalog.

Modeling the Business Capabilities catalog

The purpose of catalogs is to contain a list of elements of the same type. The list must be simple and not provide details on any elements. Apparently, there will be a catalog for each element type in the metamodel when we populate the repository with more elements and more artifacts. The repository will contain the Organization Units' catalog, Functions catalog, Processes catalog, and Course of Actions catalog, just to mention a few examples of catalogs. Our scope of work now is on the Business Capabilities catalog.

We need this diagram to contain a list of all the Business Capabilities in the enterprise. The best place that we can have this list within the repository structure would be in the project browser, under **Architecture Repository | Architecture Content | Architecture Definition | Business Architecture | Business Capabilities**. If this part of the structure has not been built or completed yet, refer to the section *Building the TOGAF content framework in steps* in *Chapter 5, Structuring the Repository,* for a quick reminder on how to add and remove packages to or from the structure. If you check the toolbox that is associated with the Business Capabilities diagram, you will see that it does not contain the elements that we need, so we need to change the diagram type to be of type Business Capabilities catalog. The following steps show how to change a diagram type:

1. In the project browser, open the package **Architecture Repository | Architecture Content | Architecture Definition | Business Architecture | Business Capabilities**.

2. Double-click on the **Business Capabilities** diagram to open it in the diagrams area. The diagram must be empty.

3. From the ribbon bar at the top of the screen, select **Design | Diagram | Options | Change Type**.

4. The **Change Diagram Type** dialog will appear with a list of available diagram types. Select **Specialized | All Specialized** under **Type**.

5. Click on **TOGAF10_MDG**, expand the list under **Diagram Types**, select **TOGAF10_ MDG::Business Capabilities Catalog**, and click **OK**. The toolbox will be adjusted to contain the elements that we need to model the Business Capabilities catalog.

6. Click on the **Business Capability** element in the **Toolbox**, click on the diagram to create one, and rename it to `Enterprise Architecture`.

7. Double-click on the diagram to open its properties window and rename the diagram to `Business Capabilities Catalog`.

Congratulations, you have just created your first artifact in the new repository using the newly created MDG. It looks simple, and it contains a single element, but this is what we know so far. We will add more Business Capabilities to this catalog as we know more about the enterprise and contribute our knowledge in the form of artifacts.

When users see a list of elements on a website or on a file system, they will immediately expect that double-clicking an element will open another screen that contains details about the selected element. To maintain the same user experience, let us create a composite child diagram for the enterprise architecture Business Capability and add more details to it.

Modeling the Business Capability

There are many ways to model the enterprise elements. Some architects tend to tell everything in one large diagram, while others prefer to have simpler, more focused diagrams, each telling one thing at a time. There are architects who are somewhere between the two. All ways are acceptable if they are consistent throughout the repository:

- The one large diagram on one hand can get seriously large and may end up having dozens of elements and relationships, which will make it difficult to understand and hard to maintain. In other words, it may easily get out of control and out of shape and become useless to its consumers.

- The focused approach, on the other hand, provides multiple smaller and focused views that tell one information per diagram. The diagrams will be easier to read, understand, and maintain, but you will have to build many of them and connect them properly.

Both the said approaches, as well as any hybrid approaches, have advantages and disadvantages that we will present to you and let you decide how you prefer to build your repository.

Create a composite child diagram for the enterprise architecture Business Capability. This diagram will be the home page of this specific element, and we will refer to it as the home page of the enterprise architecture Business Capability. It must tell the viewers everything they need to know about this capability, either in the form of a single diagram that tells everything at once, or in the form of multiple simple and focused diagrams. Here are the steps to do that:

1. Right-click on the **Enterprise Architecture** element on the diagram.
2. Select **New Child Diagram | Composite Structure Diagram**.
3. Double-click on the **Enterprise Architecture** element to open its home page.

The child diagram has been automatically set to be of type Business Capability map, and that is because we instructed the MDG in the section *Setting composite child diagram types* in *Chapter 4, Advanced Model Driven Generation,* that this is the default diagram type that we need to make as the default composite child diagrams for Business Capability elements. Check the toolbox that is associated with the diagram. It contains the Business Capability element, the related elements, and the connectors between them, so it is the toolbox that we need. That is also how we designed the MDG to be, and it is pleasing to see that it is working as desired.

The Business Capability element can be linked to six other elements, as we know from the focused metamodel in *Figure 3.15*. We will create an artifact showing how the enterprise architecture Business Capability is related to Organization Units, Functions, Processes, Value Streams, courses of action, and Business Information, and we will start with the Organization Units.

Relationships to Organization Units

An **Organization Unit** is defined by the TOGAF Standard as a *self-contained unit of resources with goals, objectives, and measures. Organization Units may include external parties and business partner organizations* (**https://pubs.opengroup.org/togaf-standard/architecture-content/chap02.html**). Under this definition, an Organization Unit can represent the entire enterprise, a unit, or a subunit within the enterprise. Self-contained does not mean that it is independent from the enterprise, but it means that it has defined boundaries, so it is well known what is in it and what is not. Organization Units will be covered in more detail in *Chapter 12, Modeling Organizations and Strategies*, but in this chapter, we will focus on how they are related to Business Capabilities in particular.

An Organization Unit element can be related to a Business Capability element using two different relationships: delivers and uses. Organization Units are responsible for delivering the Business Capabilities to be used by other Organization Units.

An Organization Unit must be responsible for delivering the enterprise architecture capability to the enterprise. In our example we will call it the enterprise architecture Organization Unit, but in your real-world, it could have a different name and it might be any other Organization Unit such as the information technology Organization Unit, the strategy and planning unit, the project/program/portfolio management office, or any other unit that your organization decided to assign the EA capability to.

Note: **Remember that the main purpose of this book is to learn how to model, not to recommend an organization structure.**

The Organization Units that deliver the Business Capability can be internal or external to the enterprise, so other Organization Units, internal or external, can use them. An example of that is when an organization decides to outsource a specific Business Capability to an external organization, and the whole enterprise will benefit from and use it.

We need to create an artifact that depicts the information that we have regarding the enterprise architecture Business Capability and the Organization Units that are related to it. The following steps will show you how:

1. In the project browser, right-click on the ‹‹**Business Capability**›› **Enterprise Architecture** element and select **Add | Add Diagram** from the menu.

2. The **New Diagram** dialog will open. Enter `Relationships to Organization Units` as the diagram's name, select **Specialized | All Specialized** from the **Type** list, click on **TOGAF10_MDG**, select **Business Capability Map** from the list of diagram types, and click **OK**.

3. From the project browser, drag the ‹‹**Business Capability**›› **Enterprise Architecture** element and drop it as a **Link** on the **Relationships to Organization Units** diagram.

4. From the **Toolbox**, click on the **Organization Unit** element, then click on the diagram.

5. A new **Organization Unit** element will be created. Name it `Enterprise Architecture Office` and use the quick linker to create a **Delivers** relationship from the Organization Unit element to the Business Capability.

6. Create two more Organization Unit elements and name them `Information Technology Department` and `Strategy Office,` and create a **Uses** relationship going from these two to the enterprise architecture Business Capability.

Note: The better approach that you should follow in real-life artifacts is to create them in a Sandbox, have them approved, then move them to the main repository.

Figure 6.1 shows the artifact that explains the relationships between the enterprise architecture Business Capability and other units within the enterprise:

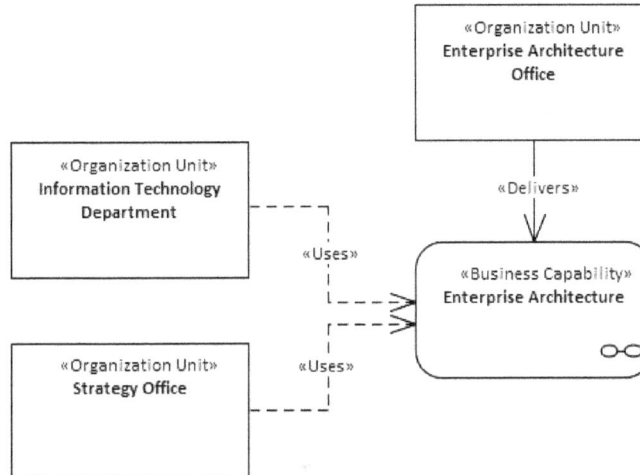

Figure 6.1: Business Capability and its relationships to Organization Units

Let us discuss a few things that can be seen in the developed artifacts. First, it is an example, and in real life, your model can look different. The goal is to explain which Organization Unit delivers the enterprise architecture Business Capability, and what Organization Units use it. If you have more Organization Units using or planning to use the enterprise architecture capability, then you must add them to your diagram. If the whole enterprise will be using this capability, then you should place one Organization Unit element representing the top-level unit in the organization structure, say for example, The XYZ Company.

Note: If you are not sure, this is where having a visual representation of your understanding can help getting answers. You can propose the artifact to the architecture review board, listen to their feedback, and act accordingly.

The second thing to notice in *Figure 6.1* is that it does not indicate how the three Organization Units are related to each other, and this is how all focused artifacts must be designed. Showing a different type of information on the same diagram such as how the Organization Units that deliver and use the Business Capability are related to each other, is against the principle of keeping the diagrams focused. If a user needs to know more about how these Organization Units are related, they need to check different artifacts that will be focusing only on that part, which will be covered in *Chapter 12, Modeling Organizations and Strategies*. Each Organization Unit will have its own homepage diagram that shows how it is related to the other Organization Units. This is how the repository grows and matures, one building block at a time, and this drives the demand to upgrade the MDG to support the new artifacts.

The third thing to pay attention to in *Figure 6.1* is in the project browser. If you look at the ‹‹**Business Capability**›› **Enterprise Architecture** element in the project browser, you will see that it contains two diagrams and three Organization Units, as you can see in *Figure 6.2*:

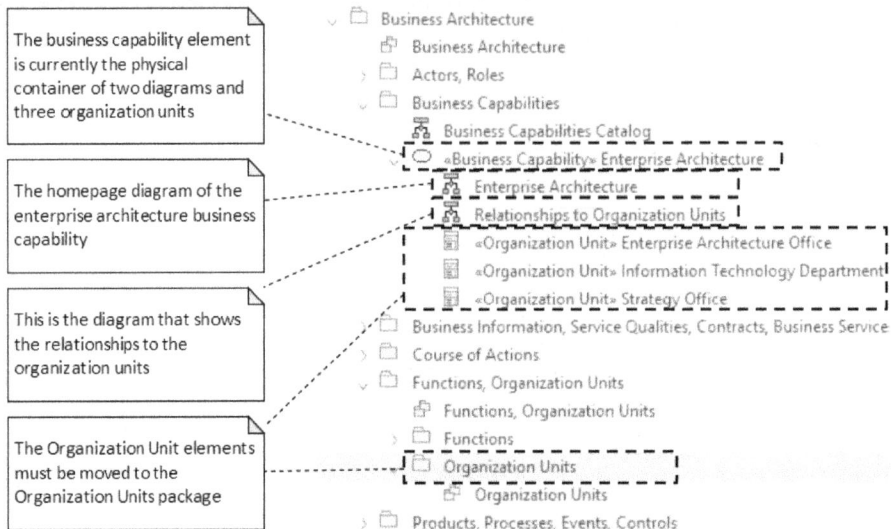

Figure 6.2: Placement of the elements in the project browser

The EA diagram is the composite child diagram, or the homepage diagram, as we call it. This is the diagram that will open by default when you double-click on the Business Capability element from any diagram in the repository. By default, composite child diagrams have the same names as their elements unless they are manually renamed. The **Relationships to Organization Units** diagram will not respond to double clicking on the element because it is not the homepage diagram; therefore, we must make it accessible to users in different ways, and we will introduce one of these ways at the end of this subsection.

The fourth and last thing in this discussion is also in the project browser. Notice how any new element that we create from the **Toolbox** is, by default, contained in the element that contains the diagram. We placed the three new Organization Unit elements on the **Relationships to Organization Units** diagram, which is contained in the enterprise architecture Business Capability. Any new element will by default be placed under the same parent that contains the diagram, so the three new Organization Unit elements became child elements of the Business Capability element, which is not the correct place for them. According to the repository structure that we built, we have a dedicated package to contain Organization Units, and we need to move the three newly created Organization Units to it. To do that, drag the elements from where they are and drop them where they should be. Use *Figure 6.2* to guide you to the target location.

We now have a new artifact in the repository, and it shows what Organization Units are related to the enterprise architecture Business Capability has now been completed. We may come back and change it when needed, because every artifact in the repository is a living artifact.

The last step is to add the new artifact to the composite child diagram to make it accessible to users, so follow these steps:

1. Close the **Relationships to Organization Units** diagram.

2. Make sure that the **Enterprise Architecture** composite child diagram is opened or open it if it is not.

3. In the project browser, find the **Relationships to Organization Units** diagram element. It should be contained in the ‹‹**Business Capability**›› **Enterprise Architecture** element.

4. Do not open the diagram, but click and hold it, drag it, and drop it on the opened diagram in the diagrams area, as explained in *Figure 6.3*:

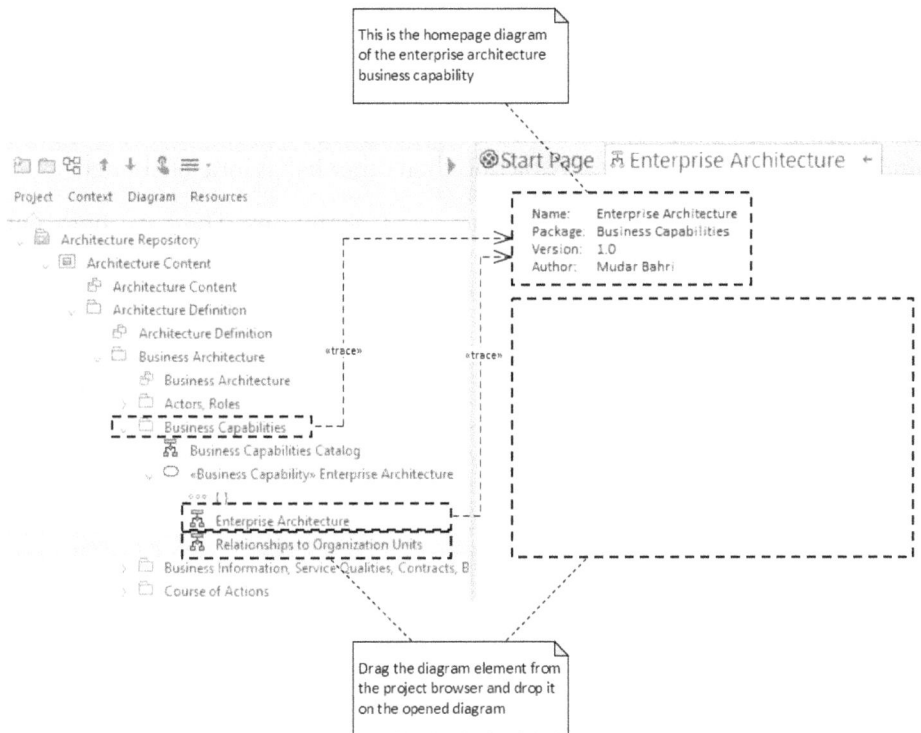

Figure 6.3: Placing a diagram on a diagram

5. The **Select Type** dialog box will give you five different types for creating a reference of a diagram on another diagram. Select **Navigation Cell** from the list and click **OK**.

6. Another dialog box will give the option to **Select Image** for the navigation cell. Find an image that is suitable for Organization Units and click **OK**.

This will place a rectangular-shaped navigation cell on the homepage diagram. Double-clicking the navigation cell will open the diagram behind it. This is one way of connecting diagrams together.

Note: **As a side exercise, try the other options of dropping a diagram over a diagram and note the differences between each choice. They all give the same results, and we will use some of the other options in different places when needed.**

We are back to the homepage of the enterprise architecture Business Capability. It is time to add another artifact to the repository, which is how this Business Capability is related to Functions.

Relationships to Functions

Starting with the definition, TOGAF defines a Function as *a set of business behaviors based on a chosen set of criteria. Functions are usually close-coupled to/with organizational units.* (**https://pubs. opengroup.org/togaf-standard/architecture-content/chap02.html**). Behavioral elements are the actions, interactions, and Processes that describe the dynamic behavior of an enterprise, as we explained in *Understanding structural and behavioral elements* section in *Chapter 1, Introduction to Enterprise Architecture Repositories*. A Function is defined as a set, which means that Functions are a grouping and a higher level of abstraction than other behavioral elements.

It is very easy to confuse Functions and Business Capabilities. They are both behavioral elements, both are at a high and abstracted level, both are influenced by the Course of Actions, both are related to Organization Units, both are related to Processes, and they have a direct relationship between them. *Figure 6.4* shows a side-by-side comparison between Business Capabilities and Functions at the metamodel level and what elements connect to each one:

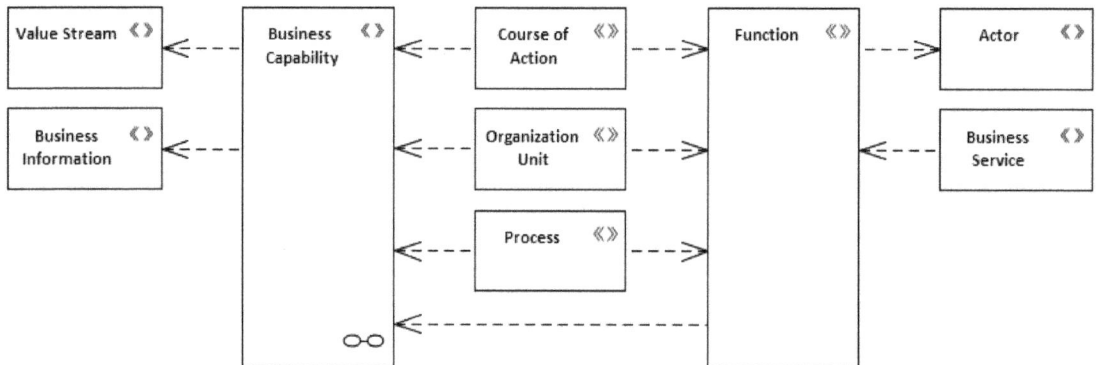

Figure 6.4: Comparing Business Capabilities to Functions

The biggest difference between the two is that Business Capabilities are more abstract than Functions and are more toward enabling and realizing a Value Stream that the organization has or is targeting to have. Functions, on the other hand, are about making things happen; yet still at a grouping and abstract level, so that business services can be provided. Functions are abstract, which means that they do not involve step-by-step instructions on how to perform things, because that is what Processes are for. Still, Functions in general describe the outcome of performing a set of Processes.

Going back to our enterprise architecture Business Capability. To identify the Functions that are related to it, ask yourself what the enterprise architecture unit must do to make the enterprise capable of performing the EA practice. The answers to this question can be obtained from the documents that were published on the establishment of the EA unit, by interviewing the managers who were behind the unit's establishment decision, and from your knowledge and experience in the EA domain. For an organization to be capable of practicing EA, it needs to adopt a framework like TOGAF, make the people aware and familiar with it by providing awareness and training sessions, provide a tool to users of all types, provide help and consultation to every unit in the organization to get their interest in EA, and populate the repository. You can think of additional Functions that the EA unit must do, but we can extract Functions from the previous statements and rephrase them in a more architectural format.

Adapting a framework or a methodology needs to be governed to ensure that everyone is following, and to identify what to do in case not everyone is following. This is simply an *EA Governance* Function. To spread awareness about EA, providing training classes and mentoring sessions about it can be called the *EA Training and Mentoring* Function. *EA Consulting* is a more advanced Function that can be provided to other Organization Units to support their efforts to contribute to the repository with artifacts. Finally, due to the importance of EA tools to successfully deliver an EA Business Capability, *EA Tool Management* is another Function that is required too.

The steps for creating a diagram that shows what Functions are related to the enterprise architecture Business Capability are similar to the steps that we followed in the previous subsection for creating the relationships to the Organization Units' diagram. Here is reminder of the steps, but you must be familiar with them from now on:

1. Add a new diagram of type **Business Capability Map** under the enterprise architecture Business Capability element, and name it as `Relationships to Functions`.

2. From the project browser, drag the ‹‹**Business Capability**›› **Enterprise Architecture** element and drop it as a **Link** on the **Relationships to Functions** diagram.

3. From the **Toolbox**, create three Function elements on the diagram, and give them the names `EA Training`, `EA Tool Management`, and `EA Consulting`.

4. Use the quick linker to create a **Delivers** relationship from the Function elements to the Business Capability, one at a time.

5. Move the three Function elements to the designated package in the structure, at **Business Architecture | Functions, Organization Units | Functions**. Add this branch to the repository structure if it does not exist yet.

6. Add a navigation cell from the **Relationships to Functions** diagram to the enterprise architecture Business Capability home page diagram.

Figure 6.5 suggests an artifact that shows what Functions deliver the enterprise architecture Business Capability:

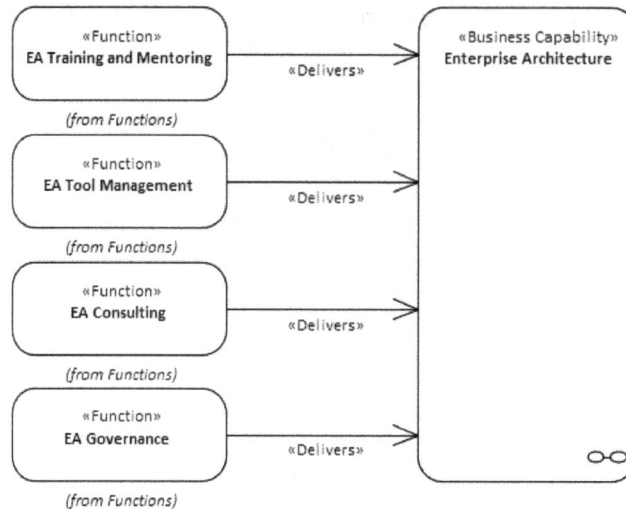

Figure 6.5: Relationships to Functions artifact

Each of the defined Functions indicates at a high-level of abstraction how to deliver the capability, but without telling exactly how in the form of steps. It is common to identify something as a Function, but finding out later that it is a Process, and vice versa. Looking at elements in the enterprise can be perceived differently by different people, and this is why the architecture review board must include representatives from all Organization Units as there is something to learn from each board member.

Another thing to remember when identifying Functions is that Functions can be composed of smaller Functions. In a large enterprise, the EA consulting Function, for example, can be composed of TOGAF Consulting, ArchiMate Consulting, and MITA Consulting Functions. You can even break down the TOGAF Consulting Function into smaller Functions each is specialized by an architecture layer, such as business architecture consulting, application architecture consulting, and so on. The important rule to keep in mind is to create artifacts that are realistic to your enterprise. If the EA Organization Unit is new or small, it is better to keep things more generic, so they do not become overwhelming.

Whenever we start listing steps of actions or sequences of flows, then we are talking about Processes, not Functions anymore. The next subsection will tell us more about relationships to Processes.

Relationships to Processes

According to TOGAF, a *Process represents a sequence of activities that together achieve a specified outcome, can be decomposed into sub-processes, and can show operation of a Business Capability or service (at next level of detail)* (**https://pubs.opengroup.org/togaf-standard/architecture-content/chap02.html**). Processes are also behavioral elements just like Functions, but the main difference between the two is that Processes are about how to do things by providing steps and sequences of flow. A Function such as EA tool management can be realized by a set of Processes, such as:

- Build and maintain the MDG

- Back up project files

- Provide technical support

- Onboard new users to the tool

Each of these Processes can be composed of smaller and more specific subprocesses, which themselves can be composed of smaller and more specific subprocesses. You can keep drilling down level after level until you reach a level that makes sense and does not need to be detailed any further. There is no rule of thumb that provides a measurement of how much detail is sufficient, because every environment has different requirements that need different levels of detailing. This is why the best level of detail in any diagram is the level that makes sense. *Chapter 13, Repository Management Processes,* will provide more detail on some of these Functions, Processes, and their subprocesses.

Figure 6.6 shows a list of Processes that operationalize the enterprise architecture Business Capability:

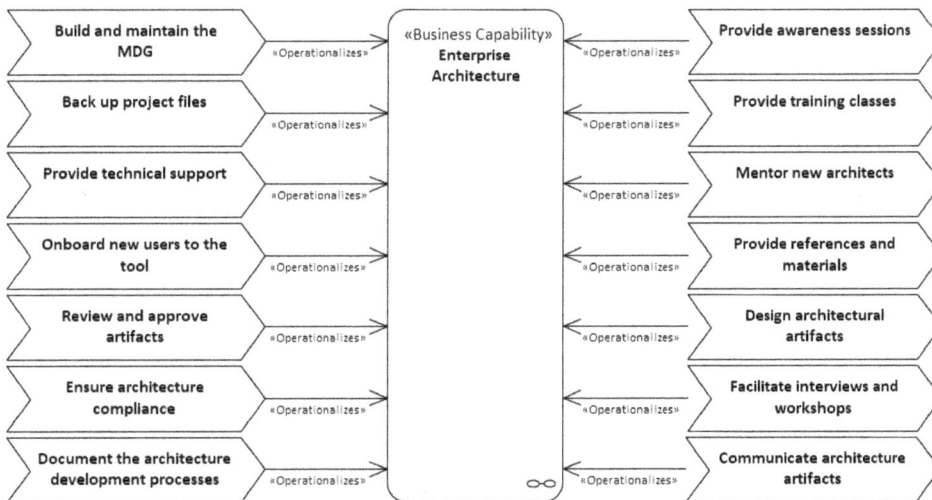

Figure 6.6: Processes that operationalize a Business Capability

More Processes can be added at any time to this list and existing Processes can be removed as well. You should be in a good shape now to perform the following steps without instructions:

1. Create the diagram in *Figure 6.6* on a new diagram and give it the name **Relationships to Processes**.

2. Do not forget to move the newly created Processes to their location in the repository under **Business Architecture | Products, Processes, Events, Controls | Processes**.

3. Also, remember to add a navigation cell on the Business Capability's homepage to direct users to the **Relationships to Processes** diagram.

The relationship between Processes and Business Capabilities is of the type *Operationalizes*, which means that Processes enable Business Capabilities to operate. The list of Processes that operationalize a certain Business Capability can get very long, so you may consider grouping them into higher-level Processes and adding them to this diagram instead of the more detailed ones. Remember that each of the listed Functions must be detailed later. Enterprise architecture is like an endless number of connected diagrams, each telling part of the story.

Relationships to Value Streams

A Value Stream is a *representation of an end-to-end collection of activities that create an overall result for a customer, stakeholder, or end-user* (**https://pubs.opengroup.org/togaf-standard/architecture-content/chap02.html**). The easiest way to understand Value Streams is to perceive them as top-level processes generating value for the stakeholders in the organization. Values can take the form of revenue, production of products, increment in stock value, making a social impact, or gains on any aspect of interest to stakeholders that include owners, employees, customers, and end users.

A Value Stream can be composed of smaller Value Streams that form phases. Value Streams and their phases must remain at the top level of process abstraction and should only answer what generates value rather than answering how. Once you start describing how to generate the value, then you have reached the process level. Value Streams and Processes are connected to each other, and they are both connected to Business Capabilities. *Figure 6.7* shows how the enterprise architecture Business Capability enables a Value Stream:

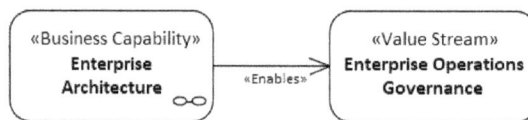

Figure 6.7: Business Capability enabling a Value Stream

The **Enterprise Operations Governance** Value Stream brings the value of having the enterprise operations properly governed, which is what the top management officers in the organization are looking for. To deliver the value of having the enterprise operations governed, the enterprise architecture Organization Unit was established to deliver the enterprise architecture Business Capability, which enables the Value Stream. You can see how the artifacts that we are contributing to the repository are already starting to answer questions and bring up more, and this is how the repository is built, one artifact connecting to the other.

Be careful when you model Value Streams, as talking about this topic may open doors to defining or refining the documented strategy of the organization or even creating a new one. This topic can divert you from where your effort is and will consume your time on a different topic. It is okay to move your efforts to another topic if the project manager and the stakeholders are aware of this shift and are approving it in the form of a scope of work statement. Knowing how to remain focused while modeling parts of the enterprise is key.

Perform the following steps to contribute the new artifact to the repository:

1. Create the diagram in *Figure 6.7* and give it the name **Relationships to Value Streams**.

2. Move the newly created Value Stream element to its location in the repository under **Business Architecture | Value Streams**.

3. Add a navigation cell on the Business Capability's homepage to the new diagram.

The next element is the Course of Action element.

Relationships to Course of Actions

Starting with another definition from TOGAF, a Course of Action is *a direction and focus provided by strategic goals and objectives, often to deliver the value proposition characterized in the business model* (**https://pubs.opengroup.org/togaf-standard/architecture-content/chap02.html**). A Course of Action can be any ongoing activity in the organization, such as a project, a program, or an initiative. The description of a Course of Action usually contains a problem statement, problem analysis, proposed solutions, a justification of the chosen solution, an estimated budget, a desired outcome, and a high-level timeline.

Course of Actions are created to realize strategic goals, and they influence many business architecture elements such as the Business Capabilities, Organization Units, Functions, products, Value Streams, and Business Information. An organization may require introducing a new product, for example. This requires either establishing a new business unit to deliver it or at least upgrading the capabilities of an existing business unit to deliver it. The Organization Unit may need to establish new Functions or upgrade the current ones to accommodate the new product; some strategic-level Value Streams will be defined, and some Business Information may be introduced to the enterprise.

To properly identify what Course of Action influences the enterprise architecture Business Capability, you need to ask for the documents, charters, letters, and anything that helps you understand why enterprise architecture was established. *Figure 6.8* shows an example, but again your real-world model could be different:

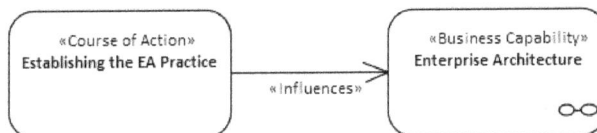

Figure 6.8: Course of Action influences Business Capability

Keep in mind that all the artifacts that we are providing in this chapter are looking from the enterprise architecture Business Capability perspective. If the same Course of Action influences other elements such as Organization Units, Functions, or even other Business Capabilities, this is not the right artifact to show these elements on. Other artifacts will be developed under the Establishing the EA Practice Course of Action element itself, as we will see in *Chapter 7, Modeling Projects*. The Course of Action will have its own homepage diagram that links to different other artifacts, just like what we are doing here for the Business Capability.

The last element that we will talk about in this chapter is Business Information, but as usual, let us start with its definition.

Relationships to Business Information

TOGAF defines Business Information as *it represents a concept and its semantics used within the business* (**https://pubs.opengroup.org/togaf-standard/architecture-content/chap02.html**). Business Information is the information that means something for the business. Most reports and documents are considered Business Information, as they combine data from different sources into a form that business users understand and use. Do not confuse Business Information with data or databases. Data entities will be covered in *Chapter 8, Modeling Applications*, and in that chapter, we will see how data entities realize Business Information. Business Information is a more human consumable form of data than data entities. *Figure 6.9* lists some Business Information that are used by the enterprise architecture Business Capability:

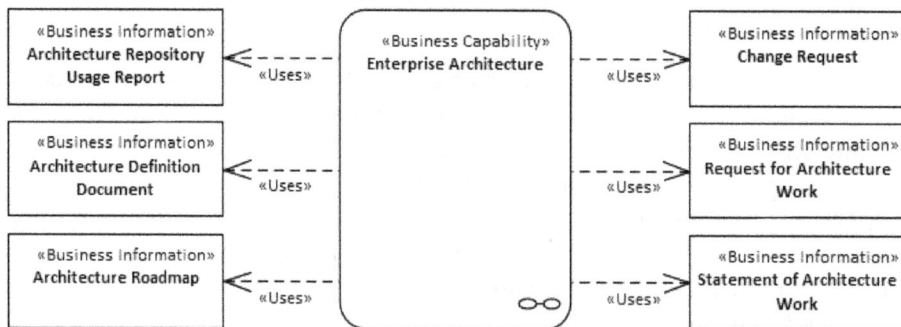

Figure 6.9: Enterprise architecture Business Information

You can use the notes section in the properties dialog box to type the complete definition of each Business Information element. You can add links to internal or external resources to direct the users to additional readings on the topic. Business Information was the last element that can connect to a Business Capability. Now, let us put everything we know about the enterprise architecture Business Capability in one diagram and see how it looks.

Building the all-in-one artifact

At the beginning of this section, *Modeling the Business Capability*, we indicated that one way of modeling is to keep the artifacts small and focused on one topic at a time, and another way to model is to put everything we know in one diagram that tells many things in one place. Both approaches, and everything in between, are right, but to have a clear comparison between the two, we put together everything we know about the enterprise architecture Business Capability in the diagram in *Figure 6.10*:

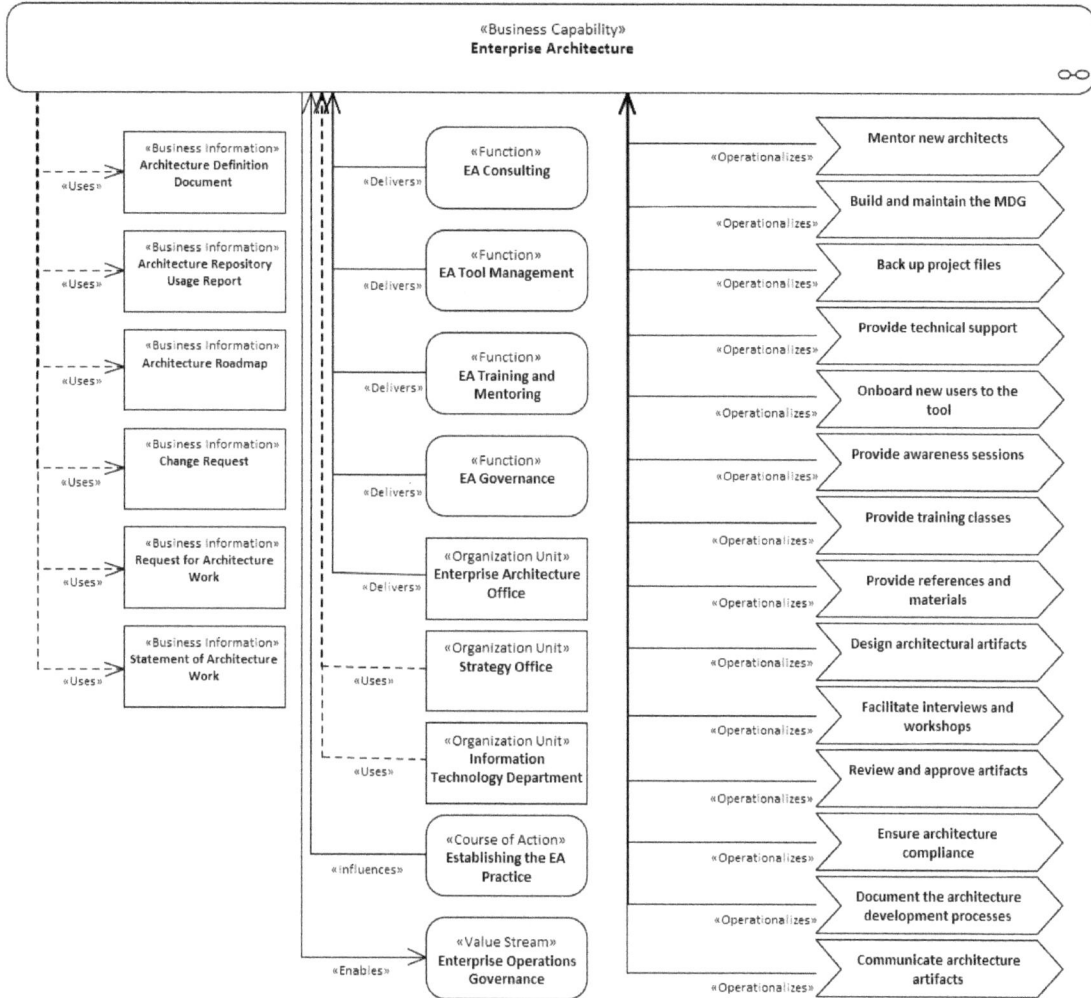

Figure 6.10: An all-in-one artifact

The diagram tells us everything we have documented so far about the enterprise architecture Business Capability, all in one place. It is good on the one hand because it saves a lot of clicking and navigating back and forth from one diagram to another. On the other hand, it made the diagram large, difficult to maintain, and difficult to read and understand. All this size and we were documenting the enterprise architecture Business Capability, which is relatively smaller than other Business Capabilities like accounting and marketing. Trying to put everything we know about accounting in one diagram will result in a diagram that is difficult to maintain and not comfortable for many users to look at and understand.

The focused artifacts that we have built are more scalable, simpler, and easier to read, but they lack the complete picture view. *Figure 6.5,* for example, tells us what Functions deliver the Business Capability; *Figure 6.6* tells what Processes operationalize it, but there is no artifact yet that tells us how the Functions and the Processes are related. This information requires a set of additional artifacts to show how Functions and business processes are related.

Having focused artifacts requires having a nicely designed homepage to provide smooth navigation and easy movement from one element to another. Let us have a final look at the Business Capability homepage to make sure that it looks the way it should be.

Finalizing the Business Capability homepage

If you followed all the examples that have been provided in this chapter, you should have a homepage for the enterprise architecture Business Capability that contains six navigation cells, each of which navigates us to a specific artifact. You may have selected different images for the navigation cells, placed the navigation cells in a different order, but it should look like the homepage in *Figure 6.11*:

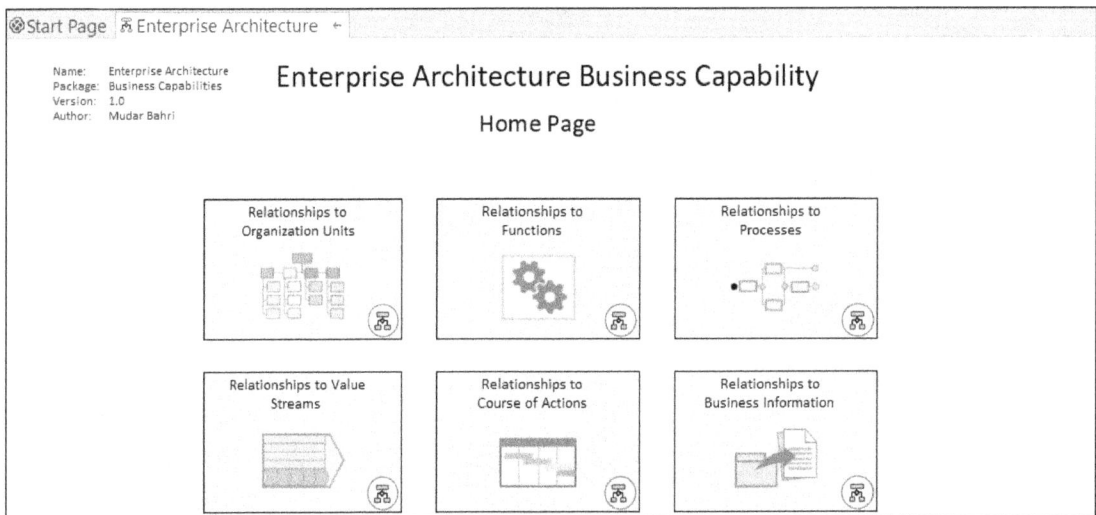

Figure 6.11: Business Capability homepage

We added two labels at the top of the diagram to introduce the users to the page. To add similar labels to your homepage, use the **Common Elements | Text** element from the **Toolbox** and adjust the font as desired. Most of the elements in the repository will have a homepage like that. You are free to add any additional diagrams to the homepage, like an all-in-one diagram or any other diagram that you think is valuable. You are also free to remove any diagram that does not have value in your workplace, but in this chapter, we have introduced a pattern that you can follow and enhance as desired. There is no one right way to build a repository, but rest assured, this pattern is one right way.

Conclusion

The enterprise is a large collection of interconnected elements. The enterprise architecture repository is a large web of interconnected diagrams reflecting the elements of the enterprise and how they are connected. We saw how we started with a single Business Capability element and how we ended up with multiple diagrams and elements in the repository. This is why enterprise architecture is a lengthy investment that not every organization recognizes. If you do not remain focused on the tasks that you need to complete within the predefined scope of work, you can easily lose your way in the maze of enterprise architecture.

If you do not have all the elements that you need, do not force defining them because this must be the scope of work of a different effort. If you cannot find an element, do not waste too much time trying to make one up, because this will distract you from finishing what you need to finish. We provided six different example models in this chapter, but in your case, if you only have information about the business processes, then this is where you need to put your effort in. All diagrams are living things in the repository, so it is best to document what you know, skip what you do not, and update later when you have more information available. If defining the Business Capabilities is very challenging to start with, and it is indeed, there is no shame at all to start with a different topic where you can find more information available, like modeling applications, Processes, or Organization Units. It is a large enterprise, and you will learn more about it by contributing more artifacts to the repository.

In the next chapter, we will learn how to break down your work into small iterations and define the scope of work for one iteration at a time. Then, we will learn how to incorporate the project's iterations within the enterprise, because every change to the enterprise needs to be tracked and documented.

Points to remember

- Business Capability is an advanced topic in enterprise architecture. If you decide to start with it, it is better to start with a Business Capability that you are familiar with, such as the enterprise architecture Business Capability.

- Building a repository is not just about collecting information and keeping it in spreadsheets, but it is about converting the knowledge that you collect into the form of EA artifacts, one artifact at a time.

- Composite child diagrams will be used as homepages for the elements that are documented in the repository.

- Focused artifacts show how an element is related to a specific type of other elements, one at a time. They are simple and easy to maintain and understand, and we will use them throughout the repository.

- All-in-one diagrams show all the relationships in one diagram, but this makes them large, complex, and difficult to maintain and understand.

- Business Capabilities can be delivered by internal or external Organization Units.

- Business Capabilities and Functions can be easily confused with each other. The Business Capability is at a higher level of abstraction than a Function.

- The best level of detail in any artifact is the level that makes sense for you, for the users, and within your environment. There is no actual measurement for it.

Key terms

- **Business Capability**: The ability that makes an enterprise capable of doing what it is doing or planning to do.

- **A catalog**: It is a diagram that contains a list of items of the same type.

- **Organization Unit**: It can mean the entire enterprise, a unit within the enterprise, or a subunit.

- **Function**: A grouping of other behavioral elements, mainly Processes.

- **Process**: The steps and sequences of flow telling how things can be done.

- **Value Stream**: A strategic top-level Process that results in creating value.

- **Course of Action**: An ongoing activity in the organization, such as a project, a program, or an initiative.

- **Business Information**: It is the information that means something for the business.

Join our Discord space

Join our Discord workspace for latest updates, offers, tech happenings around the world, new releases, and sessions with the authors:

https://discord.bpbonline.com

CHAPTER 7
Modeling Projects

Introduction

Modeling projects as a part of populating an EA repository with artifacts may sound unfamiliar at first because projects have always been managed using specialized project management tools such as Microsoft Project, Atlassian Jira, Monday, or others, which is true. Replacing project management tools with Sparx EA or replacing the **Project Management Body of Knowledge** (**PMBOK**) with TOGAF is not the purpose of this chapter, and it is not advisable to do so at any time. However, projects are components of the enterprise, which means that they are linked to other enterprise elements, to realize strategic goals or to influence how other enterprise elements are structured or should behave.

In *Chapter 3, Introducing Model Driven Generation,* and *Chapter 4, Advanced Model Driven Generation,* we created an MDG using step-by-step instructions. The MDG enabled us to create the Business Capability diagrams that we needed in *Chapter 6, Modeling Business Capabilities.* In this chapter, there is a need to create different types of artifacts that our MDG does not currently support, which means that we need to update the MDG first to enable it to create the new artifacts. Updating the MDG is a project by itself, or to be more precise, an iteration of a project. Therefore, we will use this project iteration for the examples that will be covered in this chapter, so we can learn how to model projects while working on updating the MDG project iteration.

Structure

This chapter will include the following topics:

- Updating the MDG
- Building the Course of Action artifacts

Objectives

By the end of this chapter, you will learn how to update an existing MDG to include additional stereotypes, diagram types, and toolboxes. Then, you will use the new version of the MDG to contribute new artifacts to the repository.

Updating the MDG

In TOGAF, the Course of Action element represents an ongoing activity or direction in the enterprise to deliver a value proposition, which makes it the element of choice for modeling projects at the strategic level. The MDG needs to be updated before we can model projects, so we will follow the MDG development lifecycle that was proposed in *Chapter 3, Introducing Model Driven Generation*, which starts by defining the MDG **Scope of Work** (**SOW**).

Defining the MDG SOW

Refer to the TOGAF metamodel diagram (**https://pubs.opengroup.org/togaf-standard/ architecture-content/Figures/34_contentfwk8.png**), and follow these steps to define the MDG SOW:

1. Find the **Course of Action** element on the metamodel diagram. It is a very wide rectangle near the top of the diagram.

2. Trace relationships from the Course of Action element to the elements that are connected to it.

3. Write down how the Course of Action element is related to the other elements. Also, write down how the other elements are related to it. This will be the list of requirements for the SOW.

The requirements list must contain the following:

- The Course of Action realizes the **goal**. The goal is realized by a Course of Action.
- The Course of Action influences the **Organization Unit**. The Organization Unit participates in the Course of Action.
- The Course of Action influences **Business Capability**. Business Capability is influenced by the Course of Action.

- The Course of Action influences the **Value Stream**. Value Stream is influenced by the Course of Action.

- The Course of Action influences **Business Information**. Business Information is influenced by the Course of Action.

- The Course of Action influences the **product**. The product is produced by the Course of Action.

- The Course of Action influences **Function**. Function is influenced by the Course of Action.

Some of the preceding elements and relationships are already in the MDG. We must avoid duplicating any of them and only add the new ones or update the existing ones. Additionally, if you look at the TOGAF metamodel diagram, you will see an orange box at the very top containing the *General Entities* that connect to all entities in the metamodel. TOGAF placed them separately to avoid having a huge number of crossing lines on the diagram, but we need to keep them in mind when we update the MDG and remember to connect them to every new element we add. The MDG SOW must include the general entities as identified in the following list:

- Course of Action is associated with **principle**. Principle is associated with Course of Action.

- Course of Action is associated with **constraint**. Constraint is associated with Course of Action.

- Course of Action is associated with **assumption**. Assumption is associated with Course of Action.

- Course of Action is associated with **requirement**. Requirement is associated with Course of Action.

- Course of Action is associated with **location**. Location is associated with Course of Action.

- Course of Action is associated with **gap**. Gap is associated with Course of Action.

- Course of Action is associated with **work package**. Work package is associated with Course of Action.

Finally, we need to add the following requirements too:

- Make all element stereotypes self-composed, which means having a *Composition* relationship with themselves.

- Make all element stereotypes have a *Usage* relationship with themselves.

- Make all element stereotypes have an *InformationFlow* relationship with themselves.

- Create the Course of Action diagram type.

- Create the Course of Action toolbox.

Once we have all the requirements for a new iteration of updating the MDG, we will begin by updating the stereotypes.

Working on stereotypes

We will go through the steps of updating the stereotypes at a much faster pace than we did in *Chapter 3, Introducing Model Driven Generation,* and *Chapter 4, Advanced Model Driven Generation.* Please refer to these two chapters whenever you find that you need more detailed instructions. From the list of requirements in the MDG SOW, there are nine new element stereotypes that must be created, and they are the **goal**, **product**, **principle**, **constraint**, **assumption**, **requirement**, **location**, **gap**, and **work package**. There are also four connector stereotypes, which are **realized**, **associated with**, **participates in**, and **produces**.

The MDG already contains some of the stereotypes of the elements and the connections that we need, and there are new stereotypes that need to be added, so let us start by adding the new elements stereotypes.

Adding new elements stereotypes to the MDG

Starting with the goal stereotype, follow these steps to create the nine new element stereotypes:

1. Make sure that the MDG project is open.

2. Open the ‹‹**profile**›› package and open the **TOGAF10_MDG** diagram.

3. In the **Toolbox**, click on the **Stereotype** element, click on the diagram to create a new stereotype, and give it the name **Goal**. Alternatively, we could have used the **Add Stereotype profile helper** from the **Toolbox**.

4. Click the **Metaclass** element in the **Toolbox** and click on the diagram.

5. Keep the **Core Elements** tab selected on the left, select **Class** from the list, and click **OK**.

6. Create an **Extension** relation from the **Goal** stereotype to the **Class** metaclass.

7. Right-click on the **Goal** stereotype and select **Copy / Paste I Copy**.

8. Right-click on it again and select **New Child Diagram I Composite Structure Diagram**.

9. Double-click on the **Goal** stereotype to open the empty child diagram.

10. Right-click on the empty child diagram and select **Paste I Element(s) as Link**. This will place the goal element on its composite structure diagram. Alternatively, instead of using copy/paste, you can drag the goal stereotype from the **Project Browser**, drop it on the composite structure diagram, and select **Drop as I Link**.

11. From **Toolbox I Metamodel**, click once on **Meta-Relationship**.

12. Click once on the **Goal** stereotype to create a relationship to self.

13. Right-click on the relationship and select **Visibility I Hide Connector in Other Diagrams**.

14. Click **Suppress All** to hide this connector from all other diagrams, then click **OK**.

15. Double-click on the line of the relationship to open the **Dependency Properties** dialog.

16. Click on the **Tags** tab near the bottom right corner of the dialog and enter `Composition` in the **metaclass** tag. The relationship must now show that it uses the composition metaclass.

17. We finished working on the goal stereotype, and we need to repeat the same for all other stereotype elements. Use the small back arrow of the diagram's window to go back to the **TOGAF10_MDG** diagram.

18. Repeat *Steps 1* through *17* to create the **Product**, **Gap,** and **Location** stereotypes, all extending the **Class** metaclass.

19. Repeat *Steps 1* through *17* to create the **Work Package** that extends the **PackagingComponent** metaclass. You can use any metaclass you prefer, but the packaging component metaclass acts as a component that can contain packages, unlike other metaclass types.

20. Repeat *Steps 1* through *17* to create the **Principle**, **Constraint**, **Assumption**, and **Requirement** stereotypes, all extending the **Requirement** metaclass. Make sure that the **Include Extended** checkbox is checked in the **Extend Metaclass** dialog. You will not be able to see the **Requirement** metaclass if it is unchecked.

21. Finally, make all the stereotypes we created as self-composed, self-usage, and self-information flow, and do not forget to hide these relationships so they do not appear on other diagrams.

The reason for creating a TOGAF stereotype for requirements, even though UML already has a metaclass called requirement, is that both standards have their own version of the type of *requirement*. The meaning of a requirement in TOGAF can be very close to its meaning in UML, but because the two definitions belong to two different worlds, requirements in UML connect to UML elements, while requirements in TOGAF connect to TOGAF elements. Therefore, we need to create a custom stereotype that extends the standard UML metaclass, inherits all its specifications, and then customize it as desired.

Do not forget to create the self-composition, self-usage, and self-information flow relationships to the elements that we created in *Chapter 3, Introducing Model Driven Generation,* if you have not done that yet, or add a note to the tasks backlog to do it in a later iteration. We intentionally skipped this step earlier to avoid any possible complications, but we must keep track of the steps we skip so they do not get forgotten.

The last thing that we need to do in this subsection is to hide the original UML links from their quick link menu. We already did this for the activity metaclass that the Business Capability element extends, but now we need to apply it to all the existing stereotypes. The following are the steps to do that:

1. Open the ‹‹**profile**›› package and open the **TOGAF10_MDG** diagram.

2. Right-click on the ‹‹**metaclass**›› **Activity** that is extended by the **Course of Action** stereotype.

3. Select **Features | Attributes** from the menu.

4. In the **Features** window, enter **_HideUmlLinks** under the **Name** column, and enter **True** under the **Initial Value** column.

5. Repeat *Steps 1 through 4* for all other elements' metaclasses created so far. You do not have to do it for the connectors' metaclasses.

Remember that all the attributes that are entered in the features window are case sensitive. If you enter a value such as **_HideUMLLinks**, with UML all uppercase letters, Sparx EA will not give you any error, but will not recognize the value either, and the MDG will not work properly. Be careful of mistakes like this, as they can consume some precious time before being discovered.

We have all the element stereotypes required. What we need to do next is to create the connector stereotypes.

Adding the new connector stereotypes to the MDG

As per the MDG SOW, we have two new connectors that need to be added to the MDG, the realizes and the associated with. Follow these steps to add the new connector stereotypes:

1. Open the ‹‹**profile**›› package and open the **TOGAF10_MDG** diagram.

2. From the **Toolbox**, click on **Metaclass**, click on the diagram, pick **Realization** from the list, and click **OK**.

3. Add a **Stereotype** element from the **Toolbox** and name it **Realizes**.

4. Right-click on the ‹‹**metaclass**›› **Realization** and select **Features | Attributes**.

5. Add **_MeaningForwards** attribute and give it an initial value of **Realizes**.

6. Add **_MeaningBackwards** attribute and give it an initial value of **Is realized** by.

7. Repeat *Steps 1 through 6* to create the **Associated with** connector stereotypes that extend the **Association** metaclass.

8. The associated relationship has the same meaning forwards and backwards, so enter **Associated with** in both attributes' initial values.

9. Set the **Direction** value in the associated connector to **Unspecified**. The reason for setting the direction value to unspecified is that the meaning associated with the relationship is mainly about an equal level of association between two elements, with no preference or influence of one over the other. Keeping the direction to its default value, **Source -> Destination**, is still acceptable.

10. Repeat *Steps 1 through 6* to create the **Participates in** connector stereotype and make it extend the **Association** metaclass.

11. Set the meaning forward to **Participates in** and set the meaning backwards to **Is participated by**.

12. Repeat *Steps 1 through 6* to create the **Produces** by connector stereotype and make it extend the **Association** metaclass.

13. Set the meaning forward to **Produces** in and set the meaning backwards to **Is produced by**.

Figure 7.1 shows the TOGAF10_MDG diagram, which includes all the stereotypes that have been created so far. It might be difficult to read everything on the diagram, but use it as an overview diagram that shows all the stereotypes in one place:

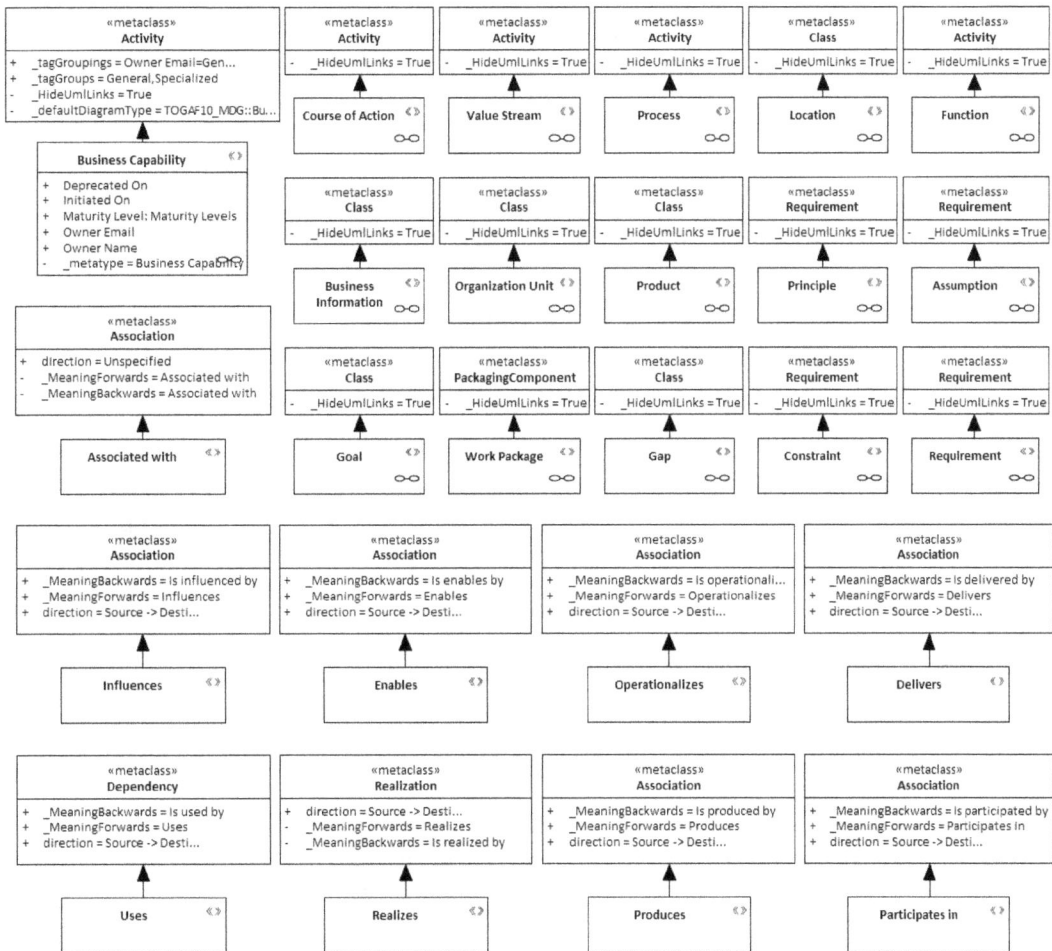

Figure 7.1: MDG's stereotypes

In *Chapter 6, Modeling Business Capabilities*, we talked about two types of diagrams. The first type fits everything in one diagram to show an all-in-one picture, and the other type is the focused diagrams that are focused and tell the viewer one thing at a time. *Figure 7.1* is an example of the first type of diagrams. It is large, shows all the stereotypes in one place, but it becomes difficult to read, especially if the diagram is used outside Sparx EA, such as on a printed page.

A diagram that cannot be read and understood is a bad diagram. Smaller and more focused diagrams that can fit in a single letter-sized page without losing readability are better than diagrams that must be shrunk by half to fit in a page, therefore, losing their quality.

To increase the readability of the preceding diagram, let us take a note and add a task to the backlog of the MDG maintenance iterations. The task should state that we need to simplify the MDG's stereotypes diagram in *Figure 7.1* by dividing it into smaller diagrams. We can have a diagram for the general entities' stereotypes, business architecture stereotypes, data architecture stereotypes, application architecture stereotypes, technology architecture stereotypes, and one for the connectors' stereotypes.

Note: **Having a scope creep while building a repository and populating it with artifacts is very easy to occur because you can easily get deviated. Controlling the scope of work is key to successfully delivering value from the repository.**

Going back to the SOW of the current iteration, we have finished adding the stereotypes that we need. Now, we are ready to customize the Course of Action stereotype.

Customizing the Course of Action stereotype

We need to configure the MDG and define how the Course of Action stereotype is related to the other stereotypes that have been created. We should already have a composite child diagram for the Course of Action stereotype that defines the self-composition relationship. We need to continue working on the same child diagram, and to do so, we need to do the following:

1. Open the composite structure diagram of the Course of Action stereotype.

2. In the **Project Browser**, find the **Principle**, **Constraint**, **Assumption**, **Location**, **Requirement**, **Gap**, **Work Package**, **Goal**, **Business Capability**, **Organization Unit**, **Business Information**, **Product**, **Function**, and **Value Stream** stereotypes, drag them, and drop them as links on the diagram.

3. You will see many relationships that exist from other diagrams. We will keep only the ones that are directly connected to the Course of Action stereotype and hide all the others.

4. To hide a single relationship, right-click on it, select **Delete Connector** from the list, select **Hide the connector** from the dialog box, then click **OK**. Alternatively, click on the relationship, then press the **Delete** button on the keyboard.

5. To hide multiple relationships at once, go to the **Layout** menu bar and click on **Layout | Diagram | Appearance | Set Visible Relationships**.

6. A dialog box like the one in *Figure 7.2* will pop up with a list of all the relationships that exist on the current diagram:

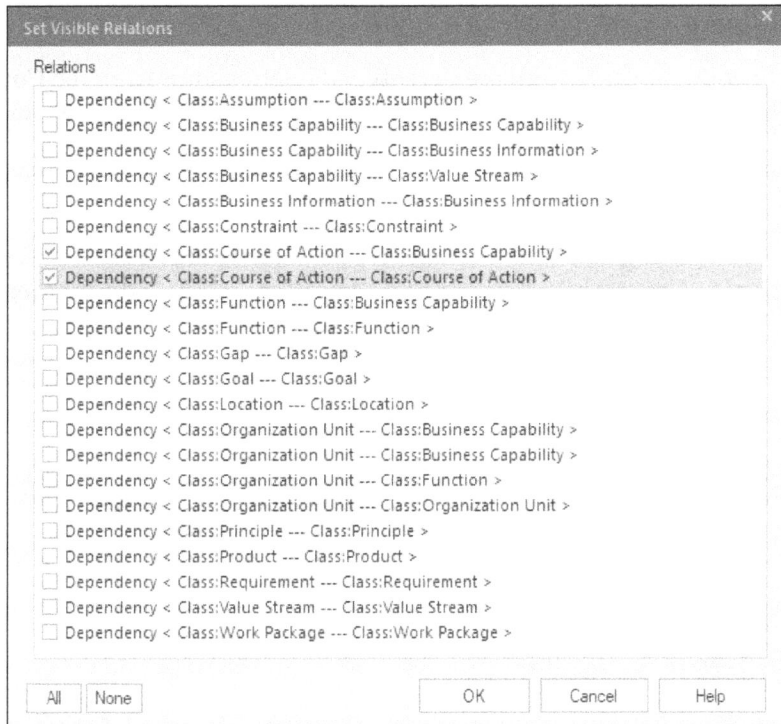

Figure 7.2: Set visible relations popup

7. Click **None** to uncheck all the relationships in the list, then check the two relationships that are associated with the Course of Action stereotype, because these two are the only ones that we need to keep on this diagram.

8. Click **OK** to close the dialog.

    Note: **Hiding relationships from a diagram keeps them available and visible in other diagrams.**

    After hiding the relationships that we do not need to see on this diagram, we need to add new relationships to the diagram, so continue with the following steps:

9. From the **Toolbox**, click on the **Metamodel | Stereotyped Relationship**, click and hold on the Course of Action stereotype on the diagram, and release the mouse on the **Organization Unit** stereotype.

10. Double-click on the newly created connector to open the **Dependency Properties** dialog box.

11. Click on the **Tags** tab and enter the value `Influences` in the stereotype value.

12. Right-click on the connector, select **Visibility | Hide Connector in Other Diagrams**, click **Suppress All**, then click **OK**.

13. Repeat *Steps 9 through 12* to create stereotyped relationships from the **Course of Action** to the **Product, Function, Value Stream**, and **Business Information** stereotypes.

14. Repeat *Steps 9 through 12* to create a stereotyped relationship from the **Course of Action** to the **Goal**, and enter the value `Realizes` in the **Tags** tab.

15. Repeat *Steps 9 through 12* to create stereotyped relationships from the **Course of Action** to **Principle, Constraint, Assumption, Location, Gap, Requirement**, and **Work Package** stereotypes, and enter the value `Associated with` in the **Tags** tab.

16. Repeat *Steps 9 through 12* to create a stereotyped relationship from the **Course of Action** to the **Product**, and enter the value `Produces` in the **Tags** tab.

17. Repeat *Steps 9 through 12* to create a stereotyped relationship from the **Organization Unit** to the **Course of Action**, and enter the value `Participates` in the **Tags** tab.

Next, we will add some Tagged Values to the Course of Action stereotype and to its activity metaclass.

Adding Tagged Values

We have a set of Tagged Values that we need to set to the Course of Action stereotype, and there is another set of Tagged Values that we need to set to the metaclass that it extends. We will add the same Tagged Values that we have added to the Business Capability stereotype. We can either right-click on the stereotype element, select **Features | Attributes**, and type the tag names and the initial values in the window, or use the **Edit with Profile Helper** menu option. We will use the profile helper in the following steps, but always make yourself familiar with both ways:

1. Right-click on the Course of Action stereotype and select **Edit with Profile Helper** from the menu.

2. Open the **Tagged Values** tab, right-click on the empty area to the right of the window, select **Add Tagged Value**, enter `_metatype`, and click **OK**.

3. Under the **Default Value** column, click and enter `Course of Action`.

4. Right-click on the empty area again, select **Add Specialized Tagged Value | Predefined**, and select the first item on the list. The list of predefined tags has been created in *Chapter 4, Advanced Model Driven Generation*, and it should contain **Deprecated On, Initiated On, Owner Email**, and **Owner Name**.

5. Repeat *Step 4* to add all the predefined Tagged Values to the Course of Action stereotype.

6. Right-click on the empty area, select **Create Tag Group**, enter `General`, then click **OK**.

7. Right-click on the first Tagged Value, select **Move to Tag Group**, select **General** from the list, and click **OK**. Alternatively, you can double-click on **General** to select it and close the dialog in one action.

8. Repeat for the Tagged Values so they are all moved to the **General** tag group.

9. Click **OK** to close the **Stereotype Properties** dialog box.

10. Resize, align, and organize your diagram, and it should look something like *Figure 7.3*:

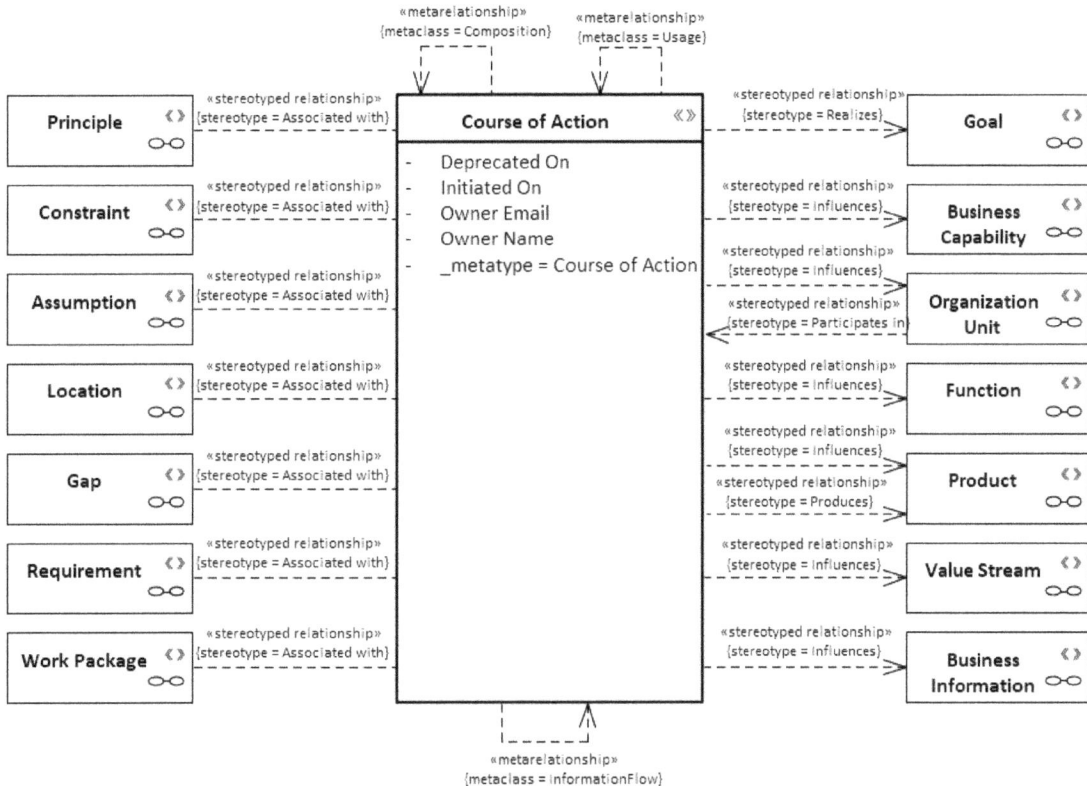

Figure 7.3: Course of Action focused metamodel

There is one last Tagged Value that we need to add for the metaclass which is the default diagram type that will be associated with the Course of Action stereotype. Since we have not created that diagram yet, we will pause adding this Tagged Value until after we create the Course of Action diagram type, but first, it is better to create the toolbox.

Creating the Course of Action toolbox

For creating the Course of Action toolbox, we will follow the same approach we followed for creating the Business Capability toolbox, which is a toolbox that contains the Course of Action element and only the elements that can connect to it. You may prefer following a different approach, such as having a single toolbox for all the business architecture layer elements. A third approach would be to have one gigantic toolbox with all the elements and the connectors in it and use it for all the diagrams.

As we always mention, there is no one right way, but different ways and approaches to do things are all right. It is up to you to decide how you prefer to do it. The following steps will create a separate toolbox for the Course of Action:

1. Open the ‹‹**toolbox profile**››**TOGAF10_MDG** package and open the **TOGAF10_ MDG** diagram.

2. Click on **Toolbox | Profile Helper | Create Custom Toolbox**.

3. **Select a Toolbox Profile Package**, and a dialog box will open. Click on the ‹‹**toolbox profile**›› and click **OK**.

4. Enter a name for the toolbox, such as `Course of Action Toolbox,` in the **Toolbox Name** field, provide an optional description, and click **OK**.

5. A new diagram will be created and opened with a ‹‹**metaclass**›› **Toolbox Page** element on it.

6. Click on **Toolbox | Profile Helpers | Add Toolbox Page** and click on the diagram.

7. In the **Add Toolbox Page**, enter `Course of Action Elements` in the **Name** field.

8. Click on **Add | Add Stereotype**.

9. From the list in the **Select a Profile Element** dialog box, select the **Business Capability**, **Business Information**, **Course of Action**, **Function**, **Goal**, **Organization Unit**, **Product**, and **Value Stream** stereotypes.

10. Provide values in the **Alias** column for each stereotype, then click **OK** to close the dialog.

11. Repeat *Steps 6* through *10* to add the general entities to the toolbox, but in a different toolbox group (toolbox page), and we will name it the `General Entities`.

12. Add the **Assumption**, **Constraint**, **Gap**, **Location**, **Principle**, **Requirement**, and **Work Package** stereotypes to the **General Entities** toolbox page.

13. Repeat *Steps 6* through *10* again to add a new toolbox page for the connectors. Make sure to include the **Associated with**, **Influences**, **Realizes**, **Produces**, and **Participates in** connectors stereotypes.

14. Click **Add | Add Built-In Type | Connector**, enter `Composes` in the **Alias** field, select **Composition** from the list, and click **OK**.

Figure 7.4 shows how the Course of Action toolbox may look:

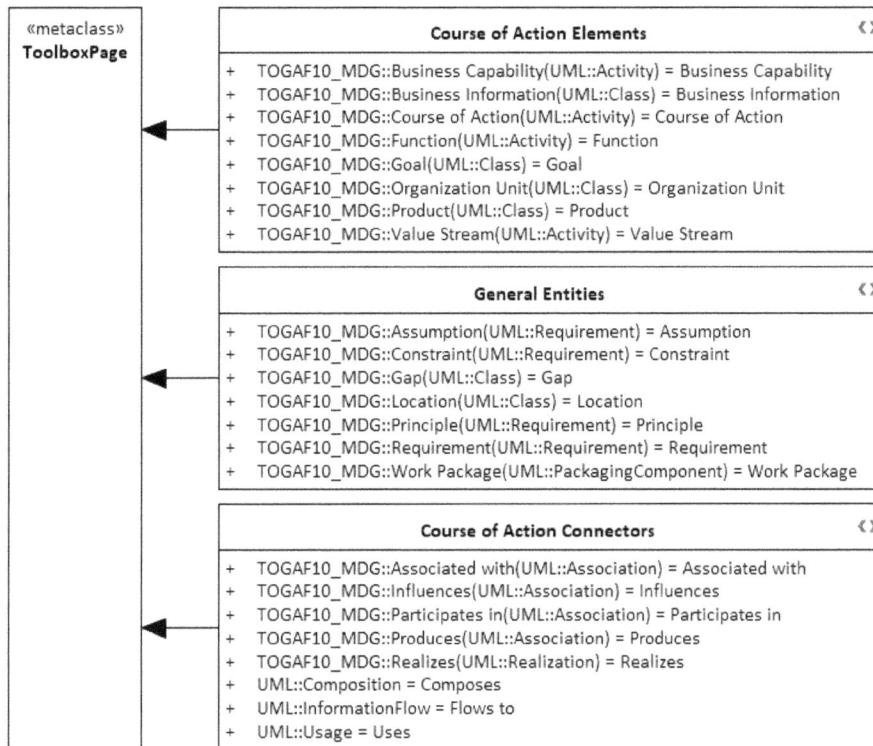

Figure 7.4: *Course of Action toolbox*

Something to pay attention to when you look at the ‹‹**toolbox profile**››**TOGAF10_MDG** package after creating two toolboxes in it is that there are three diagrams: **TOGAF10_MDG,** which is empty, and two other diagrams, each of which contains the profile of a specific toolbox. Currently, there is no link from the empty diagram to the toolbox profile diagrams, which means the navigation is not connected, so we need to fix this before moving to the next subsection. To add navigation cells from the empty **TOGAF10_MDG** diagram to the two toolboxes that we have created, perform the following steps:

1. In the **Project Browser**, open the ‹‹**toolbox profile**››**TOGAF10_MDG** package and open the **TOGAF10_MDG** diagram in it.

2. Drag the **TOGAF10_MDG_Course_of_Action_Toolbox** diagram from the **Project Browser** and drop it onto the empty **TOGAF10_MDG** diagram.

3. Select **Navigation Cell** from the list of options, select a meaningful image from the available images, and click **OK**.

Figure 7.5 suggests one way to design the toolbox profiles homepage, more toolbox profiles and more navigation cells will be added as we keep updating our MDG:

> 📁 «profile» TOGAF10_MDG
> 📁 «diagram profile» TOGAF10_MDG
∨ 📁 «toolbox profile» TOGAF10_MDG
　> ∘∘∘ { }
　　🗗 TOGAF10_MDG
　　🗗 TOGAF10_MDG_Business_Capability_Toolbox
　　🗗 TOGAF10_MDG_Course_of_Action_Toolbox
　> 🗐 «stereotype» Connectors
　> 🗐 «stereotype» Course of Action Connectors
　> 🗐 «stereotype» Course of Action Elements
　> 🗐 «stereotype» Elements
　> 🗐 «stereotype» General Entities
　　🗐 «metaclass» ToolboxPage

Toolbox Profiles

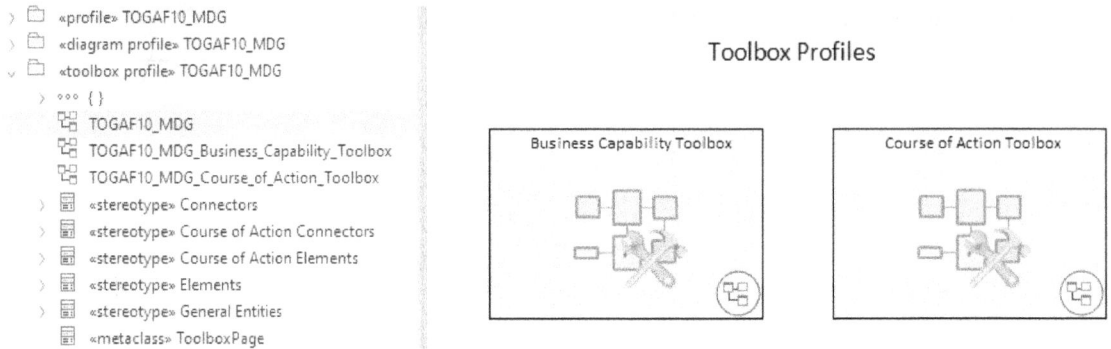

Figure 7.5: Toolbox profiles home page

Note: **Remember that each toolbox must be created in its own diagram, and upon publishing the MDG, each toolbox must be published separately at the diagram level, not at the package level.**

Now that we have created the toolbox, we need to create a diagram type and associate it with the toolbox.

Creating the Course of Action diagram type

The Course of Action diagram type is a diagram that will be specialized for building Course of Action artifacts and will use the Course of Action toolbox as the default toolbox. The steps for creating the diagram type are as follows:

1. Open the ‹‹**toolbox profile**››**TOGAF10_MDG** package and open the **TOGAF10_MDG** diagram in it. You will see the Business Capability map diagram type extending the diagram activity metaclass.

2. Click on **Toolbox | Profile Helpers | Add Diagram Extension,** then click on the diagram.

3. The **Add Diagram Extension** dialog will pop up. Enter `Course of Action Diagram` in the **Name** field, keep **Extension Type** set to **Activity**, and optionally add a description.

4. Under properties, set **Toolbox Profile** to **TOGAF10_MDG_Course_of_Action_Toolbox**, then click **OK**.

Use *Figure 7.6* as a reference to compare to your work:

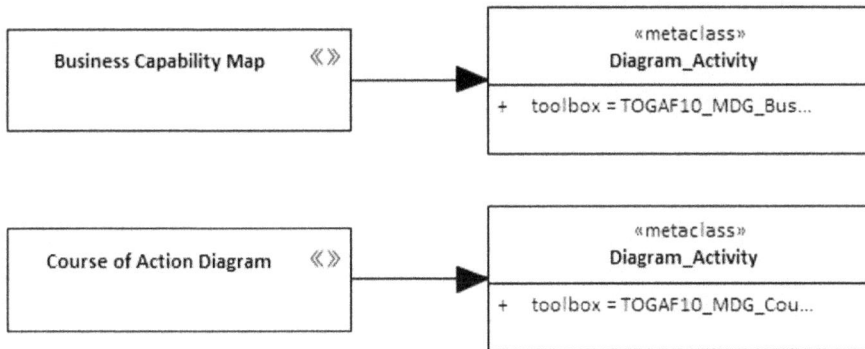

Figure 7.6: *Diagram profiles*

Now that we have the Course of Action diagram type defined, we need to make it the default diagram type when we create a new composite structure diagram for Course of Action elements. To do this, perform these simple steps:

1. Click on the **Activity** metaclass that the Course of Action stereotype extends.

2. In the **Features** window, add the attribute **_defaultDiagramType** and type **TOGAF10_ MDG::Course of Action Diagram** as the initial value.

Since we do not have a clear need for creating sub-diagram types, which are also known as view specifications within the MDG context, we will not create any. *Chapter 4, Advanced Model Driven Generation,* describes how to add view specifications in the *Customizing diagram types* section. Refer to that section whenever the need to add diagram subtypes emerges.

At this point, we have created all the items on the SOW list, so we are ready to republish the MDG.

Publishing the MDG

In *Chapter 3, Introducing MDG,* we explained in detail how to publish the profiles, the diagram types, and the toolbox. The same steps will be used every time we publish the profiles and regenerate the MDG. The only difference is in the number of toolbox profiles that we have, as we need to publish each toolbox separately. The following steps serve as quick reminders of the publishing steps:

1. In the **Project Browser**, click on the ‹‹**profile**››**TOGAF10_MDG** package. From the menu bar, select **Specialize | Technologies | Publish Technology | Publish Package as UML Profile**.

2. You do not need to change anything in this dialog, so accept the values as they are, click **Save**, and select **Yes** to overwrite the existing file.

3. Click on the ‹‹**diagram profile**››**TOGAF10_MDG** package, select the same menu option from step 1, then save and overwrite the existing file.

4. Open the ‹‹**toolbox profile**››**TOGAF10_MDG** package, double-click on **TOGAF10_ MDG_Course_of_Action_Toolbox** diagram to open it.

5. From the menu bar, select **Specialize | Technologies | Publish Technology | Publish Diagram as UML Profile**, enter `TOGAF10_MDG_Course_of_Action_Toolbox` as a Profile Name, and click Save.

6. Since we did not change anything in the Business Capabilities toolbox diagram, we do not need to republish it; otherwise, we must republish it, or the changes will not be available in the MDG.

7. From the menu bar, select **Specialize | Technologies | Publish Technology | Generate MDG Technology**.

8. Click **Next**, select **Open an existing MTS file**, and select the same file that we used in the previous chapters.

9. Optionally change the **Version** number of the MDG to a new number, such as **1.1**.

10. The MTS will remember all the settings, so you mainly need to keep clicking **Next** until reaching the toolboxes page, where you must add the new toolbox from the **Available Files** list to the **Selected Files** list.

11. When you finish, you will get a message indicating that the MDG generation has succeeded.

Import the MDG to the testing project, make sure that everything works as desired, and if so, import it to the main content repository, and let us build some Course of Action artifacts.

Building the Course of Action artifacts

The Course of Action in TOGAF can represent any ongoing activity within the enterprise to achieve a goal. It can be a project, a plan, a program, an initiative, or an ongoing operation. Examples of courses of action can be a plan to provide a new product, a direction to increase the capability maturity level of the organization, a decision to research a cure for some disease, or the activation of a business continuity plan in response to a disaster. Course of Action realizes strategic goals and influences other enterprise elements. In the business continuity plan activation, a Course of Action can be realized to achieve a strategic goal, such as providing uninterrupted services even in the case of disasters. It can influence the establishment of a new Organization Unit, such as a disaster recovery committee. It can influence the usage of Business Capabilities and Functions designed especially for this Course of Action.

In this section, we will model the Course of Action that influenced the establishment of the enterprise architecture practice in the organization. To practice with real-world examples, you need to ask your management for the documentation that preceded the decision to establish the EA practice. This will explain why the decision was made, a high-level approach to the problem, the organization structure responsible for it, and what information is needed. It does not have to be a formally signed document. It can be a presentation, a memorandum, an email, or even a Zoom recording, which will suffice. Having this type of information in hand is very helpful and will keep you away from making things up to fit in a diagram, which is not a wrong approach, but could be time-consuming, as multiple rounds of discussions will take place between you and the other parties involved.

In this section, we will also provide some examples of elements that relate to a Course of Action element. We will start by modeling the Course of Action catalog, which is supposed to contain a list of all the courses of action in the enterprise. So far, we only know about one Course of Action, and that is what we will start with.

Modeling the Course of Action catalog

The steps for creating the Course of Action catalog can be summarized as follows:

1. Open the main repository project in Sparx EA, open the **Architecture Repository | Architecture Content | Architecture Definition | Business Architecture | Course of Actions** package, then open the **Course of Action** diagram.

2. From the menu bar, select **Design | Diagram | Options | Change Type**.

3. Select **Specialized | All Specialized** from the diagram type list.

4. Click on **TOGAF10_MDG**, select **Course of Action Diagram** from the diagram type list, then click **OK**.

5. Rename the diagram to `Course of Actions Catalog`.

6. Drag-drop ‹‹**Course of Action**›› **Establishing the EA Practice** and drop it on the Course of Action catalog.

7. Create a new composite structure diagram for the ‹‹**Course of Action**›› **Establishing the EA Practice**.

The steps for creating the Course of Action catalog are the same as those for creating any catalog. We followed the same for creating the Business Capabilities catalog, so refer to the *Modeling the Business Capabilities catalog* section in *Chapter 6, Modeling Business Capabilities*. Do not be disappointed to see that both our catalogs contain a single element in each, and remember that the best EA practice is the incremental practice, where things are built one step after another.

Modeling the Course of Action

Open the composite structure diagram of **Establishing the EA Practice** Course of Action element that we created in *Chapter 6, Modeling Business Capabilities*, in the section *Relationships* *to Course of Actions*. This will be the Course of Action's home page. We will follow a similar pattern to the one we used for the Business Capability home page. The pattern, in short, is to create multiple focused diagrams and add navigation cells from the home page to these focused diagrams. We do not have to create all the diagrams showing all the relationships to the Course of Action, but we model what we need to model and add the rest to the backlog.

Realizing goals by initiating Course of Action

A goal is *a high-level statement of intent or direction for an organization. Typically used to measure success of an organization,* (**https://pubs.opengroup.org/togaf-standard/architecture-content/ chap02.html**). Organizations usually define their goals as part of their strategies, and achieving these goals is a healthy sign of how the strategy is working.

To achieve and realize goals, organizations need to do things, and these things are what are known within the enterprise as the Course of Action. Having a goal such as increasing the organization's maturity level requires a set of courses of action to realize it, such as the ones in *Figure 7.7*:

Figure 7.7: *Courses of action realizing a goal*

The diagram in *Figure 7.7* shows a set of courses of action realizing, or aiming to realize, a goal. This diagram belongs to the goal's perspective because the goal is in focus, not the Course of Action. We will look at more examples focusing on goals and other strategy elements in *Chapter 12, Modeling Organizations and Strategies.* You may have noticed that we ended up defining three more courses of action, realizing the same strategic goal, which **Establishing the EA Practice** Course of Action realizes. These three other courses of action would easily cause our scope of work to deviate from its track if we started detailing them, hence we had better keep them defined without details for now and come back to detail them in a later iteration when needed.

On the other hand, to model what goals are realized by a specific Course of Action, the diagram will look like the example in *Figure 7.8* with the Course of Action in focus:

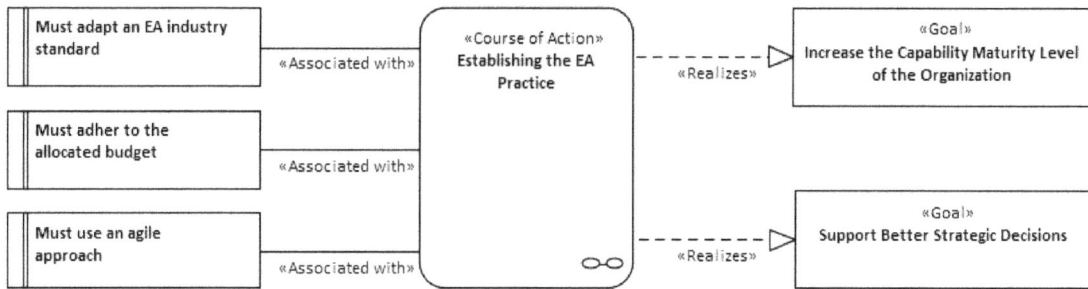

Figure 7.8: Course of Action realizing goals

The same diagram can contain the requirements or constraints that affect how the Course of Action will realize the goals. You can separate the requirements in their own diagram if their numbers increase and the diagram becomes complicated and unreadable.

Since a Course of Action requires a business unit to take ownership of and execute it, the Organization Units are the first enterprise element that will be influenced by the Course of Action.

Influencing Organization Units

A Course of Action cannot act by itself, and it needs an Organization Unit to *participate in,* from the initial planning to its completion. Organization Units can be internal, or external units to the organization. They can be committees with few members, or departments with multiple levels of organizations hierarchies and thousands of members. Participating Organization Units can be existing units, which means that their responsibilities will expand, or they can be new business units that need to be established from the ground up. In either case, an artifact must show this participation relationship.

Organization Units can be influenced by a Course of Action. The influences relationship means inspires, affects, or motivates. A Course of Action can influence Organization Units that are not necessarily participating in it. Organization Units may find themselves in need to change their Functions or update the existing ones to remain in compliance, which will end up with them participating in the Course of Action as stakeholders. It is a recursive relationship between the two types of elements, where influence derives participation, and participation derives influence in return. *Figure 7.9* shows an example of how a single Course of Action influences four Organization Units and they all participate in it:

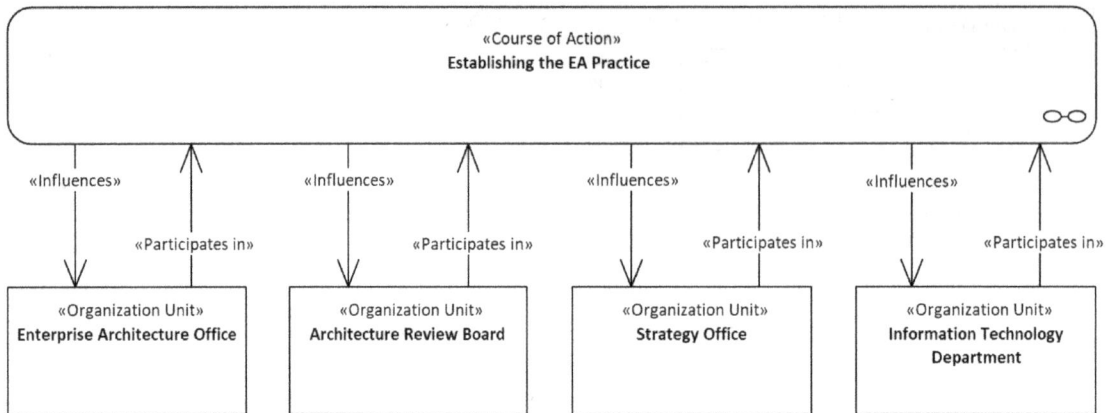

Figure 7.9: *Organization Units influenced by a Course of Action*

Notice how the names of the Organization Units on the diagram are preceded by the name of the package that contains them. This is because the Organization Unit elements are physically located in a different package with respect to the one that contains the current diagram, so Sparx EA is telling us that these elements are physically located in a different package. To hide the package prefix in object names, simply open the diagram's **Properties** dialog and uncheck **Diagram | Show Namespace** box, then click **OK**. This will hide all the prefixes and the labels that indicate the package names and will keep only the objects' names.

A Course of Action can be decomposed into multiple smaller courses of action, or it can be part of a larger Course of Action. This is how multiple phases or iterations are defined, so let us see how to model them.

Modeling Course of Actions' hierarchy

Almost every element in the enterprise can be decomposed into smaller elements of its type, and this is why we made all the stereotypes in the MDG self-composed. Course of Actions can be composed of smaller courses of action, each of which can represent a project, a phase, or an iteration, as shown in the example in *Figure 7.10*:

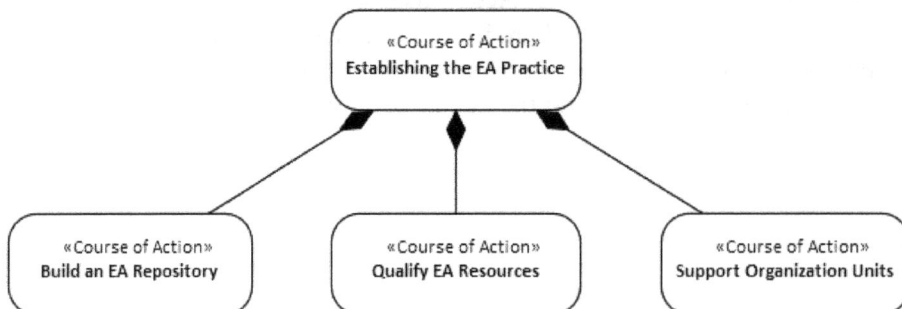

Figure 7.10: *Courses of action hierarchy*

Each child Course of Action from the preceding figure can be further decomposed into a smaller set of Course of Actions. The **Build an EA Repository** Course of Action can be decomposed into **Build and Maintain the MDG** and **Populate the Repository with Artifacts**, for example. A question that comes to mind when having a hierarchy of elements is whether we need to connect all children elements to the same enterprise elements that the parent connects to, or just connect them to the parent.

The composition relationship is transitive, which means that if element A composed element B, and element B composes elements C and D, then element A composes elements C and D. Therefore, it is more accurate to avoid having direct relationships from A to C and D, because it is already inclusive, unless there is a value in showing them with a direct relationship. In our example, we have the top parent Course of Action realizing the two strategic goals, and this is sufficient because all the child Course of Actions are, by default, realizing the same goals, so there is no need to create separate relationships from each child Course of Action to the goals.

However, you need to be careful when modeling which enterprise elements are influenced by which Course of Action, the parent or the child. In some cases, you will find that each child Course of Action influences a different set of Business Information, Functions, or products. In this case, it makes more sense to connect each child Course of Action to the elements that it directly influences rather than connecting them to the parent.

Figure 7.11 shows how the **Build an EA Repository** Course of Action, which is a child to **Establishing the EA Practice**, has two more child Course of Actions, and it directly influences the **EA Tool Management** Function as well as directly produces the **EA Repository** product:

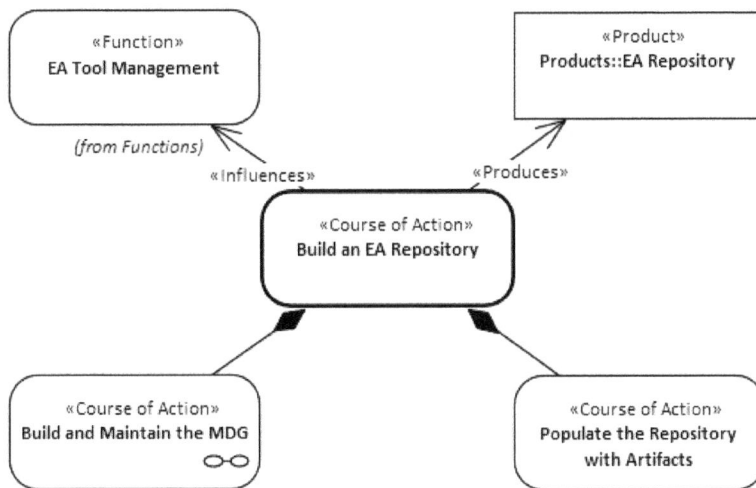

Figure 7.11: *Child Course of Action is connected to different elements*

This is a Course of Action that we are practicing in this book. We want to create an EA repository, which resulted in two separate but dependent courses of action: building and maintaining the MDG and populating the repository with artifacts.

Notice, the **EA Tool Management** Function has the label **(from Functions)** underneath the element, and the product has the package name prefixing the product name. Both the label and the prefixes can be hidden from the diagram by unchecking the **Diagram | Show Namespace** box from the diagram's properties dialog. It is useful, sometimes, to know where the element is located, so it is up to your preference to hide the package name or to show it.

The **Build and Maintain the MDG** can be further detailed and have its own hierarchy. There is no actual limit to how many levels are allowed, but once your model starts to describe tasks and actions to do, rather than describing projects, you have either reached the work package level or even to the requirements level. Let us take a closer look at these two and how they can relate to a Course of Action.

Association with work packages

A work package is defined as *a set of actions identified to achieve one or more objectives for the business. A work package can be a part of a project, a complete project, or a program.* (**https://pubs. opengroup.org/togaf-standard/architecture-content/chap02.html**). As you can see from the definition, the courses of action and the work packages share a lot of similarities, which makes it easy to be confused between them. Both can be a complete project, part of a project, or a program. Work packages contain the set of elements that will be used to perform the Course of Action, such as the requirements, constraints, and principles, or the elements that will result from performing it, such as artifacts and documents. Let us see how to utilize work packages for better models, starting by learning how to properly associate them to the Course of Action.

Associations with work packages

Figure 7.12 shows **Build and Maintain the MDG** Course of Action and how it is associated with two work packages, the MDG iterations and MDG product backlog:

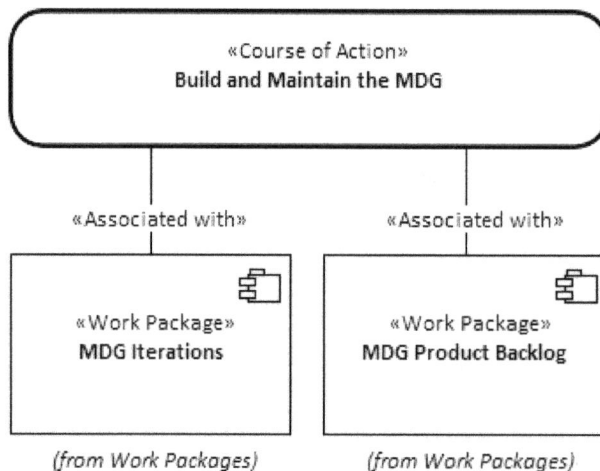

Figure 7.12: *Work packages associated with a Course of Action*

The **MDG Iterations** work package will contain the requirements of each MDG development iteration. It can contain any number of sub-packages, so it can be used as a folder that can have any structure that a specific element requires. The second work package is the MDG Product Backlog, which we will use to hold the requirements of future iterations. This Course of Action and the two packages that are associated with it, represent the MDG development that we have been doing so far in this book.

Drilling down into the **MDG Iterations** work package shows its contents, so let us see what content can be modeled there.

Modeling work packages' content

Since work packages can be structured like any other package element, we need to make them as meaningful and useful as we can. If a package name is MDG iterations, the first thing that comes to the user's mind is that double-clicking it will show a list of iterations. *Figure 7.13* depicts how the contents of the **MDG Iterations** work package can be modeled:

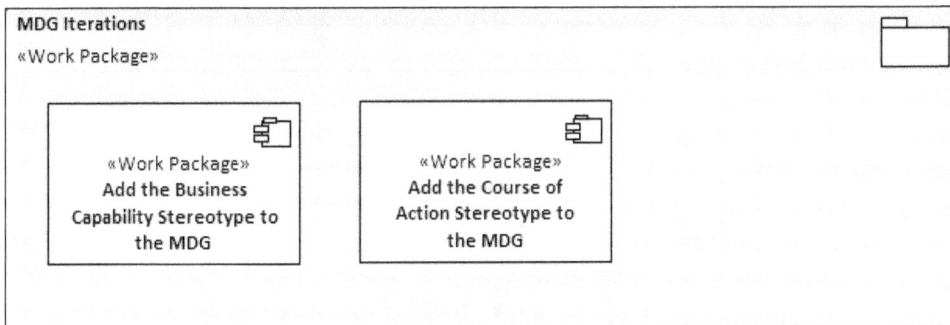

Figure 7.13: *MDG Iterations work package contents*

The MDG Iterations work package will contain all the tasks for updating and developing the TOGAF MDG that we are building. Each iteration can be packaged in its own work package, too. So far, we have done two MDG development iterations:

- The first work package is **Add the Business Capability Stereotype to the MDG,** which must contain the requirements we have captured for that iteration in the MDG scope of work statements. Each statement is a requirement that must be realized to consider our work on it as done. This work package is currently empty because we created it after we finished the iteration. We can add a backlog requirement to do this at some time, but if we have higher priority requirements to be included in our next iteration, we will focus our effort on them. Adding the requirement now to the product backlog will save it from being forgotten.

- The second work package is **Add the Course of Action Stereotype to the MDG,** which must contain the requirements of the iteration that we conducted in the first section of this chapter.

The statements that were defined in the *Defining the MDG SOW* section can be modeled as depicted in *Figure 7.14*:

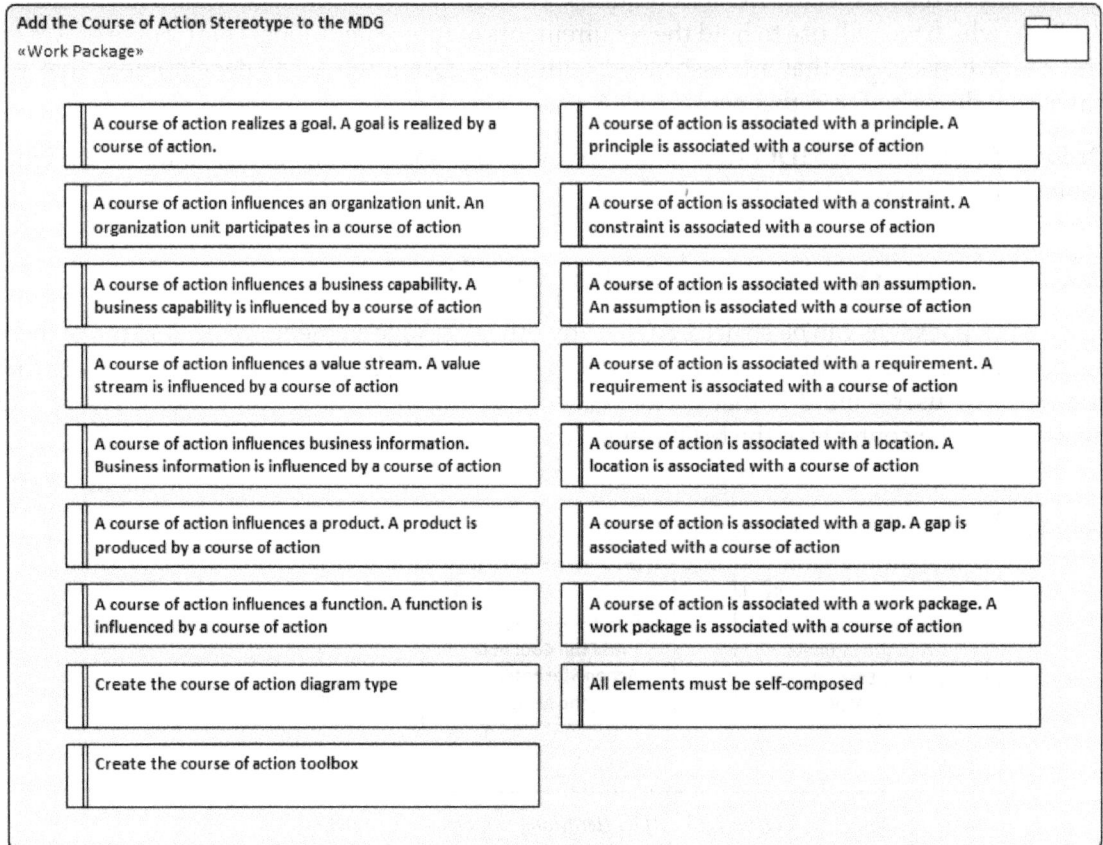

Add the Course of Action Stereotype to the MDG
«Work Package»

A course of action realizes a goal. A goal is realized by a course of action.

A course of action is associated with a principle. A principle is associated with a course of action

A course of action influences an organization unit. An organization unit participates in a course of action

A course of action is associated with a constraint. A constraint is associated with a course of action

A course of action influences a business capability. A business capability is influenced by a course of action

A course of action is associated with an assumption. An assumption is associated with a course of action

A course of action influences a value stream. A value stream is influenced by a course of action

A course of action is associated with a requirement. A requirement is associated with a course of action

A course of action influences business information. Business information is influenced by a course of action

A course of action is associated with a location. A location is associated with a course of action

A course of action influences a product. A product is produced by a course of action

A course of action is associated with a gap. A gap is associated with a course of action

A course of action influences a function. A function is influenced by a course of action

A course of action is associated with a work package. A work package is associated with a course of action

Create the course of action diagram type

All elements must be self-composed

Create the course of action toolbox

Figure 7.14: Work package associated with requirements

The last thing that we want to cover in this chapter is to finalize the home page of the **Establishing the EA Practice** Course of Action.

Finalizing the Course of Action homepage

The homepage design that we followed in *Figure 6.11*, uses navigation cells to connect diagrams to the homepage. In this chapter, we will use hyperlinks instead of navigation cells, which is depicted in *Figure 7.15*:

Establishing the EA Practice Course of Action

Home Page

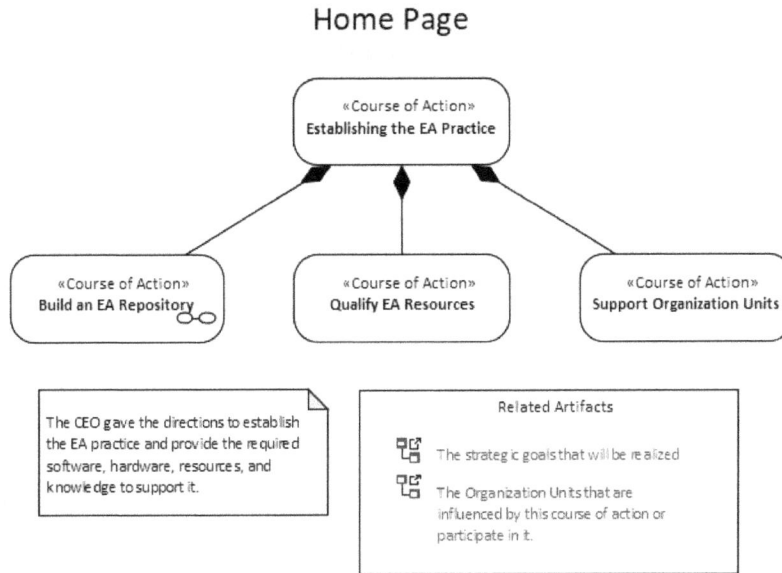

Figure 7.15: Homepage for a Course of Action

As you can see, the diagram contains a note describing the Course of Action to the readers. It also made one level of hierarchy visible on the homepage, so the viewers can see three courses of action, comprising their parent. There are also two links, one links to the goals that will be realized, which is the diagram in *Figure 7.8*, and the other link leads to the Organization Units that are influenced or participate in the Course of Action, which is the diagram in *Figure 7.9*. To create a hyperlink to a diagram, simply do the following:

1. From any **Toolbox**, use **Toolbox | Common Elements | Hyperlink** element and place it on the diagram.

2. Double-click on the hyperlink element to open the **Hyperlink Details** dialog.

3. From the **Type** dropdown, select **Diagram**.

4. Select the diagram that you want to link to.

5. Add descriptive text to the hyperlink.

We will try to provide you with multiple options to choose from, and the choice is what you and the users in your organization find comfortable.

Conclusion

We started this chapter by expanding the capabilities of our MDG by adding new stereotypes, connections, diagram types, and toolboxes. We used the updated MDG to contribute more artifacts to the EA repository. We started with a single Course of Action, establishing the EA Practice, added three siblings courses of action that realize the same goal, added three children courses of action, then started detailing one of them and detailing its sub-components one at a time. All that work started from one element, and all these diagrams resulted from describing that element, so imagine what a mature repository would contain.

In the next chapter, we will add new stereotypes to our MDG to create various types of diagrams. We will also model artifacts from the application and the data architecture layers.

Points to remember

- Projects are integral parts of the enterprise. They affect some elements and are affected by other elements; therefore, these relationships must be modeled as EA artifacts.

- You can use any metaclass for your custom MDG, and you are not required to use the metaclasses that we used.

- The enterprise is huge and is full of elements that are connected to other elements. A complete EA repository that covers every element in the enterprise can take years of development in some large organizations.

- While building an EA repository, you can easily deviate from what you are working on because everything in the enterprise is connected, and you will find that there are more models to build than what you finished.

- The proper management of the scope of work for every iteration is a key success factor.

- You do not need to fully complete all the MDG work to create useful diagrams. We were still able to create some valuable diagrams with an MDG that is being developed.

- Diagrams that represent catalogs must be updated regularly as elements get added and deleted daily in an active repository.

Key terms

- **Course of Action**: An ongoing activity in the organization, such as a project, a program, or an initiative, is termed a Course of Action.

- **Organization Unit**: It can mean the entire enterprise, a unit within the enterprise, or a subunit of it.

- **Function**: Function is a grouping of other behavioral elements, mainly Processes.

- **Business Information**: It refers to the information that means something or is crucial for the business.

- **Goal**: A high-level strategic statement that requires one, or many Course of Actions, to realize it is termed as goal. Realizing strategic goals is a sign of an organization's success.

- **Business Capability**: Business Capability is the ability that makes an enterprise capable of doing what it is doing or planning to do.

- **Value Stream**: Value Stream is a strategic top-level level Process that results in creating values.

- **Product**: A tangible or an intangible item that is provided to customers is termed as product.

- **Principle**: A high-level requirement that must be met by architecture is known as principle.

- **Requirement**: A Requirement is a statement that must be met by the work that is contained in a work package.

- **Constraint**: Constraint is a statement that identifies a specific limitation to do something. Constraints must be treated like requirements and must be considered in any architectural design.

- **Assumption**: Assumptions are statements about things that we are not yet sure about.

- **Location**: A place where any element in the enterprise exists, refers to location. It can be a physical or a virtual place.

- **Gap**: A gap in the context of EA is a difference between two states of architecture, such as the difference between the As-Is and the To-Be, or the difference between two architecture versions.

- **Work package**: A Work package is a set of work actions, requirements, constraints, or documents that are needed to achieve an outcome. It can be associated with any enterprise element.

Join our Discord space

Join our Discord workspace for latest updates, offers, tech happenings around the world, new releases, and sessions with the authors:

https://discord.bpbonline.com

CHAPTER 8

Modeling Applications

Introduction

Application architecture is an essential layer of enterprise architecture in modern enterprises, as most businesses have a decent amount of automation in their operations and service offerings, which is provided through applications. A good and trustworthy EA repository not only contains a list of all applications in the enterprise, but also must contain enough documentation about the architecture of every application as well. The golden rule is to document what is enough, which is a very vague word, but discovering its meaning for your enterprise makes up the difference between a successful EA practice and a useless and overwhelming one. It is you who needs to discover these dividing guardrails and set the expectations accordingly. For a legacy system with no current plans to replace it, enough architecture could mean listing it in the applications catalog as a single element until a new need to upgrade it or replace it develops. Enough architecture for a solution that needs to be built means defining everything that needs to be told to the developers.

Since application architecture can be documented at different levels of detail, TOGAF provides three application architecture components, each of which can be used to model a different level of abstraction about applications. In this chapter, we will start by modifying the MDG to include the new elements that we will need for our models, and then we will use it to make new application architecture artifacts.

Structure

This chapter will include the following topics:

- Updating the MDG
- Building the application architecture artifacts

Objectives

By the end of this chapter, you will learn how to model applications at different levels of abstraction as per business needs.

Updating the MDG

The first thing we need to do is update the MDG to include the three application architecture elements in the TOGAF metamodel and define the MDG SOW accordingly. The three metamodel elements are the application service, logical application component, and physical application component. We will start by defining the scope of work for a new iteration of updating the MDG.

Defining the MDG SOW

Since our repository is getting more mature and contains an ongoing Course of Action for building and maintaining the MDG, which is depicted in *Figure 7.12*, we will build the MDG SOW as a set of diagrams instead of a narrative text. Logging our development requirements in the repository is commendable because we are part of the enterprise, and our work is part of the EA practice we implement in our organization. We will create a new work package under **MDG Iterations** for this new iteration, so follow these steps:

1. In the EA repository, open the **MDG Iterations** work package. Your screen should look like *Figure 7.13*.

2. If the **Toolbox** does not contain the custom Course of Actions toolbox, change the diagram type by clicking **Design I Diagram I Options I Change Type** and choosing **TOGAF10_MDG I Course of Action Diagram**. The **Toolbox** must now show the elements and the connectors that support Course of Action diagrams.

3. Add a new **Work Package** from the **Toolbox** to the diagram, name it `Add Application Architecture Stereotypes to the MDG`, and keep the **Create Diagram** option selected.

4. From the **New Diagram** dialog, **select TOGAF10_MDG I Course of Action Diagram**.

5. Double-click on the newly created package to open its empty diagram.

6. From the **Toolbox**, create four new work packages on the diagram and name them **Create the Application Service Stereotype**, **Create the Logical Application Component Stereotype**, **Create the Physical Application Component Stereotype**, and **Create the Toolbox and Diagram Types**.

The final diagram must look something like the one shown in *Figure 8.1*:

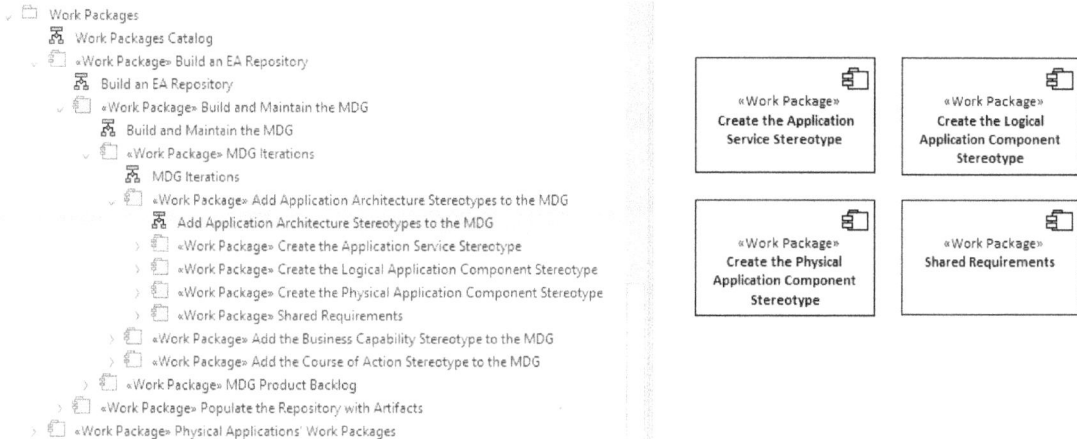

Figure 8.1: *Work sub work packages for this iteration*

To know what the parent container work package of the four sub work packages is, you will need to find the diagram in the **Project Browser** and look at the package's name. Another way is to add the parent work package as a container to the entire diagram and visually show the four sub work packages surrounded by their parent work package, like *Figure 8.2*:

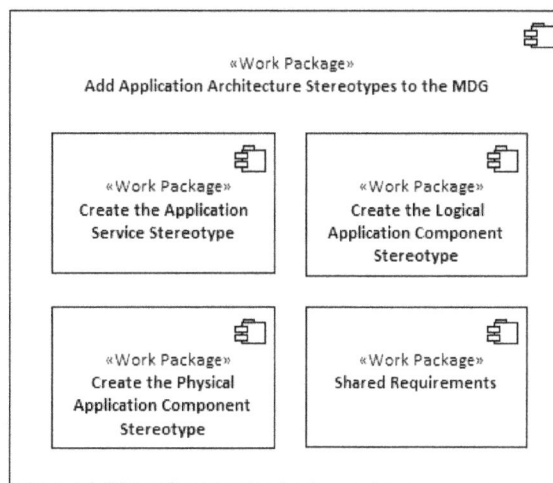

Figure 8.2: *Sub work packages contained in their parent work package*

The parent work package also has a label underneath it to indicate its parent work package. In one view, we can see three levels of work package hierarchy: the package, its children, and its parent. If you like the second diagram more, here is how to add the parent work package:

7. In the **Project Browser**, find the **Add Application Architecture Stereotypes to the MDG** work package, drag it, drop it onto the opened diagram, and select **Package Element** from the menu.

8. Right-click on the newly added package on the diagram and select **Z-Order | Send to Bottom**. This will send the element to the bottom of the diagram, which means that placing elements on it will make them appear on top of it.

9. Resize the work package to visually fit the four sub work packages.

10. Move the four sub work packages inside the borders of the parent package.

Now that we have the work packages defined, we need to add the requirements that form the MDG SOW to each one of them. Since we have four packages, the list of requirements will be longer than in previous chapters.

Defining the SOW of the first work package

The first work package will contain the requirements for creating the application service stereotype. *Figure 8.3* shows the requirements of **Create the Application Service Stereotype** work package:

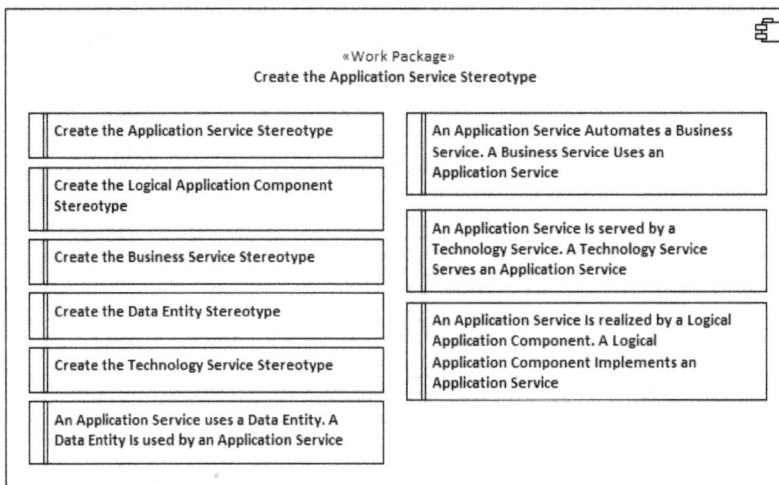

(from Add Application Architecture Stereotypes to the MDG)

Figure 8.3: *Requirements of the first work package*

We placed the work package on the diagram first, enlarged it to the desired size, set the **Z-Order** value to **Send to Bottom**, then started adding requirements from **Toolbox | General**

Entities | Requirements. If you feel that you need more details on how to do these steps, refer to *Chapter 7, Modeling Projects*, in the *Modeling work packages' content* section.

Next, we will define the SOW of the second work package by adding the requirements to it.

Defining the SOW of the second work package

The second work package is about defining the SOW of the logical application component stereotype. *Figure 8.4* lists the requirements for **Create the Logical Application Component Stereotype** work package:

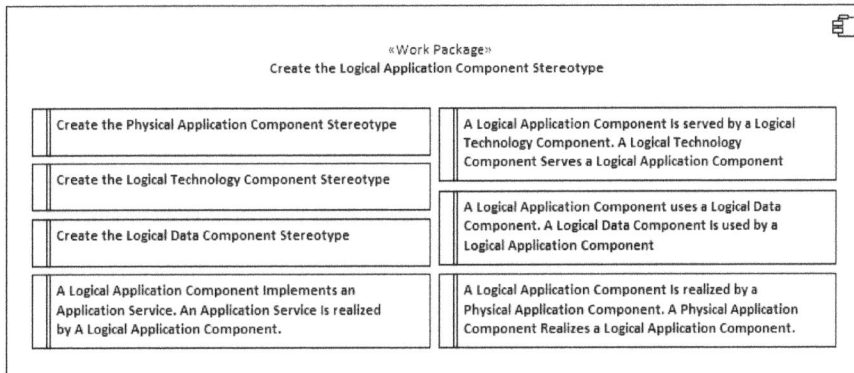

(from Add Application Architecture Stereotypes to the MDG)

Figure 8.4: *Requirements of the second work package*

Following the same approach, we will define the requirements of the third work package.

Defining the SOW of the third work package

This package will contain the MDG SOW requirements to **Create the Physical Application Component Stereotype**. The requirements of the third work package are shown in *Figure 8.5*:

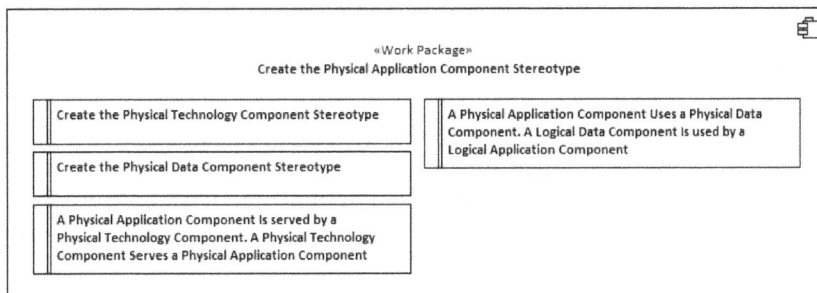

(from Add Application Architecture Stereotypes to the MDG)

Figure 8.5: *Requirements of the third work package*

Next, we will define the requirements of the fourth package.

Defining the SOW of the fourth work package

The fourth work package will contain the general requirements that are shared across the other work packages. *Figure 8.6* lists these requirements:

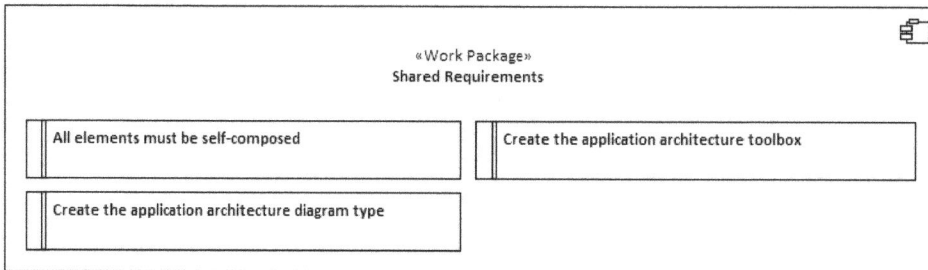

(from Add Application Architecture Stereotypes to the MDG)

Figure 8.6: *Fourth work package*

The last thing we need to do before having the MDG SOW approved is to look at the product backlog and check if anything needs to be included.

Revisiting the MDG product backlog

In the previous chapters, and while we were working on the MDG, we identified two requirements that we said we would add to the MDG product backlog so we do not forget them. These requirements are listed in *Figure 8.7*:

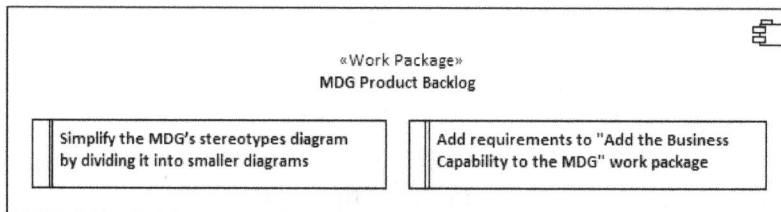

(from Work Packages)

Figure 8.7: *MDG product backlog*

The items in the backlog are important but not urgent. The requirements list in the current MDG SOW is already long, and including more requirements will not be a wise decision; therefore, they can wait until we have sufficient time to do them in a different iteration. Now that we have the requirements defined, we can start working on the MDG project.

Working on stereotypes

Our work on the MDG update project is part of **Build and Maintain the MDG** Course of Action that is depicted in *Figure 7.12*. It is important to understand the relationship between the two Sparx EA projects that we work on. They are both building each other in a gradual and iterative way. The repository project is where we are modeling our enterprise architecture artifacts. We started with the Business Capability that is influenced by a Course of Action that influences multiple courses of action. One sub Course of Action is building the MDG project, which produces the MDG files that we import into the repository project to be able to build more EA artifacts. Some of these artifacts are the requirements diagrams that define the scope of work of this MDG iteration. It is a mind-twisting relationship, but it is easy to understand once you get more familiar with it. The first thing to begin with is to add the required stereotypes to the MDG.

Adding the required stereotypes to the MDG

The MDG SOW contains requirements to create ten new element stereotypes and three connector stereotypes. We need the **Application Service**, **Logical Application**, **Physical Application**, **Business Service**, **Data Entity**, **Logical Data**, **Physical Data**, **Technology Service**, **Logical Technology**, and **Physical Technology**. *Figure 8.8* shows the list of the new application architecture stereotypes that have been added, the metaclasses they extend, the metaclasses' custom attributes, and the stereotypes' custom attributes:

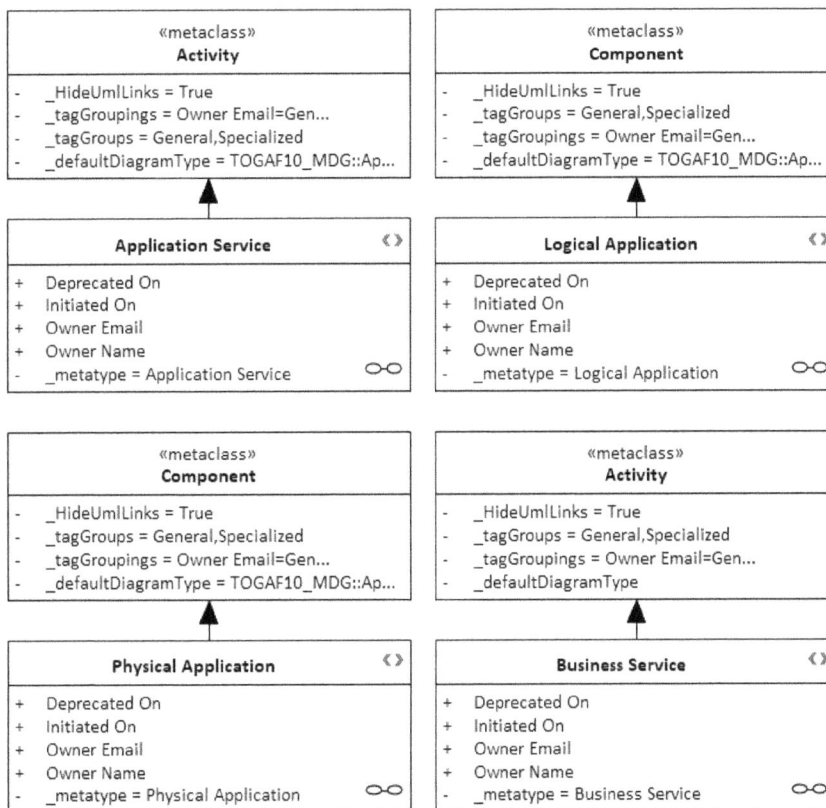

Figure 8.8: Application architecture elements' stereotypes

Figure 8.9 shows the newly added data architecture stereotypes, their metaclasses, and their custom attributes:

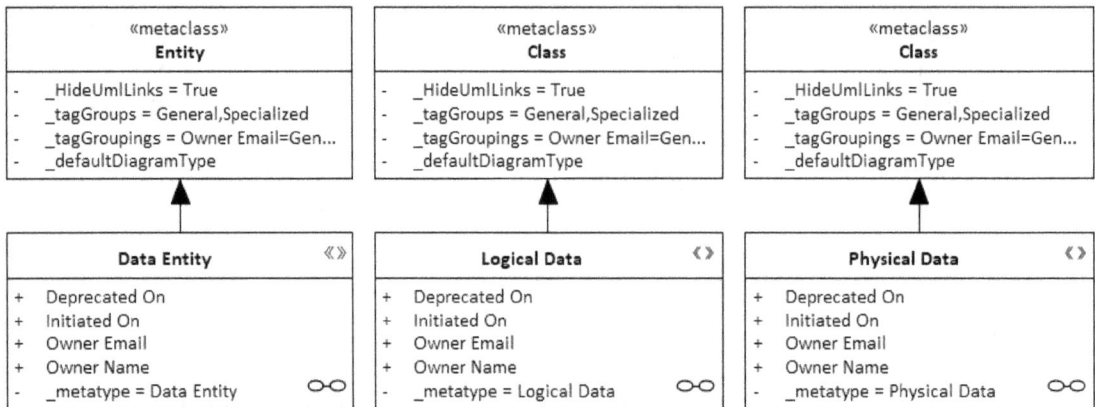

Figure 8.9: *Data architecture elements' stereotypes*

Figure 8.10 shows the technology architecture stereotypes, their metaclasses, and their custom attributes:

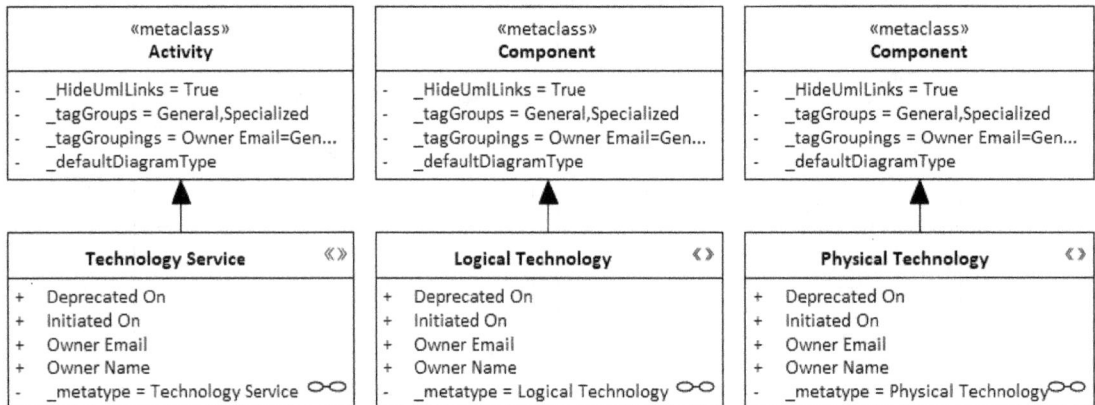

Figure 8.10: *Technology architecture elements' stereotypes*

For step-by-step instructions on how to create stereotypes in the MDG, refer to *Chapter 3, Beginning Model Driven Generation,* and *Chapter 4, Advanced Model Driven Generation*. Also, keep in mind that *Figure 8.8, Figure 8.9, Figure 8.10* are part of the entire MDG stereotypes diagram that is in *Figure 7.1*, which will not fit on a printed page and is getting busier, very crowded, and less readable. We already have an action item in our backlog to simplify it, and it seems like the need to do that is becoming more important.

We did not use the term *component* in logical application, physical application, logical data, physical data, logical technology, and physical technology stereotype names as they are defined in the TOGAF metamodel. This is simply because the full stereotype name is too long and will be truncated by Sparx EA unless we make the element on the diagram very large. It is up to you to use the full stereotype name or make it shorter, but remember that using acronyms like LAC to refer to logical application component is not recommended at all, because it is not a common abbreviation, and it will make your diagrams less readable and less understandable.

Note: **Stereotypes are meant to explain what an element is, not to make it look more mysterious.**

The following steps quickly explain, at a high level, how to define the stereotypes that are in *Figure 8.8*:

1. Make sure that the MDG project is open, then open the profiles diagram.

2. Add a new stereotype, name it **Application Service**, and make it extend to any metaclass of your choice, such as the **Activity** metaclass in our example.

3. Delete all the default attributes from the stereotype and from the metaclass.

4. Add **_defaultDiagramType** attribute to the metaclass and keep its default value empty. We will update this value after we create the diagram type.

5. Add **_HideUmlLinks** attribute to the metaclass and set its default value to **True**.

6. Add **_tagGroupings** attribute to the metaclass and set its default value to **Owner Email=General; Initiated On=General; Owner Name=General; Deprecated On=General; Maturity Level=Specialized;**

7. Add **_tagGroups** attribute to the metaclass and set its default value to **General,Specialized**

8. Add **_metatype** attribute to the stereotype and set its default value to **Application Service**.

9. Add **Deprecated On**, **Initiated On**, **Owner Email**, and **Owner Name** attributes, and keep the default value empty for all of them.

10. Make the application service stereotype self-composable.

11. Repeat *Steps 2* through *10* to add the remaining nine stereotypes using the proper names and metaclasses for each.

Some stereotypes extended the **Activity** metaclass, some extended the **Class** metaclass, and some extended the **Component** metaclass. You can change the metaclasses to other metaclasses if, for example, you did not like how the elements appear in the repository. In addition to the element's stereotypes, we need to add three connectors' stereotypes for the three new relationships that we have in the MDG SOW. *Figure 8.11* shows these new stereotypes and the metaclasses that they extend, and *Figure 8.11* is also part of the bigger *Figure 7.1* so keep that in mind:

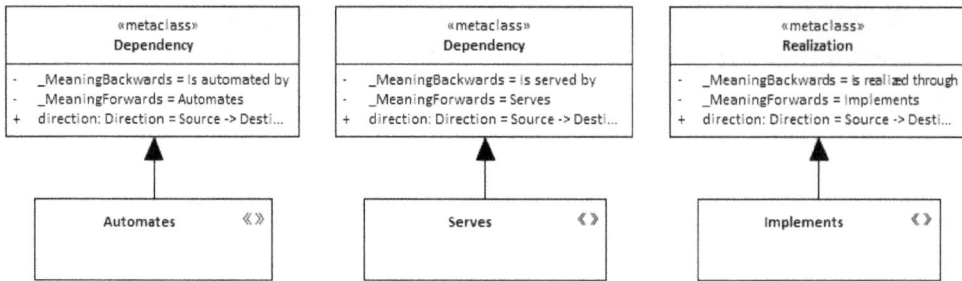

Figure 8.11: New connectors' stereotypes

After we have all the stereotypes that we need defined, we need to define the focused-metamodels for the stereotypes that belong to the application architecture layer and leave the remaining ones for future iterations, and the first on the list is the application service.

Application service focused-metamodel

Based on the requirements that are defined in **Add Application Architecture Stereotypes to the MDG** work package in *Figure 8.2*, and based on the fact that each stereotype is associated to the general entities, the application service focused-metamodel should look the one in *Figure 8.12*:

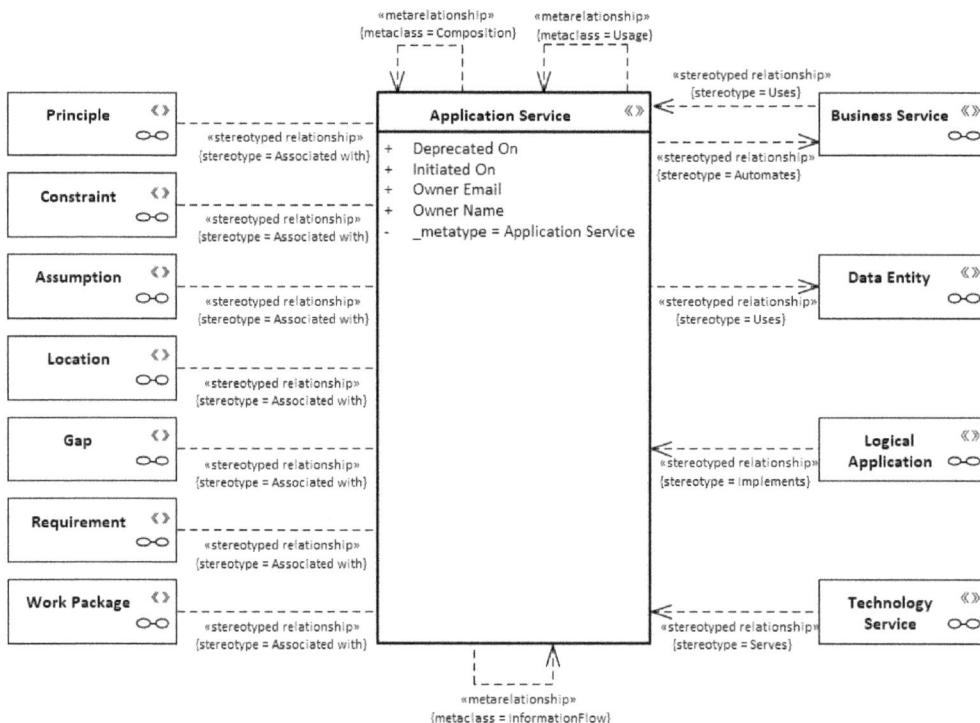

Figure 8.12: Application service focused-metamodel

You should be familiar by now with the creation of the focused-metamodels; so, we will not list the steps for creating them and will only show the result in diagrams. If you struggle with any details, refer to *Chapter 3, Introducing Model Driven Generation*, and *Chapter 4, Advanced Model Driven Generation* for a step-by-step instructions. The next focused-metamodel is the logical application component. Let us see how it looks.

Logical application component focused-metamodel

The logical application component focused-metamodel in *Figure 8.13* is based on the requirements that are defined in **Add Application Architecture Stereotypes to the MDG** work package:

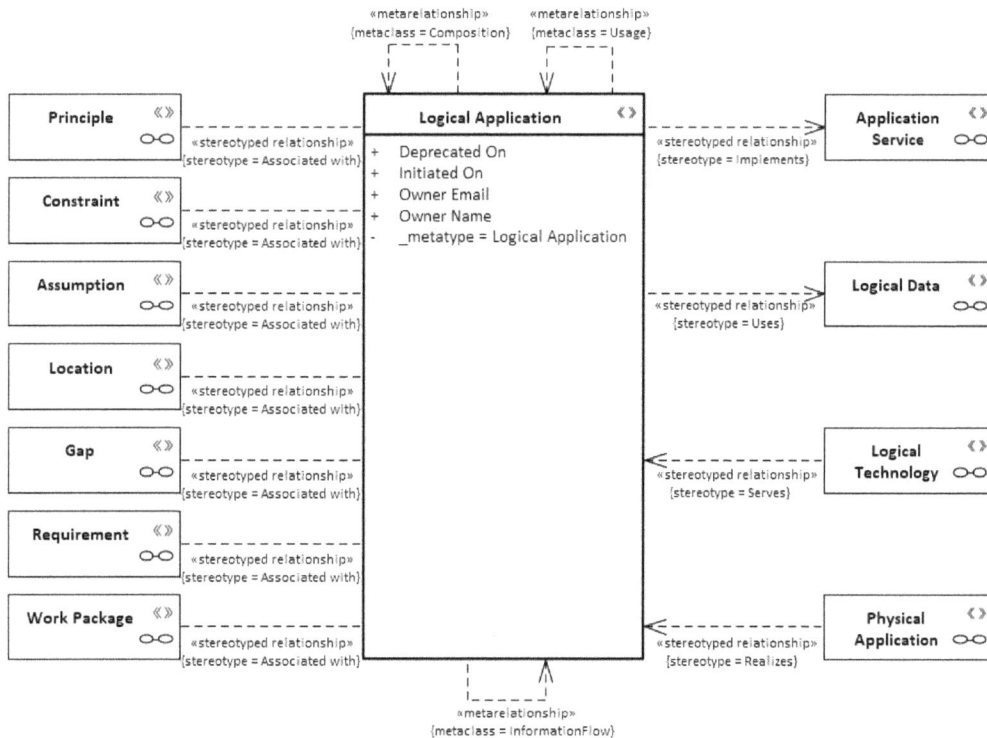

Figure 8.13: Logical application focused-metamodel

The last focused-metamodel for this iteration is the physical application component focused metamodel.

Physical application component focused-metamodel

The logical application component focused-metamodel in *Figure 8.14* is based on the requirements that are defined in **Add Application Architecture Stereotypes to the MDG** work package:

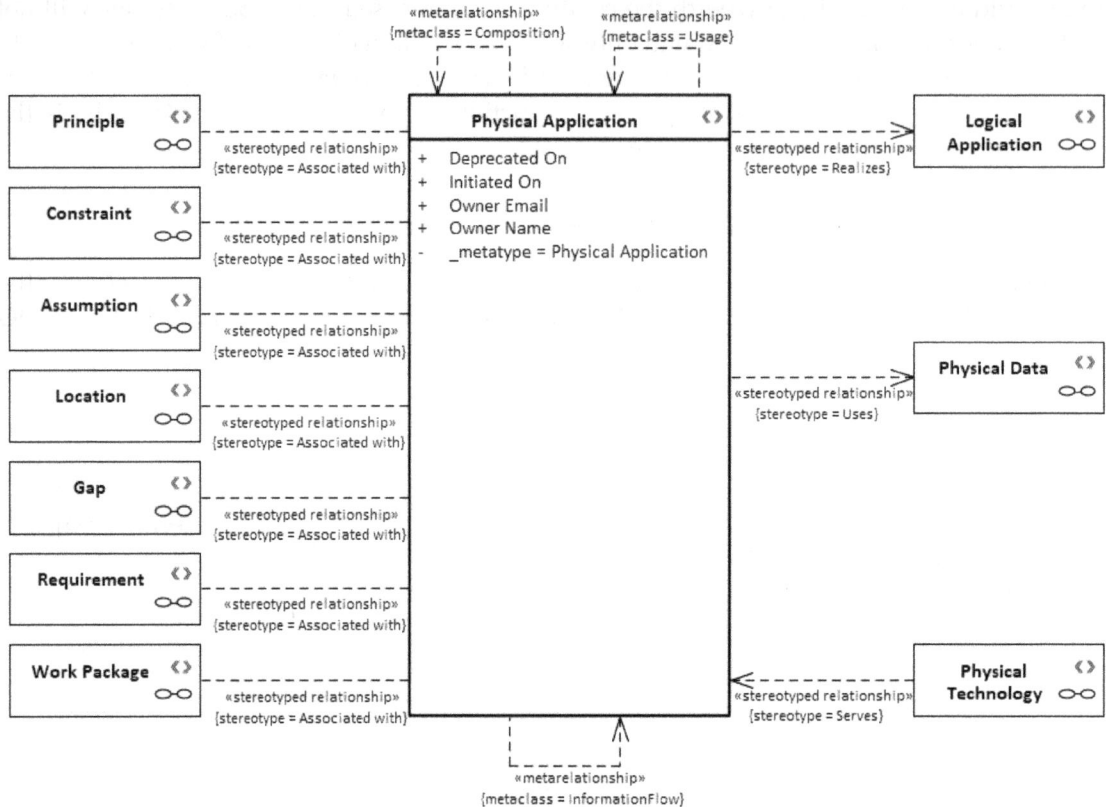

Figure 8.14: Physical application focused-metamodel

We have all the stereotypes that we need, so the next step is to create the application architecture toolbox.

Creating the application architecture toolbox

You can either create one toolbox to contain all three stereotypes in the application architecture layer or a separate toolbox for each stereotype. We will choose the first option and create a toolbox to contain all the application architecture stereotypes.

We need a new diagram for the new toolbox. We will create four toolbox pages or groups. One toolbox page for the application architecture stereotypes, one for the elements in the metamodel that are related to the application architecture stereotypes, one for the application architecture connectors, and the last one for the general entities. We can reuse the same general entities toolbox page by dragging it from the **Project Browser** and adding it to the diagram that represents the application architecture toolbox instead of duplicating the general entities toolbox group. The application architecture toolbox should look like the one depicted in *Figure 8.15*:

«metaclass»
ToolboxPage

Application Architecture Elements ‹ ›

+ TOGAF10_MDG::Application Service(UML::Activity) = Application Service
+ TOGAF10_MDG::Logical Application(UML::Component) = Logical Applica...
+ TOGAF10_MDG::Physical Application(UML::Component) = Physical Applic...

Application Architecture Related Elements ‹ ›

+ TOGAF10_MDG::Business Service(UML::Activity) = Business Service
+ TOGAF10_MDG::Data Entity(UML::Entity) = Data Entity
+ TOGAF10_MDG::Logical Data(UML::Class) = Logical Data Co...
+ TOGAF10_MDG::Logical Technology(UML::Component) = Logical Technol...
+ TOGAF10_MDG::Physical Data(UML::Class) = Physical Data C...
+ TOGAF10_MDG::Physical Technology(UML::Component) = Physical Techno...
+ TOGAF10_MDG::Technology Service(UML::Activity) = Technology Service

General Entities ‹ ›

+ TOGAF10_MDG::Assumption(UML::Requirement) = Assumption
+ TOGAF10_MDG::Constraint(UML::Requirement) = Constraint
+ TOGAF10_MDG::Gap(UML::Class) = Gap
+ TOGAF10_MDG::Location(UML::Class) = Location
+ TOGAF10_MDG::Principle(UML::Requirement) = Principle
+ TOGAF10_MDG::Requirement(UML::Requirement) = Requirement
+ TOGAF10_MDG::Work Package(UML::PackagingComponent) = Work Package

Application Architecture Connectors ‹ ›

+ TOGAF10_MDG::Associated with(UML::Association) = Associated with
+ TOGAF10_MDG::Automates(UML::Dependency) = Automates
+ TOGAF10_MDG::Implements(UML::Realization) = Implements
+ TOGAF10_MDG::Realizes(UML::Realization) = Realizes
+ TOGAF10_MDG::Serves(UML::Dependency) = Serves
+ TOGAF10_MDG::Uses(UML::Dependency) = Uses
+ UML::Composition = Composes
+ UML::InformationFlow = InformationFlow

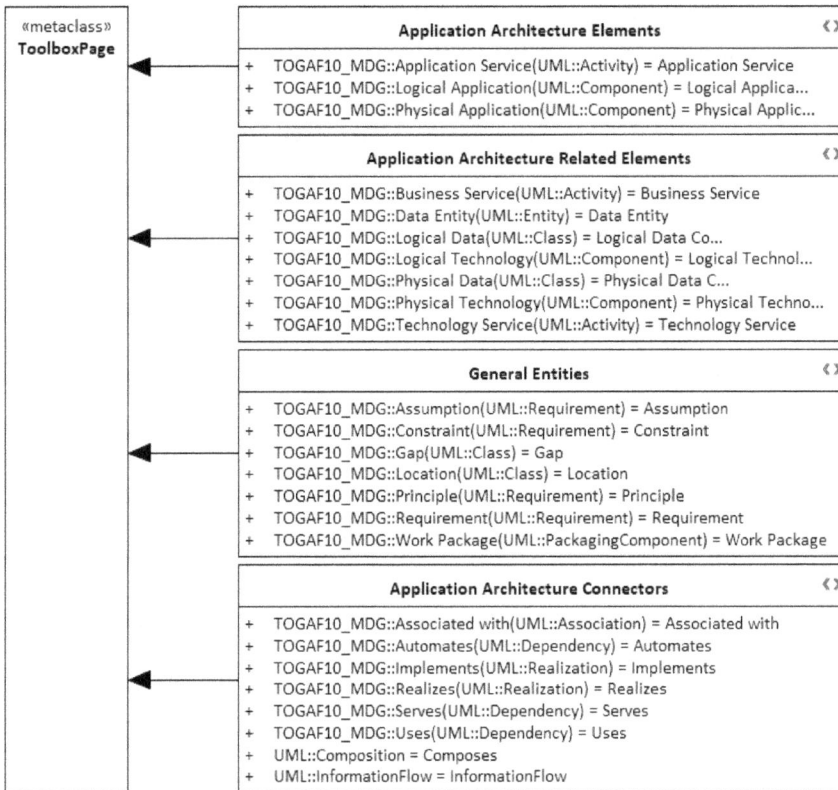

Figure 8.15: Application architecture toolbox

As you can see, we have four toolbox pages, each containing a group of elements. There is one important thing that you must remember when creating a toolbox with multiple pages. The order of the toolbox pages that you see on the diagram is not necessarily the same order that will appear in the toolbox when you generate and then import the MDG to a project. The diagram shows the **Application Architecture Elements** page on top, but when you generate the MDG and import it into a project, it may not be the top one. The way that Sparx EA decides the order of the pages in a custom toolbox is by using the toolbox pages' z-order values.

Diagrams, as we all know, are two-dimensional drawing areas. They have width and height, and so are the elements placed on them. They are all two-dimensional objects. The z-order is a value that tells Sparx EA the depth dimension, which determines the order of objects when placed above each other on a diagram. Sparx EA uses the order in which objects are placed on a diagram to set their z-order. By default, the latest object to be added to a diagram will have the lowest z-order, meaning it will appear on top of the other objects if it overlaps. Every time an object is placed on a diagram, either from the **Toolbox** or the **Project Browser**, the z-order value of 1 is assigned to it, and the z-order of all the other elements on the diagrams will be incremented by 1. As a result, the element placed first on the diagram will have the highest z-order value, which means it will be at the bottom.

To change the z-order of an object on a diagram, follow these steps:

1. Right-click on the diagram object, and select **Z-Order**.

2. You can choose whether to **Send Back** by one step, **Bring Forward** by one step, **Send to the Bottom** all the way back, or **Bring to the Top** all the way up.

   a. The **Bring to Top** option will set the z-order to 1, which puts the selected object on top of every other object on the diagram.

   b. **Send to Bottom** does the complete opposite.

   c. Further, **Send Back** will increase the z-order by 1.

   d. **Bring Forward** options will decrease it by 1.

The z-order of toolbox pages on a toolbox diagram plays an important role. The toolbox page that has the highest z-order value will be placed on top of the toolbox when the MDG is generated and imported, while the toolbox page with the lowest z-order value will be placed last in the toolbox. This is not very clear, but it is worth remembering because it could save you hours of debugging effort.

Note: **Toolbox pages with higher z-order values will be placed above the ones with lower values in a toolbox.**

To view the z-order of all the objects on a diagram, click on the diagram, then from the ribbon bar, click on **Design | Diagram | Options | Configure Z Order**. This will open a small window within the properties window, as explained in *Figure 8.16*:

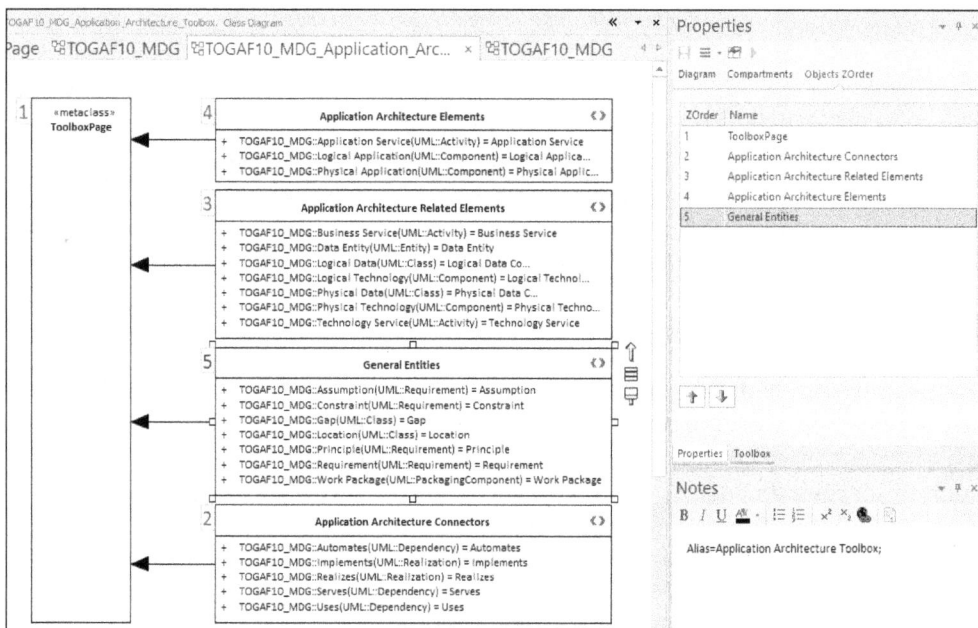

Figure 8.16: Z-order of toolbox pages

Clicking on an object in the **Objects Z Order** window will highlight it on the diagram and will show its z-order value in blue, while showing other z-order values in red. If we build the MDG as it is now, the **General Entities** toolbox page will be placed first in the toolbox, followed by **Application Architecture Elements**, **Application Architecture Related Elements**, and **Application Architecture Connector**. This is because of the z-order values. To change the z-order values, use the green up and down arrows that are placed at the bottom of the **Objects ZOrder** window.

When you finish adding and defining the application architecture toolbox and its toolbox pages, add a navigation cell on the main toolboxes' profiles diagram as depicted in *Figure 8.17*:

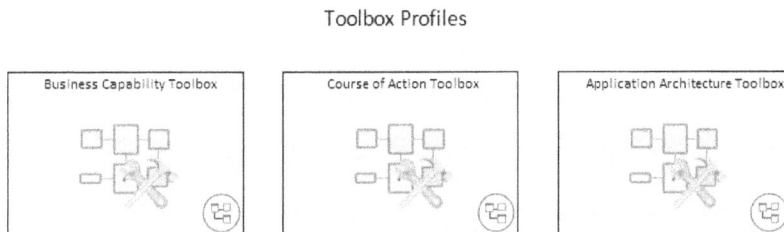

Figure 8.17: *Toolboxes profiles*

Next, we will create a diagram type for application architecture artifacts and associate it with the application architecture toolbox.

Creating the application architecture diagram type

Creating a new diagram type for the application architecture diagrams is straightforward. If you forgot how, please refer to *Chapter 3, Introducing Model Driven Generation*. In case you need to create sub diagram types, which are known as view specifications, refer to *Chapter 4, Advanced Model Driven Generation*. In *Figure 8.18*, we used the **Diagram_Component** metaclass to extend the application architecture diagram, but you can use different types, if preferred:

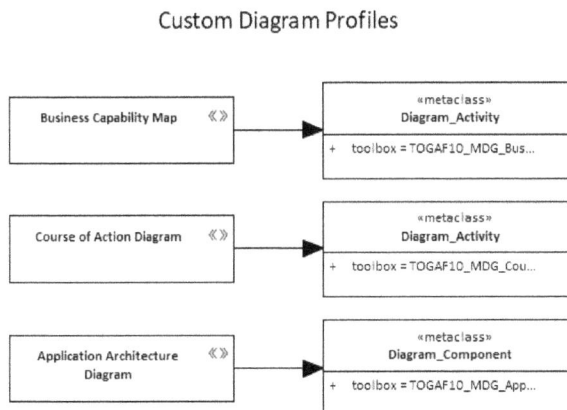

Figure 8.18: *Custom diagram profiles*

Link the application architecture diagram type to the application architecture toolbox by adding the **toolbox** attribute to the metaclass and setting its initial value to **TOGAF10_MDG_ Application_Architecture_Toolbox** or to the name that you assigned to the application architecture toolbox if in case it is different.

Lastly, you need to go back to the three application architecture stereotypes, the application service, logical application, and physical application, and set the initial value of the _ **defaultDiagramType** attribute to **TOGAF10_MDG::Application Architecture Diagram**.

Now we have realized all the requirements in the MDG SOW, hence we are ready to publish the MDG and use it to create application architecture artifacts. Open the testing project in Sparx EA, use the **Resources** tab to import the newly generated MDG, test it, and if everything works as desired, import the MDG to the main repository and let us create some new artifacts.

Building the application architecture artifacts

The application architecture can describe the applications in the enterprise at three different levels of detail, i.e., physical, logical, and conceptual. The physical models describe the actual deployable components, the logical models describe the application at a functional level, and the conceptual models describe applications at a service level. Each of these levels provides not only a different level of detail but also different perspectives to look at applications within the enterprise. Let us start with the physical level because it is the easiest to understand and the most tangible part of the application layer.

Modeling physical application components

The physical application component is defined by TOGAF as a *realization of logical application functionality using components of functionality in applications that may be hired, procured, or built* (**https://pubs.opengroup.org/togaf-standard/architecture-content/chap02.html**). The key here at the physical level is that the physical application component is what can be hired, procured, or built. An important thing to remember is that physical architecture models are not meant to show deployments. If you have multiple environments, each containing multiple instances of a physical application component, deployed on multiple servers, this is usually beyond what EA is about. This is more about IT operations and asset management practices. EA artifacts need to remain at the architecture and design level and not the deployment.

Sparx EA is an example of a physical application component. It realizes application functionalities that make it the modeling application of our choice; we procured it online and deployed it on physical technology components such as a Windows Desktop machine and a SQL Server database. We used it to create physical data components like the artifacts and the MDG files. If we put all this information in a diagram, we should get something that looks like *Figure 8.19*:

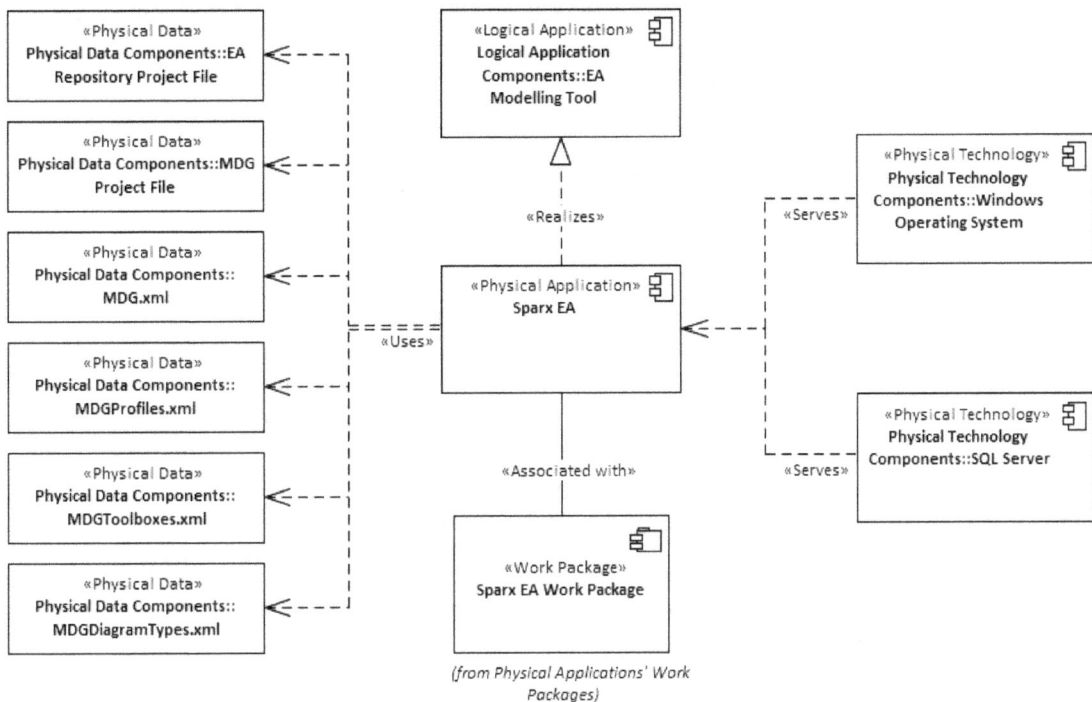

Figure 8.19: Sparx EA physical application component model

An optional but useful work package has been associated with the Sparx EA physical application component. This can contain any information that helps with the hiring, procurement, or building of the component. It can contain requirements, use cases, activity diagrams, sequence diagrams, or user interface designs, and they can be modelled using any modeling standard such as UML, SysML, ArchiMate, or any other Modeling standard of your choice.

Physical application components can be composed of other physical application components, and there is no limit to the level of decomposition hierarchy that you can create. The physical subcomponents can represent smaller modules, application programming interfaces, or batch jobs. If you are Modeling a large solution that is comprised of multiple smaller subcomponents, APIs, and batch files, it would be a good idea to model the physical hierarchy of the components on one diagram, and detail each of them in its own diagram showing its subcomponents, the physical data components they use, and the physical technology components that serve them. When modeling, it is advisable to avoid repeating the same level of information in subsequent levels of a diagram if it is unnecessary. This repetition may lead to confusion rather than providing clarification.

Note: **Application programming interfaces (APIs), microservices, SOA services, and batch jobs are all examples of physical application components and subcomponents.**

If the model in *Figure 8.19* became busy due to having more elements in it, you need to consider turning it into a home page of the component and have the physical data components and the physical technology components into separate diagrams that are linked to the home page through navigation cells or hyperlinks.

Sparx EA physical application component realizes the **EA Modeling Tool** logical application component, so let us better understand what logical application components are.

Modeling logical application components

The logical application component is defined by TOGAF as a*n encapsulation of application functionality that is definable by services offered and data maintained, independently of implementation and technology.* (**https://pubs.opengroup.org/togaf-standard/architecture-content/chap02. html**). Therefore, a logical application component is a grouping, or an encapsulation of functionality, and it is not an actual application. This is why they are called logical. The actual applications are represented by the physical application components.

A logical application component can be realized by many physical components. The **EA Modeling Tool** logical application component in *Figure 8.20*, is realized by Sparx EA, Archi, and BizzDesign:

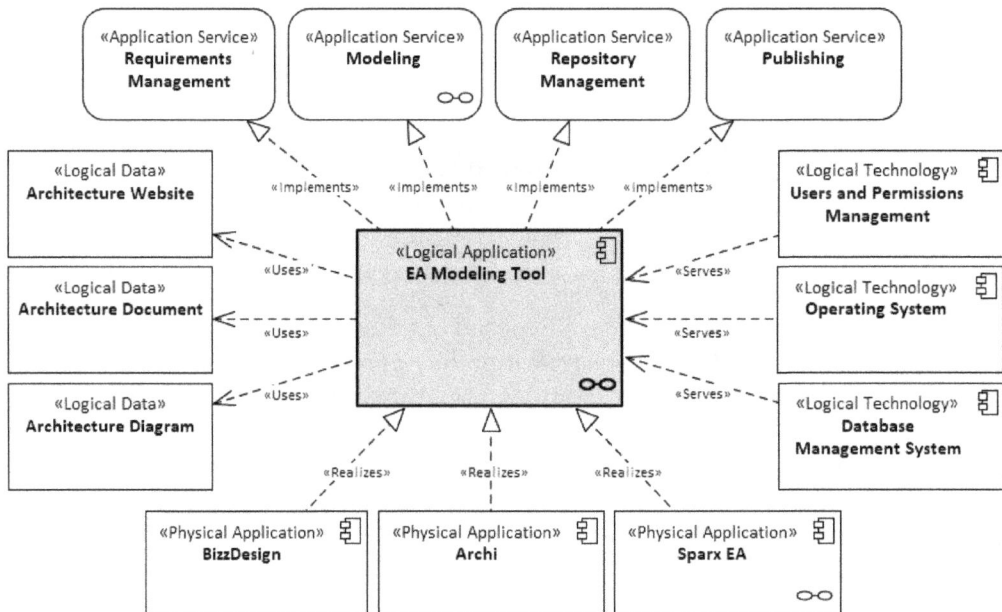

Figure 8.20: EA modeling tool

They can all realize the same logical application component if they offer the same services. Visio, for example, is not listed on the diagram because it does not have a repository and cannot implement the repository management application service.

Note: You only need to model what your enterprise contains, not every modeling tool that is on the market. So, if your organization does not use Archi, do not list it.

The EA Modeling tool logical application component uses multiple logical data components and is served by multiple logical technology components. The logical application components can only be related to logical data and technology components. They cannot be served directly by physical technology components, and they cannot directly use the physical data components. We will talk more about logical data components in *Chapter 9, Modeling Application Integrations*, and we will talk more about logical technology components in *Chapter 10, Modeling Cloud Environments*.

In real-world models, a logical application component diagram can easily get very busy, because there are usually many physical application components within the enterprise realizing the same logical component, and there are many application services that are automated by a logical application component. Therefore, a home page style with hyperlinks or navigation cells could be a better choice, as you can see in *Figure 8.21*:

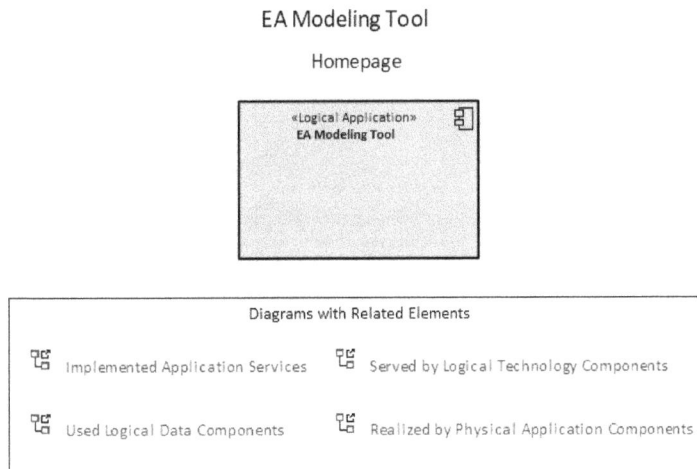

EA Modeling Tool

Homepage

«Logical Application»
EA Modeling Tool

Diagrams with Related Elements

Implemented Application Services   Served by Logical Technology Components

Used Logical Data Components   Realized by Physical Application Components

Figure 8.21: A logical application component's homepage

The main purpose for application components in organizations is to automate business services, either partially, or entirely, and this automation is provided through application services, so let us learn how to model them.

Automating business services with application services

An application service is defined as *the automated elements of a business service. An application service may deliver or support part or all of one or more business services.* Therefore, to understand the definition, we need to define the business service too. A business service is defined as *a service which supports the business by encapsulating a unique element of business behavior; a service offered external to the enterprise may be supported by business services.* Both definitions are quoted from the TOGAF standard (**https://pubs.opengroup.org/togaf-standard/architecture-content/ chap02.html**).

To simplify, a business service is what a specific business offers to its consumers. Business services are what the consumers see from the business, the services offered to them. Business services are what make business organizations exist, because every business exists to provide services or to sell products. Big or small, modern or old-fashioned, automated or manual, all businesses have their business services to offer.

Application services automate all or part of these business services, so if a specific business service is fully automated, many architects will find it difficult to differentiate between the two. In today's modern organizations, a business service can be fully automated, which makes differentiating it from the application services that automate it very difficult. Business services exist with or without applications. Application services are only the automated part of these business services. In *Chapter 11, Modeling Business Services*, we will look at more business service examples and how to properly model them.

In *Figure 8.20*, we identified that the **EA Modeling Tool** logical application implements four application services. One of them is the **Modeling** application service, which we can model in as shown in *Figure 8.22*:

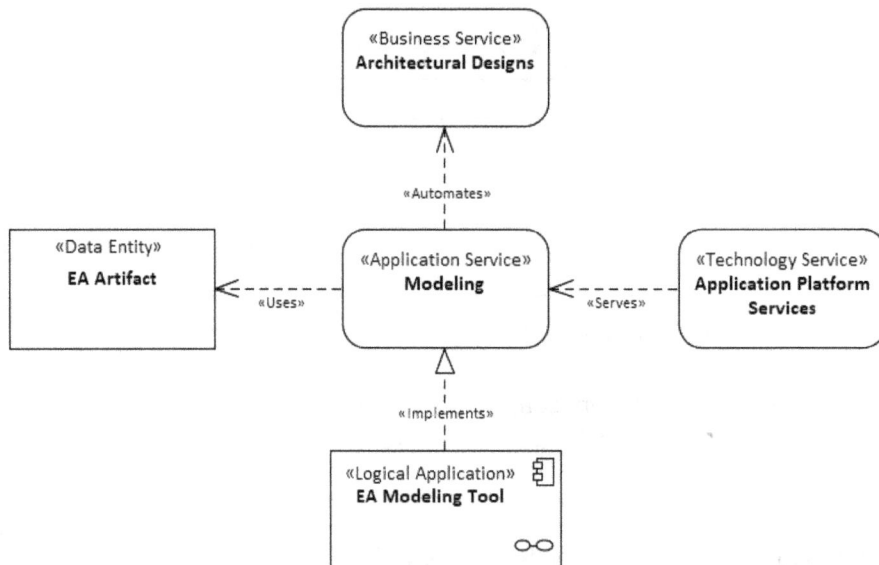

Figure 8.22: Modeling application service

Providing architectural design business service can be done using paper, but it is more efficient to use modeling software. Therefore, the **Modeling** application service automates the **Architectural Designs** business service. Having application services in the repository that do not automate any business service means they are not used, and there is a possibility that the application component that implements the said services can be retired if it does not have other application services to implement.

The **Modelling** application service uses the **EA Artifacts** data entity, which is another abstract definition of data that is used by the application service. More on data architecture will come in *Chapter 9, Modeling Application Integrations*. Application services need to be served by technology services. The **Application Platform Services** serve the **Modelling** application service. *Chapter 10, Modeling Cloud Environments,* will talk more about modeling the technology architecture components.

Application service diagrams provide a conceptual description of application services, which business services they automate, which data entities they use, which application services they are served by, and which application components implement them. The application services catalog can list all the application services that are available in the enterprise. As an exercise, you can model the requirements management, repository management, and the publishing application services, and then create an application services catalog diagram that contains all four application services that have been defined.

Conclusion

Applications can be modelled at three different levels of detail: the service level, the logical level, and the physical level. The service level reflects the level of automation that a business service has, the logical level shows applications as groups of functionalities, and the physical level shows the actual build or procured components.

Applications do not live in silos but in environments that contain many other applications, where they integrate with each other to exchange data, and this is what we will learn in the next chapter.

Points to remember

- Building the repository is a gradual and iterative Process. We used the Course of Action's work packages to document the requirements that we used in this chapter.

- The z-order value of elements on a diagram determines which element appears above or below the other elements. Elements with a lower z-order value appear on top of elements with higher z-order values.

- The z-order value within the context of an MDG toolbox plays another role as it determines the order of the toolbox pages in a custom toolbox. Toolbox pages with higher z-order values will be placed above the ones with lower values in a toolbox.

- It is not recommended to use acronyms as stereotype names because it reduces the readability and the understandability of your diagrams.

- APIs, microservices, SOA services, and batch jobs are all examples of physical application components and subcomponents.

- You only need to model what your enterprise contains, not every modeling tool that is in the market, so if your organization does not use Archi, do not list it.

- Business services exist with or without applications. Application services are the automated elements of business services.

- Every business provides services to its consumers, whether that is done manually or automated, fully or partially.

Key terms

- **Physical application component**: What can be hired, procured, or built from an application.

- **Logical application component**: It is a grouping or an encapsulation of functionality, and not an actual application.

- **Application service**: It is the automated part of a business service.

- **Business service**: It is what a specific business offers to its consumers.

Join our Discord space

Join our Discord workspace for latest updates, offers, tech happenings around the world, new releases, and sessions with the authors:

https://discord.bpbonline.com

CHAPTER 9
Modeling Application Integrations

Introduction

Data architecture is tightly related to application architecture. TOGAF even groups the two architecture layers into one and calls it the **information systems architecture** because of their strong coupling. Data cannot be meaningful for business without applications that consume it and present it to users. Applications without data are useless for business. Data in an enterprise can exist for multiple applications to use, process, and provide results. Using data from different data sources and sharing data back with them requires proper data integration. Data integration is a whole separate topic from an enterprise architecture repository; therefore, we will not discuss any integration patterns or recommend one over the other. What you need to keep in mind is that whatever integration pattern you follow in the real-world enterprise, you must document how it works. You must document how data flows from one application to another, how data is structured in different formats, and how data is transformed from one format to another. All of these are forms of data architecture artifacts, which we will learn how to model in this chapter.

Data architecture can provide artifacts at three different levels of detail: conceptual, logical, and physical, and each level targets a different set of audiences. Business actors, for example, are interested in the conceptual level because this is what data means for them. Application integrations happen at the physical level, so integration architects will be more interested in developing or consuming this type of artifact. The logical data architecture artifacts are between the two, which makes them ideal for information technology managers. A complete repository must address the needs of every consumer in the enterprise to keep and maintain their trust.

Structure

This chapter will include the following topics:

- Updating the MDG
- Building the data architecture artifacts

Objectives

By the end of this chapter, you will learn how to differentiate between the three types of data architecture artifacts and to learn how to build useful models out of them.

Updating the MDG

As we did in the previous chapters, we need to update the MDG to include the three data architecture elements that are in the TOGAF metamodel, which are the data entity, logical data component, and physical data component, and we will need to define the scope of work for the new iteration to update the MDG.

Defining the MDG SOW

In the main repository project, we have an ongoing Course of Action for building and maintaining the MDG, as shown in *Figure 7.12*. We will add a new work package for the new MDG development iteration and define the scope of work as a set of requirements diagrams. The steps for creating the new work package have been explained in *Chapter 8, Modeling Applications*, so follow the same steps to create a new work package under the **MDG Iterations** package, and name it **Add Data Architecture Stereotypes to the MDG**, then add four sub work packages in it as depicted in *Figure 9.1*:

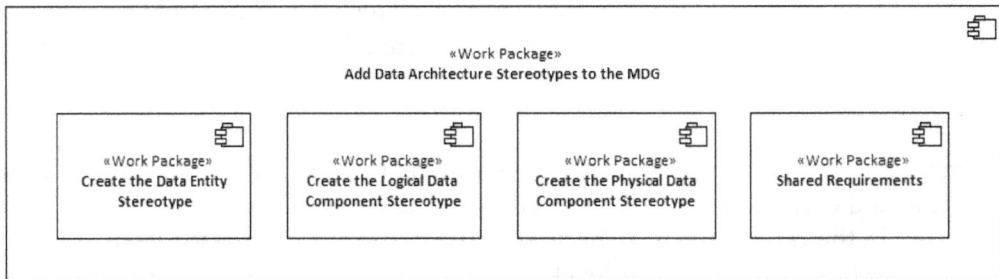

(from MDG Iterations)

Figure 9.1: *Sub work packages contained in their parent work package*

Since the work packages have been created, we need to add the requirements to them to form the MDG SOW, let us start with the first work package.

Defining the SOW of the first work package

The first work package will contain the requirements for **Create the Data Entity Stereotype** as depicted in *Figure 9.2*:

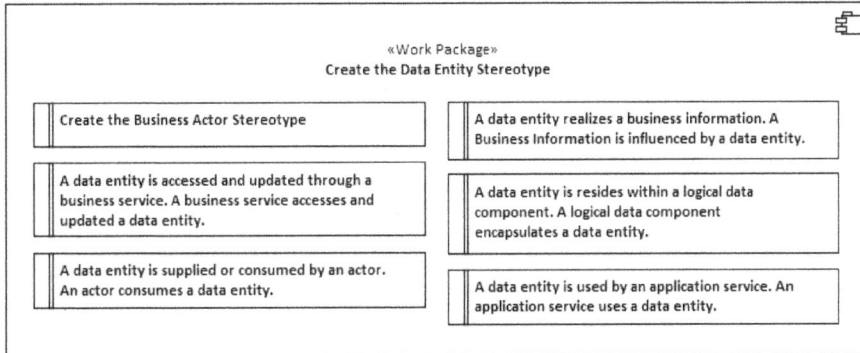

(from Add Data Architecture Stereotypes to the MDG)

Figure 9.2: *Requirements for creating the data entity stereotype*

By now, you should be familiar with defining the SOW requirements in work packages; hence, we will not repeat the steps for doing that and will provide a diagram that shows how the result should be. However, we advise you to look back at the detailed steps in *Chapter 8, Modeling Applications*, if you face any difficulties.

Next, we need to define the requirements of the SOW of the second work package.

Defining the SOW of the second work package

The second work package is **Create the Logical Data Component Stereotype,** which is depicted in *Figure 9.3*:

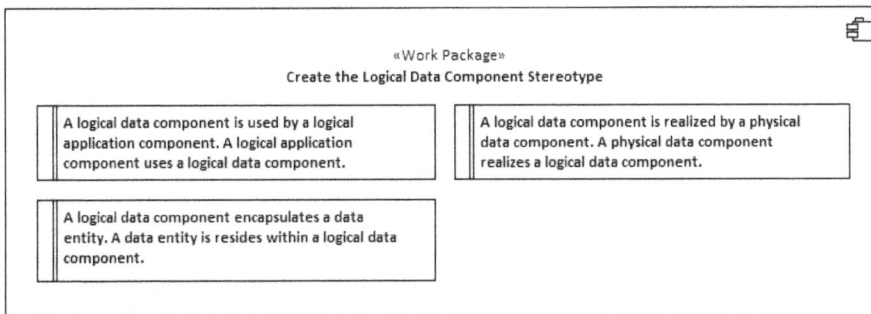

(from Add Data Architecture Stereotypes to the MDG)

Figure 9.3: *Requirements for creating the logical data component stereotype*

Continuing with the same approach, we will define the requirements of the third work package.

Defining the SOW of the third work package

This package will contain the MDG SOW requirements to **Create the Physical Data Component Stereotype**. The package content should be like *Figure 9.4*:

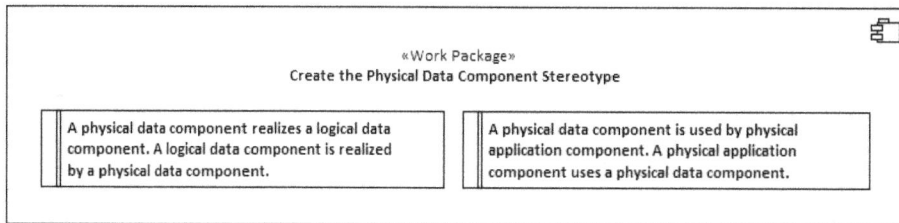

(from Add Data Architecture Stereotypes to the MDG)

Figure 9.4: Requirements for creating the physical data component stereotype

Finally, we will define the requirements of the fourth SOW work package.

Defining the SOW of the fourth work package

The fourth work package will contain the general shared requirements that are not specific to one stereotype. We think that it is time to pull the requirement for simplifying the MDG stereotypes diagram out from the backlog and add it to the SOW of the current MDG iteration. *Figure 9.5* lists these requirements:

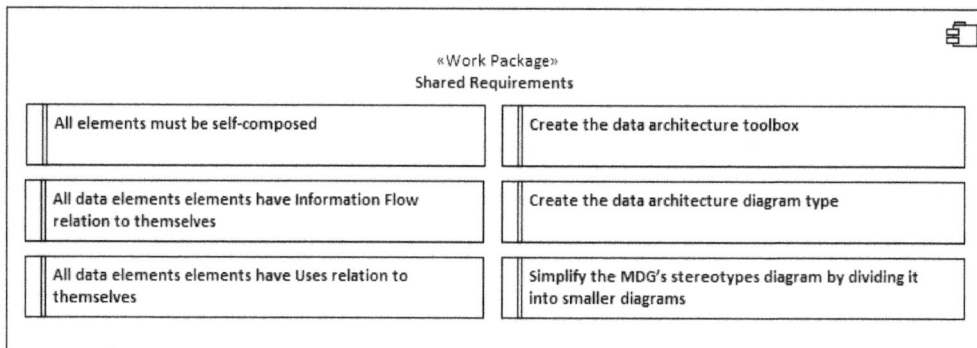

(from Add Data Architecture Stereotypes to the MDG)

Figure 9.5: Shared requirements for the current MDG iteration

We have all the requirements defined. In the real-world, you must get these requirements approved before you start working on them. This is part of the governance that you must define around making changes to the MDG project or to the repository project. We will start with the task that we pulled out from the product backlog because the main profiles diagram is getting busy and less readable, so let us see how.

Simplifying the MDG profiles page

If you look back at *Figure 7.1*, which contains the complete list of stereotypes at that time, you will see that it was getting too large, which affected its readability and, therefore, usefulness. We even added more than a dozen other stereotypes in *Chapter 8, Modeling Applications*, which made it even worse. A diagram that users cannot read is a useless diagram, and the last thing that you want to hear is that the diagrams that you worked so hard to make are useless. We will fix this by creating a separate diagram for each architecture layer.

Creating the sub diagrams

Our approach is to separate the elements that are on the **TOGAF10_MDG** diagram in the profile package into multiple diagrams, each focusing on a specific architecture layer or stereotypes. We will then move the stereotypes that belong to each layer into their designated diagrams. Follow these steps to learn how:

1. Make sure that the MDG project is open.

2. Open the profile package and create six new UML class diagrams in it with any names of your choice, but preferably names that self-describe the diagrams, such as **Application Architecture Stereotypes** diagram.

3. The newly created diagrams will be sorted alphabetically in the profile package.

   When having multiple diagrams in one package, the first diagram becomes the default diagram, which means it will be the diagram that responds to double-clicking the package, which is not the desired behavior. To make the **TOGAF10_MDG** the default diagram, we must move it to the top of the list, and this is how to do that.

4. Use the up and down arrows in the browser's toolbar to move the **TOGAF10_MDG** diagram to the top of the list as indicated in *Figure 9.6*:

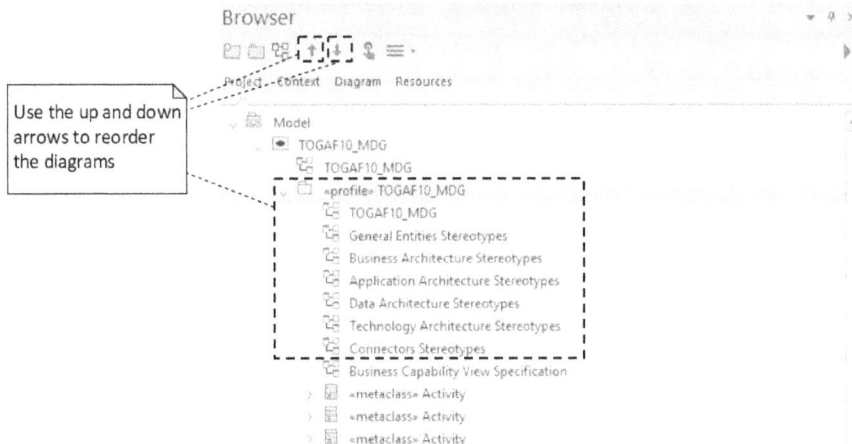

Figure 9.6: TOGAF10_MDG diagram must be on top of the list

5. Open the **TOGAF10_MDG** diagram.

6. Starting with the application architecture stereotypes, select the three application architecture stereotypes and their metaclasses. Remember that holding the *Ctrl* key while clicking allows you to multiselect.

7. Right-click on one of the selected elements and select **Copy** from the context menu.

8. Open the **Application Architecture Stereotypes** diagram, right-click on the empty diagram, and select **Paste | Element(s) as Link** from the context menu.

9. The copied elements will be placed on the new diagram with the same size and format they had on the first diagram, as you can see in *Figure 9.7*:

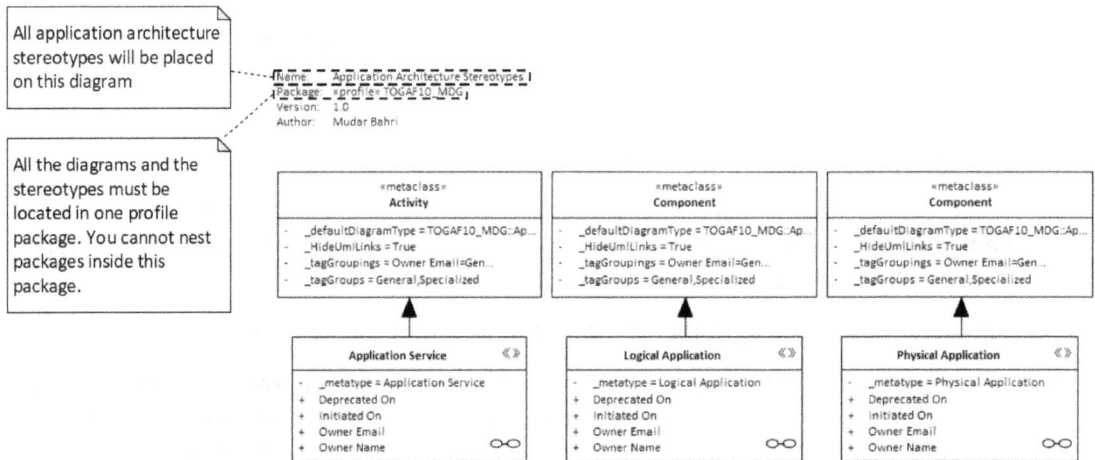

Figure 9.7: *The application architecture stereotypes diagram*

10. Go back to the **TOGAF10_MDG** and delete the elements that you just copied by clicking on each of them and hitting the Delete button on the keyboard. Remember that we need to delete the elements only from the **TOGAF10_MDG** diagram, so do not delete them from the **Project Browser**.

11. Repeat *Steps 6* through *10* to copy the stereotypes from the main **TOGAF10_MDG** diagram to the general entities, business architecture, data architecture, technology architecture, and the connectors stereotypes sub diagrams.

After finishing all these steps, the main diagram should be empty after moving all the stereotypes from it to the sub diagrams. We need to turn this main diagram into a homepage diagram that navigates the users to the desired sub diagram.

Turning the main diagram into a homepage diagram

Every time we have a single package or element that contains multiple diagrams, only one of them can be assigned as the default diagram for that package or element, which will open in response to the double-click action. In the previous chapters, we learned how to turn the default diagram into a homepage diagram that contains either navigation cells or hyperlinks that navigate the user to other sub diagrams.

We will do the same here, but we will introduce a third way to build a home page. The steps are very simple:

1. Make sure that the main **TOGAF10_MDG** diagram is opened.

2. From the **Project Browser**, drag one of the sub diagrams and drop it on the main diagram.

3. Select **Diagram Reference** from the popup dialog.

4. Resize and align the diagram references as desired. *Figure 9.8* suggests a way to build the MDG profiles homepage, but you can design it in any other preferred way:

MDG Profiles Homepage

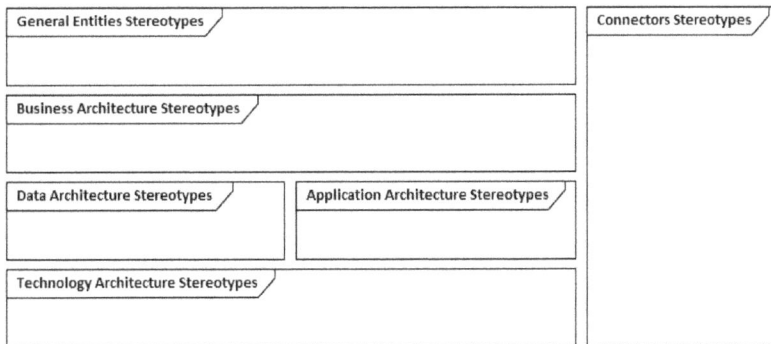

Figure 9.8: MDG profiles homepage

The diagram references act the same way as the navigation cells and the hyperlinks. Double-clicking on a diagram reference will open the diagram that is behind it. Now that our profiles homepage is organized, let us continue working on the MDG SOW by working on the stereotypes.

Working on the stereotypes

If we look at the requirements of the current iteration's work packages, we will see that all the stereotypes in the data architecture layer and the application architecture layer have been created in *Chapter 8, Modeling Applications*. We also created the business service stereotype in the same chapter and created the Business Information stereotype in *Chapter 6, Modeling Business Capabilities*. This means that the only stereotype that is missing from the SOW requirements is the actor stereotype. We also have four new connector stereotypes that we need to define on the connectors stereotypes diagram, which are the consumes, supplies, accesses, and encapsulates, and this is what we will do in the next subsection.

Adding the required stereotypes to the MDG

The actor stereotype belongs to the business architecture layer, so we need to open the business architecture stereotypes diagram and add a new stereotype to it, extend the Class metamodel, and give it the name Actor. You can extend different metaclasses, such as the UML Actor metaclass, to inherit the famous stickman's appearance. We prefer to use a different appearance than the UML actor's appearance because actors have different meanings between TOGAF and UML and we did not want the readers to be confused.

For step-by-step instructions on how to create stereotypes in the MDG, please refer to *Chapter 3, Beginning Model Driven Generation*, and *Chapter 4, Advanced Model Driven Generation*. *Figure 9.9* shows how the **Actor** stereotype will look like:

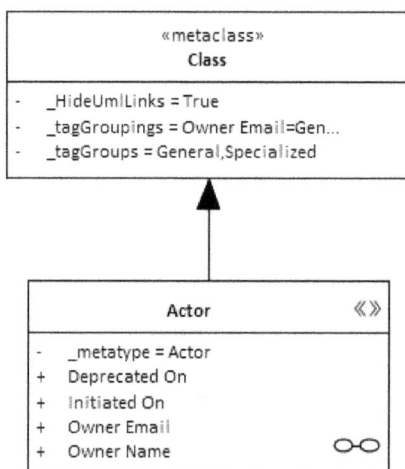

Figure 9.9: New elements' stereotypes

After defining the actor's stereotype, we need to add four connectors' stereotypes for the new relationships that we have in the MDG SOW. *Figure 9.10* shows these new stereotypes and the metaclasses that they extend:

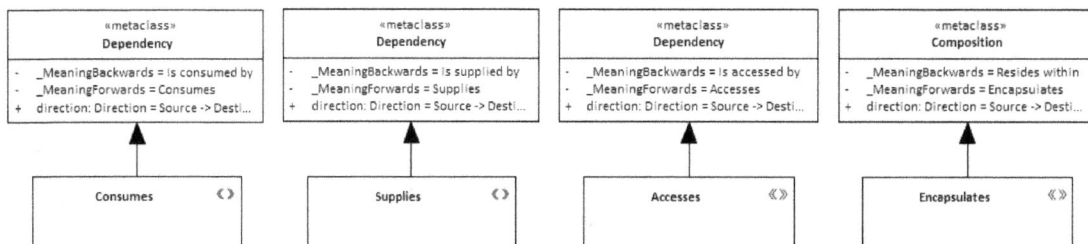

Figure 9.10: New connectors' stereotypes

Next, we need to define the focused metamodels for the data architecture layer stereotypes, starting with the data entity.

Data entity focused metamodel

Based on the requirements that are defined in **Add Data Architecture Stereotypes to the MDG** work package in *Figure 9.1*, and based on the fact that each stereotype is associated with the general entities, the data entity focused metamodel should look like the one in *Figure 9.11*:

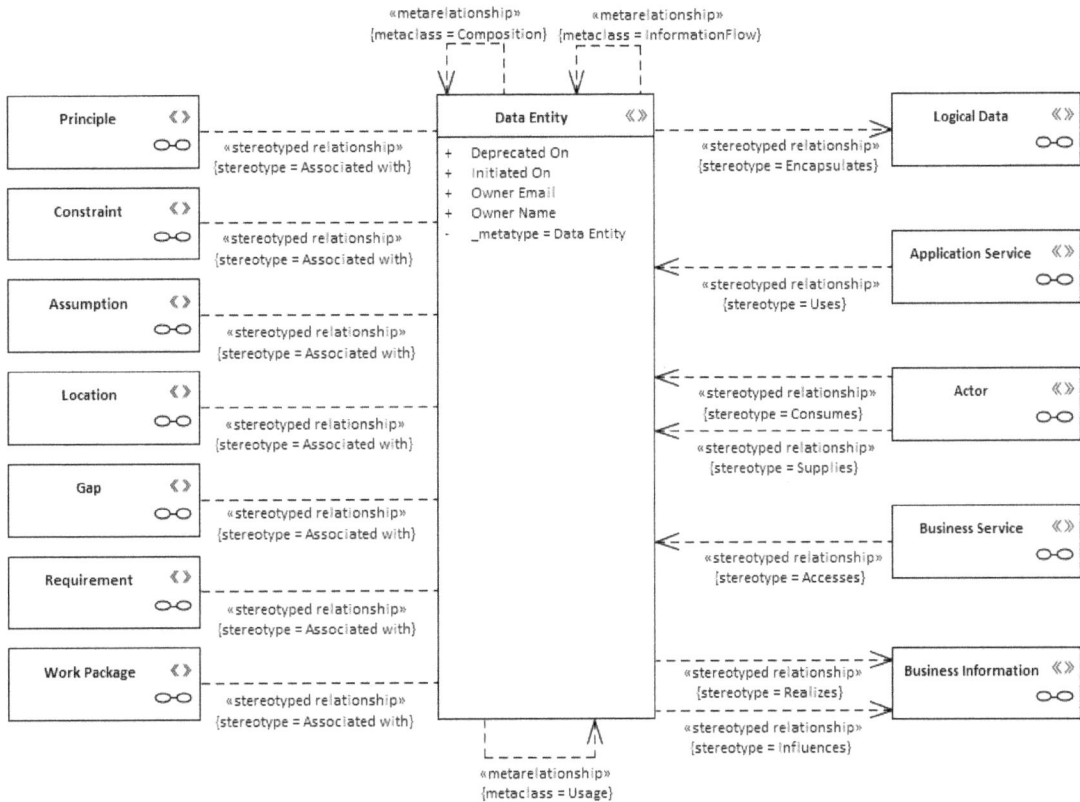

Figure 9.11: *Data entity focused metamodel*

The next focused metamodel is the logical data component. Let us see how it looks.

Logical data component focused metamodel

The logical data component focused metamodel in *Figure 9.12* is based on the requirements that are defined in **Add Data Architecture Stereotypes to the MDG** work package:

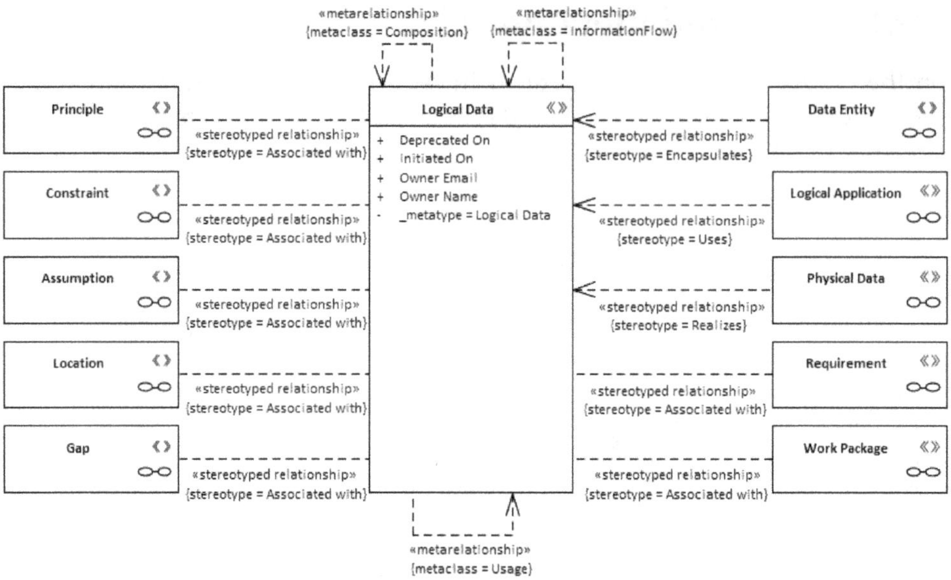

Figure 9.12: Logical data component focused metamodel

The last focused metamodel for this iteration is the physical data component focused metamodel.

Physical data component focused metamodel

The physical data component focused metamodel in *Figure 9.13* is based on the requirements that are defined in **Add Data Architecture Stereotypes to the MDG** work package:

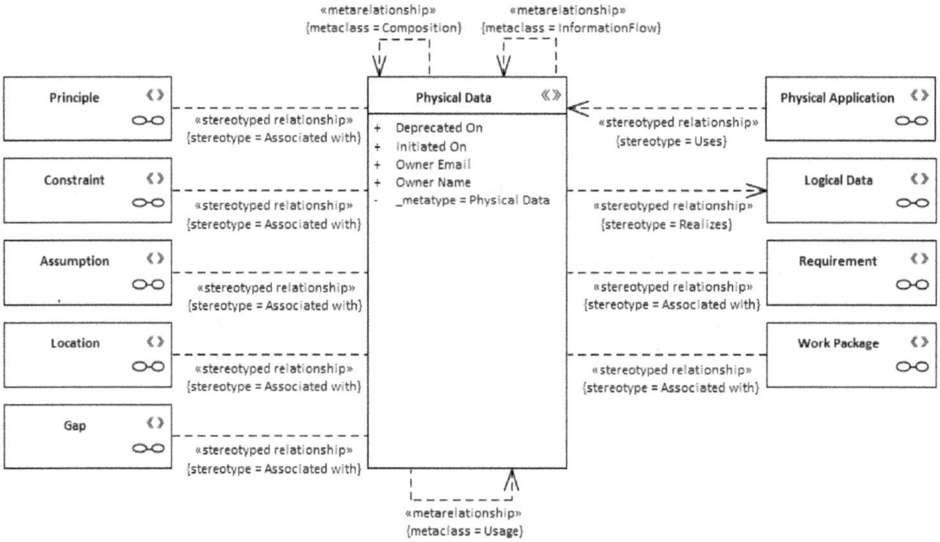

Figure 9.13: Physical data focused metamodel

We have all the stereotypes that we need, so the next step is to create the data architecture toolbox.

Creating the data architecture toolbox

In the same way we did for the application architecture toolbox, we can either create one toolbox to contain all three stereotypes in the data architecture layer or create a separate toolbox for each stereotype. We will create a toolbox to contain all the data architecture stereotypes. We need a new diagram for the new toolbox. The data architecture toolbox should look like the one depicted in *Figure 9.14*:

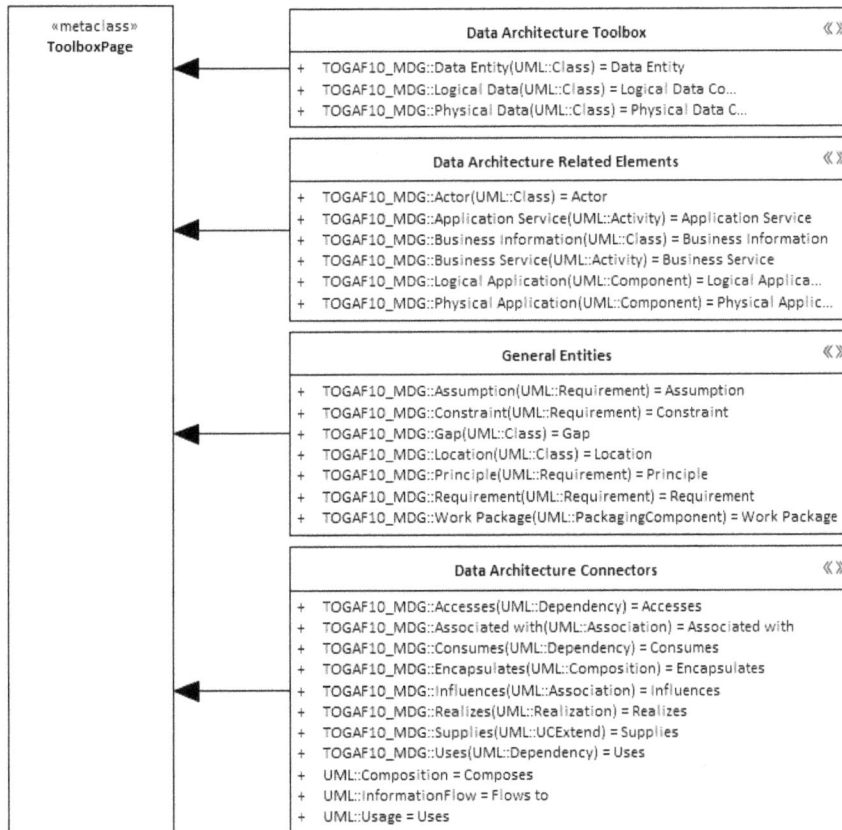

Figure 9.14: Data architecture toolbox

Change the z-order of the objects on the diagram to make their order in the toolbox the same as their order on the diagram. We explained the effect of the z-order value in custom toolboxes in the *Creating the application architecture toolbox* section in *Chapter 8, Modeling Applications,* so refer to that section for more details. When you finish defining the data architecture toolbox and its toolbox pages, add a navigation cell on the main toolboxes' profiles diagram as depicted in *Figure 9.15*:

Toolbox Profiles

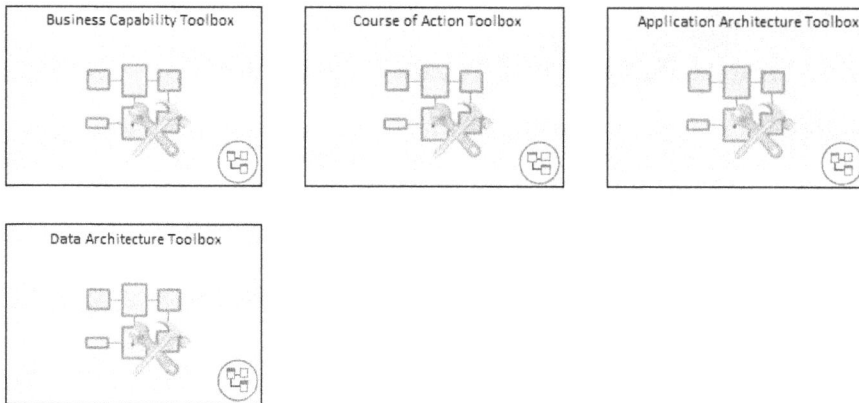

Figure 9.15: Toolboxes profiles

Next, we will create a diagram type for data architecture artifacts and associate it with the data architecture toolbox.

Creating the data architecture diagram type

In *Figure 9.16*, we used the **Diagram_Logical** metaclass to extend the data architecture diagram:

Custom Diagram Profiles

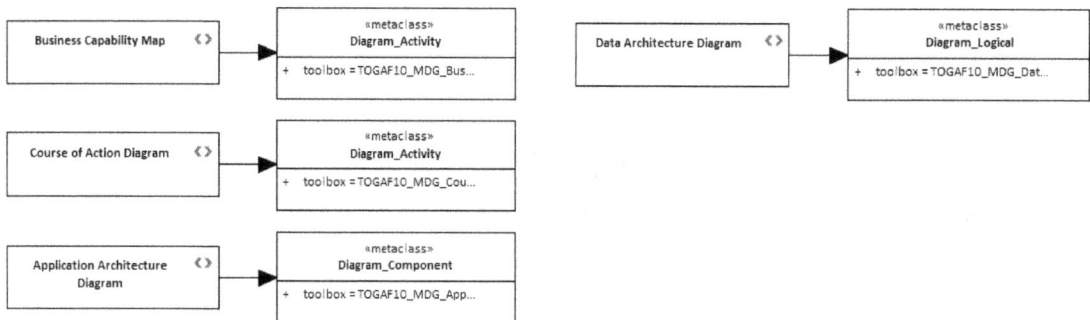

Figure 9.16: Custom diagram profiles

To extend the same, choose **Class** from the **Extension Type** dropdown list from the **Add Diagram Extension** dialog when prompted, but you can use different types if preferred.

Link the data architecture diagram type to the data architecture toolbox by adding the `toolbox` attribute to the metaclass and setting its initial value to `TOGAF10_MDG_Data_Architecture_Toolbox` or to the name that you have used for the data architecture toolbox if it is different.

The final step is to go back to the three data architecture stereotypes, the data entity, logical data, and physical data, and set the initial value of the **_defaultDiagramType** attribute to **TOGAF10_MDG::Data Architecture Diagram**.

After realizing all the requirements in the MDG SOW, we need to publish and test the MDG before using it to build data architecture artifacts. When everything works as desired, import the MDG to the main repository and let us use it to create new artifacts.

Building the data architecture artifacts

The data architecture can describe enterprise data at three different levels of detail: conceptual, logical, and physical. The conceptual level describes data in a way that is understandable by the business, regardless of how it is implemented. The logical level describes the data at a functional level without telling every attribute in it. The physical level describes the actual structure of the data, such as the tables in a relational database, the structure of a class, or the schema of an XML and a JSON file. We will look at these three modeling levels in more detail and will explain with examples how to model data integration at each level, starting with the conceptual.

Modeling data entities

A data entity represents data that is recognized by the business as a distinct concept (**https:// pubs.opengroup.org/togaf-standard/architecture-content/chap02.html**). This means that a data entity is data that means an unambiguous thing for the business. The easiest way to identify data entities in an organization is to look at its business glossary, where there is a definition for things that the business knows, defines, and understands. That business glossary is your source of data entities.

The business glossary varies from one organization to another, either partially or completely. One organization may differentiate, for example, between a customer and a client; another business may have the same definition for both, a third business may call one of them a beneficiary, while a fourth business may call it a patient. It all depends on the business and the type of services that it provides. Another example can be about the difference between a bill and an invoice. They could mean the same thing for one business but a different thing for another business. The only way to know that is to refer to the business glossary, if available, or help create one if it is not available.

As enterprise architects, we should not be the ones responsible for creating and maintaining the business glossary except for the data entities that belong to the enterprise architecture world. Defining the business glossary in general is a pure business exercise, that needs to be performed and governed by people who represent the business and know its definitions. We can help in facilitating the required sessions, providing tools and techniques to use, and collecting and documenting the findings, but not making definitions other than the EA definitions.

Data entity models show data at a very abstract level of detail. In fact, all that we show on the model is the data entity's name. We can show how it is related to other elements in the enterprise, such as the actors that supply or consume it, the sub data entities that comprise it, which application services use it, which business services access it, and which logical data encapsulates it. We can also show the Business Information elements that are realized by the data entity, and we can add its definition in a note element on the model as depicted in *Figure 9.17*:

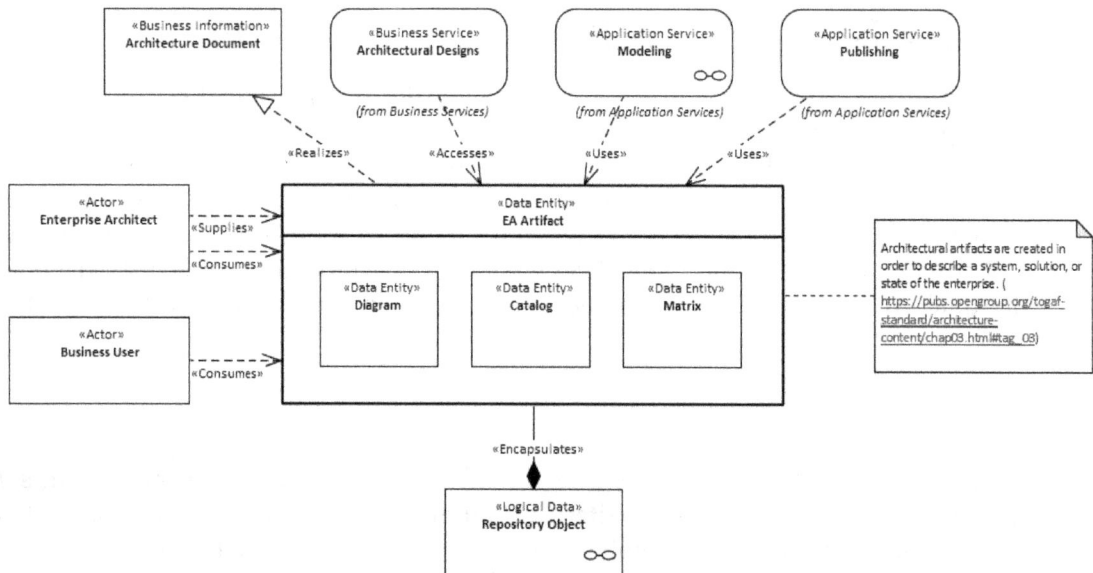

Figure 9.17: EA artifact data entity model

If this diagram got busy with so many elements on it, then it is time to consider turning it into a home page and distributing it on multiple diagrams.

For every element in your business glossary, consider having a diagram like *Figure 9.17* to describe that element. The business glossary provides a narrative definition, only while the data entity model shows more than just the definition. This added value will make you gain the trust of enterprise users in your repository.

Data integration can be modeled at the conceptual data entity level to show how data flows from one application service to another without distracting the viewers with details. *Figure 9.18* shows an example of integration at the data entity level:

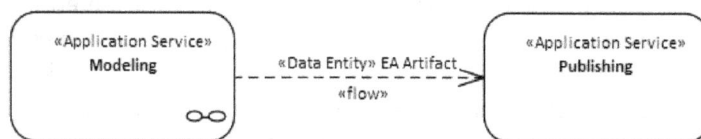

Figure 9.18: Integration at the data entity level

When you connect two application services with an information flow connector, a dialog box will pop up asking you to provide the **Information Items Conveyed**, as shown in *Figure 9.19*:

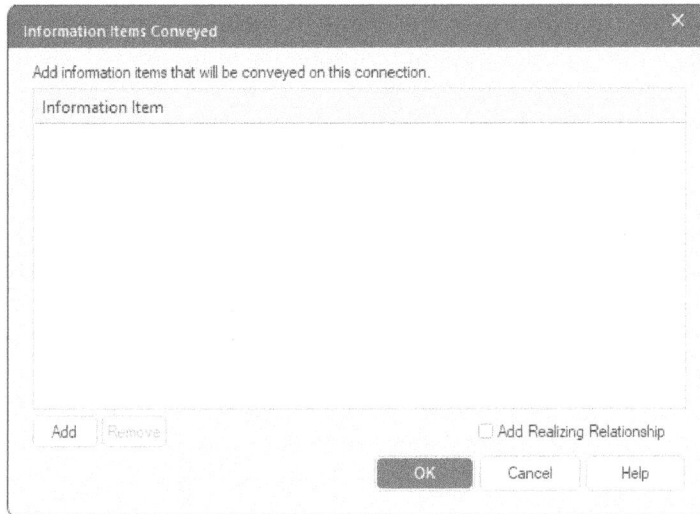

Figure 9.19: Information Items Conveyed dialog box

If you click on the **Add** button, the **Select Classifier** dialog, like the one in *Figure 9.20*, will ask you to select or create the information item, or the data entity, that flows from the source application service to the target:

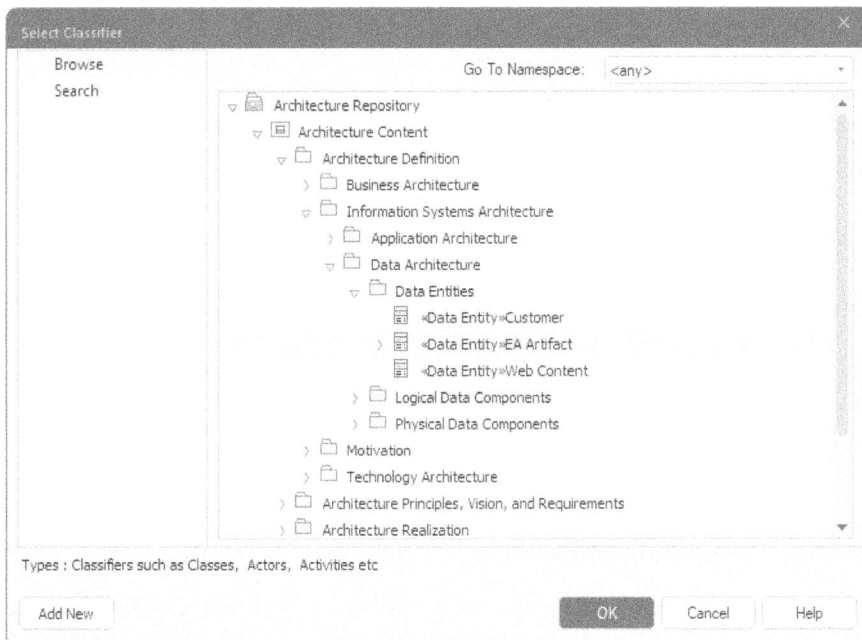

Figure 9.20: Select the data

Find the **EA Artifact** data entity, click **OK** to close the first dialog box, and click **OK** to close the second dialog box and return to the diagram.

Data entities do not exist in isolation from other data entities. Data entities that are related to each other can be combined in logical data components, so let us see how they look.

Modeling logical data components

The logical data component is defined by TOGAF as, *a data structure composed of logically related data entities.* The definition is simple; however, to elaborate, we can describe the logical data model as a diagram explaining a group of related data entities that make up a data structure. In *Chapter 5, Structuring the Repository,* we explained how the repository structure is comprised of packages that can contain other packages, diagrams, or elements. The package, diagram, and element are all data entities that should exist in the business glossary. The data model in *Figure 9.21* shows how the **Repository Structure** logical data component is composed of packages that are composed of zero-to-many packages, zero-to-many artifacts, and zero-to-many elements:

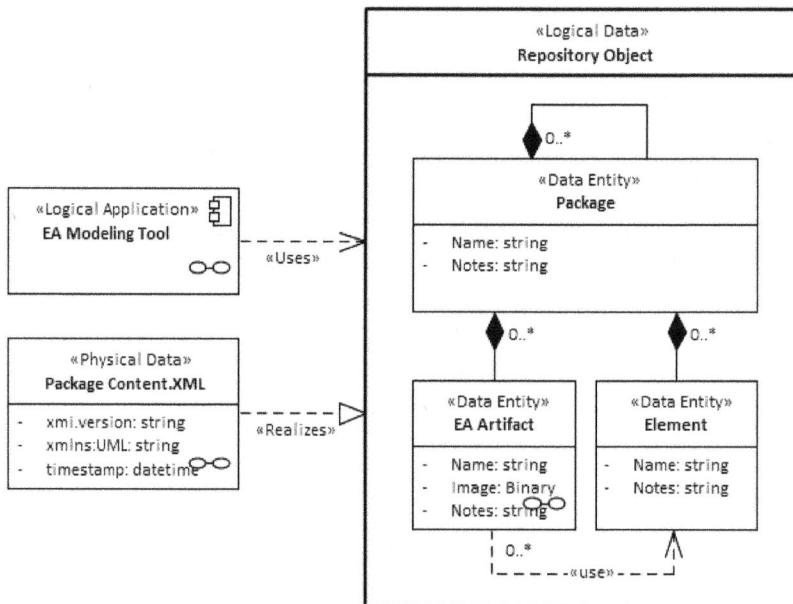

Figure 9.21: Repository structure logical data model

> Note: **A diagram is a type of EA artifact, so we used the generalized name in the model rather than using the specialized name.**

A logical data model can show attributes, relationships, and multiplicities between the data entities. It can show all or some of the attributes that an entity has, except for keys. Logical data models usually do not show primary and foreign keys or indices, because this will take the diagram to the physical level. When a physical data component realizes a logical data component, all the attributes, keys, and data types can be identified in it. Additionally, logical data models show the logical application components that use the logical data component. This provides traceability to know which logical application provides or consumes which data, which will help decision makers estimate the impacts of possible changes, either to the data or to the application components.

Logical data components are still considered abstract and do not reflect what is contained in a data component. When we look for actual technical implementation and an actual structure, then we need to look at the physical data component.

Modeling physical data components

The physical data component is defined by TOGAF as, *a data structure that realizes related logical data components represented in the format or schema required by a particular technology* (**https://pubs. opengroup.org/togaf-standard/architecture-content/chap02.html**). From the definition, we can understand that it is a data structure, just like the logical data component, but it represents the format or the schema that a specific technology needs. So, if we know that our logical data will be implemented in a relational database, then our physical model will show tables, relations, and keys. If the same logical data component is implemented in a JSON or an XML file, our physical data component will show nodes and attributes.

A single logical data component can be realized by many different physical data components based on the chosen technology. If you need your models to remain independent of how they will be implemented, you need to keep them at the logical level. If you are certain that a specific format, such as XML, will be used, then you provide models at the physical level.

Physical data models describe the structure of the data components, but it is not about listing its data. When Modeling a database table, for example, the physical data component must only show how the table is structured, not what is in it. It must show all the attributes and their data types, which keeps the model at the schema description level, but not the actual contained data. Let us take an example to elaborate more.

Modeling XML files

To learn how to model XML files, we need to have a sample file first. We can randomly get any example from the internet, but in Sparx EA, you can export any package from the **Project Browser** into XML in addition to several other formats. We will export a package from the **Project Browser** as an XML. Then, we will use it as a sample to model. Follow these steps to learn how:

1. In the **Project Browser**, click on any package, preferably one that contains packages, diagrams, and elements, such as the **Application Architecture** package.

2. In the ribbon bar, select **Publish | Model Exchange | Export | XMI Format**. A dialog box like the one in *Figure 9.22* will appear:

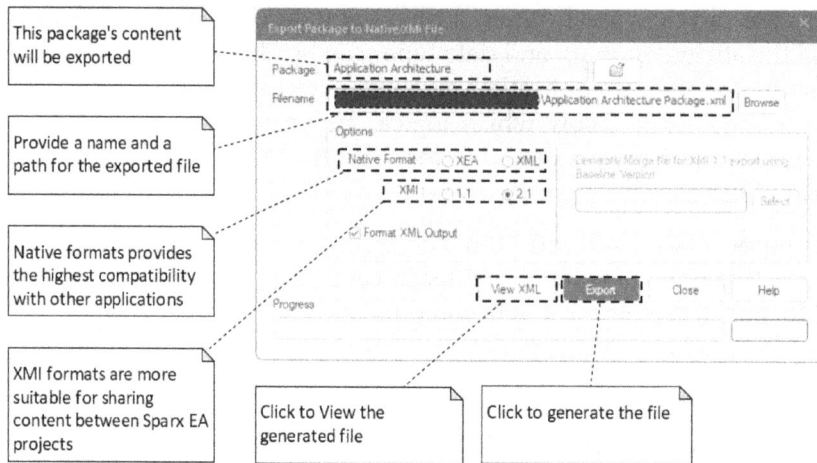

Figure 9.22: Export package dialog box

3. Export the package, then click **View XML** to view the content of the XML file. The content of the XML file will be opened in its own tab in Sparx EA, with a tree navigator on the left and a content viewer on the right side of the screen, as depicted in *Figure 9.23*:

Figure 9.23: Exported package content in XML format

This is the actual content of the file with all the data, which is not a physical data model. The physical data model must focus only on the structure and the schema of the file, so the XML file in *Figure 9.23* can be modeled as a physical data component which is shown in *Figure 9.24*:

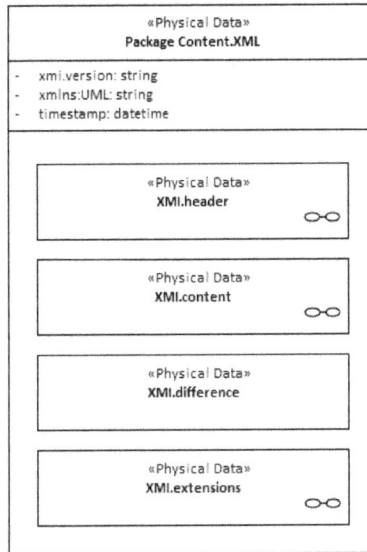

Figure 9.24: *A physical data model showing a package content*

The physical data model, as you can notice, consists of attributes and nodes; each node consists of nodes and attributes, and it keeps nesting that way. Each node will be modelled following the same pattern, and the navigation will keep drilling until reaching the desired level.

Another way to model an XML physical data component is to put the entire file hierarchy in one diagram, showing the nodes and their sub nodes all in one, like *Figure 9.25*:

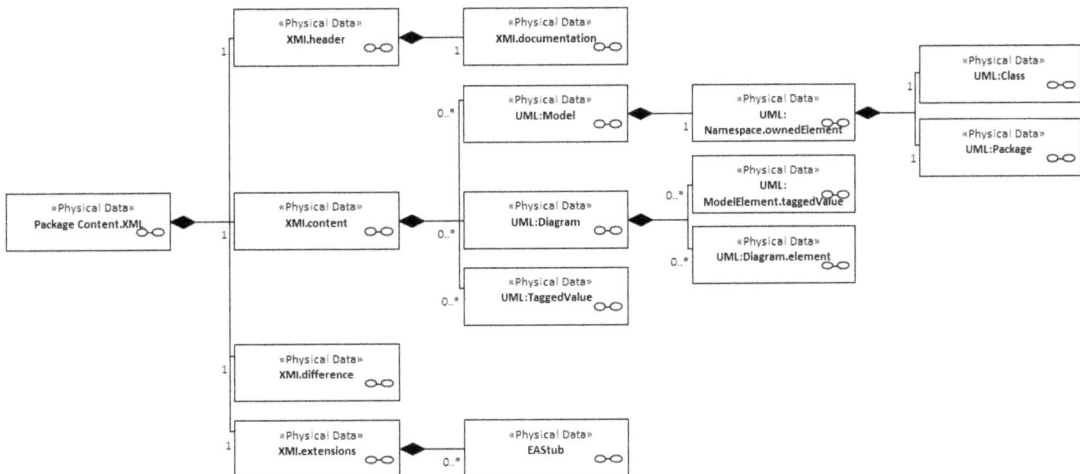

Figure 9.25: *Complete model for an XML file*

This way, the entire structure can be visualized in one diagram, and reaching the desired node will not require multiple levels of drilling down from one node to another. The only disadvantage is that it can get busy very easily, especially with complex real-life files. One way to keep it simple is by hiding the attributes of all the nodes on the complete model diagram and showing them on the child diagrams of each node. This requires every node to have a child diagram, which is a good practice anyway.

Modeling relational databases

The physical data model can vary significantly based on the technology that is used to implement it. The same repository object data component can be modeled in a completely different way in a relational database implementation. *Figure 9.26* shows a part of the internal database structure of Sparx EA:

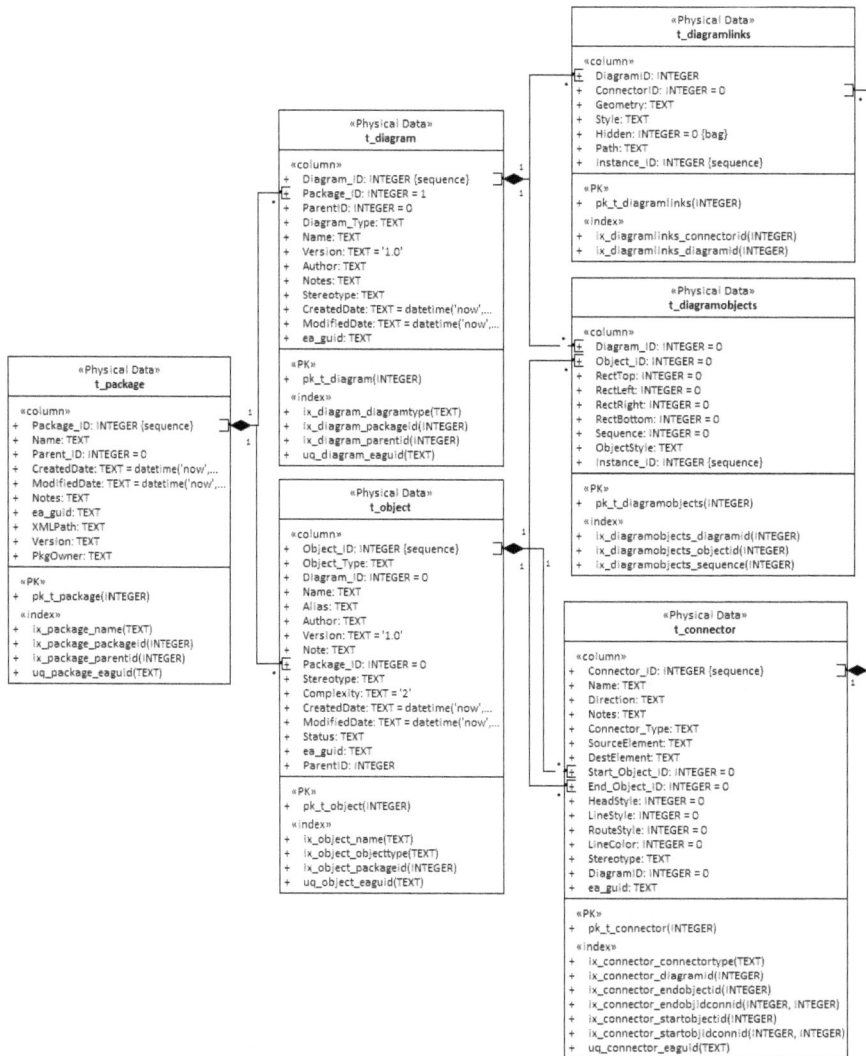

Figure 9.26: Relational model showing a package structure

Describing the internal structure of Sparx EA's database is not within the scope of this book, although we will look at it again in *Chapter 13, Repository Management Processes*, to create custom queries and dashboards. But for now, we only wanted to give an example of how to build physical data component artifacts that are implemented in a relational database.

Note: **We are not showing all the tables in the Sparx EA database, nor are we showing all the attributes and the indices in the modeled tables.**

Packages are stored in the **t_package** table, diagrams in **t_diagram**, objects in **t_object**, and connectors in **t_connector**. Tables like **t_diagramobjects** and **t_diagramlinks** are joint tables to maintain the many-to-many relationships between **t_diagram** and **t_connector**, and between **t_diagram** and **t_object**. We used the **column**, **PK**, and **index** stereotypes for attributes to give them an additional level of description. You may also extend the MDG to add new stereotypes, such as *Table*, to differentiate the physical data components of type tables from other data components in the repository.

Modeling data integration

Integration, in its simplest definition, is sending data from one application to another. It can be modeled at the logical level, where we can show how the data entities and their attributes flow from the source logical application to the target. It can also be modeled at the physical data level to show a flow of information, too, but with more detail and highlights on integration rules based on the used technologies. The mapping in both cases is not necessarily one-to-one when it comes to fields, as you can see in *Figure 9.27*:

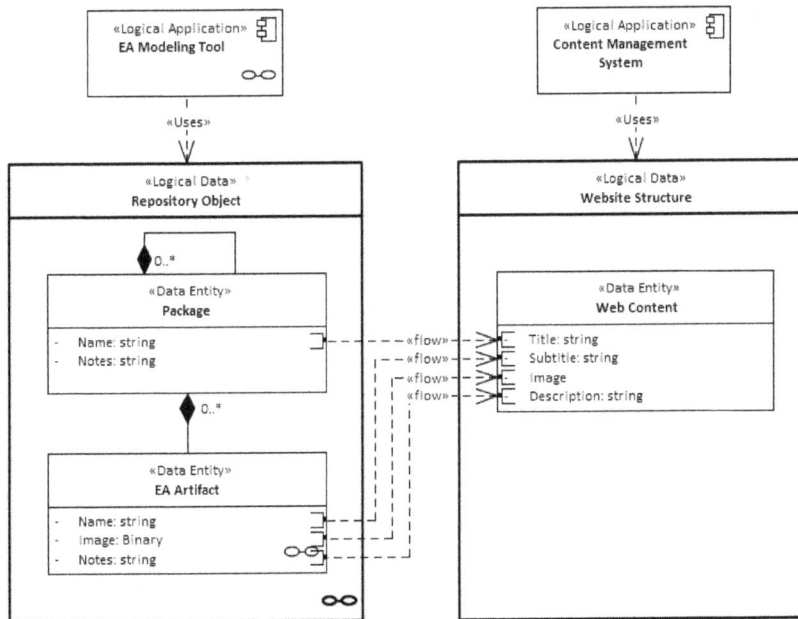

Figure 9.27: Data integration at the logical level

Two data entities from the source can be combined and mapped into one data entity at the target.

To create the flow connections between the source and the target, do the following steps:

1.   Place the source and target data entities side by side and make sure that the attributes in both are visible.

2.   Click once on the source data entity.

3.   Click once on the source attribute that you want to create the flow from. A small handle will appear on the left side of the selected attribute, as indicated in *Figure 9.28*:

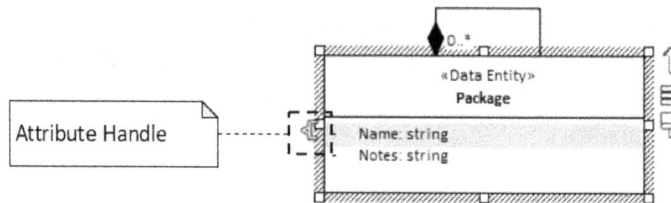

Figure 9.28: Attribute handle

4.   Click and hold the handle, drag it, and drop it on the target attribute.

5.   Select **Information Flow** from the list.

6.   A dialog box will ask you to select the information flow object. Click **OK** without selecting anything. This will close the dialog and create the flow relationship from the source attribute to the target. If the relationship's arrowhead did not connect to the desired attribute but connected to the data entity itself instead, add these extra steps to make it connect to the right attribute:

7.   Right-click on the relationship, close the arrowhead, and select **Link to Element Feature**.

8.   From the **Feature Type**, select **Attribute**.

9.   The available attributes will be listed under **Feature**. Select the desired one and click **OK**.

10. Optionally, and to hide the label, right-click on the ‹‹**Flow**›› label and select **Hide Label** from the menu.

We can show similar models at the physical level with additional levels of details. At the physical level, the same logical data can have many different physical implementations, which may require making conversions from one format to another. Let us take an example scenario to better describe how to model data integration.

Imagine having an invoicing application that uses a relational database to persist its data. To integrate the invoice data with other applications, a nightly batch job runs every day, picks up a JSON from a specific location, and sends it to an API in the integration layer to publish it.

We will model how the **Invoice.JSON** file will be structured, and how it will be extracted from the relational tables. *Figure 9.29* shows how to model it with some sample physical data components, and both sides realize the same logical data component, which is the invoice:

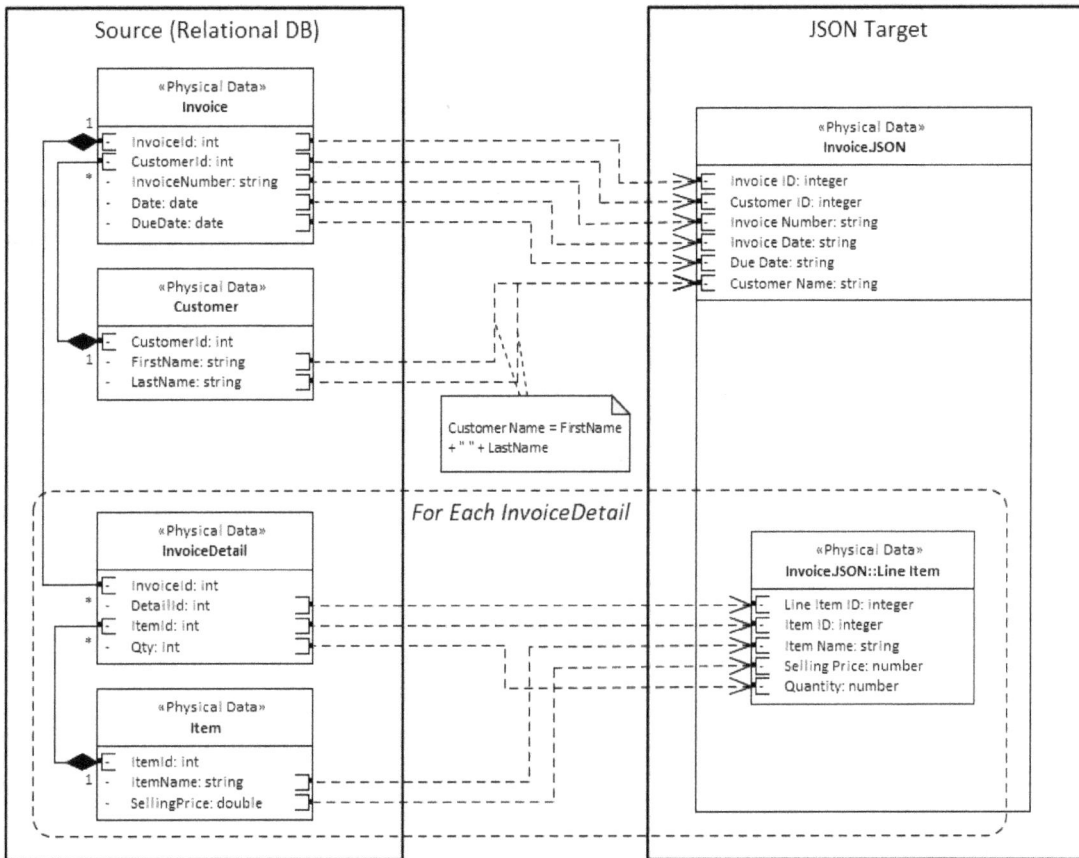

Figure 9.29: Mapping a relational source to a JSON target

Business rules for combining, splitting, or formatting fields can be mentioned on the diagram either as notes or as requirements. A loop has also been added to indicate that the highlighted section must be repeated for each invoice detail.

There will be another diagram showing how the batch job will convert the **Invoice.JSON** file into an API request, which is another JSON file. A third diagram will show how the batch job receives the response and acts according to its success or failure. We will need a separate book to model all the possible data integration patterns and what to do in case of exceptions, so we will leave that for your real-life examples, but we hope that this content will give you the kick-start that you need. A good EA repository must address the needs of its users, so you can use this example as a starting point to either go deeper with more details or keep your work at a higher level. The decision will always depend on your needs and priorities, and there is no single right way.

Conclusion

Data components can be modelled at three different levels of detail based on what we want to convey from the model and who the recipients are. Data entity models target users who are looking for definitions. Logical data models target users who want to know how data entities are logically related. The physical models target the users who need to know how data is stored or is supposed to be converted, and into what. The most important thing to keep in mind is to keep these diagrams connected so users do not lose their navigability experience.

In the following chapter, we will discuss the technology architecture layer, define the necessary stereotypes for this layer, and utilize the updated MDG to create artifacts, including examples from cloud computing environments.

Points to remember

- Integration can be modeled at the conceptual, logical, and physical levels. Every model type targets a different set of audiences.

- The business glossary is a rich source of data entities. Almost every entry in the glossary can be used to define a data entity model.

- Logical data models can show attributes, relationships, and multiplicities of the different logical data components, but they do not usually show keys or indices.

- Physical data models show the exact schema of a data store.

- EA artifact must remain at the schema description level and must not show the actual data content of a specific physical data component.

Key terms

- **Data entity**: It describes data of things that are defined or can be recognized by the business.

- **Logical data component**: A data structure that logically combines multiple data entities without concerns about how it will be implemented is known as a logical data component.

- **Physical data component**: The physical data component is a data structure that shows how a logical data component is implemented using a specific technology, such as a database table.

CHAPTER 10
Modeling Cloud Environments

Introduction

Cloud environments are forms of technology environments. Therefore, from the EA point of view, building artifacts that belong to cloud environments should not be different from building the artifacts for any on-premises technology environment. What we need to be aware of as enterprise architects is that the terminologies that the cloud industry and providers use can have a different meaning in the world of EA. What the industry defines as a service does not exactly fit within TOGAF's definition of a technology service, which can be confusing.

In this chapter, we will continue our journey in updating the MDG to include the stereotypes that we will need to build technology architecture artifacts. We will provide you with sample artifacts, and finally, we will learn how to use the image library to add a nice appearance to technology artifacts.

Structure

This chapter will include the following topics:

- Updating the MDG
- Building the technology architecture artifacts

Objectives

By the end of this chapter, you will learn how to differentiate between the three types of technology architecture artifacts, and to learn how to build useful models out of them, including the artifacts that model cloud environments.

Updating the MDG

As we did in the previous chapters, we need to update the MDG to include the three technology architecture elements that are in the TOGAF metamodel, which are the technology service, logical technology component, and physical technology component. We will start by defining the scope of work for the new iteration to update the MDG.

Defining the MDG SOW

Since we have done this section a few times in previous chapters, we will avoid repeating what we already mentioned, so let us create a new work package under the **MDG Iterations** package, and name it `Add Technology Architecture Stereotypes to the MDG`, then add four sub work packages in it as depicted in *Figure 10.1*:

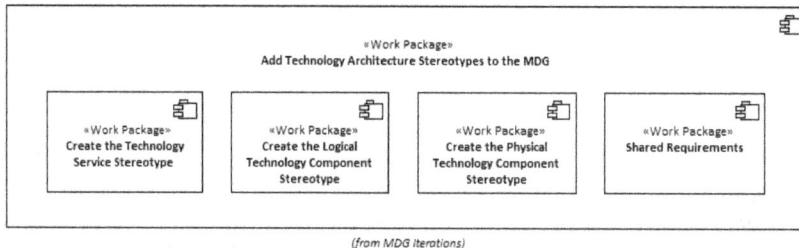

(from MDG Iterations)

Figure 10.1: Add technology architecture stereotype to the MDG work package

Now, we need to add the requirements to them to form the MDG SOW. We will start with the first work package. The first work package will contain the requirements for **Create the Technology Service Stereotype** as depicted in *Figure 10.2*:

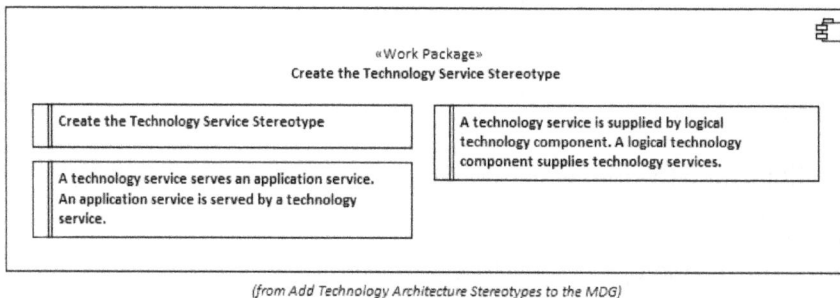

(from Add Technology Architecture Stereotypes to the MDG)

Figure 10.2: Requirements for creating the technology service stereotype

The second work package is **Create the Logical Technology Component Stereotype,** which is depicted in *Figure 10.3*:

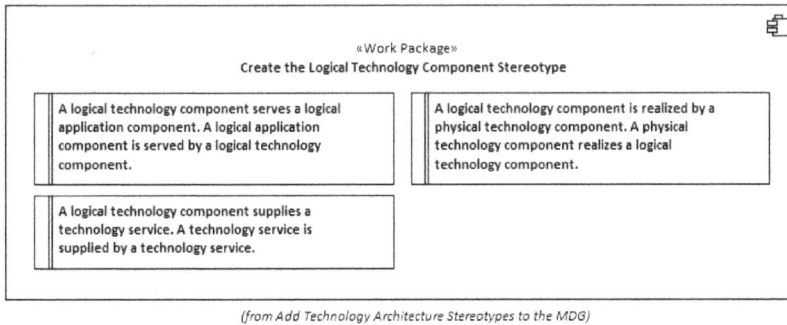

(from Add Technology Architecture Stereotypes to the MDG)

Figure 10.3: *Requirements for creating the logical technology component stereotype*

The third work package will contain the requirements to **Create the Physical Technology Component Stereotype**. The package content should be like *Figure 10.4*:

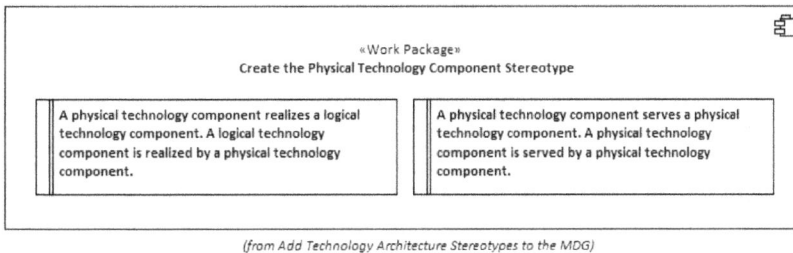

(from Add Technology Architecture Stereotypes to the MDG)

Figure 10.4: *Requirements for creating the physical technology component stereotype*

The fourth work package will contain the general shared requirements that are not specific to one stereotype, which can be seen in *Figure 10.5*:

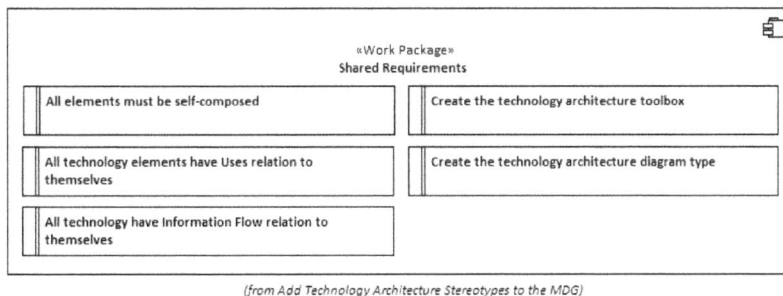

(from Add Technology Architecture Stereotypes to the MDG)

Figure 10.5: *Shared requirements for the current MDG iteration*

We have all the requirements defined. Do not forget that in the real-world, you must get these requirements approved before starting to work on them. This is part of the governance that you must define around making changes to the MDG project or to the repository project.

Working on stereotypes

If we look at the requirements of the current iteration's work packages, we will see that all the stereotypes in the business, technology, and application architecture layers have been created in *Chapter 8, Modeling Applications*. We have only one new connector stereotype that we need to define on the connector's stereotypes diagram, so let us add it.

Adding the required stereotypes to the MDG

Add a new connector stereotype for the new relationships that we have in the MDG SOW. *Figure 10.6* shows the new stereotype and its metaclass:

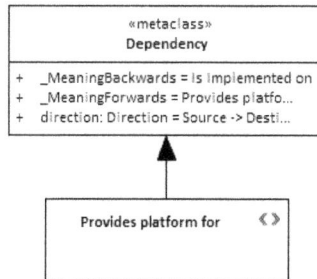

Figure 10.6: New connector stereotype

Next, we need to define the focused-metamodels for the three technology architecture layer stereotypes, starting with the technology service.

Defining the technology architecture focused-metamodels

The technology service, focused-metamodel should look like *Figure 10.7*:

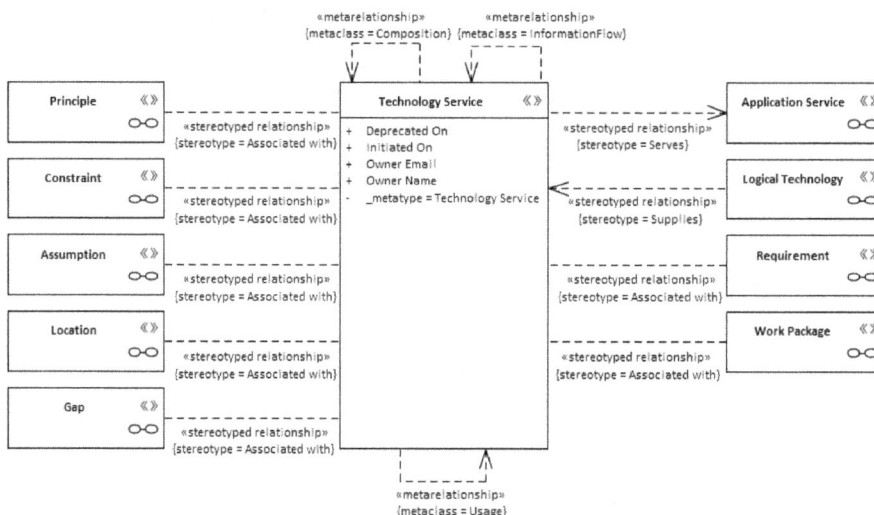

Figure 10.7: Technology service focused-metamodel

The logical technology component focused-metamodel is shown in *Figure 10.8*:

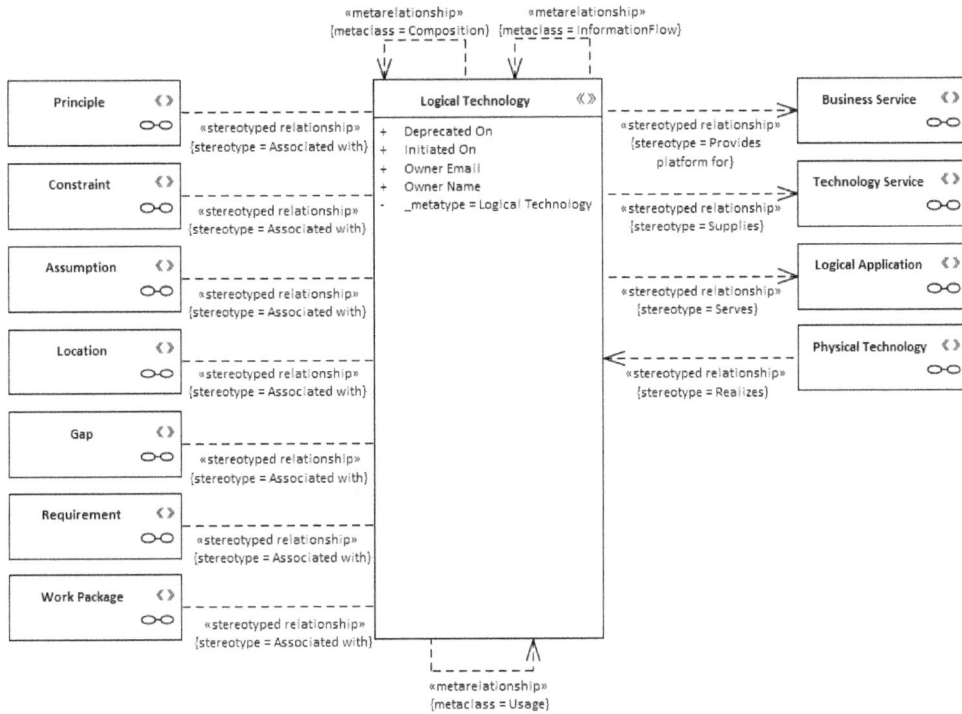

Figure 10.8: *Logical technology component focused-metamodel*

The physical technology component focused-metamodel is shown in *Figure 10.9*:

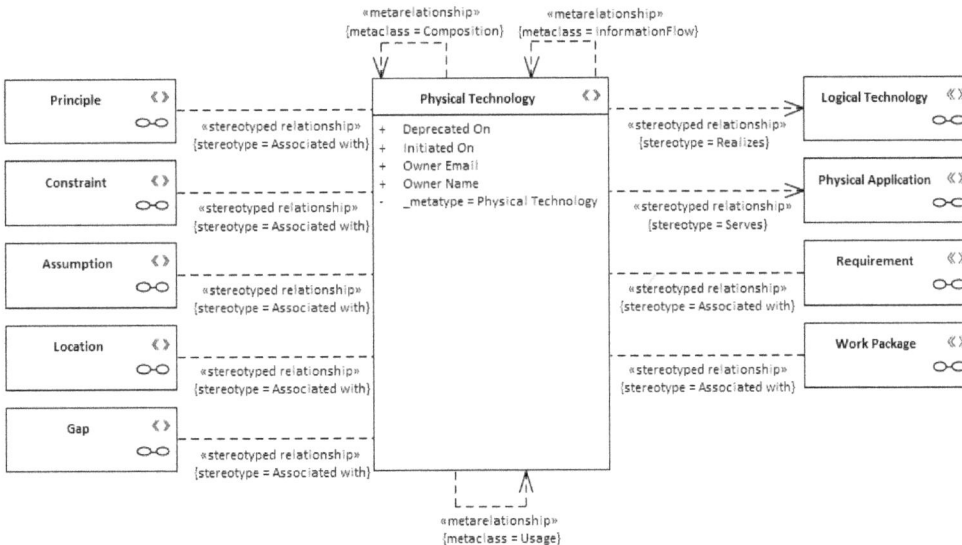

Figure 10.9: *Physical technology component focused-metamodel*

We have all the stereotypes that we need, so the next step is to create the technology architecture toolbox.

Creating the technology architecture toolbox

We will create a toolbox to contain all the technology architecture stereotypes. The technology architecture toolbox should look like *Figure 10.10*:

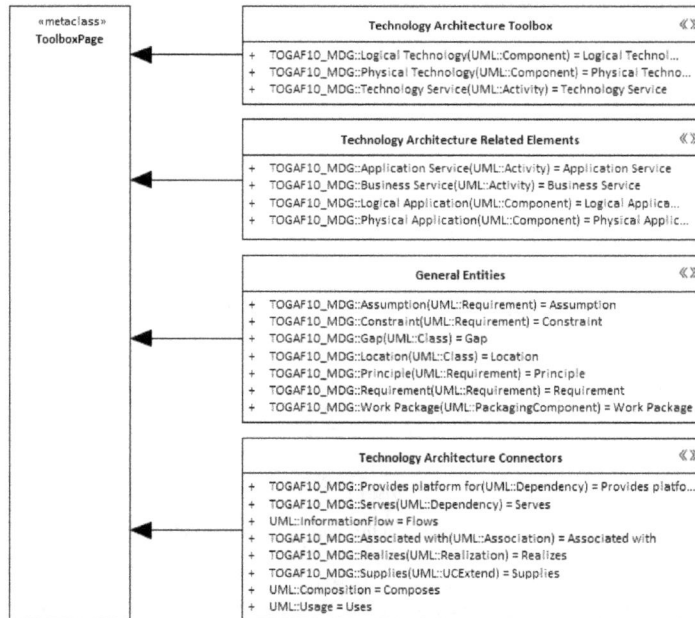

Figure 10.10: *Technology architecture toolbox*

When you finish defining the toolbox, add a navigation cell on the main toolbox's profiles diagram, as depicted in *Figure 10.11*:

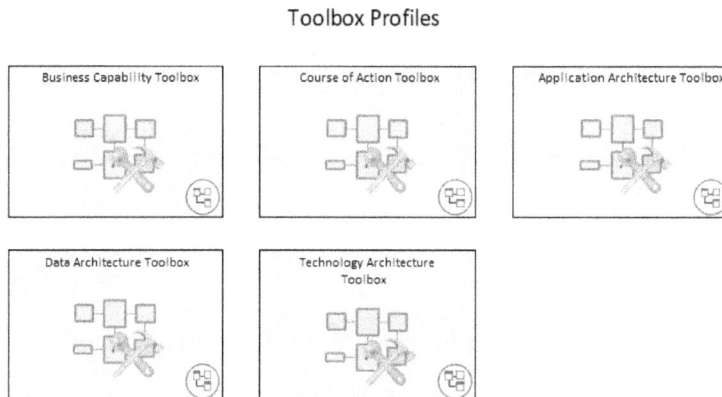

Figure 10.11: *Toolbox's profiles*

Next, we will create a diagram type for technology architecture artifacts and associate it with the technology architecture toolbox.

Creating the technology architecture diagram type

Figure 10.12 shows the custom diagram profiles page with all the diagram types on it:

Custom Diagram Profiles

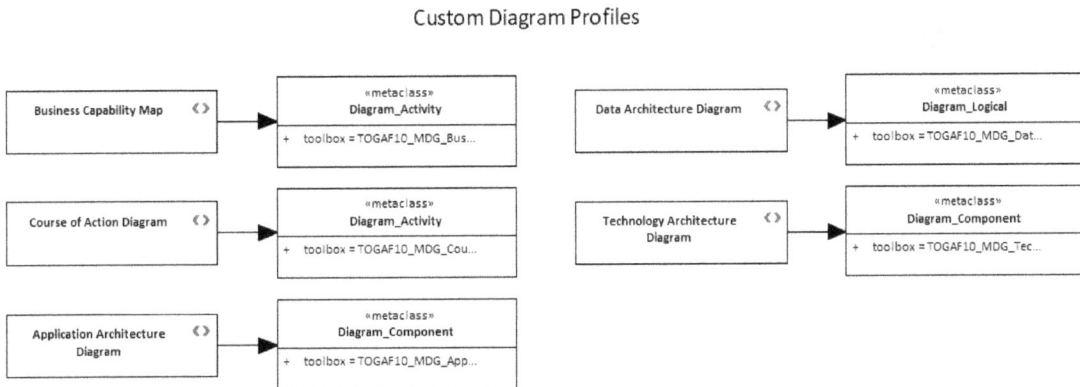

***Figure 10.12**: Custom diagram profiles*

Link the technology architecture diagram type to the technology architecture toolbox by adding the **toolbox** attribute to its metaclass and setting its initial value to **TOGAF10_MDG_ Technology_Architecture_Toolbox** or to the name that you have used if it is different.

Lastly, go back to the three technology architecture stereotypes, the technology service, logical technology component, and physical technology component, and set the initial value of the **_defaultDiagramType** attribute to **TOGAF10_MDG::Technology Architecture Diagram**.

Publish and test the MDG before using it to build technology architecture artifacts. When everything works as desired in the testing project, import the MDG to the main repository. Let us now create some technology architecture artifacts.

Building the technology architecture artifacts

The technology architecture artifacts describe the technology infrastructure components and how they can relate at three levels of abstraction: the service level or the conceptual level, the logical level, and the physical level. The technology architecture components include all the software and hardware components that serve the application architecture components. Refer to *Chapter 8, Modeling Application Components*, for a more detailed understanding of application architecture components and artifacts. When it comes to hardware components, it is very easy to identify them as technology architecture components. When it comes to software, it can be confusing to differentiate between what can be identified as an application component or a technology component.

The dividing line is to know how much the component is related to business rules. If specific software runs within your business environment in almost the same way it does in other business environments, then it is commodity software; therefore, it is a technology architecture component. Windows operating system, Norton Internet Security, Office 365, and Citrix NetScaler load balancer are examples of technology architecture software components. Some of them need configuration, of course, to work properly in their environments, but they rarely implement any specific business rules. Software components that contain business rules are considered application architecture components such as billing, customer relationship, sales, and inventory systems are all examples of application architecture components.

In this section, we will learn with examples the three abstraction levels of technology architecture artifacts, starting with the technology services.

Modeling technology services

A technology service is a *technical capability required to provide enabling infrastructure that supports the delivery of applications* (**https://pubs.opengroup.org/togaf-standard/architecture-content/ chap02.html**). A technology service is a technical capability based on the definition, which means that it is not the programmable or the configurable part of the infrastructure, but more likely the outcome, or the technical capability that we get from it.

The TOGAF **Technical Reference Model (TRM)** (**https://pubs.opengroup.org/togaf-standard/ reference-models/trm.html#_Toc513102739**) defines the technical service categories that can be applicable to any enterprise, as depicted in *Figure 10.13*:

Technology Services Catalog

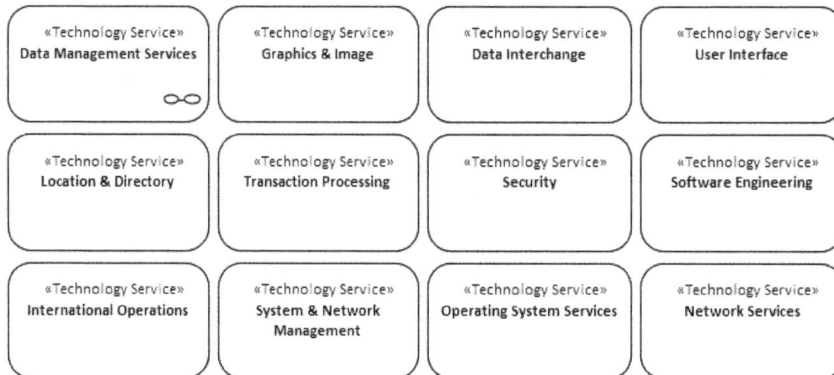

Figure 10.13: Technology services catalog

You can break down the high-level technology services in the catalog into smaller and more meaningful services if more explanation is needed. **Data Management Services** technology service, for example, can be broken down into smaller technology services, as depicted in *Figure 10.14*:

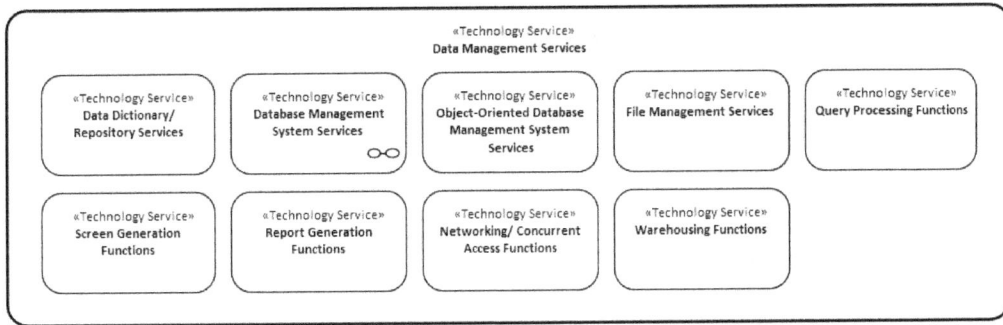

Figure 10.14: A detailed view of a technology service

You can use the TRM to build a hierarchy of technology service catalogs, or you can limit your models to the technology services that your enterprise uses and add more services when you need them. Each technology service from *Figure 10.14* can be detailed, on its own diagram depicting its sub technology services, if any, what the application services are that it serves, and which logical technology component supplies the technology service, as you can see in *Figure 10.15*:

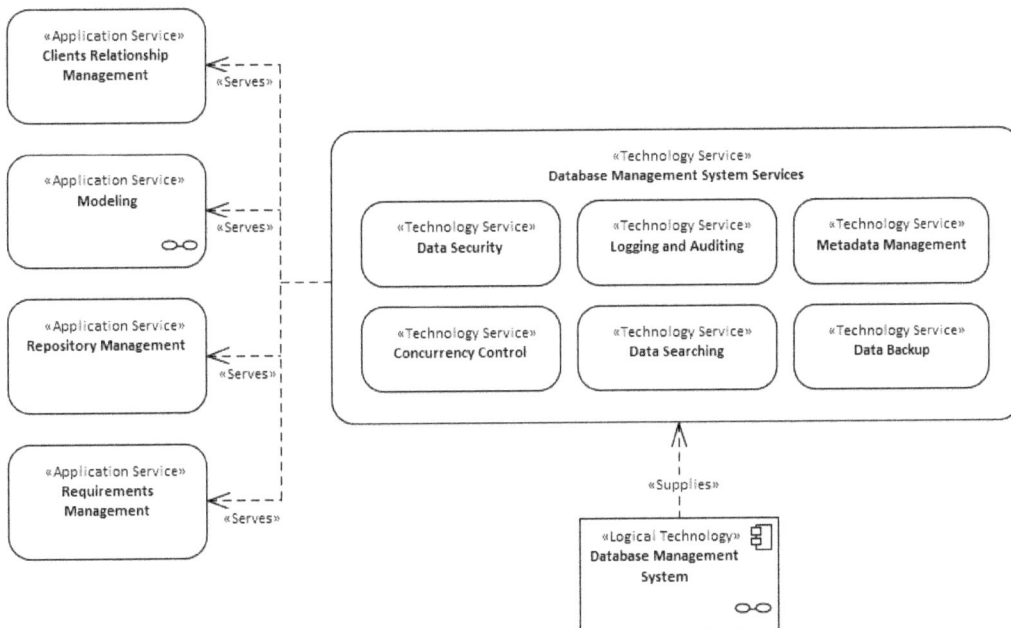

Figure 10.15: Database Management System Technology Service

Once your diagram starts to contain components that indicate a system or a physical component, then your diagram is ready to describe another level of abstraction in the technology architecture layer, which is the logical technology components. In the next section, let us learn how to model logical technology components.

Modeling logical technology components

A logical technology component is *an implementation-independent encapsulation of technology services* (**https://pubs.opengroup.org/togaf-standard/architecture-content/chap02.html**). The definition clearly indicates that it is implementation-independent, which means that a logical technology component must be defined at the functionality level without mentioning what technology or products implement it. *Figure 10.16* models the **Database Management System** logical technology component, which supplies the Database Management System Services and all its sub services, it serves the EA Modeling Tool logical application component and is realized by four specific database management system products:

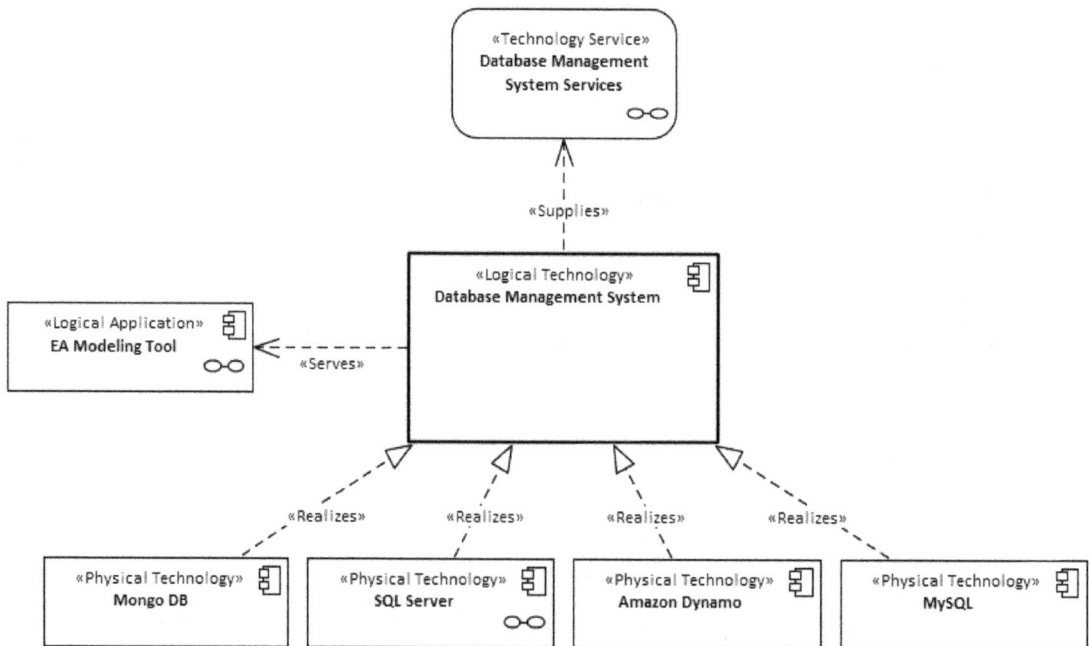

Figure 10.16: Database management system logical technology component

Keep in mind the following points regarding real-world logical technology component models:

- If the logical technology component does not supply all the sub technology services that compose the parent technology service, then the model must contain only the sub technology services that are supplied by the logical technology component.

- The actual list of the logical application components that will be served by a single logical technology component can be long. The actual list of physical technology components can easily grow. This means that *Figure 10.16* must be turned into a home page with nested sub diagrams to avoid the complexity.

- The list of the physical technology components must include only the products that your enterprise uses, not a generic list of all database products.

Other examples of logical technology components are virus protection software, message broker, load balancer, operating system, file system, and transaction manager. They are still considered abstract and do not reflect what product or tool is used, but they indicate a single entity that provides (in other words, supplies) the desired technological services. When we start describing an actual product implementation, we are describing the technology layer at the physical component level, which will be covered in the next subsection.

Modeling physical technology components

The physical technology component is defined by TOGAF as, a *realization of logical technology functionality using a particular technology product that may be deployed,* (**https://pubs.opengroup. org/togaf-standard/architecture-content/chap02.html**). As you can understand from the definition, a particular technology product is the physical technology component. *Figure 10.17* models the **SQL Server** physical technology component:

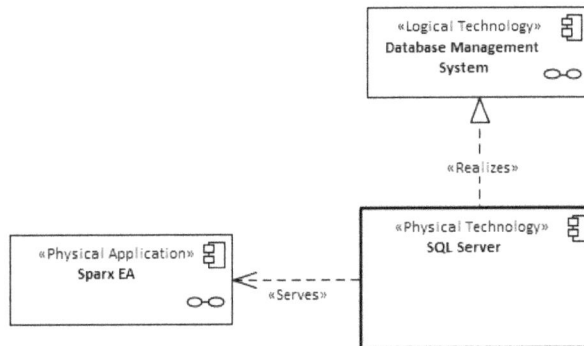

Figure 10.17: SQL Server physical technology component

It shows how it realizes the **Database Management System** logical technology component and how it serves the **Sparx EA** physical application component. In real-world examples, the diagram must list all the physical applications that use SQL Server as a backend database server. If the list becomes too long, it is always better to create a separate diagram and create a link to it.

If your enterprise uses multiple versions of a specific physical technology component, say for example, SQL Server 2016, SQL Server 2019, and SQL Server 2022, then each version can be represented by a different physical technology component since different versions may serve different physical application components and may realize different logical technology components. In other words, the different versions of a single product can be treated as different products if the enterprise uses and supports them individually.

Do not get confused between a physical technology model and a technology deployment model. For instance, if our enterprise contains several instances of this same product deployed on multiple servers, we must still have a single SQL Server physical technology component in our repository. All the deployed instances must be instantiated from the single physical technology component that we have in the architecture content package. Deployment models belong to the solutions architecture, which can be built in the Solutions Landscape package in the enterprise repository. We will take a simple example of a solution architecture artifact in the next subsection, when we talk about modeling cloud components.

Modeling cloud components

Modeling cloud artifacts is not different from modeling other physical artifacts. There are conceptual components or technology services, logical technology components, and physical technology components. The biggest confusing part, when it comes to cloud artifacts, is that what cloud providers define as services is not in alignment with TOGAF's definition of a technology service. If we take **Amazon Web Services** (**AWS**) as an example, Amazon VPC is not a technology service by the TOGAF definition but a physical technology component, since it is a realization of a logical technology component using a particular technological product. *Figure 10.18* shows how Amazon VPC fits within the hierarchy of technology architecture components:

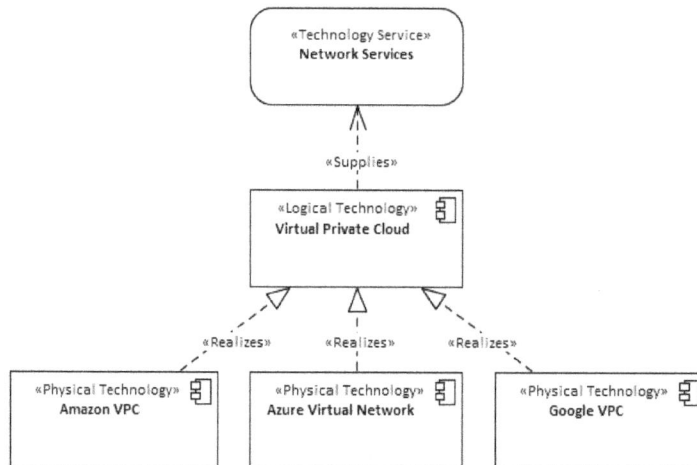

Figure 10.18: *Service vs logical vs physical cloud technology components*

If cloud environments are entirely virtual to us, then how come we have physical technology components? It may look odd and against what the cloud industry is using; however, remember that we are using TOGAF as the chosen framework, and this is how it defines services and components. Since customizing TOGAF and its metamodel is not within the scope of this book, we will accept what the definitions dictate.

As we have learned earlier in this section, the technology architecture artifacts can describe the technology layer at a conceptual, logical, and physical level of detail. The cloud artifacts are technology architecture artifacts, and therefore, everything that we learned applies to them. A model like *Figure 10.18* is perfectly acceptable as technology architecture artifact that contains components from cloud providers. However, people are used to see cloud artifacts with nice colorful and iconic symbols, so you may need to consider adding images to your diagrams just to keep your users familiar with what they used to see.

We will look at some examples to learn how to model cloud artifacts using AWS images, and the same steps can be followed for Azure and Google clouds. The first step is to import the images library of the cloud provider to give our artifacts the look and feel of cloud diagrams.

Importing the AWS library

Sparx EA comes with many image libraries, which you can use to give your diagrams a more professional and vivid look. Since there are many image libraries for many industry standards and service providers, they are not included by default; hence, you must import them into your projects before using them. You can import the image library to any package of your choice; however, in *Chapter 5, Structuring the Repository*, we created the **Reference Library** model package, which can be perfectly used for this purpose. Follow these steps to import the AWS image library to the reference library package:

1. Open the **Reference Library** model package.

2. The AWS images are considered external resources because they were not created by our organization, so open the **External** view package.

3. Create a new package and name it **Images**.

4. Right-click on the package and select **Model Builder (pattern library)** from the context menu.

5. The **Model Builder** dialog will open. Click on the hamburger menu, which is a menu icon that has three short horizontal bars and select **All** to list all the perspectives.

6. Scroll down until you find the **Amazon Web Services** package. Open it and select the desired release version, such as **Release 7,** as indicated in *Figure 10.19*:

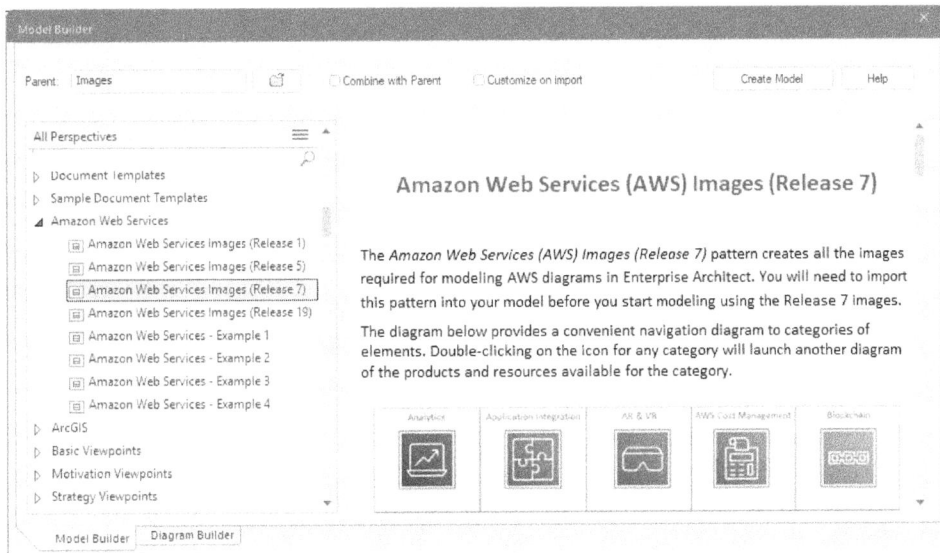

Figure 10.19: Importing the AWS image library

7. Click **Create Model** button to create the library.

Sparx EA will take a minute or two to create the image library in the selected location. Once it finishes, open the **AWS** diagram and explore the images to get yourself familiar with how they are categorized. The top-level diagram contains the service categories or groups, such as **Analytics**, **Application Integration**, and **AR & VR**. Double-clicking on any group icon will navigate you to the images of the products and the resources that belong to that service group. *Figure 10.20* shows the content of the **Compute** package on the left side, where all the elements are stereotyped as images:

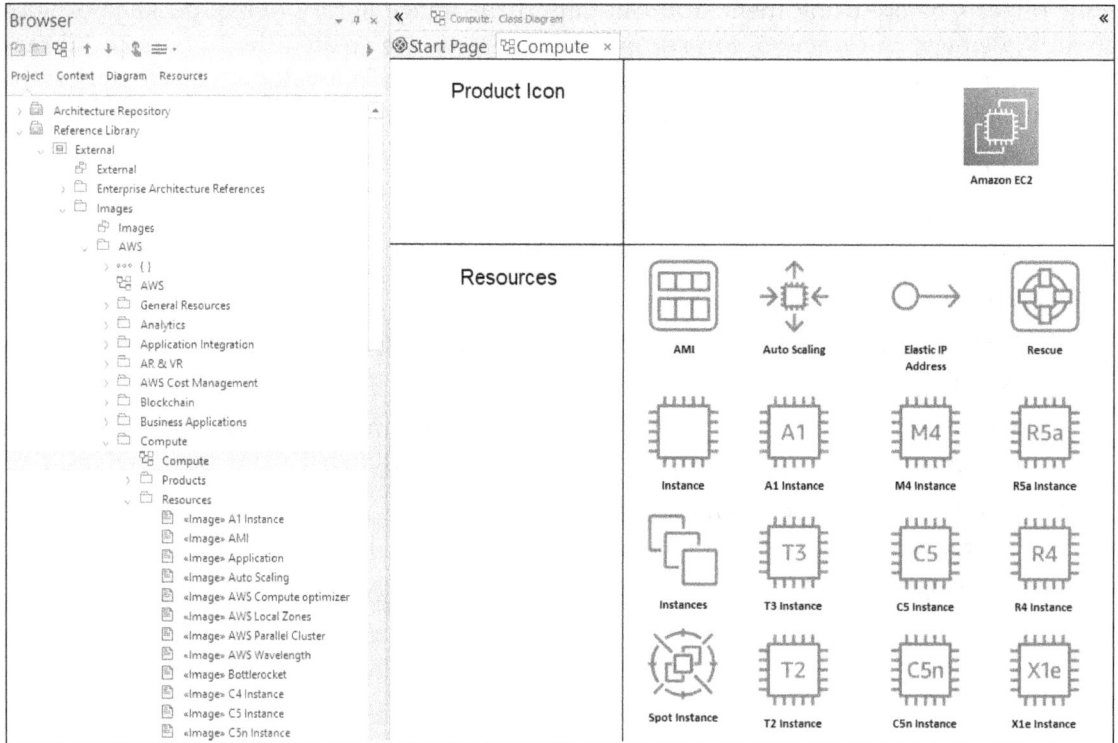

Figure 10.20: *Compute products and image resources*

On the right side of the diagram, you can see the content of the **Compute** diagram, which helps you to visually spot the icon that you are intending to use. If you want to use the **C5 Instance**, for example, right-click on the **C5 Instance** icon on the diagram, select **Find | In Project Browser,** or press **Alt+G** to highlight the image in the **Project Browser**.

Once the desired image is highlighted, it is ready to be used. Images from libraries can be used in two different ways. You can either apply them to existing elements or use them to create brand new elements. We will explore both ways of adding images to components so you can have the flexibility to choose the one that suits you best.

Adding images to components

The easiest way to apply images to a model from an image library is to locate them in the browser, drag and drop them onto the target object, and then set the images as alternate images. Keep in mind that because images are vendor-specific, we want to add them only to the physical components. Otherwise, we will be imposing a vendor-specific implementation on logical and conceptual components, which should not be the case.

Note: **Since images are vendor-specific, they must be applied to the physical components only.**

Let us take, for example, a diagram like *Figure 10.21*, which lists some of the physical subcomponents of Amazon VPC:

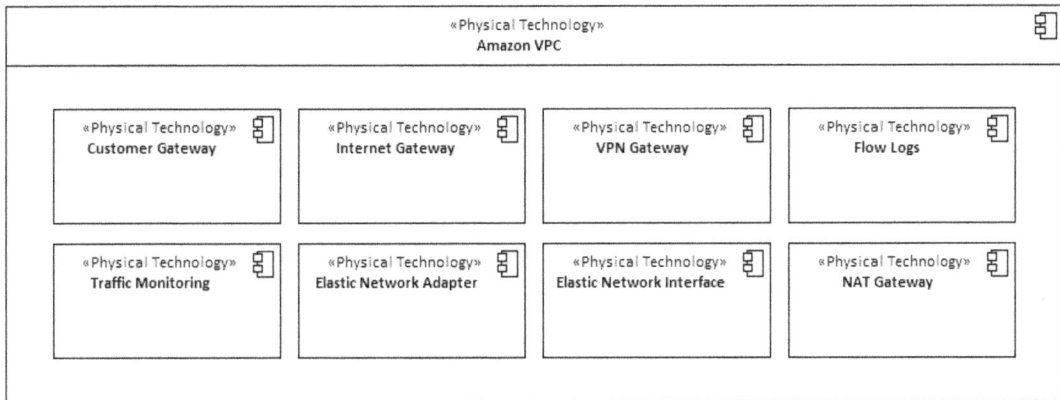

Figure 10.21: Amazon VPC subcomponents

We need to add the proper images to the existing components and add the remaining Amazon VPC subcomponents that are not listed.

Follow these steps to add the images from the library:

1. Keep the diagram in *Figure 10.21* opened in its own tab.

2. Locate the image library and locate the proper package that contains Amazon VPC, which is the **Network & Content Delivery** package.

3. Open the **Network & Content Delivery** diagram, and you will see a grid of two rows, one for the products and the other for the resources.

4. Scroll to the right until you find the **Amazon VPC** product. All the resources that are listed underneath it can be considered as Amazon VPC subcomponents.

5. Click on the **Customer Gateway** icon on the diagram and find it in the **Project Browser**.

6. Click the tab that contains the Amazon VPC diagram.

7. Drag the **Customer Gateway** image from the **Project Browser** and drop it on the **Customer Gateway** physical technology component.

8. Select **Set as Alternate Image** from the menu.

9. Adjust the size of the **Customer Gateway** physical component to a square shape instead of the standard rectangular shape. Use the **Width** and **Height** information in the status bar to make a perfect square shape.

10. Optionally, and to show the name of the component and its stereotype, right-click on the **Customer Gateway** physical technology component and select **Appearance |** **Show Name Under Image**.

11. Adjust the stereotype label and move it where it does not cover the component's name.

12. Repeat *Steps 3* through *11* for all the subcomponents.

    There are still subcomponents for Amazon VPC that are not on the diagram yet, so we need to add them with their proper images. Continue with the following steps:

13. Keep the **Amazon VPC** diagram open.

14. Open the **Network & Content Delivery** diagram if you already closed it.

15. Find the **Endpoints** resource on the diagram, click on it, then press Alt + G to find the image in the **Project Browser**.

16. Open the tab that contains the Amazon VPC diagram.

17. Click on the **Endpoints** image from the **Project Browser**, drag it, and drop it onto the diagram.

18. Select **Add as element with image** from the context menu. A dialog like *Figure 10.22* will pop up to know what type of element you want to create:

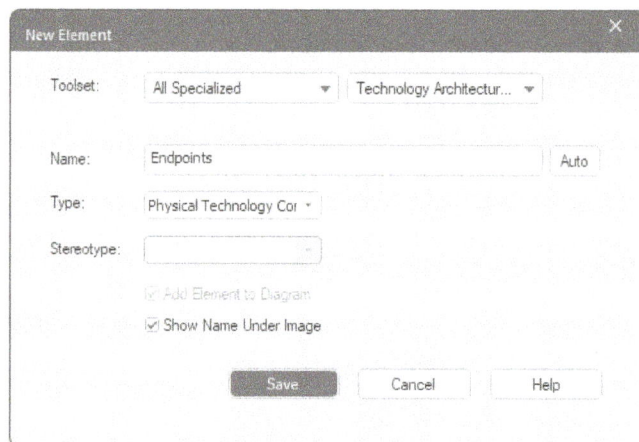

Figure 10.22: New element dialog

19. Select **All Specialized** from the **Toolset** dropdown, then select **TOGAF10_MDG |
    Technology Architecture Toolbox** to specify which toolbox your element will be
    created from.

20. Select **Physical Technology Component** from the **Type** dropdown list.

21. Click **Save** to accept the setting and create the new element with the specifications that
    we have provided. The element will automatically have the image that we dragged
    from the **Project Browser**.

22. Repeat *steps 13* through *21* to create all the remaining Amazon VPC subcomponents.

The diagram should look like *Figure 10.23*, which provides a better visual representation about
Amazon VPC than *Figure 10.21*:

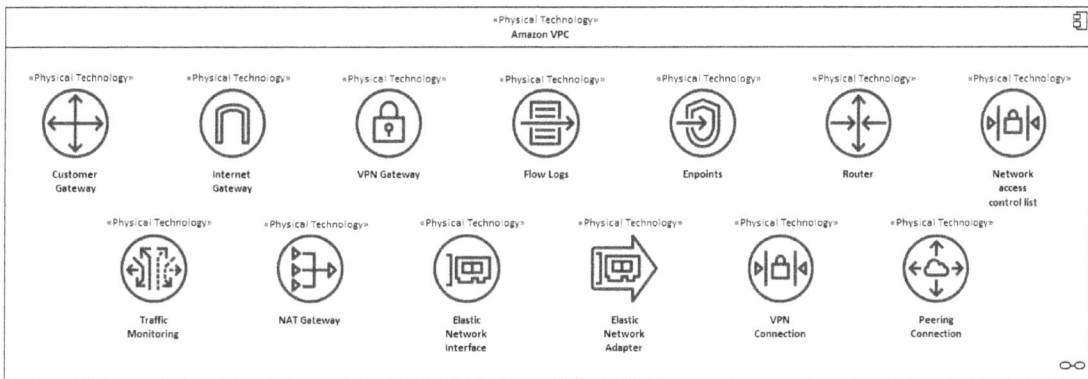

Figure 10.23: *Enhanced Amazon VPC diagram*

From an architecture perspective, the two diagrams, i.e. *Figure 10.21* and *Figure 10.23*, represent
the same component.

The only physical technology component that we need to add an image to is the Amazon VPC
itself. Since it is a container object, applying an image to it using the same way that we used for
the subcomponents will make the image fill and cover the entire area of the component, which
is not what we need. We need to have a small icon on the side of the containing component
that does not cover any content. To do this, we need to take an extra step and enable the
custom drawing style.

Enabling the custom drawing style

The custom drawing style is an extra feature that enables us to customize how components on
a diagram look. It gives us the ability to customize where a component name appears, such as
top left, top right, bottom left, bottom right, or center, instead of the default top center location.
It allows us to make the name go from the top to the bottom or from the bottom to the top. It
allows us to set an image as an icon, decide its size, and where we want it to appear.

Follow these steps to set the Amazon VPC image as an icon to the Amazon VPC component, and make it appear in the top right corner of the shape:

1. Keep the **Amazon VPC** diagram open.

2. Right-click on the Amazon VPC physical technology component and select **Appearance | Enable Custom Draw Style**.

   Now we need to add the icon to the component.

3. Open the **Network & Content Delivery** diagram if you already closed it.

4. Find the Amazon VPC image in the **Project Browser**.

5. Open the tab that contains the Amazon VPC diagram.

6. Drag the image, drop it on the Amazon VPC physical technology component, and select **Set as icon** from the menu.

   You will see that the Amazon VPC name and the physical technology stereotype have been moved to the center of the diagram, and this is not the position that we want. So we need to adjust the location of the component's labels.

7. Click again on the Amazon VPC physical component, and you will see that a new brush-shaped handle has been added to the list of handles. See *Figure 10.24* for guidance:

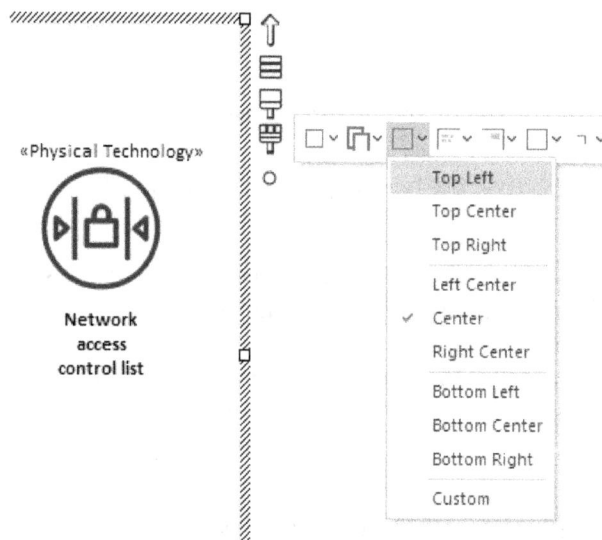

Figure 10.24: Custom drawing style menu

8. Click on the new brush icon to use the custom drawing style features.

9. Use the **Top Left** menu option to move the component's name and stereotype labels to the top left corner of the component area.

Explore the other options under the custom drawing style menu and discover the new styling flexibility that this feature provides. The final Amazon VPC diagram must look like the one shown in *Figure 10.25*:

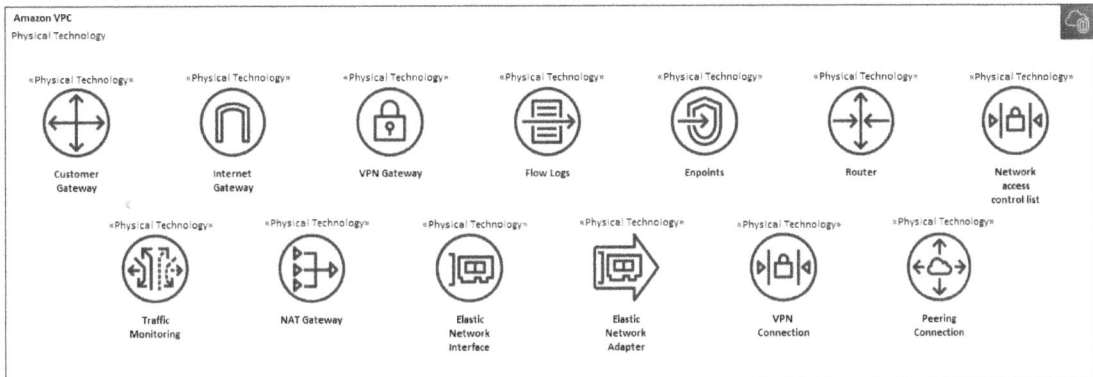

Figure 10.25: *Amazon VPC final diagram*

Many people think that Sparx EA diagrams are always dull; conversely, we have learned that with some extra effort, we can create very nice-looking diagrams while maintaining the integrity of our EA repository and its artifacts. Nothing is free, of course, so you must ask yourself and your project sponsors if they are willing to invest in the extra effort to get more appealing diagrams, or to set the effort on something else. Always remember that the key success factor when building an EA repository is managing the scope and the priorities, considering it is very easy to deviate from what you are supposed to be doing.

All the artifacts that we have built and enriched our repository with so far are architecture content artifacts that describe the components and how they are related to other components. What we have not given an example of yet is how to model a deployable solution artifact, so let us see how.

Modeling a solution artifact

Solution artifacts describe how the architecture components can fit together to make up a solution. Architecture content artifacts describe components as definitions and relationships; hence, every element has a single representation in the repository. Solution artifacts on the other hand describe how many architecture elements are needed for a solution, how these elements will be connected, and how they will be deployed. Elements of solutions artifacts are instances of architecture content elements. *Figure 10.26* shows a sample solution artifacts of a generic cloud environment:

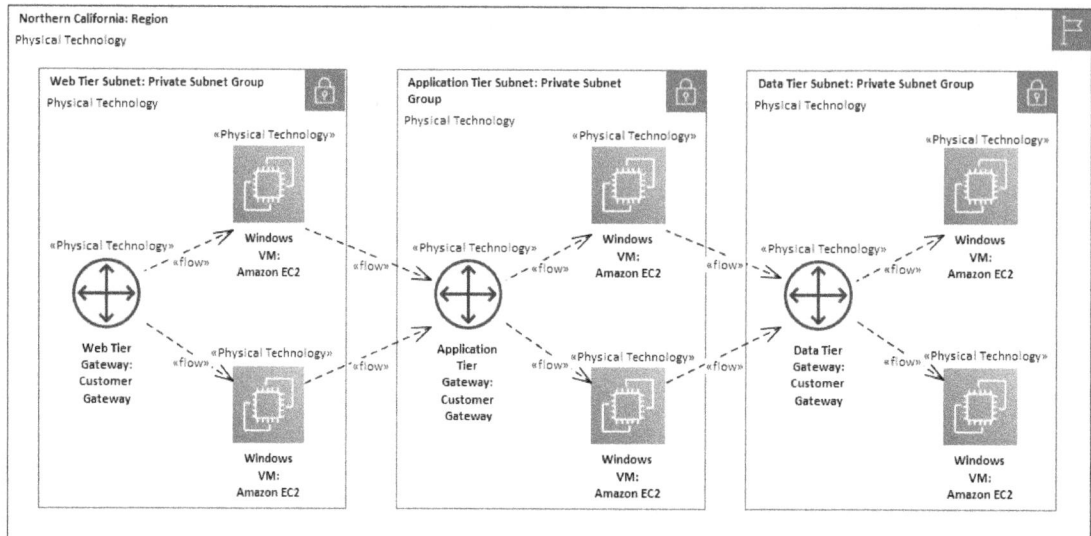

Figure 10.26: Sample AWS deployment artifact

All the elements that you see in the diagram are instances of elements in the architecture content repository. The **Web Tier Gateway**, **Application Tier Gateway**, and **Data Tier Gateway** are all instances of the **Customer Gateway** physical technology component. All the **Windows VMs** are instances of the **Amazon EC2** physical technology component, and all subnets are instances of the **Private Subnet Group** physical technology component.

To create an instance of any object in the architecture definition repository, simply drag the element, drop it on the deployment diagram, and select **Drop as | Instance (Component)** from the dialog box. A single customer gateway physical technology component can have hundreds of instances deployed by many solutions in the enterprise, so it is important to bear in mind the difference between the two.

Conclusion

Technology architecture artifacts describe the hardware and software that make up the technical infrastructure of the organization. These artifacts can be at three levels of detail, and each is targeting a different set of audiences. The conceptual level of detail describes what services a technology layer provides, the logical level of detail groups and encapsulates technology services into a logical component, and the physical level of detail describes the actual products that are used to build the technology layer.

Cloud components are specialized components of the technology architecture components. Ironically, what the cloud industry refers to as a service is considered a physical technology component from the TOGAF definition point of view, and this is something that you need to bear in mind always when using terminologies from other industries, as some of them do not align with TOGAF's definitions. We faced this issue in this chapter as well in *Chapter 8, Modeling Applications*, but since TOGAF is our chosen framework, we will adhere to its definitions and build our repository accordingly.

In the next chapter, we will learn about artifacts from the business architecture layer, such as the business services, functions, processes, and actors, and how they relate to other components in the enterprise.

Points to remember

- Technology architecture components are also known as the infrastructure components, and they represent all the software and hardware that make up the technology platform in an enterprise.

- Software technology architecture components are commodity software that do not contain business rules.

- A single technology service can be supplied by multiple logical technology components, and a single logical technology component can supply multiple technology services.

- A single logical technology component can be realized by many physical technology components, and a single physical technology component can realize many logical technology components.

- If the enterprise runs multiple versions of the same product, each version can be treated as a separate physical technology component.

- A physical technology component can be instantiated many times to create deployable solutions that comprise instances of the physical technology components.

- Most of the cloud services that we know from the big cloud computing providers are considered as physical technology components in a TOGAF EA repository, not as services.

Key terms

- **Technology service**: It is a technical capability at the infrastructure level.

- **Logical technology component**: A generic name that describes the functionality that a component must perform is termed a logical technology component.

- **Physical technology component**: The actual product used to realize the logical components is known as the physical technology component.

Join our Discord space

Join our Discord workspace for latest updates, offers, tech happenings around the world, new releases, and sessions with the authors:

https://discord.bpbonline.com

CHAPTER 11
Modeling Business Services

Introduction

For a business to exist, it needs to provide services to consumers. Business services are the external parts of a business that are available for the service consumers to interact with. When a person wants to know about a specific organization, the first thing they check is its service offering. A business service is what the consumer wants from the business without being interested in how it is internally performed. The behavioral elements that describe how business services are internally performed are the Functions and the Processes. Functions provide a conceptual internal view of how the business services are performed, while Processes provide more detailed step-by-step instructions.

In this chapter, we will understand the similarities and the differences between business services, Functions, and Processes, how they interact with each other, and how different actors interact with them, all with simple yet practical examples.

Structure

This chapter will include the following topics:

- Updating the MDG
- Building the business architecture artifacts

Objectives

The objective of this chapter is to learn how to differentiate between business services, Functions, and Processes, and learn how to model them.

Updating the MDG

Following the same trend of previous chapters, we will update the MDG to include the new stereotypes that we need for creating this chapter's artifacts, and the first step, as we know, is defining the MDG SOW.

Defining the MDG SOW

You should be familiar now with how to interpret the TOGAF metamodel and extract the MDG SOW requirements from it, so we will skip that part. We will need a work package for adding the business service stereotype to the MDG, a second for the Process stereotype, a third for the Function stereotype, and a fourth for the actor stereotype. We will need a fifth package for the shared requirements, as depicted in *Figure 11.1*:

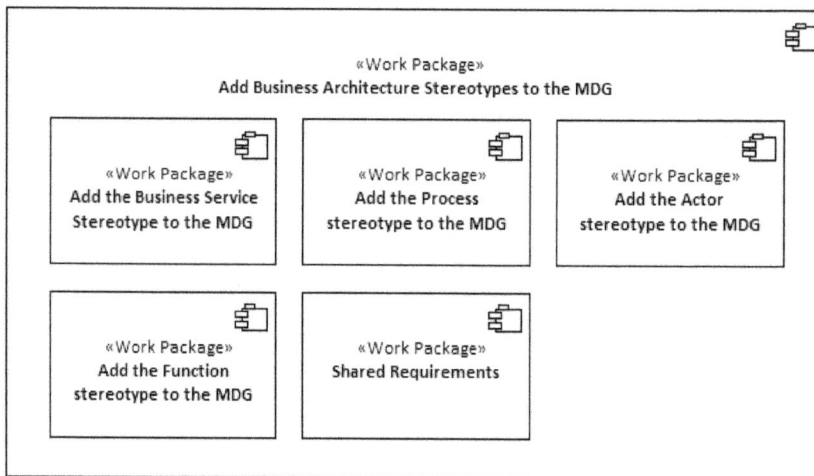

(from MDG Iterations)

Figure 11.1: Adding business architecture stereotypes to the MDG

When we have the requirements approved, we will update the MDG project accordingly, starting with the stereotypes.

Working on stereotypes

The requirements that we identify in every MDG SOW state what changes must be made to the MDG to be able to support the new types of artifacts. The stereotypes are divided into two groups: the elements stereotypes and the connectors stereotypes. Since the business service, Process, Function, and actor elements are connected to many other elements as identified in the TOGAF metamodel, the list of the new stereotypes to be created is longer than what we usually had in the previous chapters, so be ready for a large amount of work. We will start with the connectors' stereotypes first.

Adding the required connectors' stereotypes

Figure 11.2 list the new connectors' stereotypes, and their suggested metaclasses that will be added to the MDG for the current iteration:

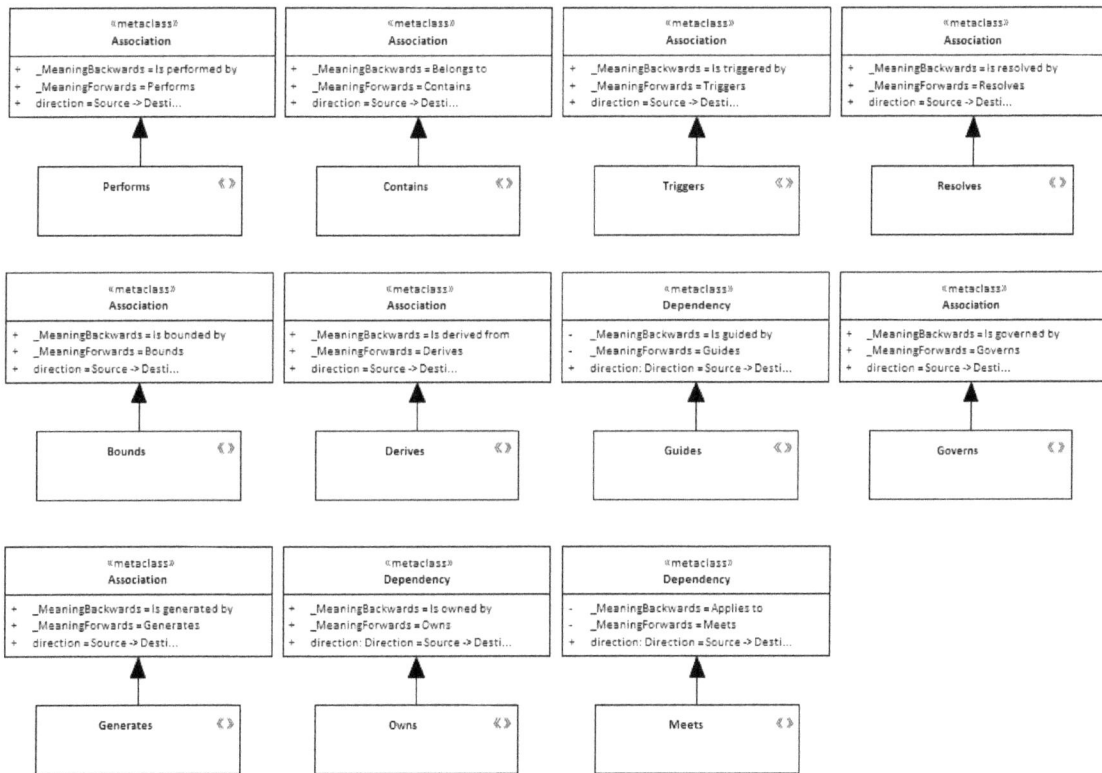

Figure 11.2: New connectors' stereotypes

Next, we need to define the focused-metamodels for the elements' stereotypes, starting with the business service.

Defining the business service focused-metamodels

The business service focused-metamodel should look like *Figure 11.3*:

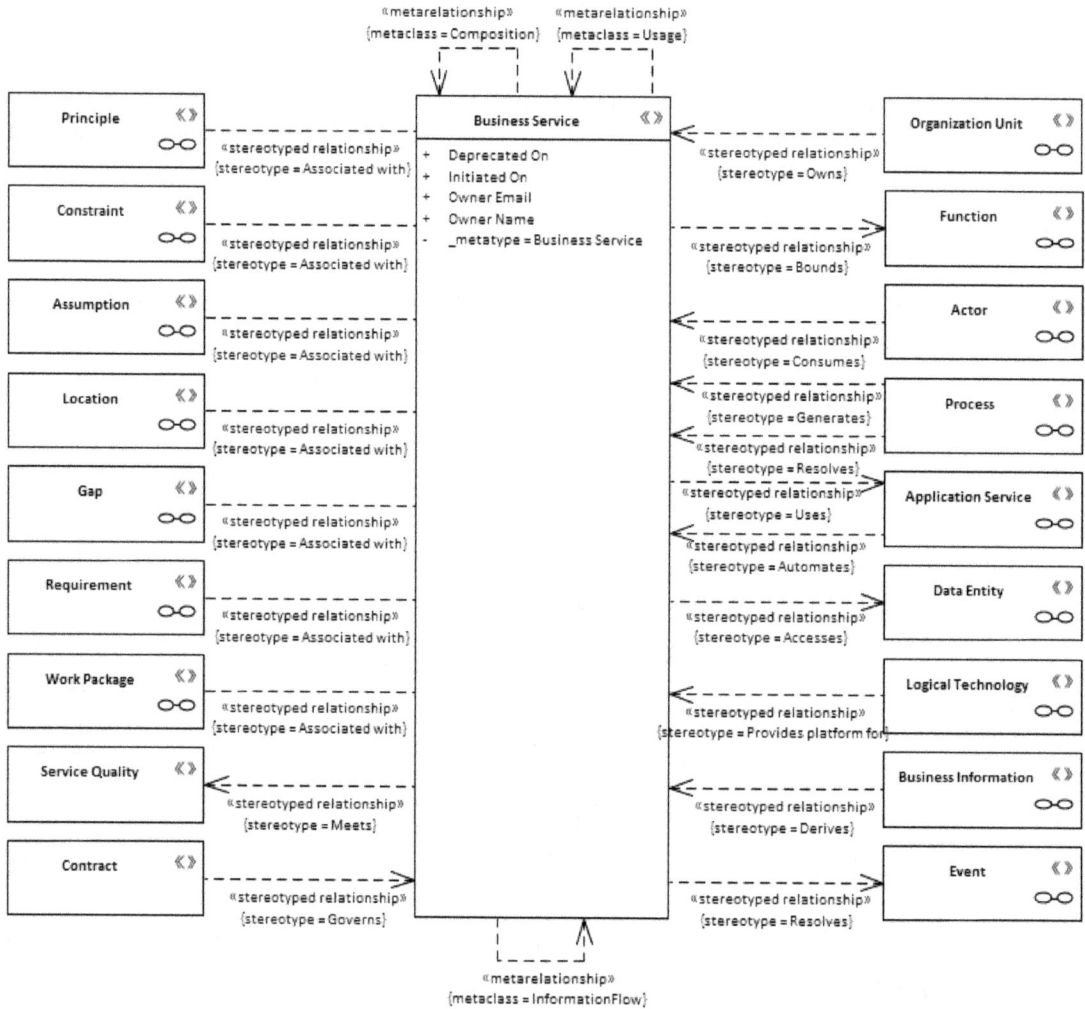

Figure 11.3: Business service focused-metamodel

The next focused-metamodel is the Function.

Defining the Function focused-metamodel

The Function focused-metamodel is depicted in *Figure 11.4*:

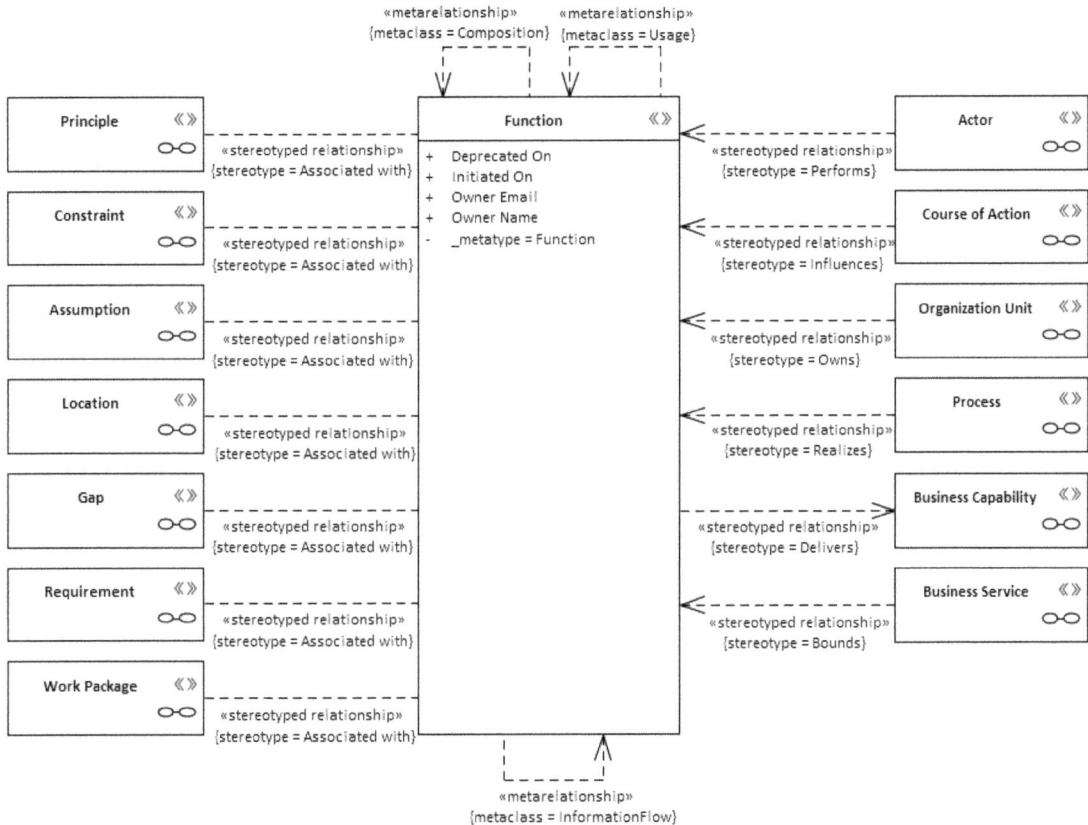

Figure 11.4: Function focused-metamodel

The next focused-metamodel is the Process.

Defining the Process focused-metamodel

The Process focused-metamodel is depicted in *Figure 11.5*:

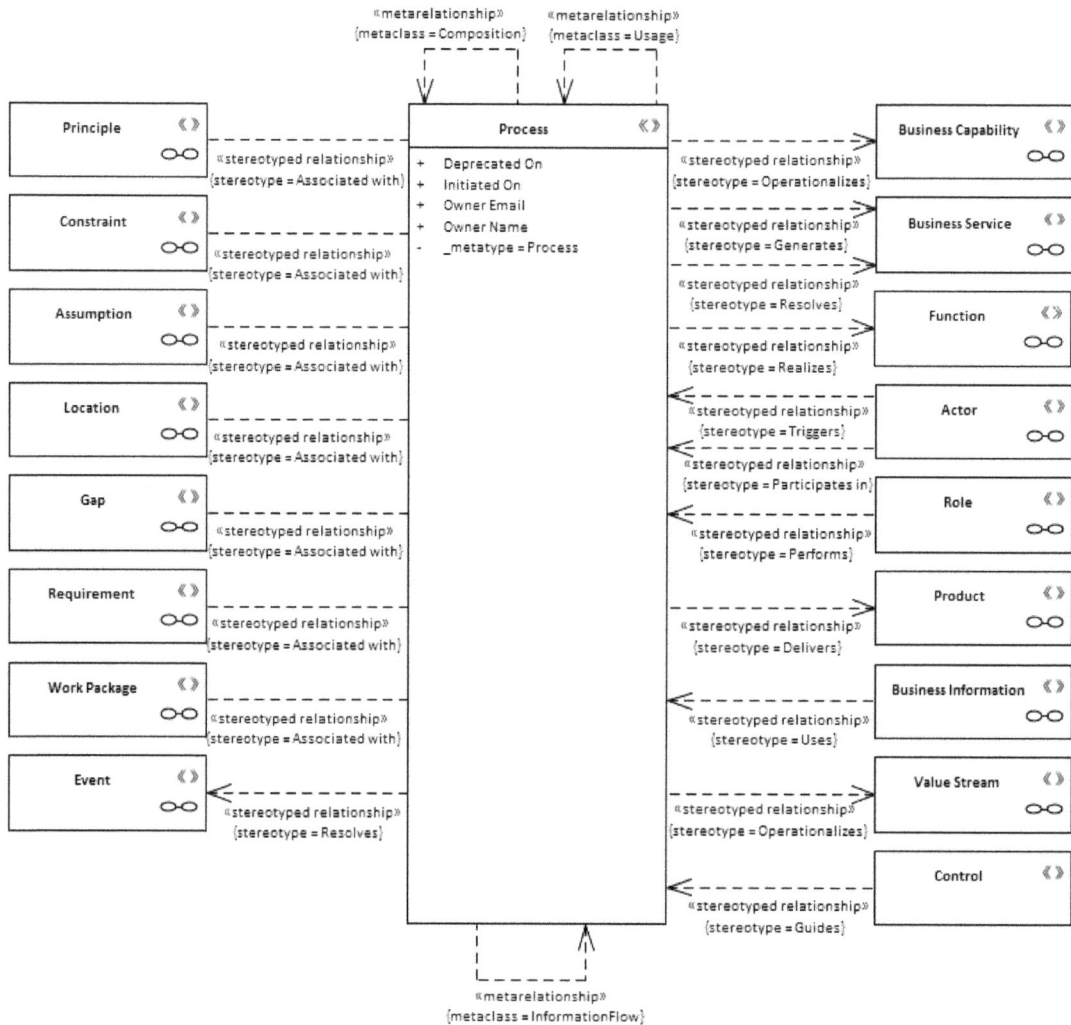

Figure 11.5: *Process focused-metamodel*

The next focused-metamodel to define is the actor.

Defining the actor focused-metamodel

The actor focused-metamodel is depicted in *Figure 11.6*:

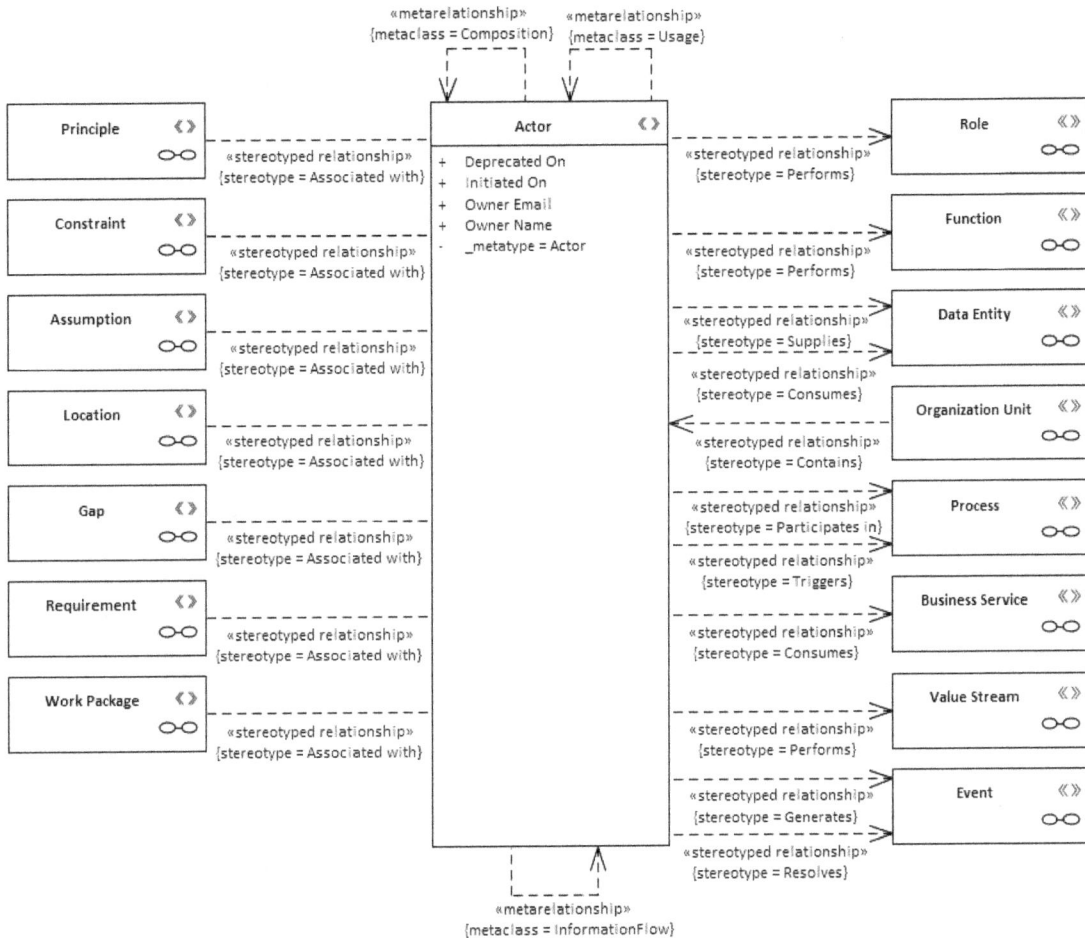

Figure 11.6: *Actor focused-metamodel*

We need to define some extra stereotypes, but only at a high level, without detailed specifications, since they would not be the main focus of our diagrams within the current scope of work. The required details can be added when needed in a future iteration.

Defining the remaining stereotypes

The stereotypes that will be defined in this section are no less important than the other stereotypes for which we had to describe the focused-metamodels, but since no artifacts will be created around them in this iteration, we will only create the minimum required definitions. If you feel that there is a need to create the focused-metamodels since you want to build artifacts that are focused on them, you can do that at your own pace by adding it to the MDG SOW either in this iteration or in further iterations. *Figure 11.7* lists the additional business architecture artifacts that are needed in this chapter:

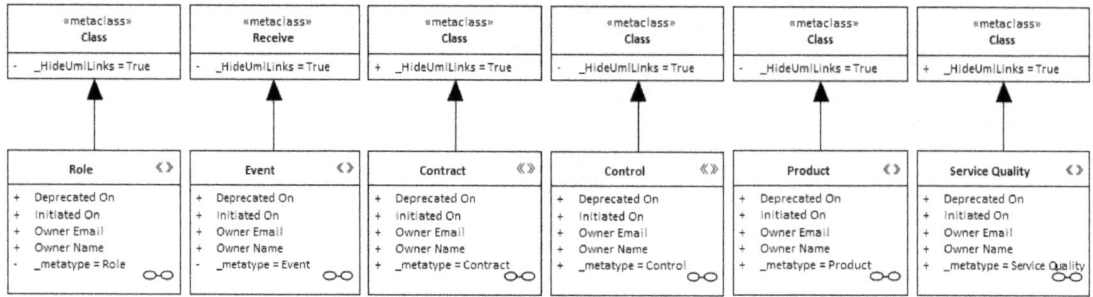

Figure 11.7: *Additional business architecture stereotypes*

We have all the stereotypes that we need, so the next step is to create the toolboxes, one for each stereotype with a focused-metamodel, starting with the business service toolbox.

Creating the required toolboxes

The business service toolbox should look like *Figure 11.8*:

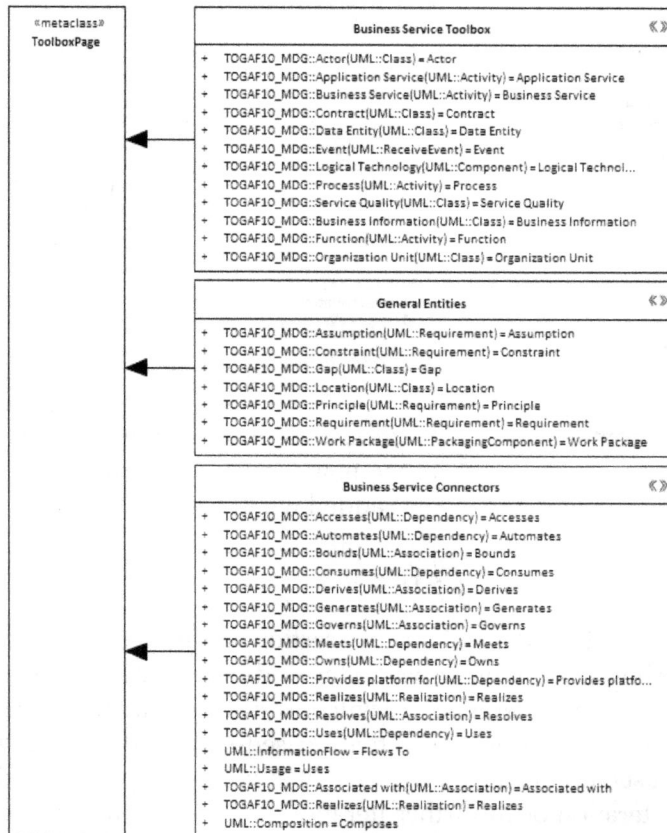

Figure 11.8: *Business service toolbox*

The Function toolbox should look like *Figure 11.9*:

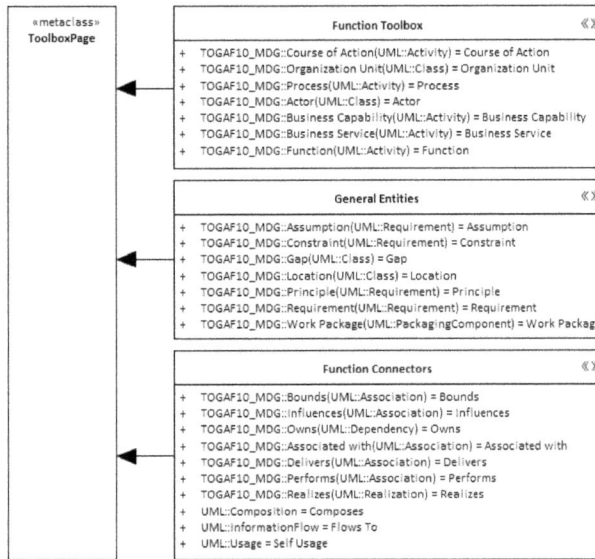

Figure 11.9: *Function toolbox*

The Process toolbox should look like *Figure 11.10*:

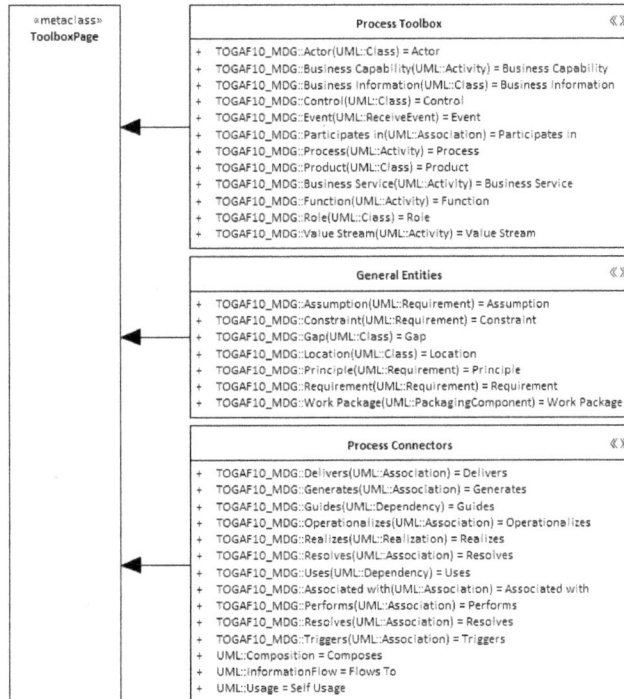

Figure 11.10: *Process toolbox*

And finally, the actor's toolbox should look like *Figure 11.11*:

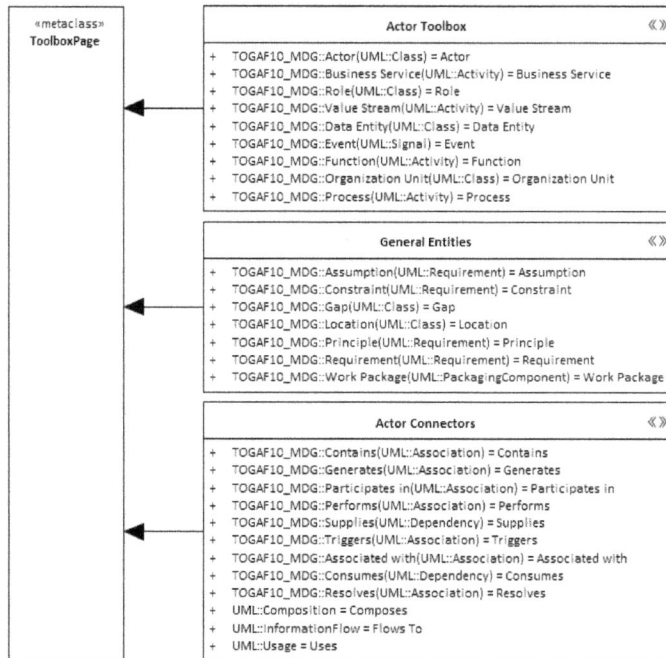

Figure 11.11: Actor toolbox

When you finish defining the toolboxes, add a navigation cell on the main toolboxes' profiles diagram for each toolbox, as depicted in *Figure 11.12*:

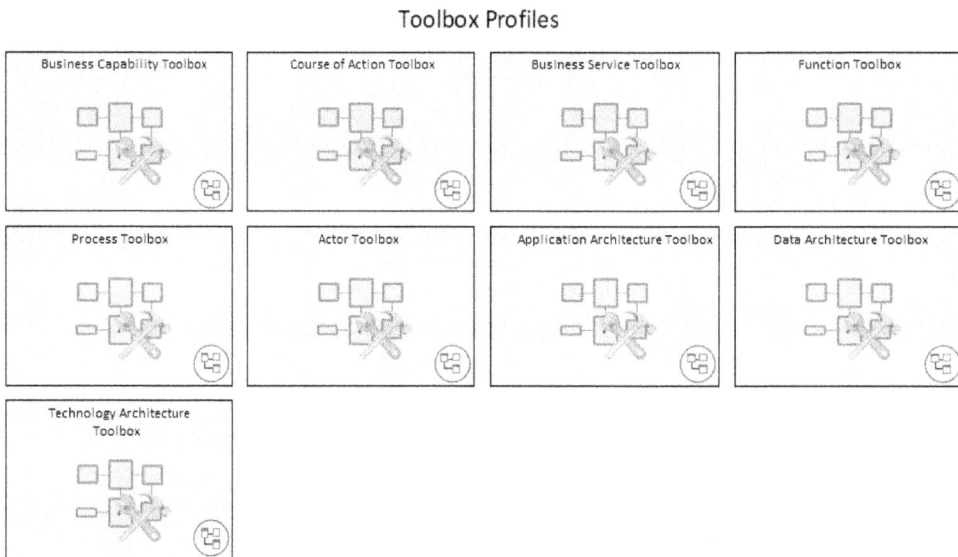

Figure 11.12: Toolboxes profiles

Next, we will create a diagram type for technology architecture artifacts and associate it with the technology architecture toolbox.

Creating the data architecture diagram type

Figure 11.13 shows the custom diagram profiles page with all the diagram types on it, including the ones that we created in previous chapters, and the ones that we need for this chapter:

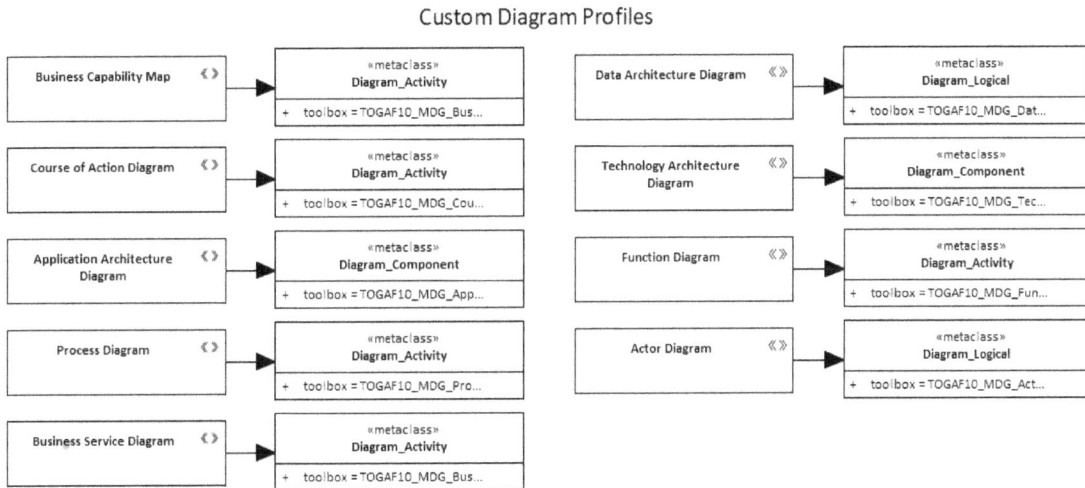

Figure 11.13: *Custom diagram profiles*

Link the Business Service Diagram, Function Diagram, Process Diagram, and Actor Diagram to their designated toolboxes by adding the **toolbox** attribute to their metaclasses and setting its initial value to **TOGAF10_MDG_Business_Service_Toolbox**, **TOGAF10_MDG_Function_Toolbox**, **TOGAF10_MDG_Process_Toolbox**, and **TOGAF10_MDG_Actor_Toolbox**, respectively, or to the names that you have used if they are different.

Finally, go back to the business service, Function, Process, and actor stereotypes; and set the initial value of the **_defaultDiagramType** attribute to **TOGAF10_MDG::Business Service Diagram**, **TOGAF10_MDG::Function Diagram**, **TOGAF10_MDG::Process Diagram**, and **TOGAF10_MDG::Actor Diagram**, respectively.

Publish and test the MDG before using it for building business architecture artifacts. When everything works as desired in the testing project, import the MDG to the main repository and let us create some interesting artifacts.

Building the business architecture artifacts

In this section, we will learn how to differentiate between a business service, a Function, and a Process, and how each of these can relate to an actor. We will learn with examples how to create useful artifacts based on these elements, and we will start with the formal definitions.

A **business service** supports the business by encapsulating a unique element of business behavior; a service offered external to the enterprise may be supported by business services. A business service represents what a specific Organization Unit provides to its external world. The external world is represented by actors. An **actor** is a person, organization, or system that has a role that initiates or interacts with activities; for example, a sales representative who travels to visit customers. Actors may be internal or external to an organization. Actors are the consumers of business services. Although it makes sense to say that Organization Unit A consumes services from Organization Unit B, when we model it, the actor is required as the median between the two Organization Units, as we will show with the examples later in this chapter.

A car repair workshop offers a car repair service to its customers, and this is what they see from that business. They will not be able to see or interact with the other organizational units that work behind the scenes to make this business work. Some large car repair chains have thousands of employees who require human resources, accounting, sales, and marketing. The Organization Units provide internal services to the other internal units, but their services are not exposed to external clients. In a large financial institute, the situation could be the complete opposite, which means that the financial services are offered to customers while the repairs of the vehicles it owns are an internal service provided to the internal Organization Units.

All the definitions are quoted from the TOGAF Standard (**https://pubs.opengroup.org/togaf-standard/architecture-content/chap02.html**), and we will look at a good amount of example diagrams, which will help you to understand these definitions and to apply your understanding to real examples in your enterprise.

Business services are the exposed parts of what an enterprise performs or does internally to provide these services. The internal parts represent the skills and the knowledge that the Organization Unit's internal actors perform to provide business services to the consuming actors. These internal parts are known as the Functions and the Processes. A **Function** is a set of business behaviors based on a chosen set of criteria. Functions are usually close coupled to/with organizational units. A Function is a high-level description of how internal jobs are performed to provide a specific service. Functions are not meant to describe the exact steps of how things are performed because this is what **Processes** are, but only a conceptual description. A Process represents a sequence of activities that together achieve a specified outcome, can be decomposed into subprocesses, and can show the operation of a Business Capability or service (at the next level of detail). Processes represent the actual steps that need to be performed, while Functions represent a grouping or a categorization of a set of Processes that perform a common job.

Note: **All definitions are quoted from The TOGAF Standard (https://pubs.opengroup.org/togaf-standard/architecture-content/chap02.html).**

Let us start modeling the business services that the enterprise architecture unit owns and use them as an example that can be applied to any business service models.

Modeling business services

Business services are owned by Organization Units. When introducing a specific Organization Unit, it is useful to provide a model, telling the audience and the possible consumers, about the business services it owns and what do they provide. This artifact is called the business services catalog. Whether the owning Organization Unit is the entire organization, or a small department within it, informing the external consumers about the owned services is valuable information. *Figure 11.14* shows the business services catalog of the enterprise architecture office Organization Unit and the same concept can be used for modeling the business services catalog of any Organization Unit:

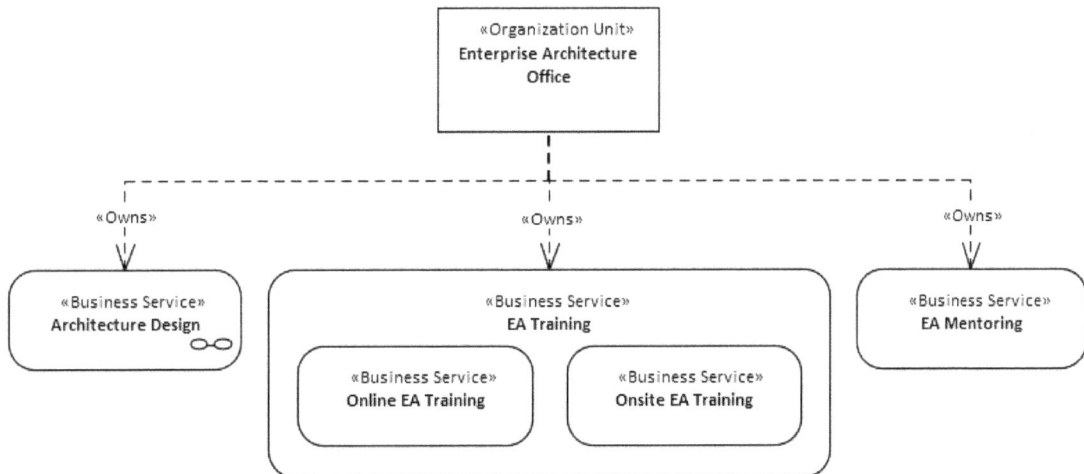

Figure 11.14: *Business services owned and provided by an Organization Unit*

Business services can be broken down further into smaller business services, if they still represent the concept of business services, which is the external exposure. For example, if we are not sure what requirements elicitation would be considered, a business service, a Function, or a Process, we need to ask ourselves, is this something that a customer can consume directly as a complete package, or not? If this is something that a consumer can directly ask your Organization Unit to provide, then it is a business service, and it needs to be listed on the business services catalog of that Organization Unit. Even if this service is provided to internal actors within the same enterprise, it is still considered a service. If it is not something that can be provided as a complete package, but a part or a phase towards the fulfillment of the business service, then it is either a Function or a Process.

Figure 11.15 shows a model for the homepage of the **Architecture Design** business service:

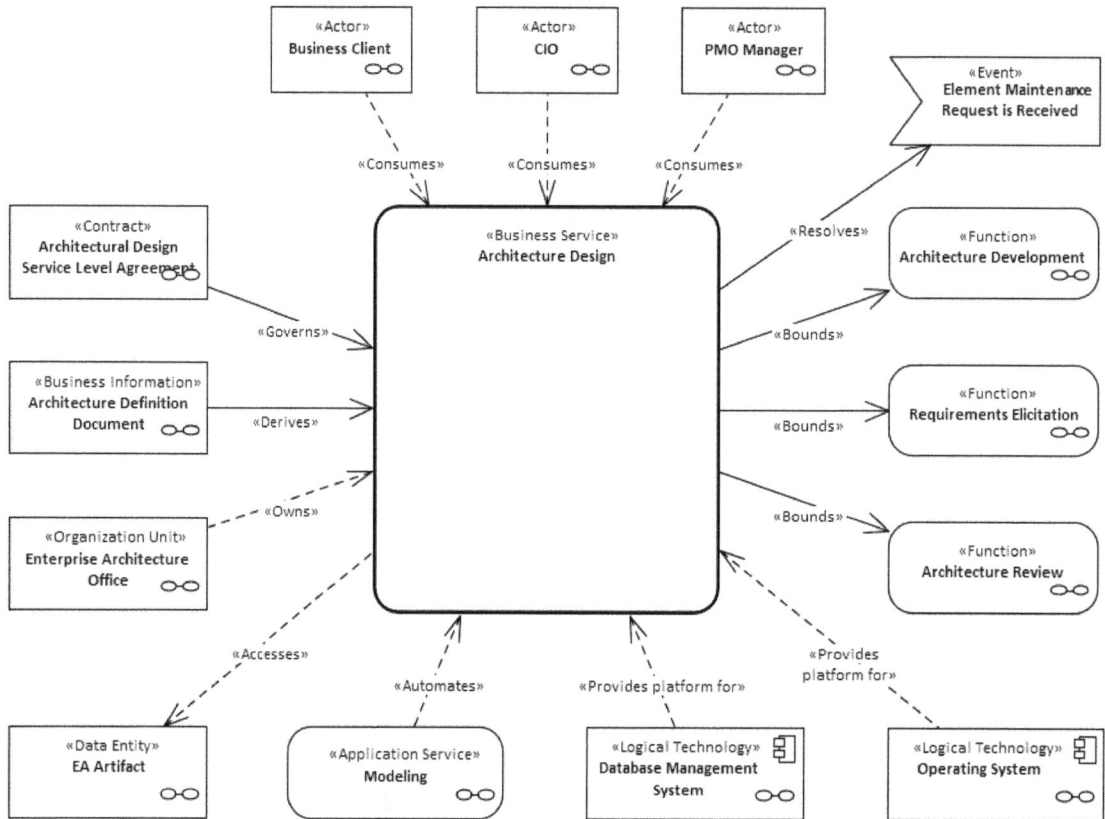

Figure 11.15: Architecture Design business service

The model is an all-in-one model that shows the **Architecture Design** business service in the center, surrounded by the elements that are related to it, such as the Organization Unit the owns it, the contract that governs it, the Business Information that derives it, the actors that consume it, the Functions that it bounds, the events that it resolves, in addition to the data entities that it accesses, the application services that automate it, and the logical technology components that provide platform for it.

One business can identify a business service in a different way than another business. If one business is a consulting or an auditing firm, they may identify **Architecture Review** as an independent business service that is provided directly to consumers as a complete service. For a retail business, reviewing architecture is most probably an internal Function that is bound by the business service.

As we kept repeating, if the diagram became very busy with elements and the ability to read and understand it became more difficult, it would be better to follow the homepage style, which can include links to more focused diagrams. *Figure 11.16* shows a model that shows the components of the **Architecture Document** Business Information, and that it derives the **Architecture Design** business service:

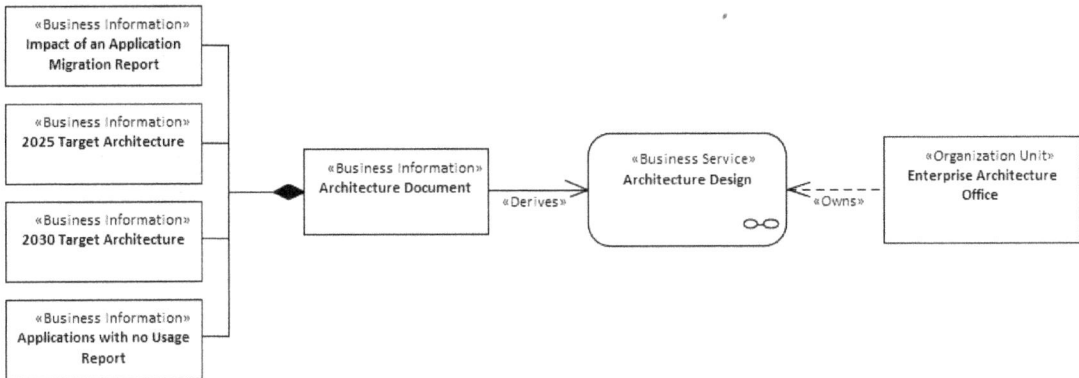

Figure 11.16: Business Information deriving a business service

Another model that consuming actors would be interested in is how much a specific business service is automated, which technologies it uses, and what data it has access to. *Figure 11.17* shows the elements that are related to the **Architecture Design** business service from the data, application, and technology architecture layers:

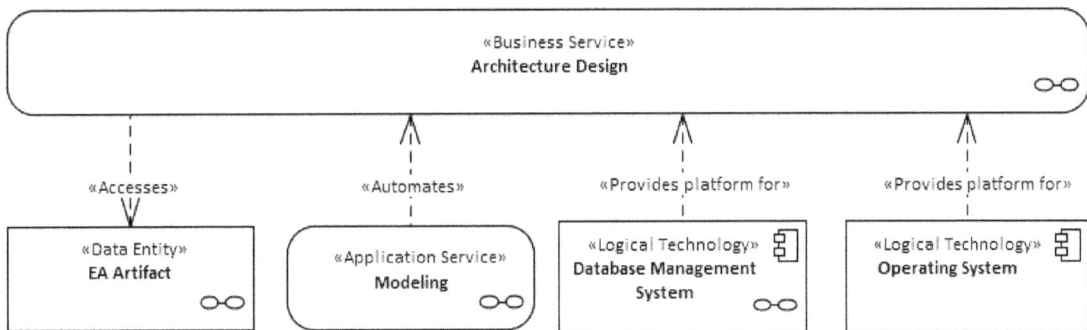

Figure 11.17: Relationships between a business service and data, application, and technology components

You may prefer to create a model showing relationships to data architecture elements only, a second model for application architecture elements, and a third showing the relationships to technology architecture elements, which is highly recommended when you have a long list of related elements.

The third aspect that is provided on the architecture design business service home page shows who the actors are that consume this business service, what the governing contract is that will govern the quality of this service, and which business events it will resolve. *Figure 11.18* shows the model that explains this:

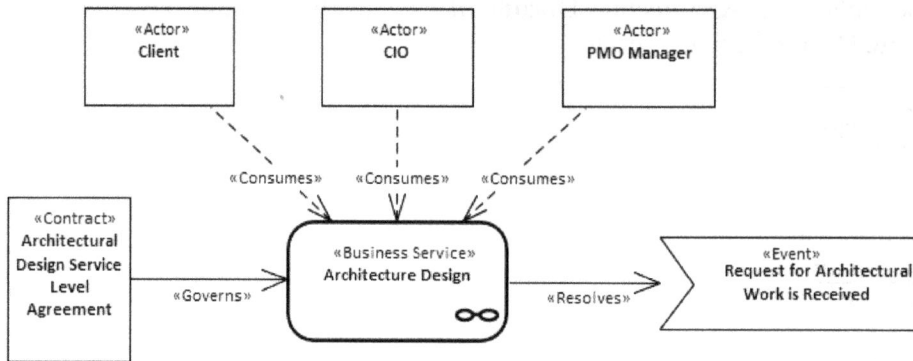

Figure 11.18: *Example of a business service consumers model*

An **event** is an organizational state change that triggers processing events; it may originate from inside or outside the organization and may be resolved inside or outside the organization. A **contract** is an agreement between a consumer and a provider that establishes functional and non-functional parameters for interaction. This applies to all types of service interactions within the metamodel (**https://pubs.opengroup.org/togaf-standard/architecture-content/chap02.html**). Events are the triggers of business services and processes. The request for specific Business Information, migrating an application from one platform to another, migrating data from one database management system to another, or the decision to merge or split business units are all examples of events that can trigger the architecture design business service. You may list all the events that you know in your real-world models.

Going back to the architecture design business service homepage, the model tells us that the business service is bound by three Functions. In the next subsection, we will have a closer look at them.

Modeling business Functions and Processes

While business service models tell *what* a specific Organization Unit provides to its consumers, Function models tell *how* the service is performed. *Figure 11.15* tells us the three main functionalities behind providing the architecture design business service. It tells how the service is provided, however, at a level of abstraction that does not involve listing the steps. The Process models describe these steps, and this is a key differentiator between a Function and a Process. They are both internal behaviors, but Processes describe steps, while Functions describe a grouping of functionality.

Figure 11.19 models the **Architecture Development** Function, which is one of the Functions that are bound by the architecture design business service:

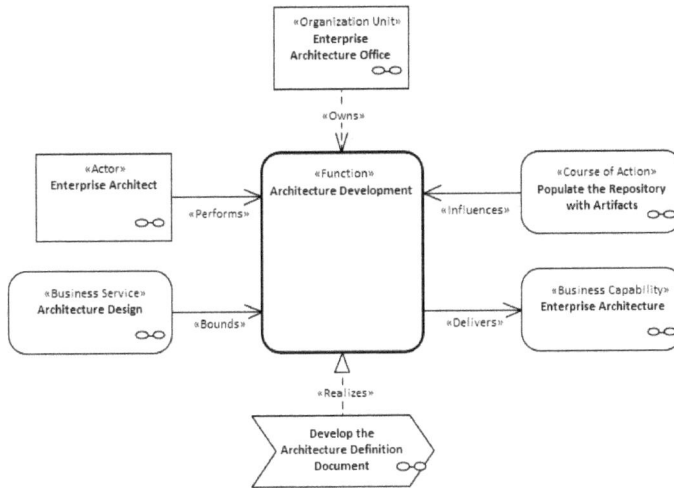

Figure 11.19: Architecture development Function model

The Function model tells which Organization Unit owns the Function, which actor performs it, which Course of Action influences it, which Business Capability it delivers, which business service bounds it, and which Process details and realizes it. Some elements have child diagrams describing them and providing more information about them. Each Process can contain multiple Processes, and each of them can be decomposed into smaller subprocesses until the desired level of detail is reached. *Figure 11.20* models `Develop the Architecture Definition Document` Process at a level that can be sufficient if the purpose is to describe the main steps of the Process:

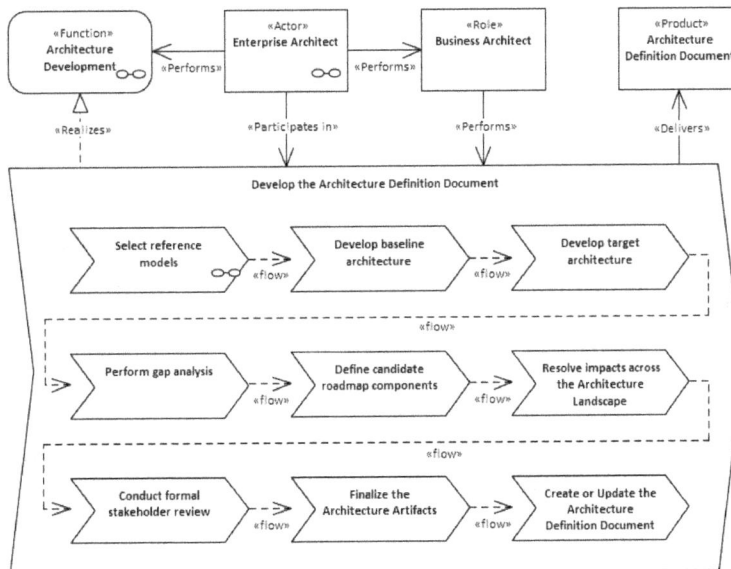

Figure 11.20: A business Process model

However, if the purpose of the model is to detail for a business architect, what are the exact steps to be performed, then more levels of detail for each subprocess and possibly their child subprocesses will be required.

You can use other modeling notations to model Processes, especially at detailed levels, where you need to show decisions and different flows. You can use UML activity diagrams or BPMN for this purpose. *Figure 11.21* models the detailed steps of the selection of reference models Process using UML activities:

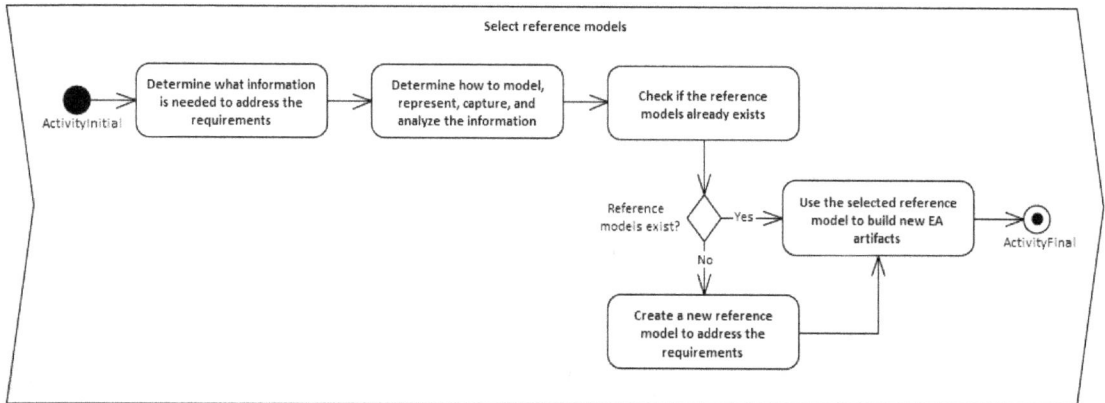

Figure 11.21: Detailed business Process model

There is no secret recipe for developing the right level of detail. The scope of work identifies stakeholders' requirements, which should define how much time and effort you are allowed to put into each diagram. Do not waste time detailing Processes that no one is interested in just for the sake of documentation; document only what matters.

Stakeholders are the actors who perform the behavioral elements of the enterprise, so let us learn more about how to model them.

Modeling actors

Actors are the living part of the enterprise. They are the people, the organizations, and the systems that perform the enterprise's behavior. They can be internal or external to the enterprise, based on the Organization Units that contain them. Organization Units without actors are nothing but a virtual setup on paper. Actors are what actualize Organization Units and make them functional. If an Organization Unit wants to consume a business service owned by another business unit, the consumption must happen through an actor. *Figure 11.22* shows how the project management office consumes the architecture design business service from the enterprise architecture office through the PMO manager actor:

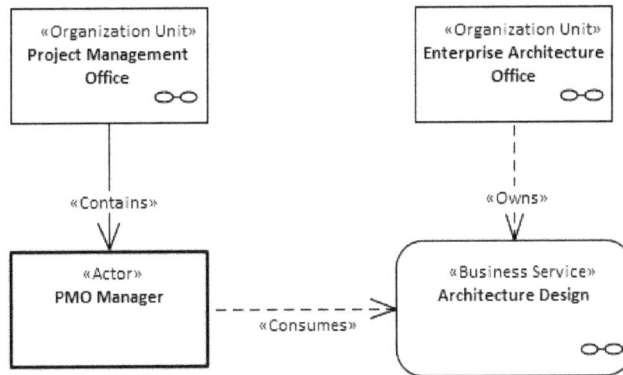

Figure 11.22: *Actor consumes a business service*

A diagram that shows the actors in each Organization Unit will be a good artifact to provide. *Figure 11.23* shows the actors that belong to the enterprise architecture office Organization Unit:

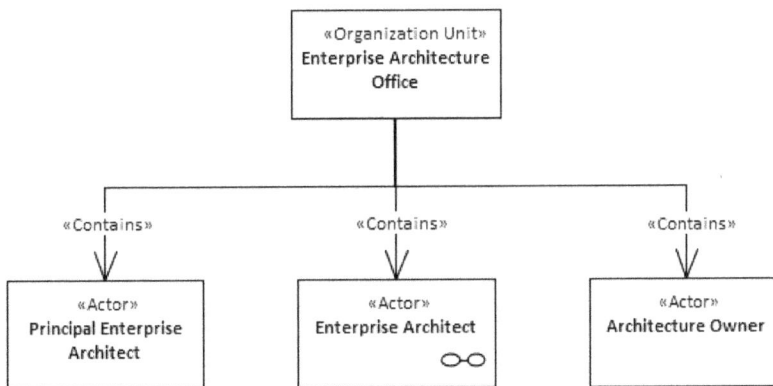

Figure 11.23: *An actor consuming a business service*

It will be beneficial for the enterprise if the repository contains a model for each Organization Unit listing the actors that belong to it.

Each actor can provide another level of detail showing what enterprise behavior it performs or participates in, what roles it performs, and which artifacts it supplies, like the example presented in *Figure 11.24*:

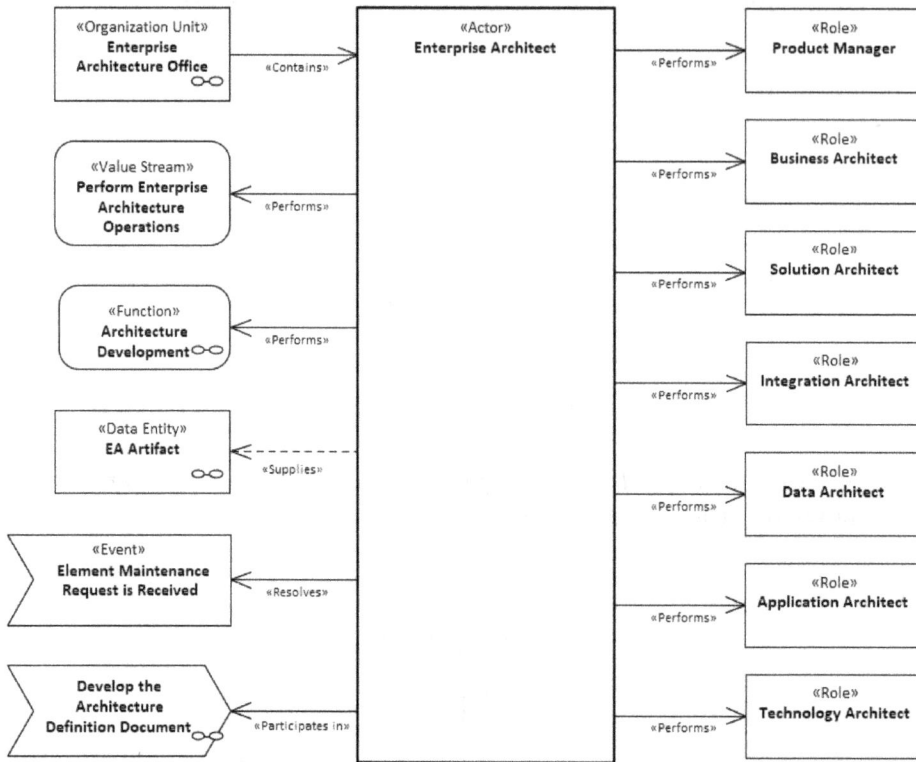

Figure 11.24: Detailed view of the enterprise architect actor

The relationship between actors and roles can be confusing to many. The simplest way to explain it is to think of actors as a generalization of roles. Let us take the business architect as an example. You may wonder, is it an actor or is it a role performed by an actor? The answer simply is that it can be classified as an actor or a role based on the elements to which it is connected to. If we imagine that the business architect is a separate actor, and it will be performing the same Value Streams, Processes, Functions, resolving the same events, and supplying the same data entities, therefore, it will be identical to the enterprise architect actor, therefore it is better to consider the business architect as a role performed by the enterprise architect. However, if the business architect and the enterprise architect each perform and participate in different behaviors and supply different data entities, then they had better be classified as two different actors.

Conclusion

As you have experienced in this chapter, elements that we have created in earlier chapters, such as the Course of Action and the Business Capability, started to appear and connect properly to this chapter's models. The more artifacts that you have in the repository, the more sense you can make out of the information in it, the more trust that stakeholders will have in it, and the more valuation and appreciation that will be developed with the enterprise architecture office Organization Unit.

Building EA artifacts is a never-ending journey. Documenting every element and every relationship in an enterprise should be an ongoing practice, not as a project with a limited time and scope. Populating the repository with artifacts must be a part of the enterprise architecture office's strategy.

In the next chapter, we will discuss modeling Organization Units and business strategies.

Points to remember

- Business services can be provided to external customers or consumers, and they can also be provided to internal enterprise consumers, who are still considered external to the Organization Unit that is providing the service.

- Business services, Functions, and Processes are all behavioral elements. Business services describe what Organization Units provide, and Functions describe how internal actors perform the services at a generalized and abstract level. In contrast, Processes provide the required sequence to perform the service.

- Processes can be modeled using UML activity diagrams, BPMN, or any other preferred standard.

- Actors are the doers of the enterprise. They are the providers and the consumers of the business services.

- Contracts govern the execution of business services. It identifies the service quality measures, conditions, and constraints.

- Actors can perform multiple roles if they have the required skills.

Key terms

- **Business service**: It is the visible part of the enterprise that consumers consume and interact with.

- **Process**: Process is the steps required to perform the business service.

- **Function**: An abstract description of a group of Processes that perform a common task is called a Function.

- **Event**: A trigger of behaviors in the enterprise is called an event, which can be internal or external.

- **Actor**: The actor is the performer of the actions in the enterprise. It can be internal or external, and it can be a person, a system, or an organization.

- **Role**: A role is a specialty that an actor performs within a specific Process or Function.

Join our Discord space

Join our Discord workspace for latest updates, offers, tech happenings around the world, new releases, and sessions with the authors:

https://discord.bpbonline.com

CHAPTER 12

Modeling Organizations and Strategies

Introduction

The most common artifact that architects use to model organizations is the organization chart, which describes the hierarchy of the Organization Units that form the organization. However, there are several other artifacts that describe the Organization Units too, and how these units play a role in the organization's strategy. Modeling organizations' strategies, on the other hand, is not different from modeling any other EA artifact. In fact, strategy elements in TOGAF are part of the business architecture layer, and they are not separated into a different architecture layer like in ArchiMate, for example. Every strategy element can be described in a set of diagrams connected to another set of diagrams, each of which shows different aspects of the strategy.

In this chapter, we will learn how to model organizations by developing artifacts that tell more than just the organization structure, but also how they connect to other elements of the enterprise, what strategies they are associated with, and how they contribute to the ongoing changes in the enterprise.

Structure

This chapter will include the following topics:

- Updating the MDG
- Building the organization strategy artifacts

Objectives

The objective of this chapter is to learn how to identify the elements that contribute to the organization's strategy, how to model them, and how to connect them to the other models in the EA repository.

Updating the MDG

As we did in previous chapters, we will update the MDG to include the new stereotypes that we need for creating this chapter's artifacts, and the first step is defining the MDG SOW.

Defining the MDG SOW

We will need two work packages for this iteration's SOW, one for the Organization Unit's stereotype, and the other for adding the motivation stereotypes as depicted in *Figure 12.1*:

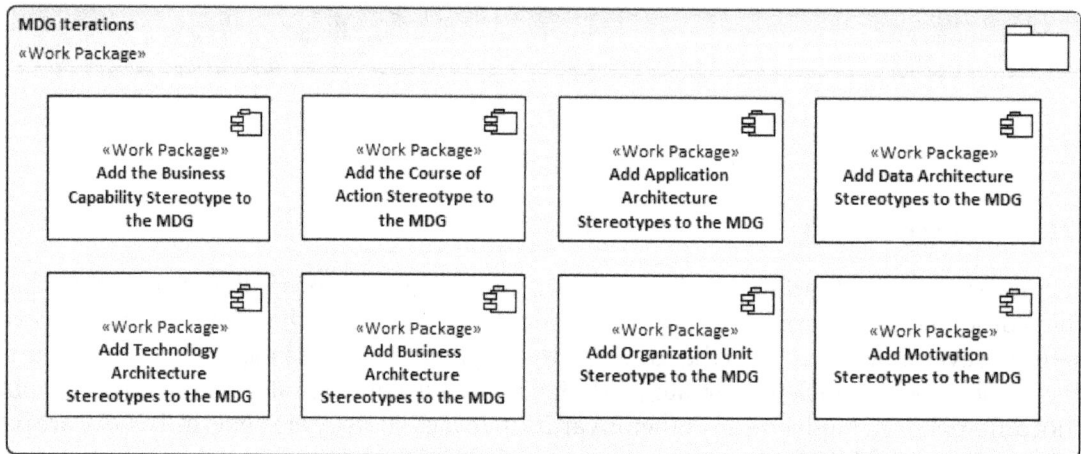

Figure 12.1: Add business architecture stereotypes to the MDG

Extracting the requirements from the metamodel should be familiar to you, so we will not spend more time explaining it; however, you can refer to *Chapter 3, Introducing Model Driven Generator,* to learn in detail how to do that. When we have the requirements approved, we will start working on the stereotypes.

Working on stereotypes

The requirements that we identify in every MDG SOW state what changes must be made to the MDG to support the new artifacts that we are planning to build. The stereotypes are divided into two groups: the elements stereotypes and the connectors stereotypes. We will start with the connectors' stereotypes first.

Adding the required connectors' stereotypes

Figure 12.2 lists the new connectors' stereotypes and their suggested metaclasses that need to be added to the MDG in the current iteration:

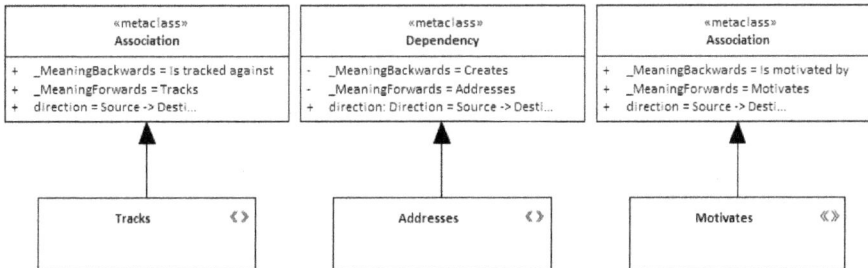

Figure 12.2: *New connectors stereotypes*

Next, we need to define the focused-metamodels of the elements' stereotypes starting with the Organization Unit.

Defining the Organization Unit focused-metamodel

The Organization Unit focused-metamodel should look like *Figure 12.3*:

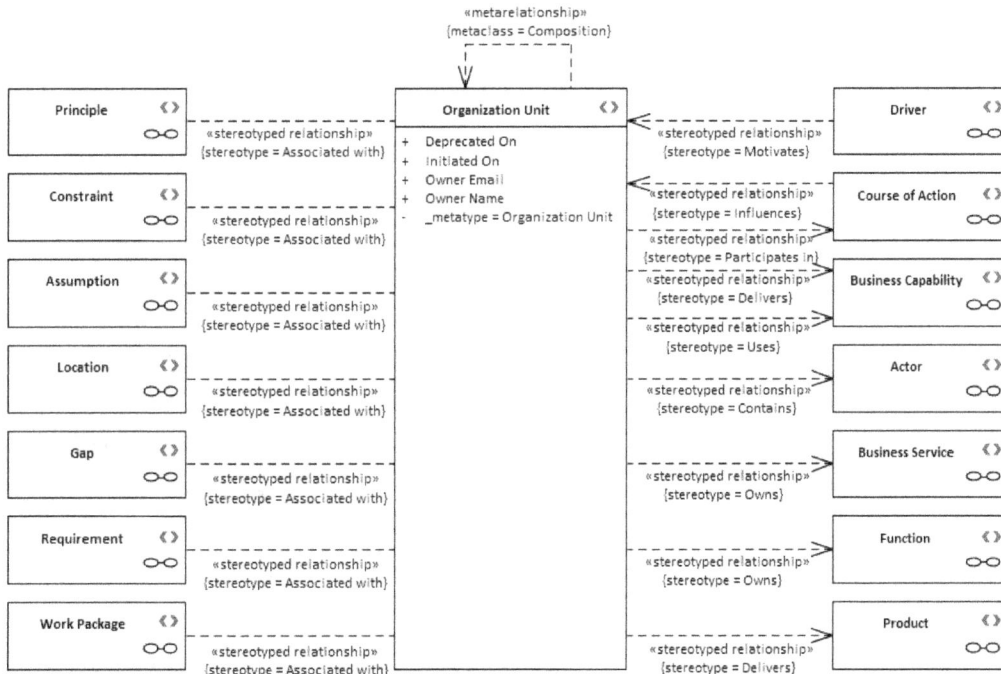

Figure 12.3: *Organization Unit focused-metamodel*

The next focused-metamodel is the driver.

Defining the driver focused-metamodel

The driver focused-metamodel is depicted in *Figure 12.4*:

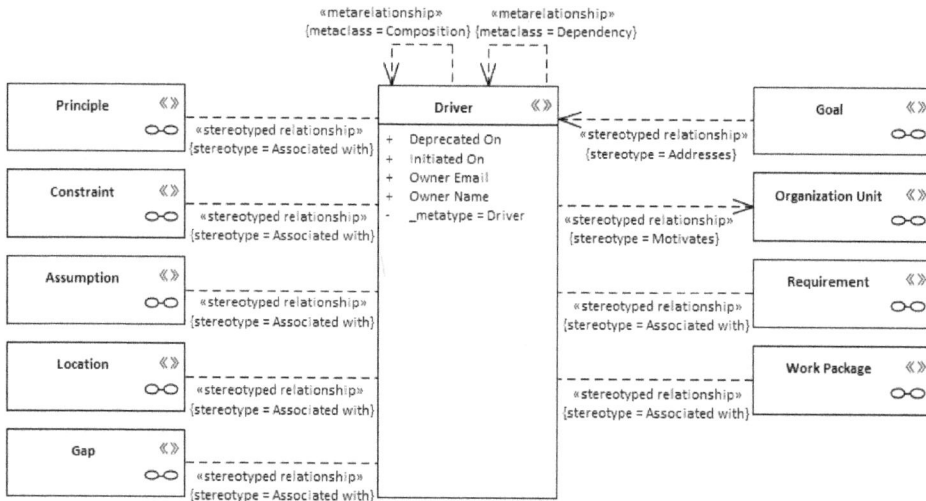

Figure 12.4: Driver focused-metamodel

The next focused-metamodel is the goal.

Defining the goal focused-metamodel

The goal focused-metamodel is depicted in *Figure 12.5*:

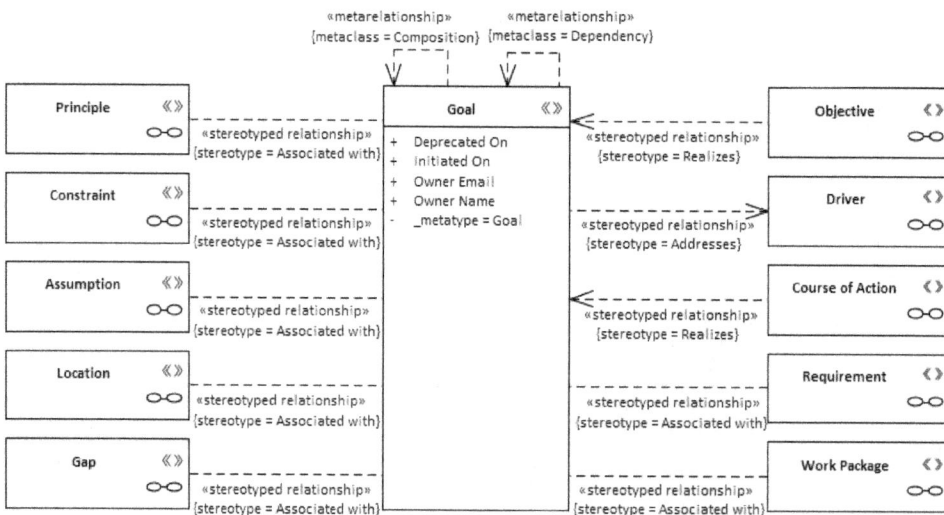

Figure 12.5: Goal focused-metamodel

The next focused-metamodel to define is the actor.

Defining the objective focused-metamodel

The objective focused-metamodel is depicted in *Figure 12.6*:

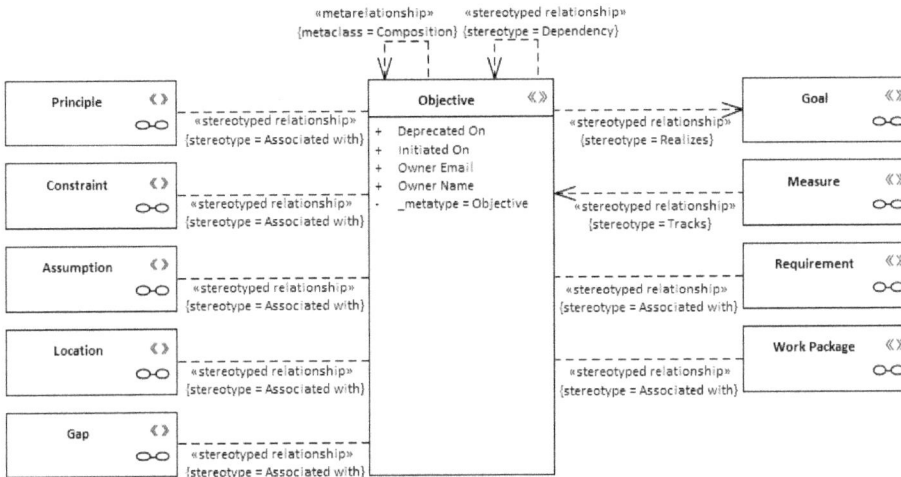

Figure 12.6: *Actor focused-metamodel*

Finally, we need to define the measure focused-metamodel.

Defining the measure focused-metamodel

Figure 12.7 shows the measure focused-metamodel:

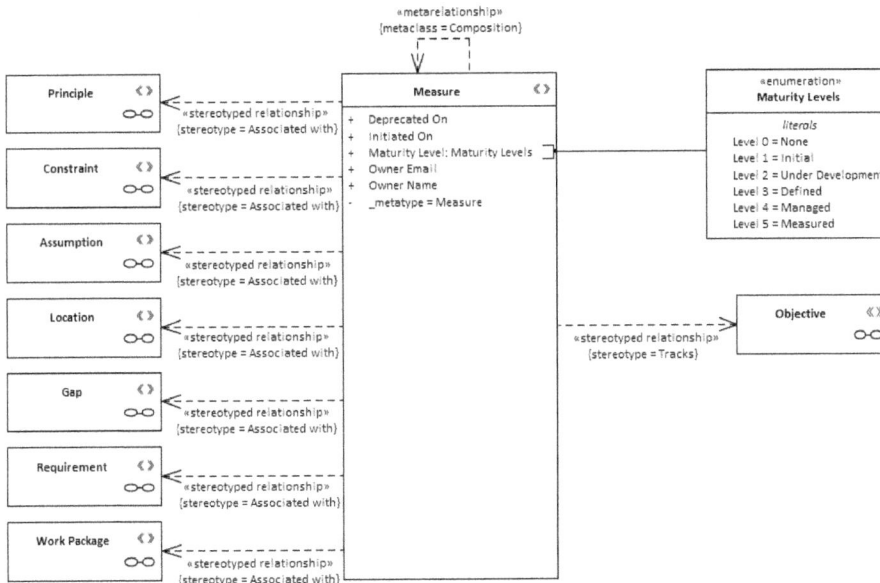

Figure 12.7: *Measure focused-metamodel*

Notice how we added a new Tagged Value with enumeration to be used to store the maturity level value. We learned how to add an enumerated Tagged Value in *Chapter 4, Advanced Model Driven Generator*, hence refer to that chapter if you want to refresh your memory.

We have all the stereotypes that we need, so the next step is to create the toolboxes, one for each stereotype.

Creating the required toolboxes

The Organization Unit toolbox should look like *Figure 12.8*:

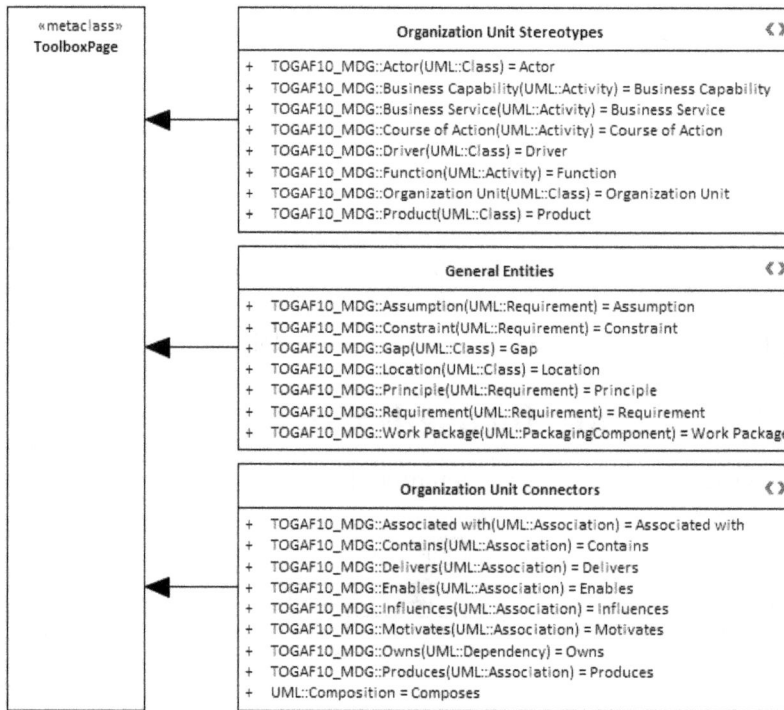

Figure 12.8: Organization Unit toolbox

The motivation stereotypes will be grouped into one toolbox, as modeled in *Figure 12.9*:

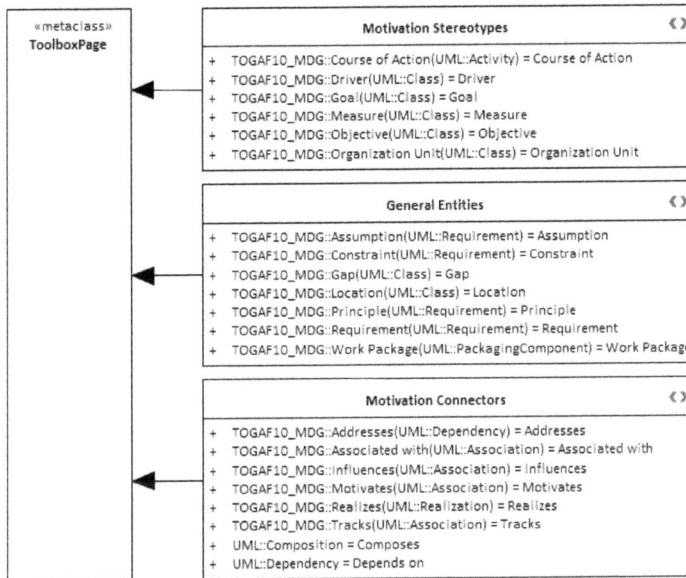

Figure 12.9: Motivation toolbox

Next, we will see the diagram types and associate them with the motivation toolbox.

Creating the diagram types

Figure 12.10 shows the custom diagram profiles page with all the diagram types listed on it, including the newly added **Organization Unit Diagram** and the **Motivation Diagram** types:

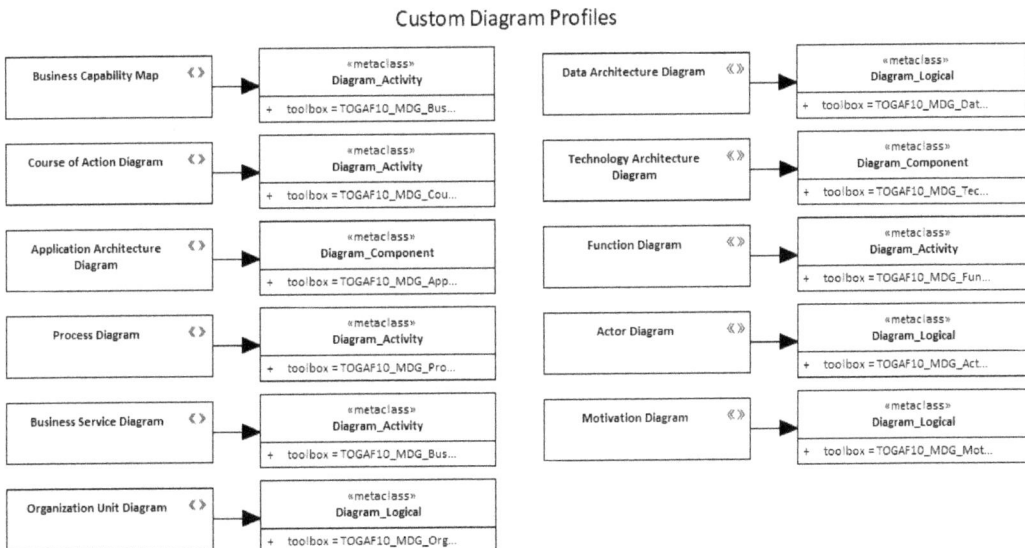

Figure 12.10: Custom diagram profiles

Link the **Organization Unit Diagram** and **Motivation Diagram** to their designated toolboxes by adding the **toolbox** attribute to their metaclasses and setting their initial values to **TOGAF10_MDG_Organization_Unit_Toolbox** and **TOGAF10_MDG_Motivation_Toolbox**, respectively, or to the names that you have used if they are different.

Finally, go back to the Organization Unit and motivation stereotypes, and set the initial value of the **_defaultDiagramType** attribute to **TOGAF10_MDG::Organization Unit Diagram** and **TOGAF10_MDG::Motivation Diagram**, respectively.

Publish and test the MDG before using it to build business architecture artifacts. When everything works as desired in the testing project, import the MDG to the main repository, and then we can proceed to create some interesting artifacts.

Building the organization strategy artifacts

When modeling Organization Units, the most common artifact is the organization structure diagram, so let us start by modeling it.

Modeling organization structures

The Organization Unit's definition has already been explained in *Chapter 6, Modeling Business Capabilities*, but to recall, it is a self-contained unit of resources with goals, objectives, and measures. Organization Units may include external parties and business partner organizations (**https://pubs.opengroup.org/togaf-standard/architecture-content/chap02.html**). As per the definition, an Organization Unit is a unit of resources that can represent the entire enterprise, a single unit, or a subunit of it. Organization Units can either be internal or external to the enterprise. *Figure 12.11* shows an organization structure example with a legend that differentiates between internal and external units:

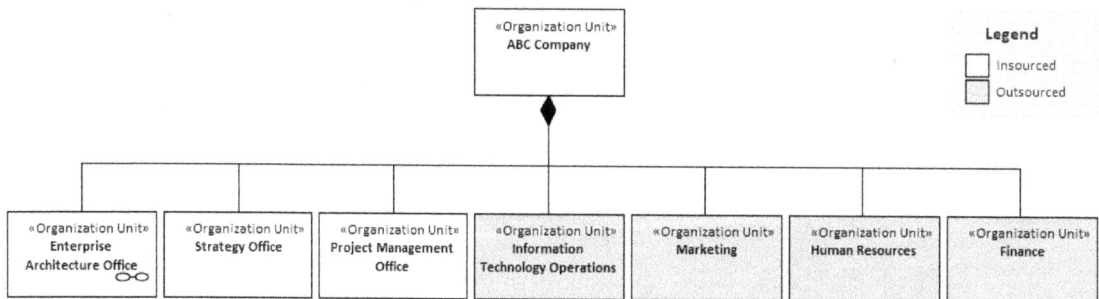

Figure 12.11: Organization structure diagram

For users who want to understand the hierarchy of the Organization Units within an organization, the organization structure is the artifact to look at. It helps to understand the reporting and escalation paths for each unit within the organization. The root node is also an Organization Unit element, and each of the units can be decomposed into subunits that can be further decomposed into smaller subunits. If the **Enterprise Architecture Office**, for example, contains four subunits for business, data, application, and technology architecture, you can show that on the model. The relationship between a parent and a child Organization Unit is always of type composition.

Some Organization Units can be external to the enterprise, such as a finance partner that takes care of all the bookkeeping and financial reporting activities. The organization structure model can optionally show the difference between internal and external Organization Units by adding a legend element to it. To add a legend to a diagram, follow these steps:

1. In the **Toolbox**, open the **Common Elements** section and find the **Diagram Legend**.

2. Drag the diagram legend and drop it on the diagram.

3. Double-click on it to open the **Legend** dialog box.

4. Keep the value **Legend** in the **Name** field or change it if needed.

5. Check the **Apply auto color** box.

6. Click on the three dots button next to the **Filter** field and select **Element | Keyword** from the menu.

7. Click the **New** button, enter `Internal` in the **Value** field, and enter `Insourced` in the **Display Value** field.

    You can enter any other values in the **Value** and **Display Value** fields, or you can enter the same value in both fields as well. The value field contains the value that the legend element will look for to apply the formatting, while the display value is the label that will appear in the legend box on the diagram.

8. Select the **Fill Color**, **Line Color**, and **Line Width**. This is where you set the format of the elements that match the legend's value.

9. Click **Save**.

10. Repeat *Steps 7* through *9* for the `External` keyword. Use *Figure 12.12* as a guide and click **Ok** when done:

Figure 12.12: Legend dialog

After the dialog box is closed, you will be returned to the diagram, but with no change to how the elements look. This is because we still need to assign values to the keyword field of each Organization Unit on the diagram. Continue with the following steps to learn how.

11. Right-click on one of the Organization Unit elements on the diagram, such as **Finance,** and select **Properties | Properties** from the context menu.

12. Enter the value **External** in the **Keywords** field, then click **OK**. Once the dialog box is closed, you will see that the selected Organization Unit will have the formatting options that we set in the legend dialog.

13. Repeat for all the Organization Units by identifying which one is internal and which one is external.

You can use fields other than the **Element.Keyword** by selecting another option from *step 6*. Explore the other values and choose the one that makes more sense to you. You can also define a custom Tagged Value to indicate the status of an Organization Unit, which requires adding a new Tagged Value to the MDG. The development of the MDG never ends because the needs of the architects and the repository users will keep evolving.

It is better to keep the organization structure models simple and focused. A large organization can have many Organization Units, each of which can have many subunits, which can make the model large and difficult to read. In a case like that, it is better to split the diagram into multiple diagrams and provide the proper navigation experience to the users.

Organization structures describe the hierarchy of an organization. However, describing an Organization Unit in a model requires more than knowing its parent and child Organization Units, so let us see how to model a single Organization Unit.

Modeling Organization Units

When describing an Organization Unit, it is useful to tell what the unit is in terms of who the actors are in this business unit, what it provides, how it performs things, and what motivates it strategically. *Figure 12.13* suggests an Organization Unit model that answers some of these questions and provides links to additional views with more information to avoid overwhelming the diagram:

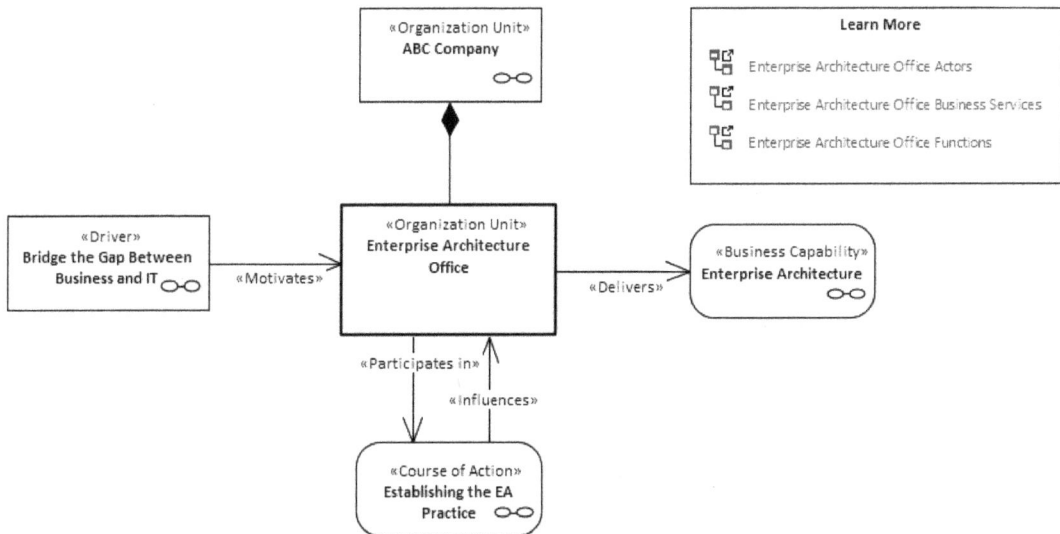

Figure 12.13: Organization Unit model

This model can be used for any Organization Unit, including the root Organization Unit, and in that case, it will show the drivers, Business Capabilities, and Course of Action of the whole enterprise.

Each of the elements on the Organization Unit model has links for additional details. Double-clicking on the parent Organization Unit will take us back to *Figure 12.11* in this chapter. Double-clicking on the Business Capability will take us to *Figure 6.14* in *Chapter 6, Modeling Business Capabilities*. Double-clicking on the Course of Action will open *Figure 7.15* in *Chapter 7, Modeling Projects*. We will discuss the driver and its model in the next subsection.

To keep the diagram simple, we added links to diagrams that provide additional information; each provides a special perspective. The **Enterprise Architecture Office Actors** link will open *Figure 11.16*, in *Chapter 11, Modeling Business Services*, while the **Enterprise Architecture Office Business Services** link will open *Figure 11.17* in the same chapter. The last link will open *Figure 12.14* showing all the Functions that are owned by the enterprise architecture Organization Unit:

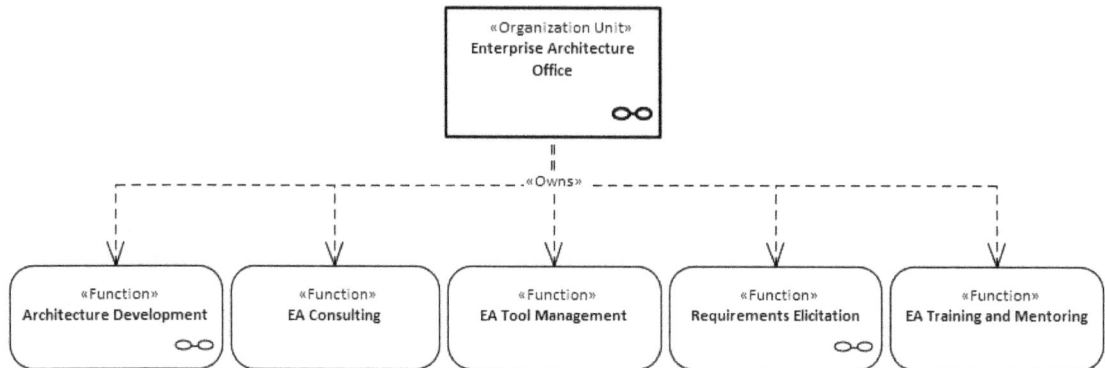

Figure 12.14: Functions owned by the Organization Unit

Double-clicking the driver in *Figure 12.13* will open the driver's model, which is one of the business strategy elements that we will learn about more in the next subsection.

Modeling business strategies

A business strategy, in general, is a plan that an organization defines to achieve its defined vision. A business strategy contains many elements, some of which are supported by TOGAF, like the drivers, goals, objectives, and measures, and some are not, like the vision, mission, and core values. There are different ways to work around this limitation. One of them is to extend the TOGAF metamodel, adding the extended elements to the MDG, and using them just like any other element. We recommend using another reference to guide the extension of the TOGAF metamodel, because there must be rules governing how the new elements will connect to the existing metamodel elements. The other way to model elements that are not supported by TOGAF is to reuse elements that already exist in it for multiple purposes, such as reusing the requirement element for the vision, and the mission; and reusing the principal element for the core values. Extending the TOGAF metamodel is not part of this book's scope; therefore, we will repurpose the existing elements to work around this limitation.

Modeling a business strategy starts with modeling its individual elements just like any other elements that we have modeled so far. Having a business strategy document is a different step that involves composing and generating the document, a topic that will be covered in *Chapter 14, Publishing EA Artifacts*. With that said, let us see how to model the driver.

Modeling drivers

A driver is, an external or internal condition that motivates the organization to define its goal (**https://pubs.opengroup.org/togaf-standard/architecture-content/chap02.html**). Organization strategies are concerned with achieving defined strategic goals. To define the strategic goals, we need a higher-level statement that identifies the purpose to achieve, which is what the driver is meant to define. *Figure 12.15* shows how the enterprise architecture office business unit is motivated by **Bridging the Gap Between Business and IT** driver:

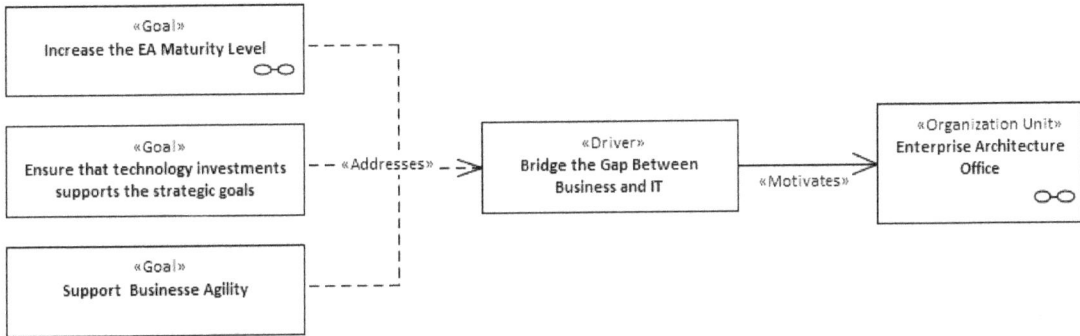

Figure 12.15: Driver and goals that address it

The driver does not tell how, but what to achieve. To define how to achieve the drivers, each driver needs to be addressed by goals, each of which describes how, but still using a high-level statement. Each goal can be further detailed in a model that provides more information about it, as we will see next.

Modeling goals, objectives, and measures

A goal is defined by TOGAF as, a high-level statement of intent or direction for an organization. Typically used to measure the success of an organization (**https://pubs.opengroup.org/togaf-standard/architecture-content/chap02.html**).

A goal is a statement of intent, so it tells how the driver will be addressed, but at a higher level. Increasing the EA Maturity is a possible goal to address, bridging the gap between business and IT. An organization with a higher maturity has more documented means of communication, which helps in bridging the business and IT communication gaps. Realizing a goal requires initiating one or more courses of action. *Figure 12.16* models **Increase the EA Maturity Level** goal, the driver that it addresses, the Course of Action, and the objectives that realize it:

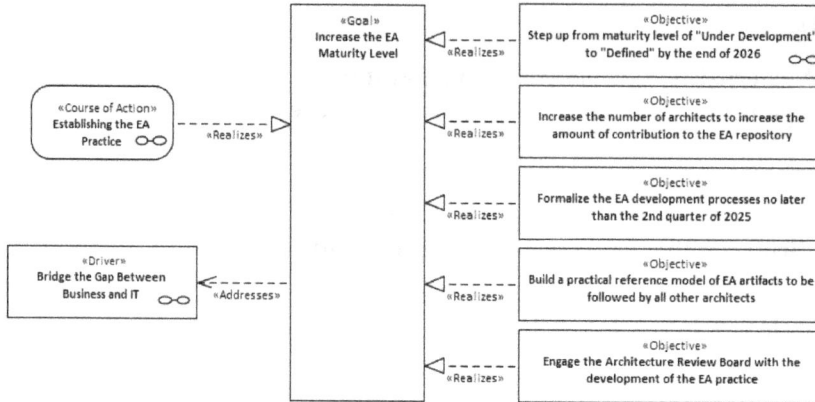

Figure 12.16: Goal to increase the EA maturity level and its objectives

Since goals are still high-level statements of intent, they must be broken down into simpler, measurable, actionable, realistic, and time-bound statements, which are known as the objectives. An objective is an organizational aim that is declared in a **Simple, Measurable, Actionable, Realistic, and Timebound (SMART)** way (**https://pubs.opengroup.org/togaf-standard/architecture-content/chap02.html**).

An objective like **Step up from the maturity level of Under Development to Defined by the end of 2026** is a simple statement that tells exactly what needs to be done in a simple, measurable, actionable, realistic, and time-bound manner. To measure the maturity level of an organization, TOGAF provides a guide to architecture maturity and how to define its measures. The guide can be found at **https://pubs.opengroup.org/togaf-standard/architecture-maturity-models/index.html**. It is recommended to read it and add the link to the external reference library in your repository. Briefly, the architecture maturity model provides nine elements to measure the EA maturity against, and these elements are depicted in *Figure 12.17*:

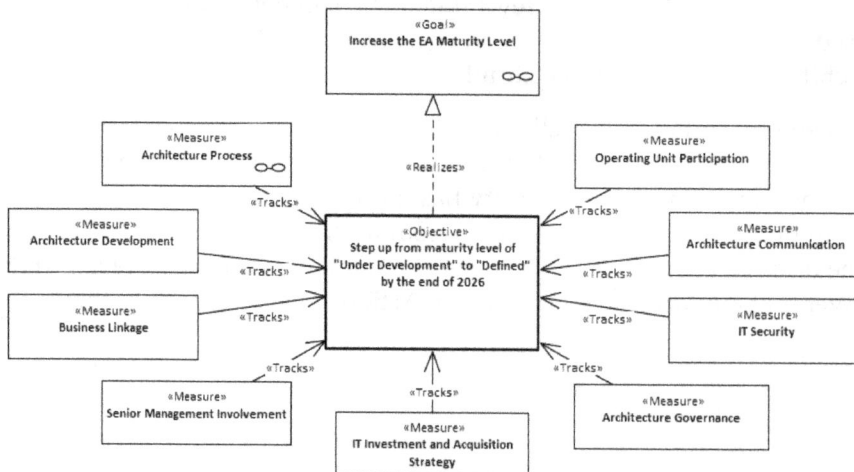

Figure 12.17: An objective and its measures

Each maturity element can have one of six maturity levels: **None**, **Initial**, **Under Development**, **Defined**, **Managed**, and **Measured**. *Figure 12.18* shows the six maturity levels of the **Architecture Process** maturity element:

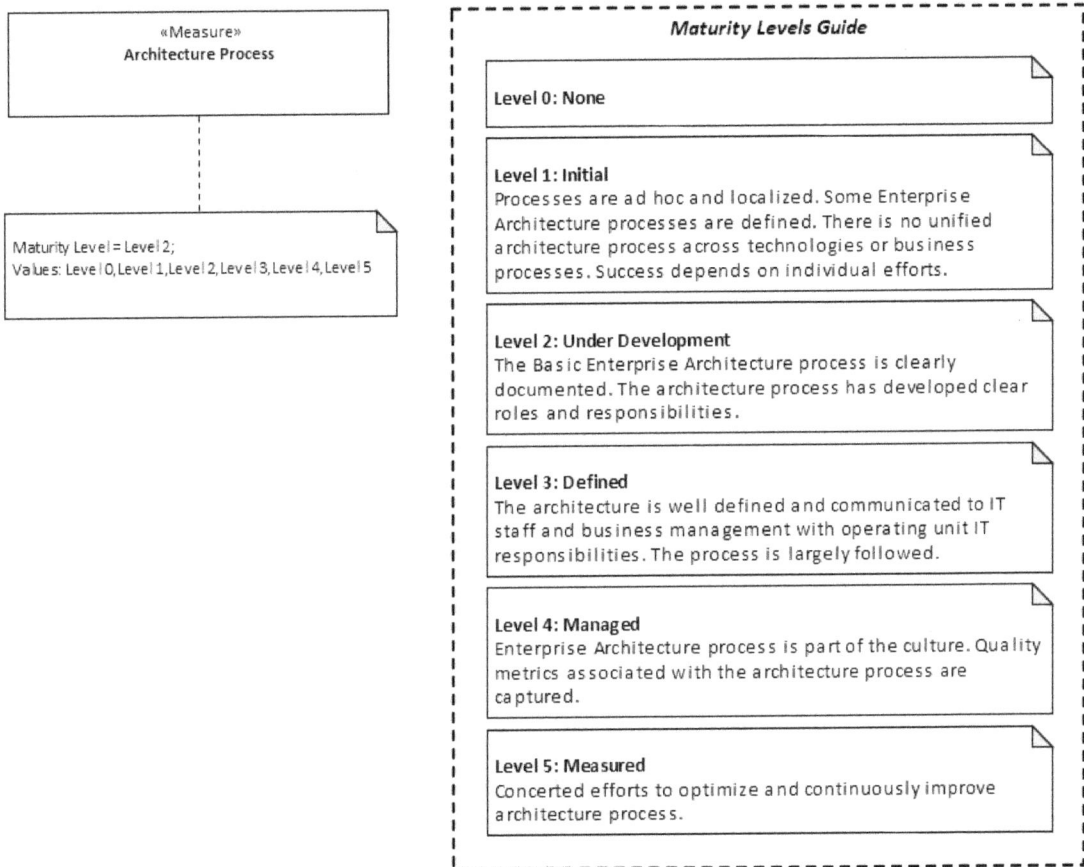

Figure 12.18: Six maturity levels of the architecture Process maturity element

The other maturity levels of the eight other maturity elements can be found in the guide, so you can model them as an exercise or add a task in the backlog to do it when you have time.

Our MDG contains a Tagged Value for the measure stereotype to store the current maturity level. Because the Tagged Value is hidden inside the properties, it will be useful to display its value on the diagram, and for that, we need to use a note element from the common elements. To display the value of the maturity level Tagged Value, do the following:

1. Link the note to the measure element.

2. Right-click on the connector that connects the note to the measure and select **Link this Note to an Element feature**. The **Link note to element feature** dialog will appear as depicted in *Figure 12.19*:

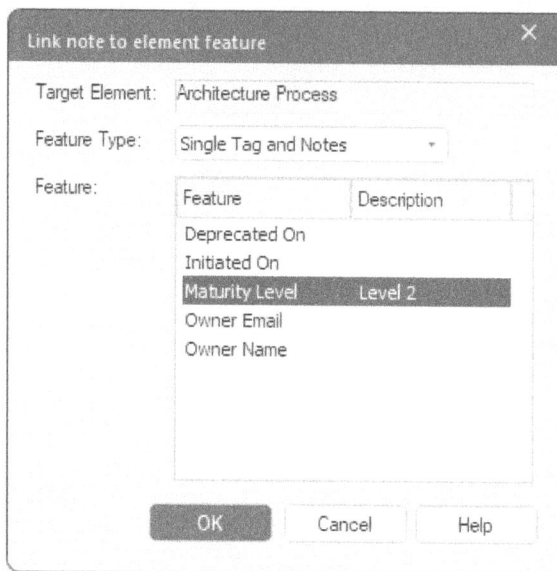

Figure 12.19: Link note to element feature

3. From the **Feature Type** dropdown list, select **Single Tag and Notes**.

4. Select the **Maturity Level** from the **Feature** list.

5. Click **OK**.

6. Resize the note to display the information properly.

Displaying Tagged Values and other element features in a note is optional, but it adds more readability and value to the diagram. Not every reader will check the Tagged Values, and if a user is looking at a diagram image from outside Sparx EA, there is no way to tell what the Tagged Value is or what its current value is. Remember that building readable and meaningful diagrams must always be your priority.

Conclusion

Modeling strategy elements is not very different than modeling any other EA element. These elements can be combined in views that make sense for the users, whether in the form of reports, documents, or diagrams. If your users are familiar with the balanced scorecards, for example, you can organize the goals and the objectives on a diagram that resembles a strategy map. If the users are more comfortable reading a strategy map document, then you need to compose and generate a report that matches their expectations. The source in both cases should be the same, which are the building elements that we learned how to model.

In the next chapter, we will learn how to model artifacts from the enterprise architecture business units and how they can form the standard of similar artifacts in the enterprise.

Points to remember

- Organization Units can be internal or external to the enterprise.
- An organization structure diagram shows the hierarchy of Organization Units.
- An Organization Unit model shows the elements that are related to a single Organization Unit.
- The development of the MDG never ends because the needs of the architects and the repository users will keep evolving.
- The driver states what to achieve at a high-level, the goal tells how at a high-level, and the objective tells how at a more detailed level.

Key terms

- **Organization Unit**: Organization Unit is a unit of resources that can represent the entire enterprise, a unit, or a subunit.
- **Driver**: Driver is a higher-level statement that identifies what to achieve.
- **Goal**: Goal is a high-level statement that identifies how to address the driver.
- **Objective**: It is a more detailed statement of intent that tells how a goal will be realized.

Join our Discord space

Join our Discord workspace for latest updates, offers, tech happenings around the world, new releases, and sessions with the authors:

https://discord.bpbonline.com

CHAPTER 13
Repository Management Processes

Introduction

Building a repository is not a task that you can finish and forget about; on the contrary, it is an ongoing operation that will continue as long as the business sponsors are happy with the results and users are trusting the quality and the accuracy of the artifacts in it. Therefore, and just like anything else, to keep the repository operational and up to the expectations of its users, some maintenance is required. If you have done every example we did in this book, and if you added more artifacts from your work environment, you should have already experienced that you always need to clean up such as deleting the unneeded elements, changing elements from one type to another, changing diagrams' types, merging duplicate elements, and many other tasks that are required to keep the repository accurate and up to date.

In this chapter, we will learn how to perform these Processes in Sparx EA using models that are built using the MDG that we started building from the third chapter of this book.

Structure

This chapter covers the following topics:

- Exploring the EA tool management Function
- Working with artifacts

- Maintaining diagrams
- Customizing user's navigation experience

Objectives

The objective of this chapter is to learn some techniques to manage the EA tool and keep the repository clean and up to date with accurate artifacts.

Exploring the EA tool management Function

In *Chapter 12, Modeling Organizations and Strategies*, we introduced the **EA Tool Management** Function in *Figure 12.14*, as one of the Functions that the enterprise architecture office Organization Unit owns. We did not provide any details about it at that time, but in this chapter, we will give it more context and will decompose it into subfunctions and Processes, so you can use them as reference architecture models when dealing with real-world examples. *Figure 13.1* shows the first level of the proposed subfunctions; each is composed of subfunctions and processes:

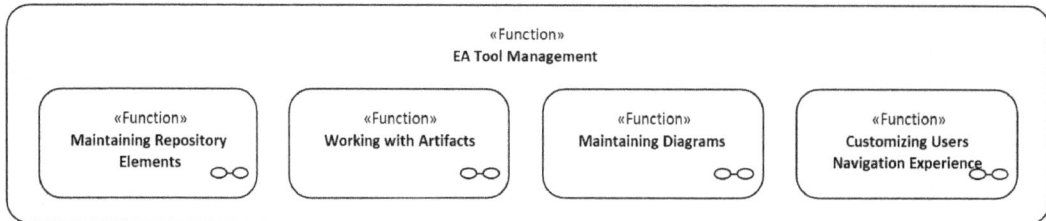

Figure 13.1: EA tool management Function

This list is not based on any standard, nor is it a list that can work for every EA unit in every enterprise; however, it is a proposed list that contains essential Functions that are needed to maintain the repository, keep it clean, and up to date. You can use the proposed Functions and Processes as references to build your own or as a starting point to expand and enhance them. Since we, as architects, must turn our thoughts into models, we will describe these Processes in models and sub-models. This way, we learn how things can be done in Sparx EA while populating the EA repository with some useful artifacts.

You must have the knowledge and the confidence to describe your Organization Unit's Functions and Processes in terms of EA artifacts, so you can guide the rest of the enterprise to follow the model that you are building. Try to put everything you learn in a model and enrich the repository, and this is how you practically and gradually develop the culture of EA. The goal is to have this level of documentation for every element in the enterprise, and that requires many contributors in every domain, which needs consistency between their deliverables; that is enhanced by reference architectures to follow.

Let us explore the list of proposed subfunctions and see how they can possibly be modeled and set as reference architectures, starting with maintaining the repository elements' Function.

Maintaining repository elements

While building an EA repository, sometimes you will face the need to change the type of elements after creating them, to move elements from one package to another, to merge two or more duplicate elements, or to delete elements that are no longer needed. **Maintaining Repository Elements** is a Function that includes a set of Processes, each of which documents a maintenance process as explained in *Figure 13.2*:

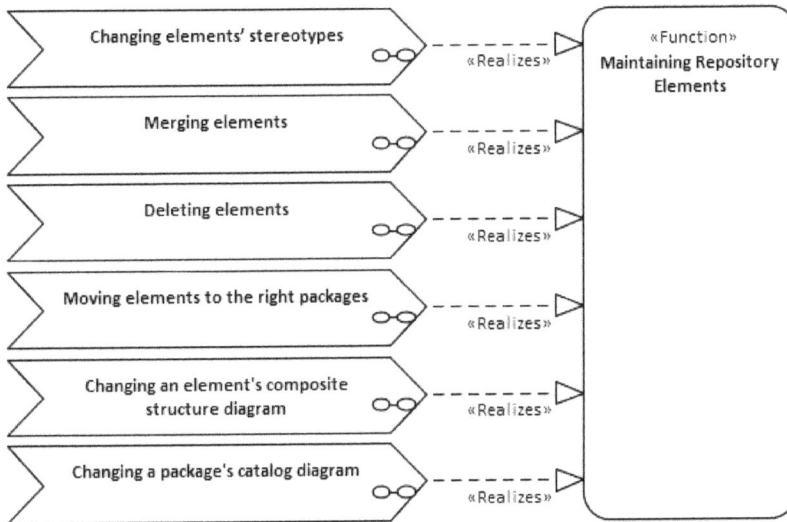

Figure 13.2: Maintaining the repository elements process

The Processes still do not represent steps at this level, so they can be easily confused with Functions, which is not wrong. However, we must have top-level Processes that act as containers to the Processes that represent the steps to simplify the diagrams. The sub processes that form the steps of each top-level Process are modeled in a composite diagram for each Process, and we will start with changing elements' stereotypes.

Changing elements' stereotypes

It is very common to identify something as a Process, for example, only to discover later that it should have been identified as a Function. The same can happen between actors and roles, Functions and business services, Functions and Business Capabilities, Processes and Value Streams, goals and objectives, goals and drivers, and many other possible mistakes that are normal to occur. The solution to correct such an issue is very simple, however, it needs to be done with caution as it may result in possible loss of some data, hence you need to understand the Process in *Figure 13.3*:

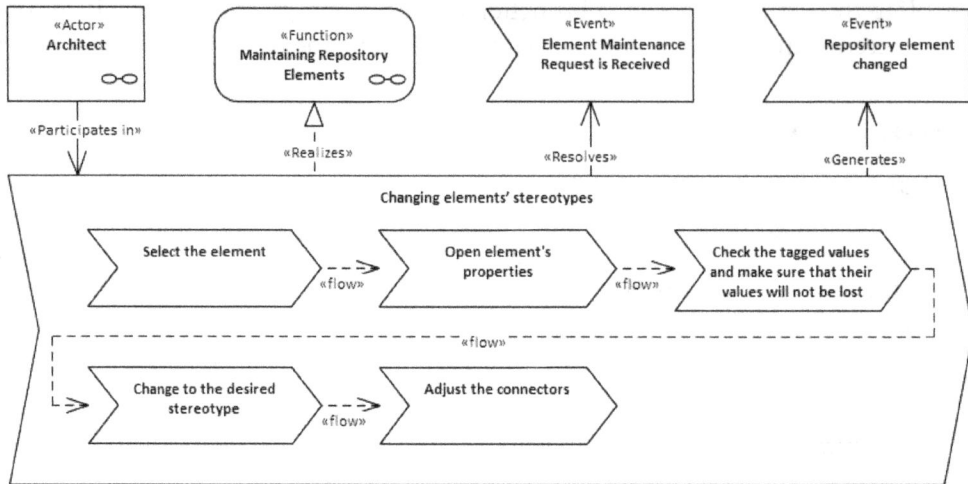

Figure 13.3: Changing elements' stereotypes process

When opening the properties dialog of an element, there is an ellipse button in the top right corner that allows you to change the element's stereotype as explained in *Figure 13.4*:

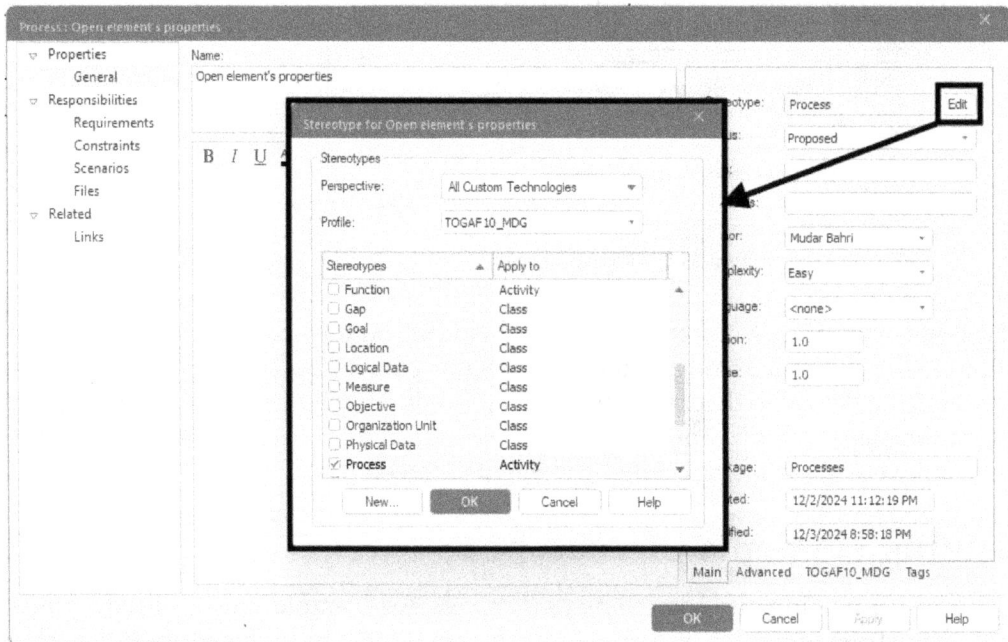

Figure 13.4: Element's stereotype

From the stereotype's popup window, you can change to any desired stereotype by easily unchecking the old stereotype's box and checking the new one. However, there are three important points that you must pay attention to:

- The first point is that values in the Tagged Values will be lost. When changing an element's stereotype, the Tagged Values will be reset to their default values, so make sure to write down any custom value you entered to manually set them in the new stereotype's Tagged Values.

  Note: **Values entered in the Notes field will be retained when changing stereotypes. Only Tagged Values will be lost.**

- The second point to pay attention to is that the existing connections between the element that is being changed and the elements that are related to it will be retained even if these relationships become invalid. For example, if a Process is linked to a Function with a *realizes* relationship, and we change its stereotype from Process to Business Capability, the Function and the Business Capability will still have the realizes relationship between them, which is invalid. Hence, manually delete the invalid relationships and add the new ones whenever you are changing an element's stereotype.

- The third point to bear in mind when changing an element's stereotype is the default diagram type that is associated with it. When we created the stereotypes in the previous chapters, we also created new diagram types for the new stereotypes. Each diagram type is associated with a toolbox that will be opened by default with this diagram type. When we change the element's stereotype, the default diagram type that is associated with it does not get automatically updated and must be updated manually. Later in this section, under the *Changing diagram type* subsection, we will learn how to change a diagram type.

Note: **Elements can have multiple stereotypes in Sparx EA. However, for consistency in an EA repository, it is suggested to restrict elements to one stereotype each by using the `_strictness=all` special attribute in MDG.**

If the level of detail in *Figure 13.3* is not sufficient, and you prefer to further detail all or some of its subprocesses, you can do that. The three important points that we asked to pay attention to can be modeled as sub or additional Processes, which is a good idea. The scope of work identifies the limit of how much detail needs to be documented. We will keep reminding you that properly managing the scope of work is a key success factor for the EA practice in any enterprise. This book is also an EA project, and it has a scope of work too. We believe that the documented level is sufficient, but it is up to you to decide in the real-world how much is good for your enterprise requirements.

The next process is merging duplicate elements.

Merging duplicate elements

When creating new elements in diagrams, you may discover later that there is another element in the repository having the same name and stereotype. You may also find that both elements were used in two different sets of diagrams, meaning that the repository contains duplicate elements, a factor that affects the reliability of the quality of the repository. Remember that the main purpose of the repository is to document which elements connect to which elements. Having duplicate elements will result in incorrect information in the form of incorrect diagrams and relationships. Some repository elements will be connected to the first occurrence, while some other elements will be connected to the second, and users will think that they both connect to the same element. They are two completely independent elements carrying the same name and having the same stereotype. To resolve this issue, we must keep one element and delete the other. To perform this task without losing any data, follow the **Merging elements** process that is modeled in *Figure 13.5*:

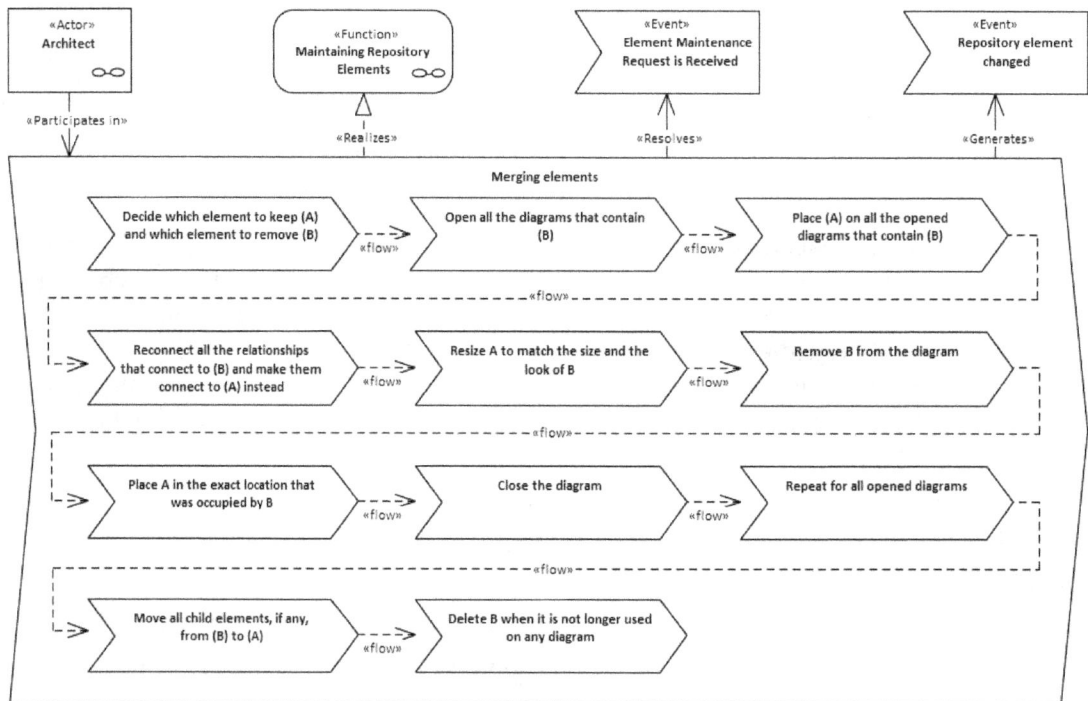

Figure 13.5: *Merging elements process*

It is up to you to decide which element to keep and which one to delete; however, it makes more sense to keep the one that is used more and delete the one that is used less, just to reduce the amount of rework needed.

To open all the diagrams that contain an element, right-click on the element and select **Find | Find in all Diagrams** or press *Ctrl + U* as a shortcut. If one of the elements is not used at all in any diagram, then you can delete it without the need for the merging process. The next subsection explains how to safely delete an element without accidentally losing data.

Deleting elements

Deleting an element from a diagram only removes it from that specific diagram but does not completely delete it from the repository. Technically, it is deleting the relationship between the diagram and the element; however, it will remain intact in the repository. This deletion can be performed by highlighting the element and pressing the Delete button on the keyboard, or right-clicking on the element and selecting **Delete** from the context menu.

On the other hand, to completely and permanently delete an element from the repository, we need to follow the process in *Figure 13.6*:

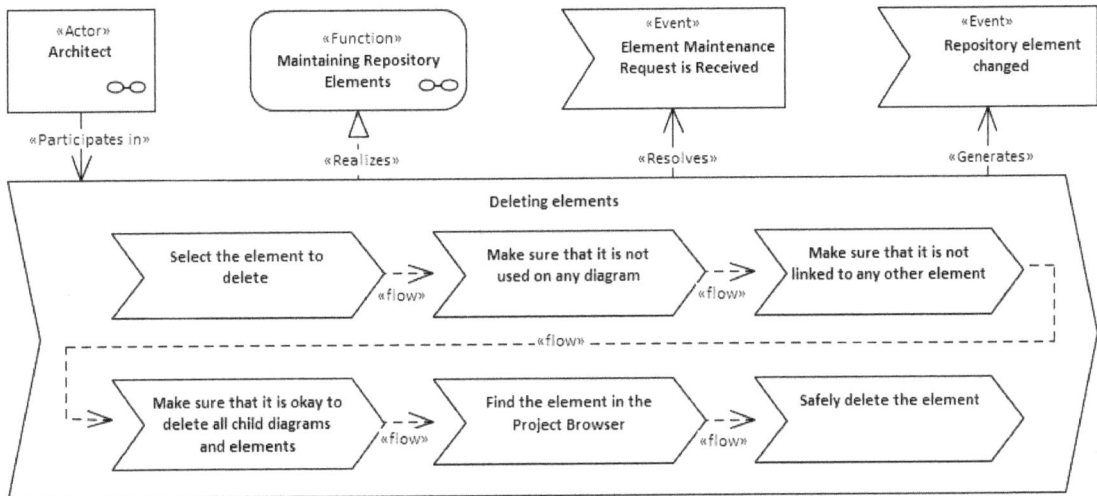

Figure 13.6: Deleting an element from the repository process

To ensure that an element is not in use in any diagram, we need to ask Sparx EA to find it in all diagrams. If the result was an empty list, then it is not used in any diagram. Keep in mind that it is possible not to have an element on any diagram, yet it is still connected to other elements. Deleting the element without checking these relationships will result in losing all of them, which might not be the intention. Therefore, you must ensure that an element is not linked to any other element before committing to deleting it.

To check the element's links to other elements, open the **Properties** dialog of the element and check the **Links** tab, as depicted in the example in *Figure 13.7:*

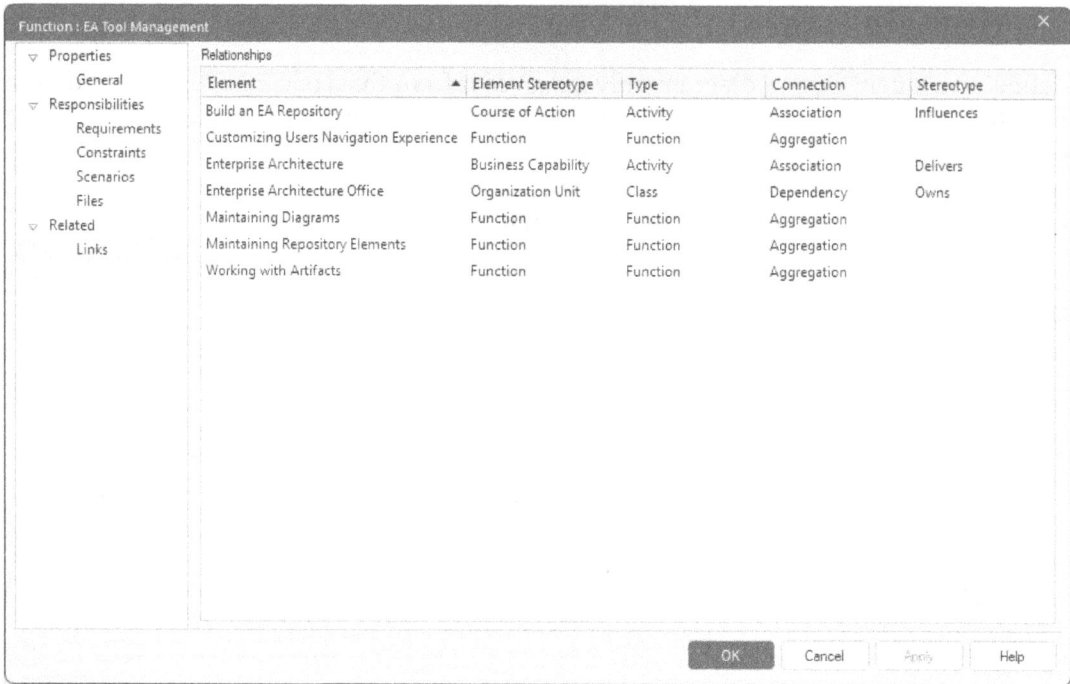

Figure 13.7: List of linked elements

You can right-click on any item in the list to take the desired action, such as locating the related element, so you can learn more about this link and decide accordingly. You can also delete the relationship by selecting **Delete relationship** from the context menu.

Once you decide that it is safe to delete the element, you can do that by either finding it in the project browser and deleting it from there or by highlighting the element on the diagram and hitting *Ctrl + Delete* on the keyboard. Once you confirm your action, the element will be permanently deleted from the repository. It will be lost forever with all its child diagrams and elements, if any, and there is no way to get it back.

Important: **Deleting an element from the repository is permanent and irreversible.**

If you are not very sure about deleting an item but still want to keep the repository clean and free of orphan elements, you can move them to a package in the **Sandboxes** package and decide later what to do with them, something like the Recycle Bin in Windows. Moving elements from one location to another is what we will discuss next.

Moving elements

Moving content is as simple as dragging and dropping it from the source location to the destination. You can move content between packages for many reasons, such as moving it from the Sandbox to the Architecture Content package after it gets approved. Another reason is to move unwanted content to an archive or a recycling bin location. The third reason is that the content was created in the wrong location, which will affect the consistency of the repository. This is mainly why we are discussing this.

Take, for example, the diagram that we created in *Figure 13.2*. We created a child diagram for the **EA Tool Management** Function, then created new Processes that realize the Function on that child diagram. Sparx EA places all new elements that are created on a diagram in the same location that contains the diagram, which in our case will result in having all the newly created Processes under the Function element, and we will end up having Processes contained in the **Functions** package and not the **Processes** package, as explained in *Figure 13.8*:

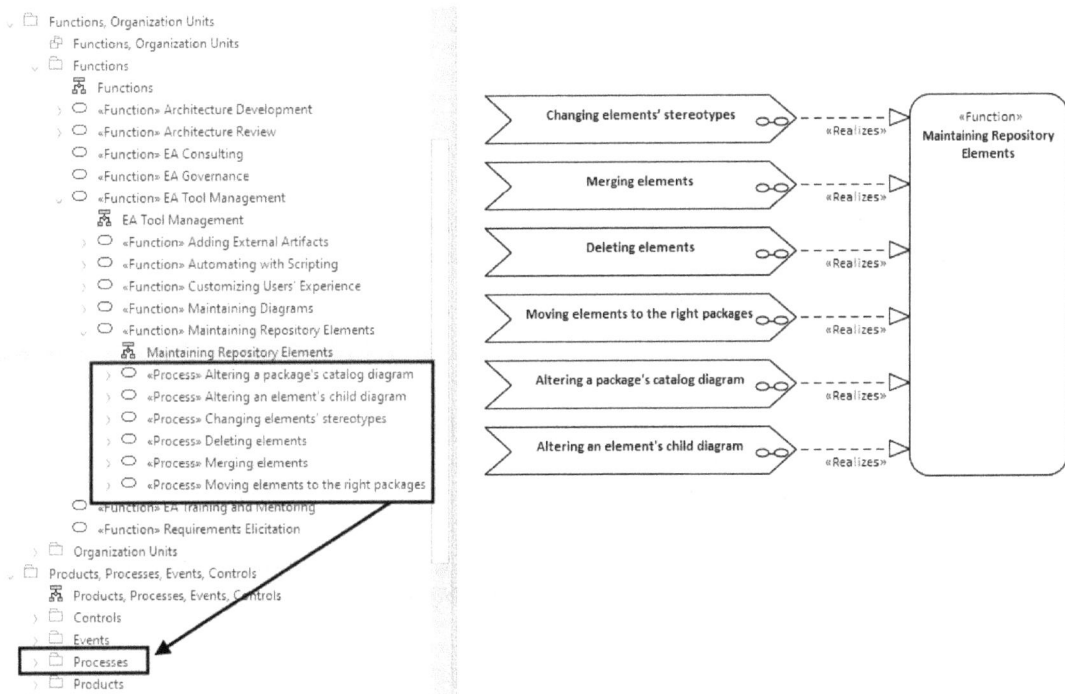

Figure 13.8: Processes contained in the incorrect location

If you do not move the diagram elements from the place where they are created to the packages that are designated for their types, the repository will end up in a mess, and finding an element in it will be like finding a needle in a haystack.

Users will expect to find the information in the locations that you trained them to look in. They will expect to find Functions in the Functions package, Processes in the Processes package, and so on. Therefore, you must meet the users' expectations to maintain their trust in the repository and its content, and it is a goal that you must achieve. *Figure 13.9* models the process of moving elements to the right packages that are designated for their stereotypes:

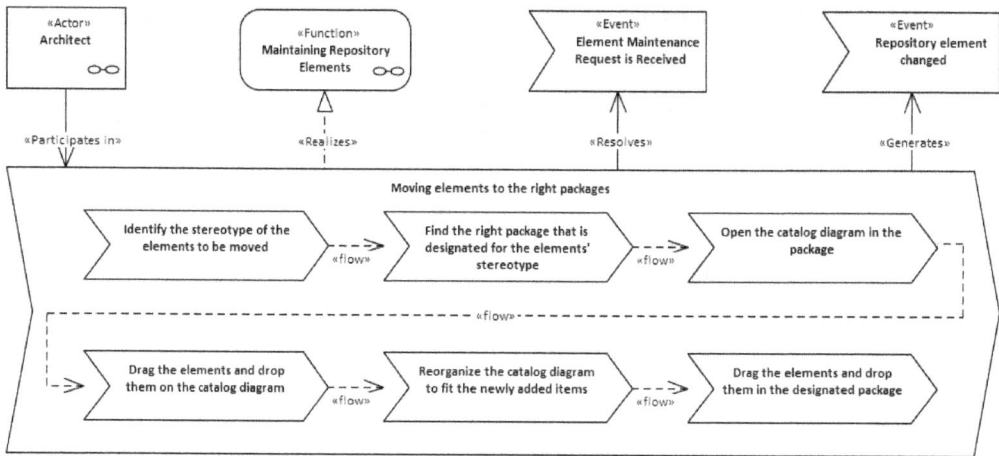

Figure 13.9: *Moving elements to the right packages process*

We have already experienced how to create a child diagram for an element, and we used it on many occasions in the previous chapters, but let us see how to change an element's child diagram to a different diagram type.

Changing an element's composite structure diagram

When creating a composite structure diagram for an element, that diagram becomes the default diagram that will respond to the double-click action on the element. Creating other child diagrams for the same element does not change the assigned composite structure diagram. This is good; on one hand, the element will not be disconnected from its composite structure diagram. However, on the other hand, we may need to change the diagram that responds to the double-click action at one time. The Process in *Figure 13.10* explains the steps for doing that:

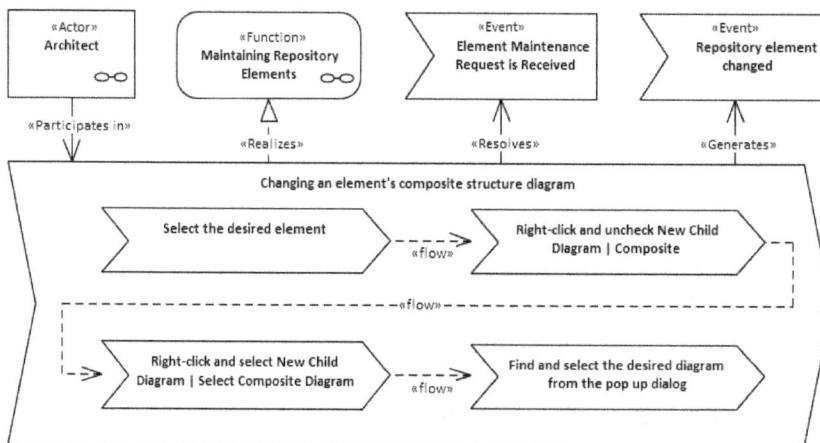

Figure 13.10: *Changing an element's composite structure diagram process*

We talked about packages' diagrams in previous chapters but let us revisit the topic to see how to change the catalog diagram of packages.

Changing a package's catalog diagram

When we create a single diagram inside a package, that diagram becomes the package's default diagram that responds to double-clicking on a package that is placed on a diagram. Take *Figure 5.3* in *Chapter 5, Structuring the Repository* for example. Double-clicking on the **Business Architecture** package that is on the diagram will open the **Business Architecture** diagram that is contained in the package by default. Unlike elements' composite structure diagrams, you do not need to assign the diagram to the package to become its default diagram or catalog diagram. Sparx EA takes the diagram that is on top of the list of diagrams and makes it the default catalog diagram. Additionally, Sparx EA sorts the package content alphabetically by default.

There will be no issues with the default behavior of Sparx EA if we have a single diagram in the package only, so by default, it will be the only diagram to be opened. If you have many diagrams, Sparx EA will keep picking the top diagram on the list, which will be the diagram that comes first in alphabetical sorting. Since it may not be the diagram that we want to be opened when we double-click on the package, we need to change this behavior. The workaround is to manually change the order of the diagrams in a package and make the default catalog diagram on top of the list, regardless of its name. *Figure 13.11* summarizes the process for doing that:

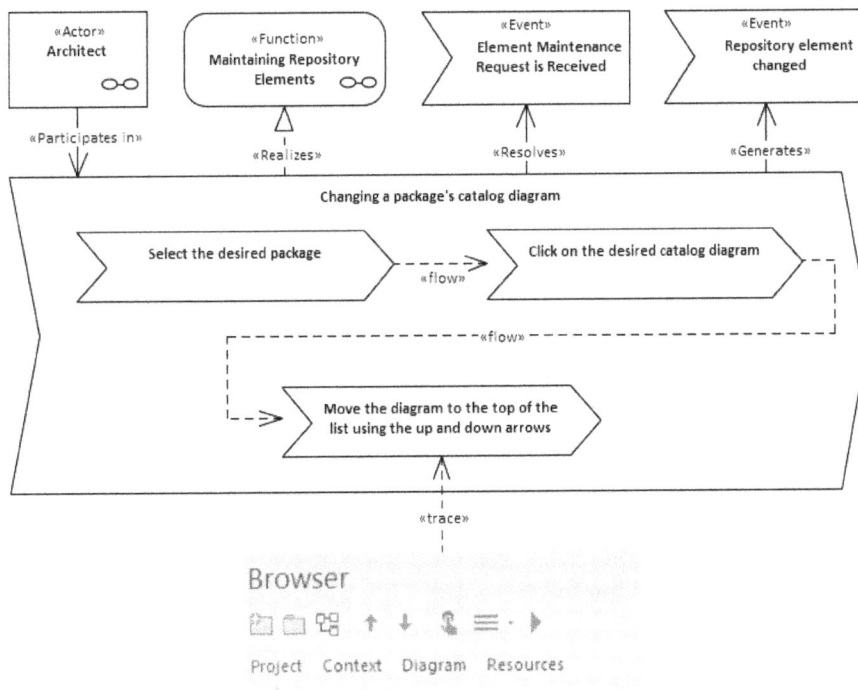

Figure 13.11: Changing a package's catalog diagram Process

Notice how we added an image to enhance the documentation of the Process so the reader of the diagram will know what the up and down buttons are. We will learn more about images and how to add them to diagrams next.

Working with artifacts

An external artifact is a file that is produced from an external application, and we want to import it and use it in Sparx EA. An image file in any format, like JPEG, PNG, BMP, or GIF, or an Office file, such as Word, Excel, or PowerPoint, are the most common files that you will use as artifacts. We have three Processes to cover in the **Working with Artifacts** Function, as modeled in *Figure 13.12*:

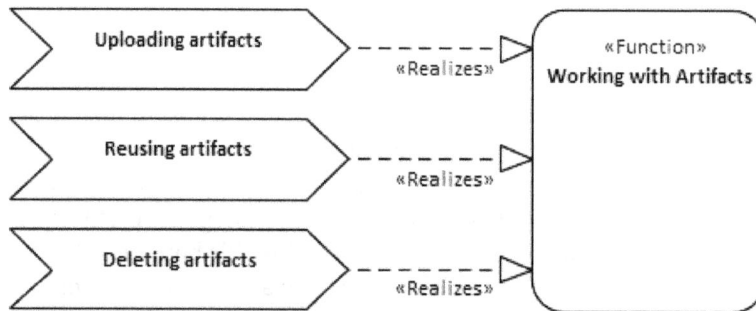

Figure 13.12: *Working with artifacts Function*

The scenarios that you will need to upload an artifact into Sparx EA and use it in a diagram can include adding the company's logo, adding a Word document that contains a reference to a diagram instead of adding a link to it, or adding an Excel spreadsheet that contains a list of data that will be converted into diagrams. This should not mean turning Sparx EA into a document management system, as this is not its purpose as software, but it can store documents in its internal database, so we can use this feature to store some important references. If you received a list of requirements in a spreadsheet, for example, storing the spreadsheet in Sparx EA and keeping it as a reference is very valuable for requirements traceability. With that being said, it makes sense to start learning more about uploading artifacts into Sparx EA before using them.

Uploading artifacts

Uploading documents and images are two similar Processes. We combined them in one Process in *Figure 13.13*, but if you prefer to model them as two separate Processes, you can do that too, the first four steps will be the same and only the fifth will be different:

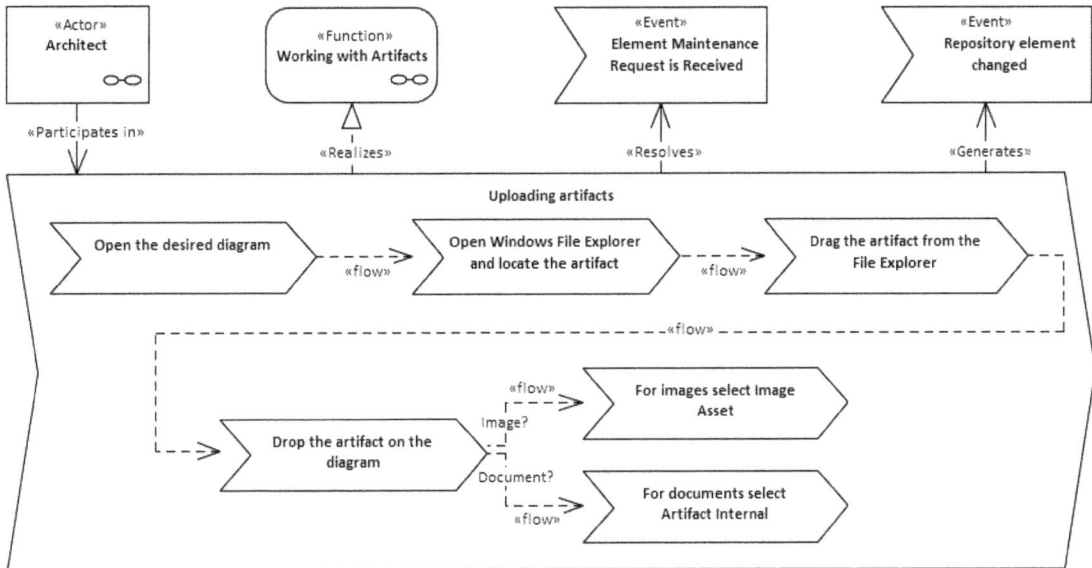

Figure 13.13: Uploading artifacts Process

Sparx EA will place the uploaded artifacts in the same package that contains the diagram. If you want to move them to a different package, use the same Process for moving elements that we modeled in *Figure 13.9*. For images that could be used in many diagrams, like the logo image, the Reference Library package can be an excellent location for them.

The next Process is how to use the artifacts on diagrams.

Reusing artifacts

When you upload an artifact to a diagram, it will automatically appear on it, so you can resize it and place it in the desired position. If you want to add the artifact to another diagram, follow the Process modeled in *Figure 13.14:*

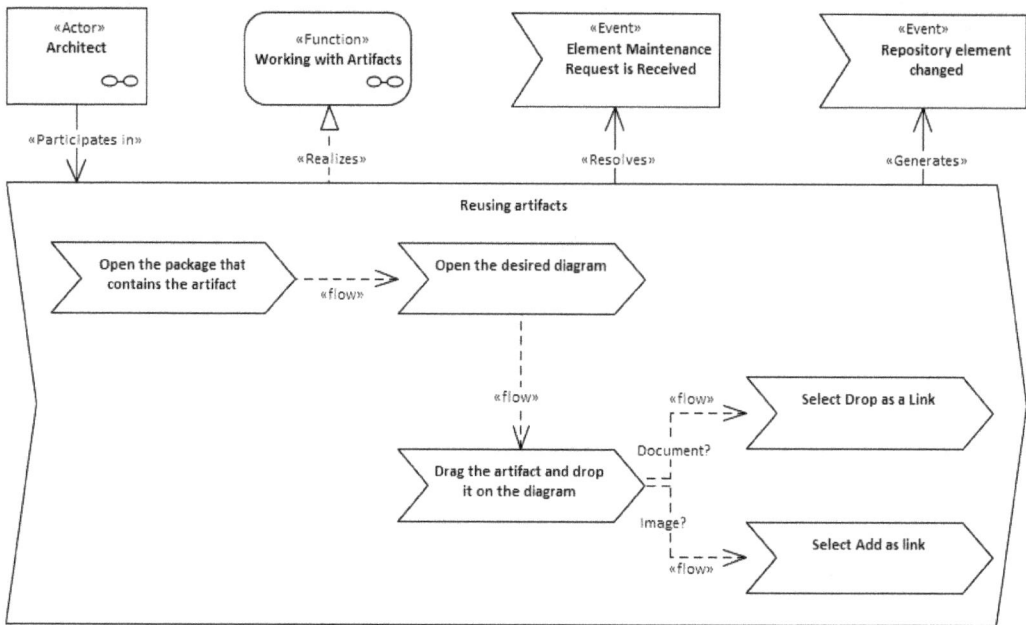

Figure 13.14: *Reusing artifacts Process*

Reusing artifacts is slightly different between documents and images, so you can also keep them as one Process, as we did, or split them into two. Next Process is for deleting artifacts.

Deleting artifacts

Artifacts are treated like any other element in the repository, so deleting them is the same as deleting elements. *Figure 13.15* shows that the deleting artifacts Process uses the same logic and steps as deleting elements, so there is no need to duplicate the model, and directing users to **Deleting elements** Process is better, but it is up to your preference:

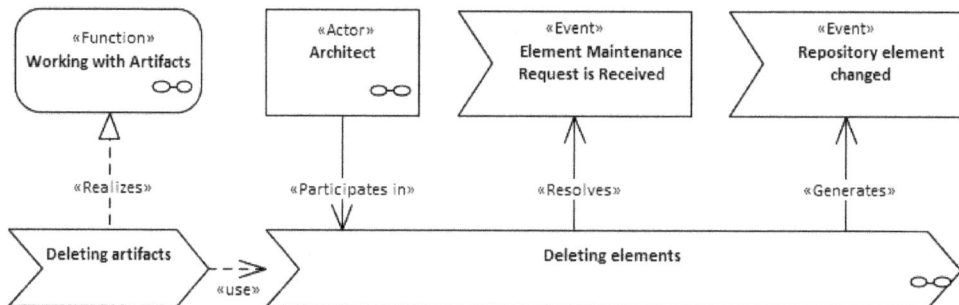

Figure 13.15: *Process of deleting artifacts*

The next Function that we will learn about is the one that documents the Processes of maintaining diagrams, so let us look at it.

Maintaining diagrams

Diagrams are special types of elements. They cannot physically contain child elements, but the elements can be placed on them, forming a relationship between diagrams and elements. Since diagrams need maintenance too, we modeled the **Maintaining Diagrams** Function and the Processes that realize it, in *Figure 13.16*:

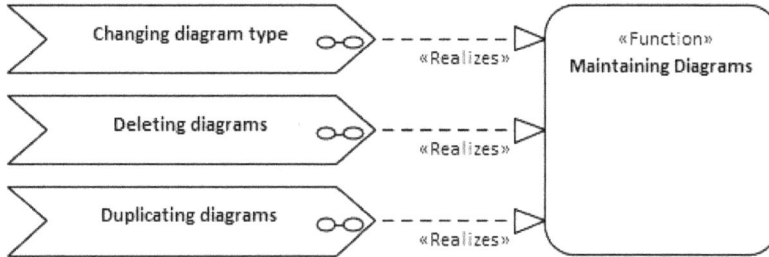

Figure 13.16: Maintaining diagrams Function

The first Process to look at is the Process that models how to change a diagram type.

Changing diagram type

Diagrams come in different types, and each diagram type is associated by default with a toolbox that contains the elements that can be used on the diagram. If a different toolbox is required to be linked with the diagram, the diagram type must be changed to the type that is associated with the toolbox. A very common use case is when we change the stereotype of an element, and we want the composite structure diagram of that element to show the toolbox that matches the new stereotype. Follow the Process in *Figure 13.17* to learn how:

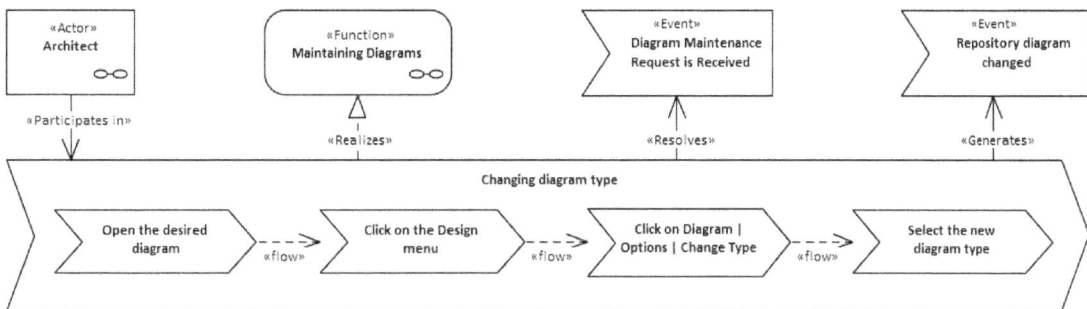

Figure 13.17: Changing diagram type Process

If a diagram is not needed anymore, they had better get deleted to avoid having unnecessary elements in the repository, and we will learn how to do that next.

Deleting diagrams

The Process for deleting a diagram from the repository is very straightforward, and it is depicted in *Figure 13.18*:

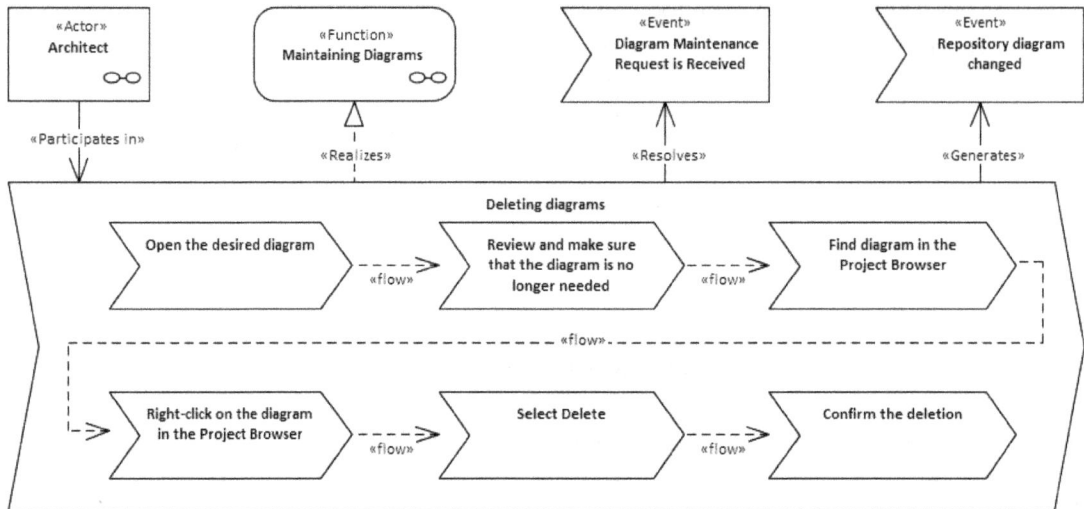

Figure 13.18: *Deleting diagrams Process*

We must warn you that once you confirm the deletion of a diagram, it will be permanently deleted, and this action is irreversible, just like deleting elements. It is good practice to make a backup copy of the diagram if you are not sure. Creating a duplicate copy of a diagram must be studied carefully, as there are three ways to do that, so let us see how in the next subsection.

Duplicating diagrams

Before looking at the Process of duplicating diagrams, we need to explain the relationships between a diagram and the elements that appear on it in more detail. If an element is placed in a diagram, and both the element and the diagram are contained within the same container, the element is described as *owned by the diagram*. If an element is in a diagram, and the element and the diagram are not contained within the same parent container, the element is described as *linked to the diagram*. The container can either be a package that contains diagrams and elements or an element that contains diagrams and elements.

Figure 13.19 models the Process for duplicating a diagram, and the part to pay extra attention to is the **Type of copy** options that appear in the **Copy Diagram** dialog box:

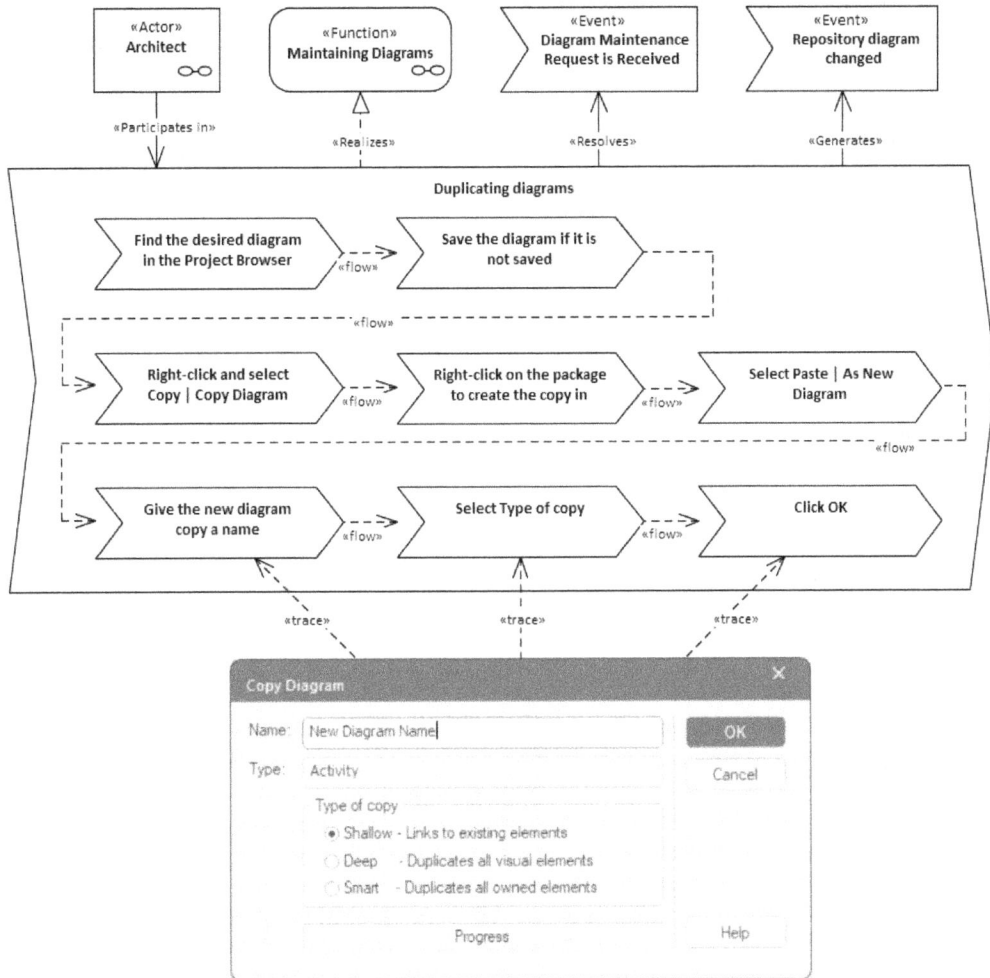

Figure 13.19: Duplicating diagrams Process

If we have a diagram that has both owned and linked elements in it, selecting **Shallow** will duplicate the diagram only, and will not duplicate any of the owned or the linked elements. The new diagram will contain links to the original elements. Selecting **Deep** will duplicate the diagram and will also duplicate all the elements that are in it, both the owned and the linked. The new diagram will also have new independent elements that are not related to the original diagram.

Selecting **Smart** will duplicate the diagram and all the elements that are owned by the diagram, but will not duplicate the elements that are linked to the diagram. Remember that when you place an element on a diagram from the toolbox, it creates a new element. The new element will be contained in the same package that contains the diagram; therefore, we say that the diagram owns the element. In short, an element is considered owned by a diagram if it is placed on it and they both reside in the same package. Linked elements, on the other hand, are the elements that are placed as links on the diagram when dragged from the project browser. They are used by the diagram but not owned by it.

Note: Press Ctrl + U to get a list of all the diagrams that use an element.

Let us take an example to clarify this important point. We have a package A that contains three Processes, and another package B that contains a diagram and a Function. If we place the Function from package B and on the diagram, then placed all the Processes from Package A on the same diagram, the Function element is considered as an element owned by the diagram because they are both contained within the same package. The Processes, on the other hand, are elements that are linked to the diagram because they are contained in a different package. Copy the diagram and paste it into **Packages X** using shallow. Paste the same diagram in **Package Y** using deep, and paste it again in **Package Z** using smart. The results are depicted in *Figure 13.20*:

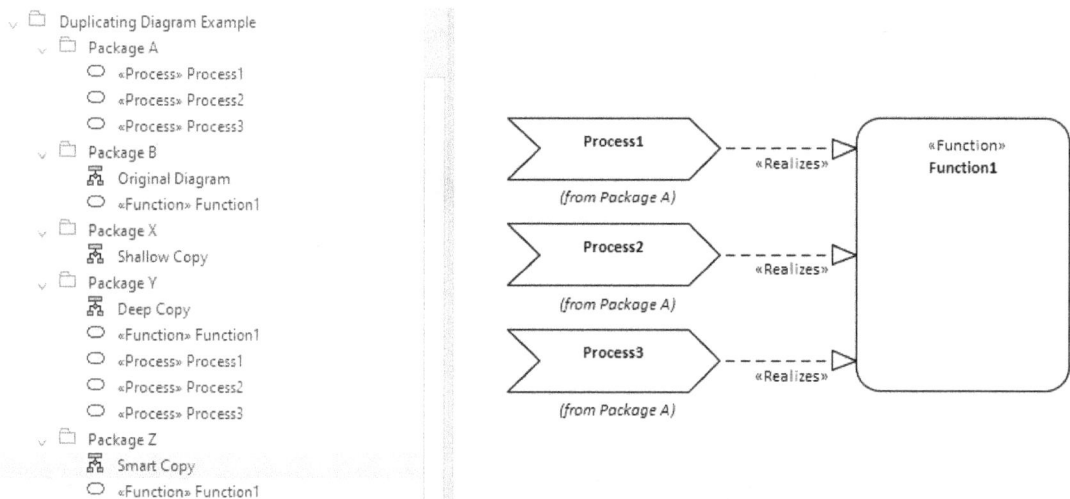

Figure 13.20: Duplicating diagram example

We used a shallow type of copy in **Package X**, which resulted in duplicating the diagram only, but did not duplicate any of the elements that were on it. All the elements on the new diagram are linked to it. We used the deep type of copy when we pasted the diagram in **Package Y**, which resulted in duplicating the diagram and everything on it, including both the owned and the linked elements. All the elements on the new diagram are owned by it, and there is are no more connections between the new elements and the original elements. The repository will contain two Functions and six Processes after a deep copy. In **Package Z**, we used the smart type of copy, which resulted in duplicating the owned element only. The elements that were linked to the original diagram are also linked to the new diagram.

Understanding the behavior of the three different types of copy is essential to avoid having unwanted duplicate elements in the repository. Use the Sandbox package to practice the different types of copying and understand the differences and similarities. There are different use cases for each, so understanding the differences will help you decide which one to choose.

Different users have different interests in an EA repository. Building different interests for each group of users in the repository requires building different navigation experiences so users will feel comfortable navigating with content that they understand; hence, let us learn how to do that.

Customizing users' navigation experience

It is easy for experienced EA practitioners to navigate a repository that is structured in a way that is aligned with the TOGAF content framework. *Figure 5.2* in *Chapter 5, Structuring the Repository*, shows that navigation will start from the Architecture Content page. If an experienced TOGAF user is looking for a place that contains all the business processes, they know that they must look inside the business architecture package and find the sub package that contains the Processes.

For users with limited experience in EA, it may be difficult to know where to go next from *Figure 5.2*, and they will prefer a different view with terminology they understand. It will also help them to have the information flat rather than needing to navigate up and down in different packages. *Figure 13.21* shows **Customizing the Users Navigation Experience** Function and the Processes that realize it.

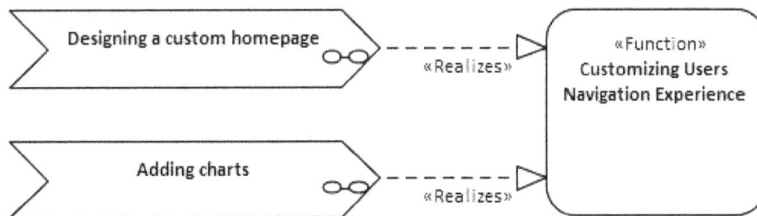

Figure 13.21: *Customizing users navigation experience Function*

Let us see what designing different views means and learn how to do it.

Designing different views

The standard navigation style that we have designed in the repository in *Chapter 5, Structuring the Repository*, starts from the top-level package, which is the Architecture Content package, and drills down to packages and subpackages where the artifacts are located. This navigation style is useful for a person who is familiar with the TOGAF content framework and knows where to go to find the information. For someone who is less familiar, providing a flat view that contains all the links to the important artifacts in one place might be easier for them to understand and use. *Figure 13.22* shows an example of a catalog diagram that contains links to other catalogs:

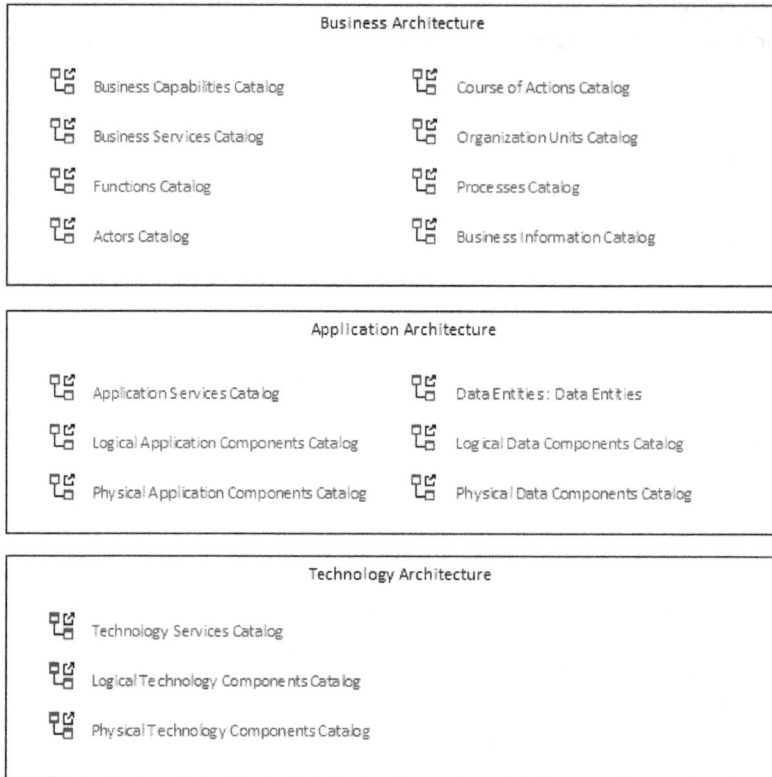

Figure 13.22: *A catalog of catalogs*

This catalog of catalogs can be customized to include or exclude any links to diagrams that users like to have on a homepage.

As you can see, users can directly navigate to the **Functions Catalog**, for example, without the need to drill down into multiple packages and subpackages to reach it. Another style of homepages is the one that is centered around a specific element, but provides a full-picture style of diagrams, where users can see not only the elements that are directly connected to that specific element, but also the elements that are connected to the connected elements too. *Figure 13.23* shows an example with everything that is related to the **Architecture Design** business service:

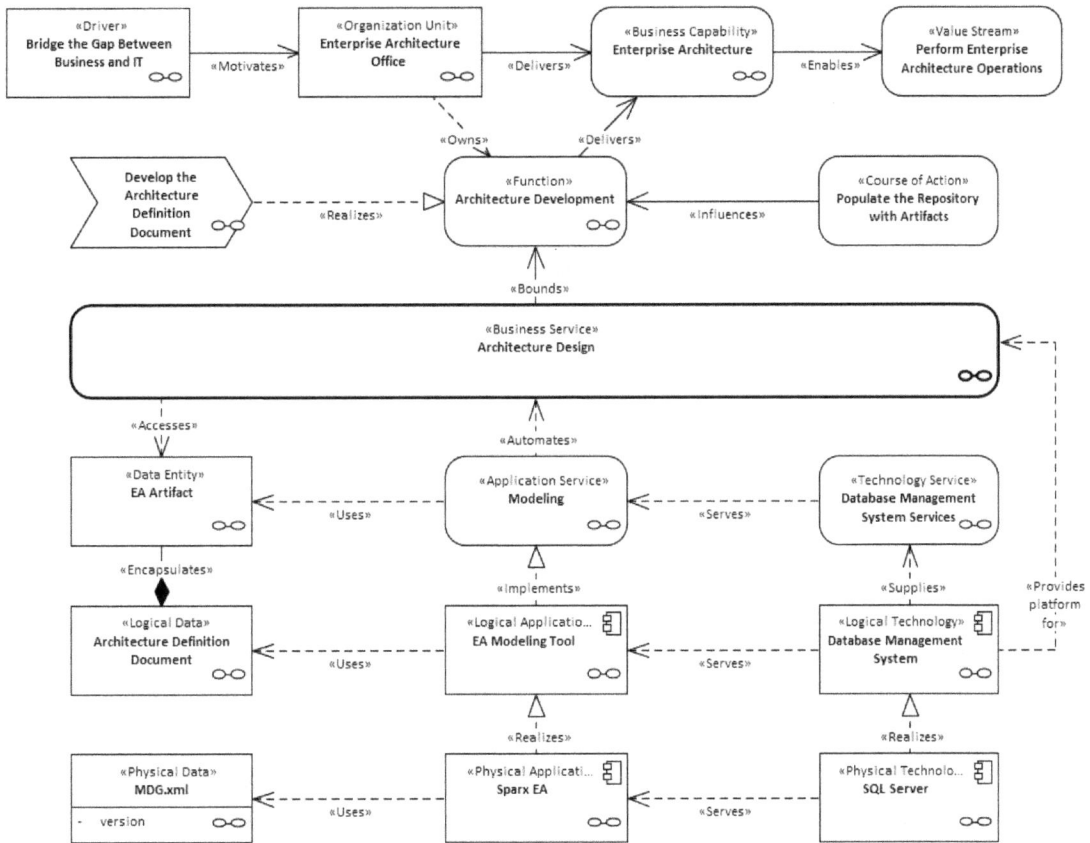

Figure 13.23: *Business service full-picture style homepage*

This style of diagrams is useful for solution architects and project managers, who would be interested in seeing everything that is related to a specific project in one place and use it as a homepage to navigate to the rest of the repository. The only take on this type of diagram is that it can easily get crowded and overwhelmed with crossing and intersecting connectors covering the entire space, so they must be used with extra care and get visited regularly to be cleaned up from unwanted connectors.

Once you decide on the style you and the users prefer to use, build the diagram in any package in the repository, including the Sandboxes, then set it as the default homepage, so Sparx EA will open it every time it is launched. *Figure 13.24* models the Process of designing a custom homepage:

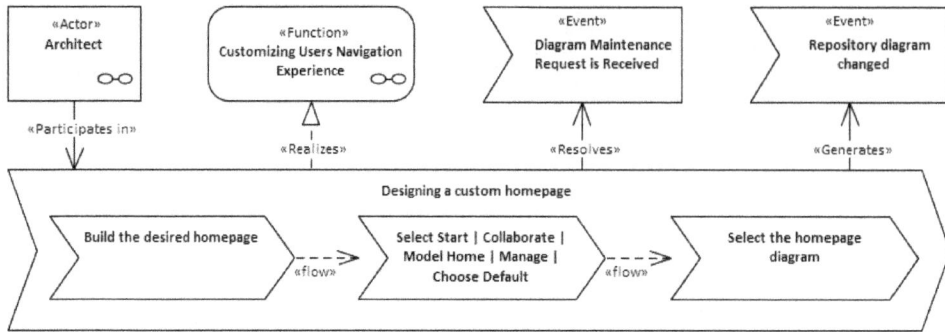

Figure 13.24: *Designing a custom homepage Process*

This Process sets the default homepage to the selected diagram for all users. However, most of the time, Sparx EA will be running on a network in your workspace, and each user will have their own profile defined in it. In this case, you can have a different homepage per user by replacing the second step in *Figure 13.23* with **Start | Personal | My Diagram | Manage | Choose Default**.

Another good feature that you can add to a repository is queries and dashboards, a topic that we will learn about next.

Adding charts

Charts are graphical representations of selected data. You can chart to any diagram, and Sparx EA provides different styles like pie charts and bar charts. In *Figure 13.25*, we added two charts to the homepage that we introduced in *Figure 13.22*:

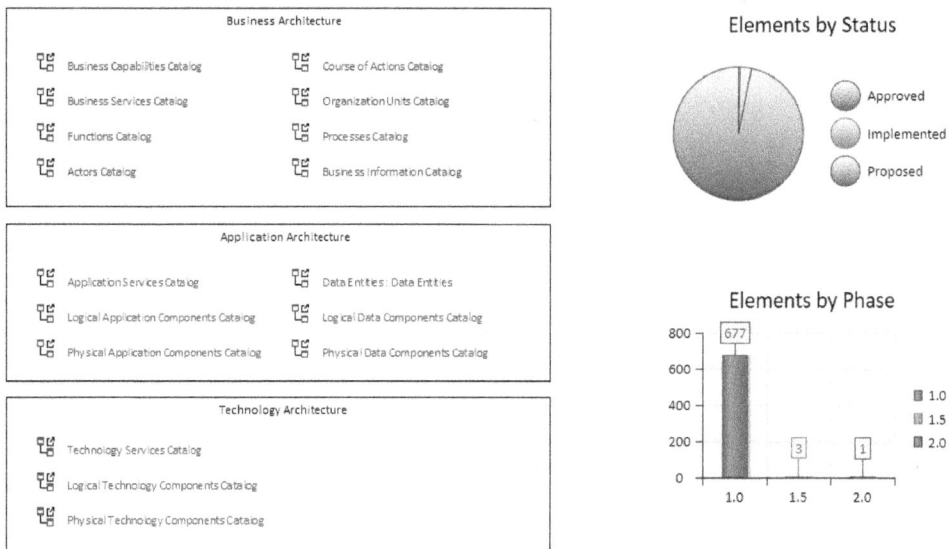

Figure 13.25: *Adding charts*

The pie chart shows a comparison of the elements' status, and the bar chart shows a comparison of the elements' phase. These two charts tell us that most of the elements in the repository are **Proposed**, and that most of the elements are in Phase 1.0. This is because these are the default values for the status and phase attributes of every new element. This is a clear indicator that we need to revisit all the elements in the repository and set these values to a value that reflects that reality. The Process for adding a chart to a diagram is modeled in *Figure 13.26*:

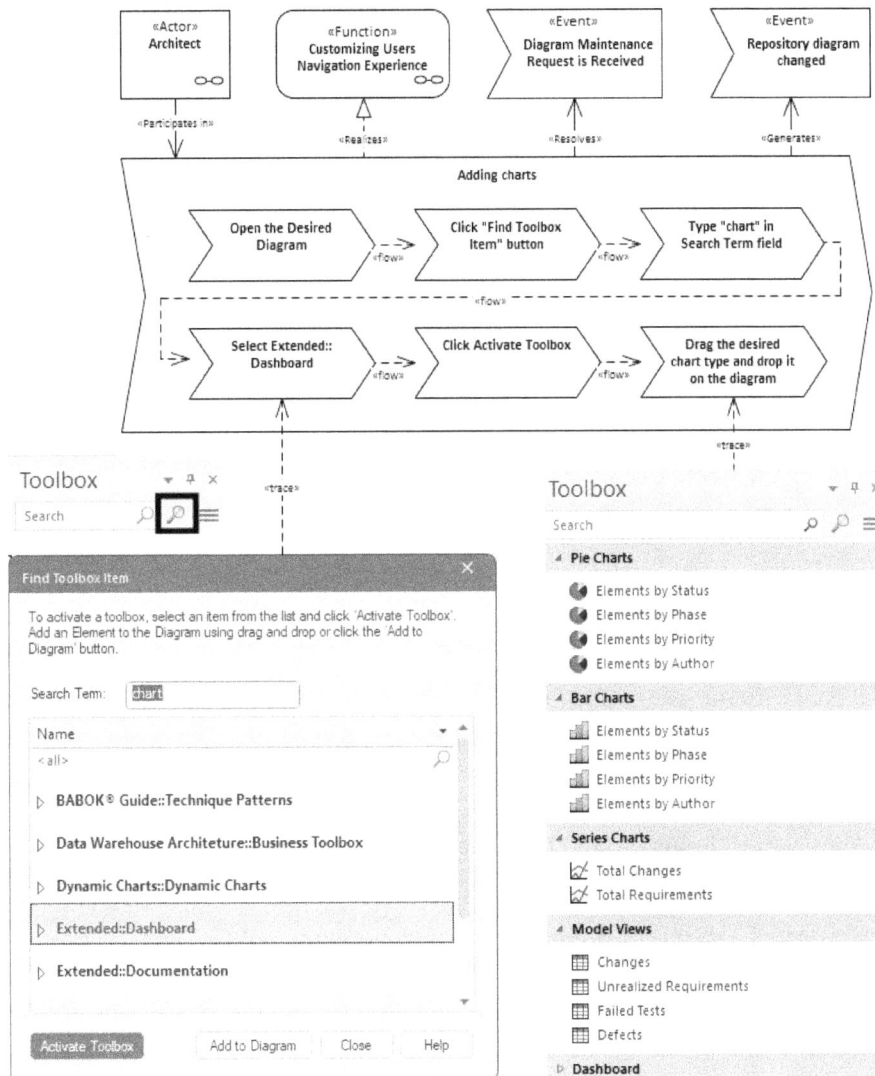

Figure 13.26: Adding charts Process

Adding screenshots to the Processes makes them easier to understand for anyone who wants to learn the Process. This way, the Process model can play the role of a training manual and a reference material too, not just dry Process documentation.

We have only scratched the surface of charts. If you right-click on any of the charts that we created, and select **Properties | Properties | Chart Details**, you can customize the appearance of the charts, the source database query that populates them, and you can filter the results to match your needs. You can read more about charts and their data in the Sparx EA user guide at **https://sparxsystems.com/enterprise_architect_user_guide/17.1/model_publishing/chart_data.html**.

Conclusion

We learned a few Processes to keep the EA repository properly maintained and attractive to its users. We could not model everything, but we hope that you learned a way to model Functions and Processes at the same time as learning how to perform the maintenance Processes. Imagine how well documented your enterprise will be if every Process is documented the way we documented our repository management Processes.

In the next chapter, we will learn how to publish architecture documents. With that ability, you can publish EA content either in HTML or document formats, and share it with people who do not have a license to access Sparx EA or do not have the proper experience to use it.

Points to remember

- When changing an element's stereotype, you need to adjust the connectors that connect to and from it, or you will end up with invalid relationships.

- It is very possible to discover duplicate elements, so make sure to learn how to merge them properly and how to delete the unneeded ones.

- Deleting elements, diagrams, and artifacts is permanent and cannot be undone.

- The default diagram in a package is the first one on top.

- Reusable elements like logos must be uploaded to one place only, but used as needed.

- Shallow copy of a diagram duplicates the diagram only, but none of its elements.

- A deep copy of a diagram duplicates every element on the diagram.

- Smart copy of a diagram duplicates owned elements only.

Key terms

- **Charts**: Graphical representations of selected data such as pie charts, bar charts, and area charts.

CHAPTER 14
Publishing EA Artifacts

Introduction

The content of an enterprise repository should not be available only to users with Sparx EA experience or only to users with a license to use it. A successful repository must be accessible by the entire enterprise and by every group having a different interest in its content. The simplest way of sharing EA artifacts with the rest of the enterprise is to copy diagrams to the clipboard and paste them into documents, then share them. This is how this book is written. All the diagrams that were included in this book were developed in Sparx EA, then embedded into Word documents using the standard screen snipping tool that comes with Windows.

The biggest advantage of this approach is that it gives more flexibility to format the document any way we want. Text can be added above, below, or around the images, and we have great control over the content flow. The biggest disadvantage to this approach, however, is that updates must be done manually, and the steps for copying and pasting the content from Sparx EA to Word must be manually repeated. In a large enterprise, where changes are constantly happening, relying on manual Processes like this is not efficient and will make the EA content and the published content out of synch very quickly. In this chapter, we will learn how to automatically generate and publish Sparx EA's content using templates that we can design and customize. They will not be as good-looking as a book, but with some investment in time and effort, you can get nicely published content that can be easily and efficiently shared with the rest of the enterprise.

Structure

This chapter will include the following topics:

- Publishing artifacts

Objectives

The objective of this chapter is to learn how to convert the EA artifacts into documents and web content that can be read by others without the need for a Sparx EA license.

Publishing artifacts

Publishing artifacts is a Function that we will be creating in this chapter to learn how to publish artifacts, and at the same time, we will learn how to fit this content properly in the EA repository as Functions and Processes. **Publishing Artifacts** is a Function that can either be considered an independent Function, that is, directly owned by the **Enterprise Architecture Office** Organization Unit. In this case, it must be added to *Figure 12.14* or as a subfunction to the **EA Tool Management** Function, which means it can be added to *Figure 13.1*. We believe that publishing artifacts is part of the **EA Tool Management** Function because it is part of using and managing the tool's functionality, but you may have a different opinion in your work environment. *Figure 14.1* shows the updated model of the **EA Tool Management** Function:

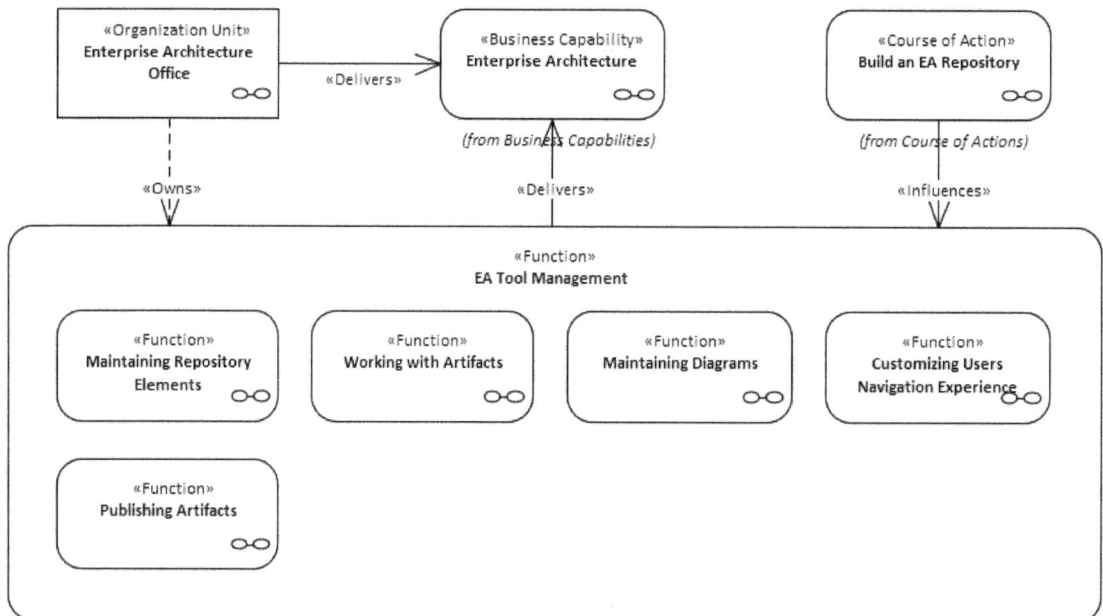

Figure 14.1: Updated view of EA tool management Function

The **Publishing Artifacts** Function can be decomposed into two main Functions: **Publishing Documents** and **Publishing Web Content**, as depicted in *Figure 14.2*:

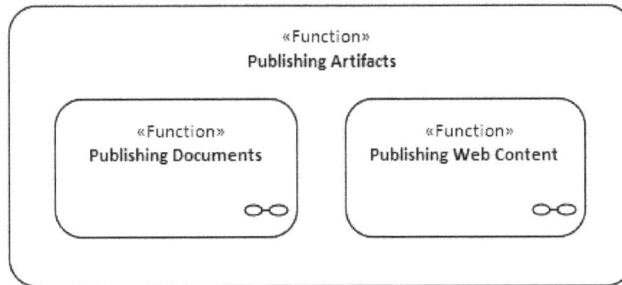

Figure 14.2: *Publishing artifacts Function*

The **Publishing Documents** Function covers converting the selected content from Sparx EA into a format that can be opened and read by a word Processor such as Microsoft Word. **Publishing Web Content** covers converting the selected EA content into HTML content that can be accessed and viewed using a web browser. We will talk about both; however, we will start by publishing documents.

Publishing documents

Document publishing converts a package and all its content from the repository into a document. Sparx EA supports **docx**, **pdf**, and **rtf** formats, which cover the needs of most enterprise audiences. Document publishing works at the package level, which adds some constraints on what can be included in the document and what cannot be. By default, every package, diagram, and element in the selected package will be included in the generated document. There are ways to customize this behavior to include or exclude elements and diagrams from different packages, and this is what we will be covering in the **Publishing Documents** Function that is modeled in *Figure 14.3*:

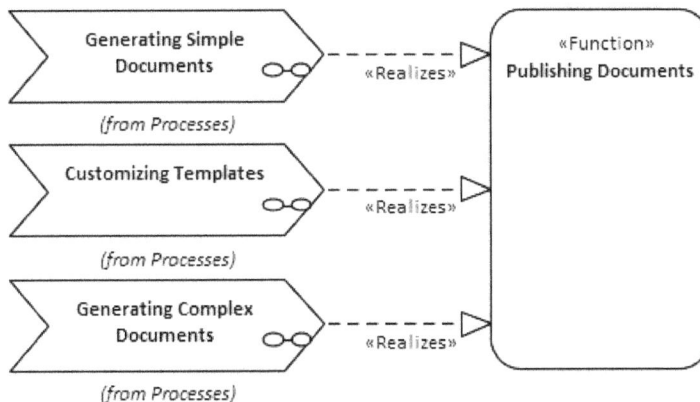

Figure 14.3: *Publishing documents Function*

Let us learn first how to generate a simple document before learning how to customize the templates and generate more complicated documents.

Generating simple documents

To generate a document, select any package in the **Project Browser**, press *F8* or select **Publish | Model Reports | Report Builder | Generate Documentation**, then follow the instructions in the **Generate Documentation** dialog box, as modeled in *Figure 14.4*:

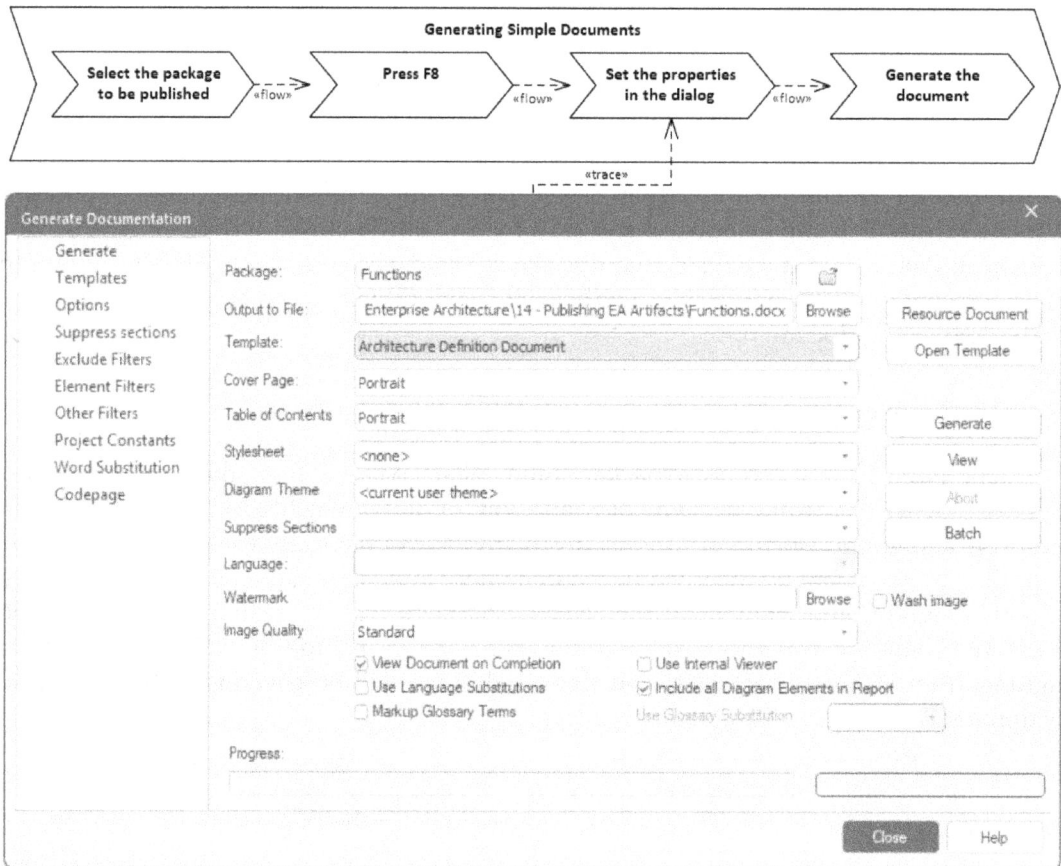

Figure 14.4: *Generating simple documents Process*

Use the ellipses button next to **Output to File** field to provide the file path, name, and type. The **Template** dropdown contains a list of predefined templates, each of which is configured and customized to provide a different set of information, based on the use case that the document is being generated for. We will select the **Data Modeling Report** template for this example, however, we highly recommend that you explore all the other templates to understand the differences between each template type, how the information is provided in each template, and to identify any adjustments or customizations if needed or required.

There are a few templates for the cover page and table of contents; select the ones that you like. Check **View Document on Completion** for the generated document, to be automatically opened for viewing after a successful generation. Uncheck **Use Internal Viewer** to launch the document in the proper document viewer that is installed on the computer, such as Microsoft Word.

Click **Generate** to start generating the document, and when the generation is successfully completed, the document will be available for you to view. *Figure 14.5* shows a comparison between the hierarchy in Sparx EA on the left side of the screen, and the hierarchy in the generated Word document on the right:

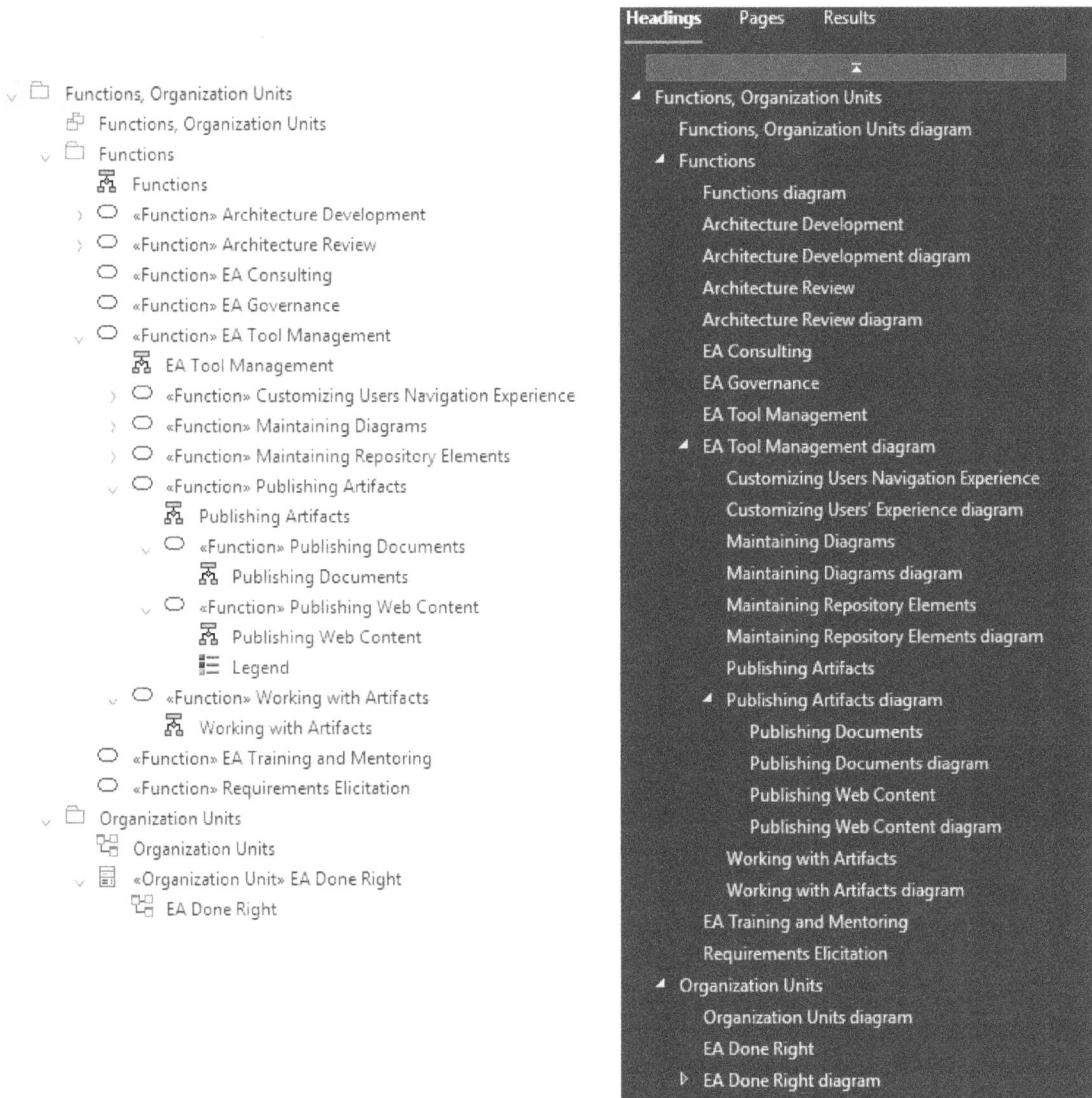

Figure 14.5: Repository structure converted to document structure

The top-level package in Sparx EA is converted into an H1 header in the document. Every diagram and subpackage is converted into an H2 header, then an H3 header for the packages' content, and so on. *Figure 14.6* shows a Word document generated from the **Functions** package in the repository:

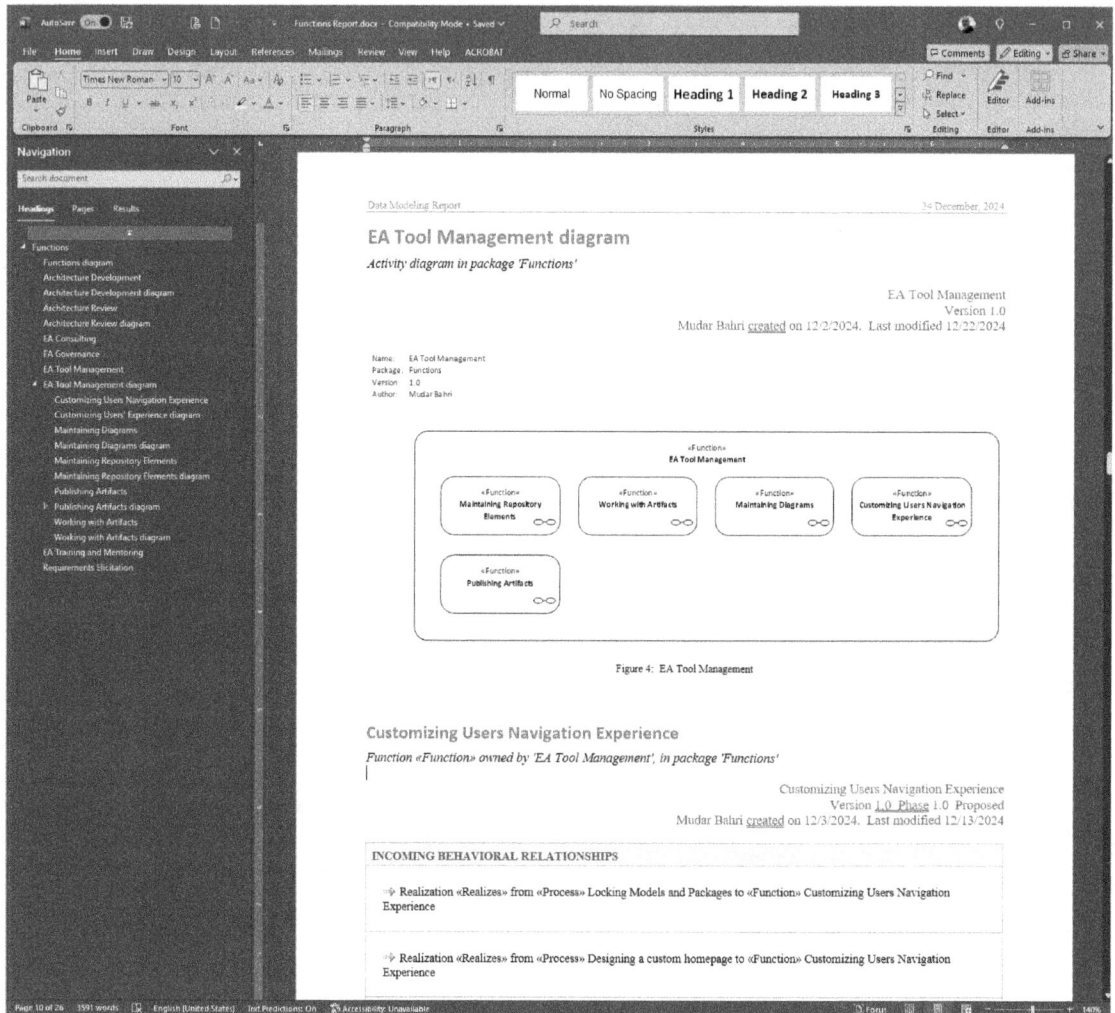

Figure 14.6: Sample from a generated document

If we look at the **EA Tool Management diagram** header, it starts with the diagram name, followed by the word diagram, followed by information about the diagram, like its version number, author, and last editor information, followed by the diagram's image. Since the **EA Tool Management** Function in EA contains subfunctions, diagrams, and other elements, a new heading will be created for each one of these contained elements, and it continues until reaching the deepest element in the selected package's hierarchy.

The order of the sections in the generated document will be determined by their order in the **Project Browser**. If you want the sections to be ordered differently, you must manually reorder the elements in the package in the **Project Browser**. This explains why the first subfunction in the generated document is **Customizing Users Navigation Experience**, and that is because it is the first among its sibling elements in the **Project Browser**.

If you like everything in the document, then you are ready to use it. If you want to add a logo on the cover page or adjust the content or the appearance of the document, you must learn how to customize templates.

Customizing templates

The Process for customizing templates is modeled in *Figure 14.7*. We must first open the **Generate Documentation** dialog either by pressing *F8* on the keyboard or selecting **Publish | Model Reports | Report Builder | Generate Documentation** from the menu. The **Templates** tab will list all the customized templates, so you can either modify an existing template, delete one, create a new one, or close the dialog box as *Figure 14.7* shows:

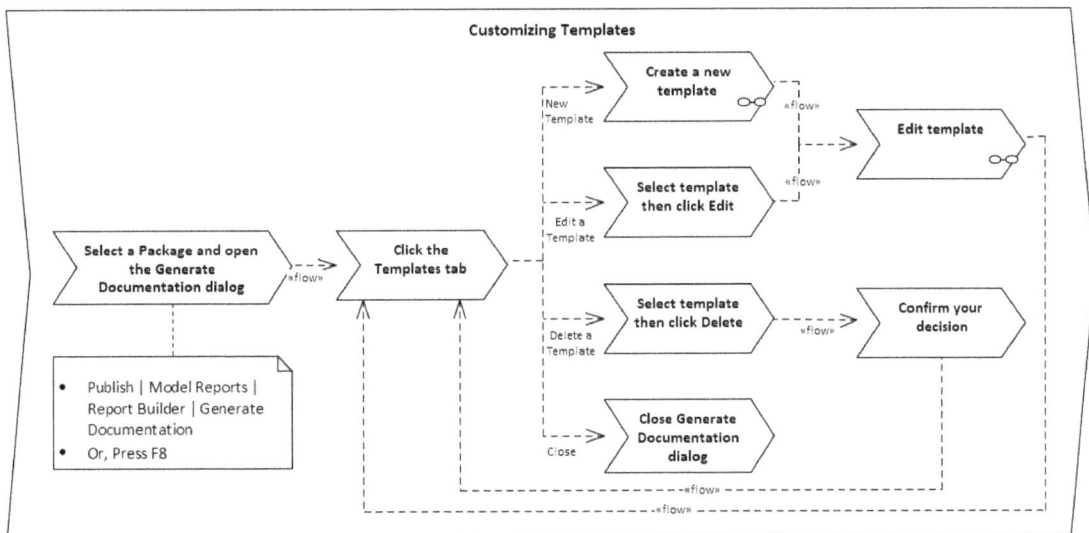

Figure 14.7: *Customizing templates Process*

If you are opening this dialog for the first time, the template list will most probably be empty. The Process for creating a new template is modeled in *Figure 14.8* with a screenshot showing the values that we used in this example:

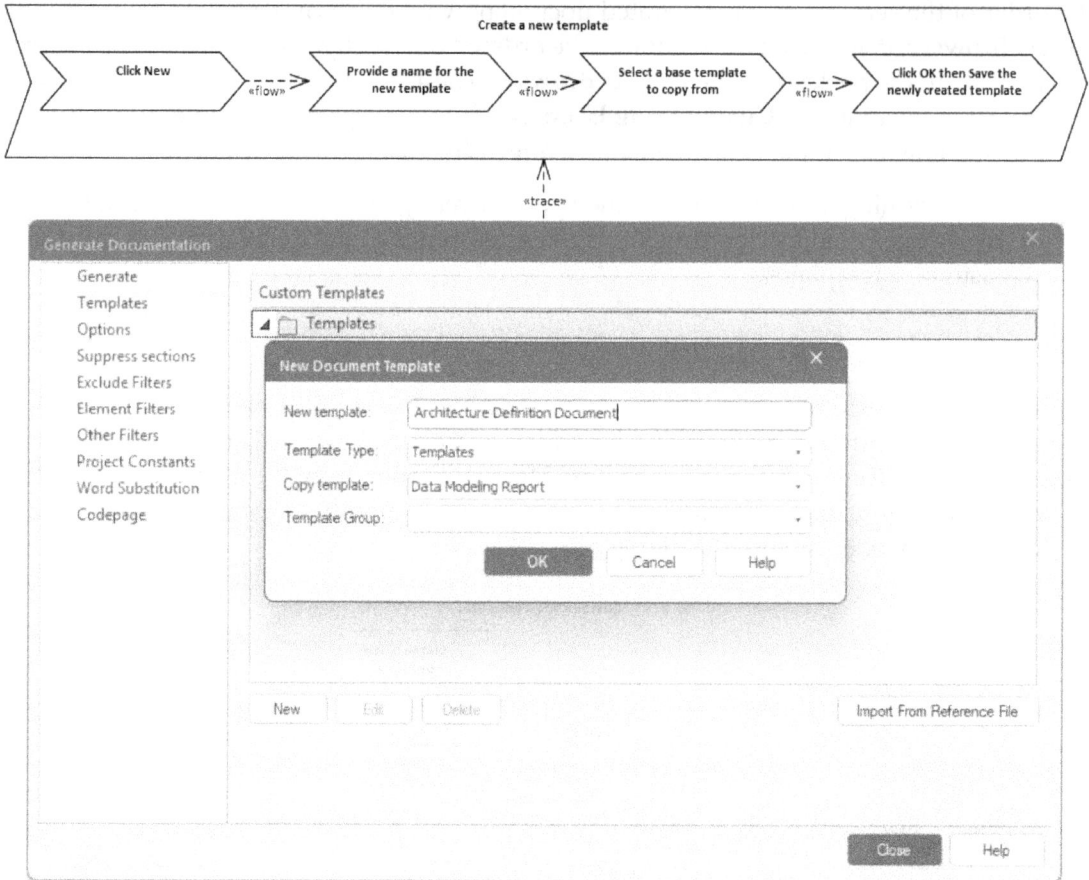

Figure 14.8: Create a new template Process

Give the document template a new name and make it self-descriptive so that you and other architects can understand what it is. If you are editing a document template, select **Templates** from the **Template Type** dropdown list, or select **Cover Pages** or **Table of Contents** if that is what the new template is supposed to be. Select a base template from the **Copy template** list and then click **OK**. The new template will be copied from the selected base template and will be opened in a new tab. *Figure 14.9* shows how the document template designer looks and shows the Process of using it:

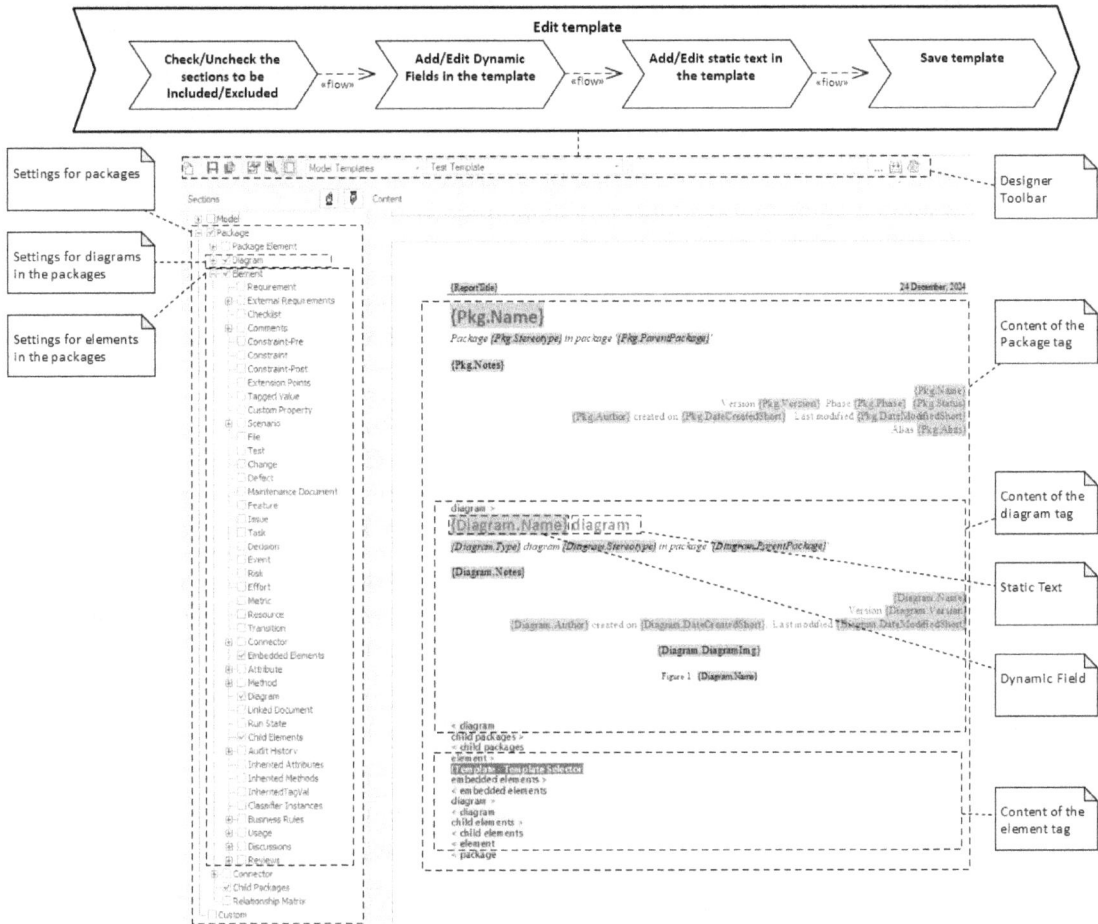

Figure 14.9: Edit template Process

The template designer screen contains two main components: the **Sections** hierarchy tree on the left and the **Content** on the right side. Checking a box from the **Sections** will create a corresponding tag in the **Content,** while unchecking the box will remove the tag from the content. *Figure 14.9* shows that because the **Element | Embedded Elements** checkbox is checked, the `embedded elements >` and `< embedded elements` tags appear between the `element >` and `< element tags`.

Having a tag in the Content side tells Sparx EA that we need this section to appear in the document. We can customize what we want to see by adding static and dynamic fields between the opening and the closing tags. For example, between the `diagram >` and the `< diagram` tags, we can define what to show about a diagram. Right-clicking in any place between the two tags will bring up a content menu that allows us to insert a dynamic field at the cursor's location.

Selecting **Select Field | Diagram Image** will insert the dynamic field `{Diagram.DiagramImg}` which means when the document is generated, the diagram image will appear at the designated location. To format the dynamic field as an image, click on it, then from **Edit | Font** menu bar at the top of Sparx EA's window, select **Diagram Image** from the list of available document formats. Notice how the template designer places the dynamic field in the middle of the page and formats it accordingly. You can change or override the provided format as needed by changing font face, size, color, highlighter color, and many other formatting options.

To add the name of the diagram as a caption, add a line underneath the `{Diagram.DiagramImg}` tag, right-click and choose **Select Field | Name**, will insert the `{Diagram.Name}` under the diagram image tag. From the **Edit | Font** menu bar, select **Diagram Label** from the list of available document formats.

There are a good number of dynamic fields that are available for each tag. There is also another set of dynamic fields that can be accessed from the **Report Constants** context menu option. These are fields that are related to the report itself, not to its content, such as report author, report date, and report file name. Showing these fields on the first page can be helpful.

When adding a dynamic field to the template, the template designer shows you the tag that tells the purpose of the field. When the document is generated, the dynamic field will show the value of the field without telling what this value is. This is why it is important to add static labels next to the dynamic fields when needed. Static labels can be added to the template by typing the label at the location where we want it to appear.

Customizing document templates is a very large topic, and the user guide of Sparx EA provides all the information that you need to customize templates at **https://sparxsystems. com/enterprise_architect_user_guide/17.1/model_publishing/rtfstyletemplateeditor.html**.

Now you know how to customize a document template, and you know where to look for more information, so all you need is to practice doing it more. Try different sections and different tags every time you generate a new document. Keep a copy of the older templates in case a look back is needed, then delete the ones that are not needed anymore.

Even the custom-designed document templates that we create will still work at a single package level and their content. If we want the generated document to have content from different packages, then we need to learn how to generate virtual documents.

Generating virtual documents

A **virtual document** is a data model that tells Sparx EA what packages will be included in the document to be generated. For example, if there is a requirement to generate a document that combines the logical application components, the logical data components, and the logical technical components in one *IT Logical Architecture Document*, we must combine the content from three different locations. The **Logical Application Components** package is located under the **Application Architecture** package. The **Logical Data Components** package is located under the **Data Architecture** package. The **Logical Technology Components** package is located under the **Technology Architecture** package. Since the document generator works at the level of a single package, we need to create a package that virtually acts as a binder of the desired packages. The Process for creating a virtual document is modeled in *Figure 14.10*:

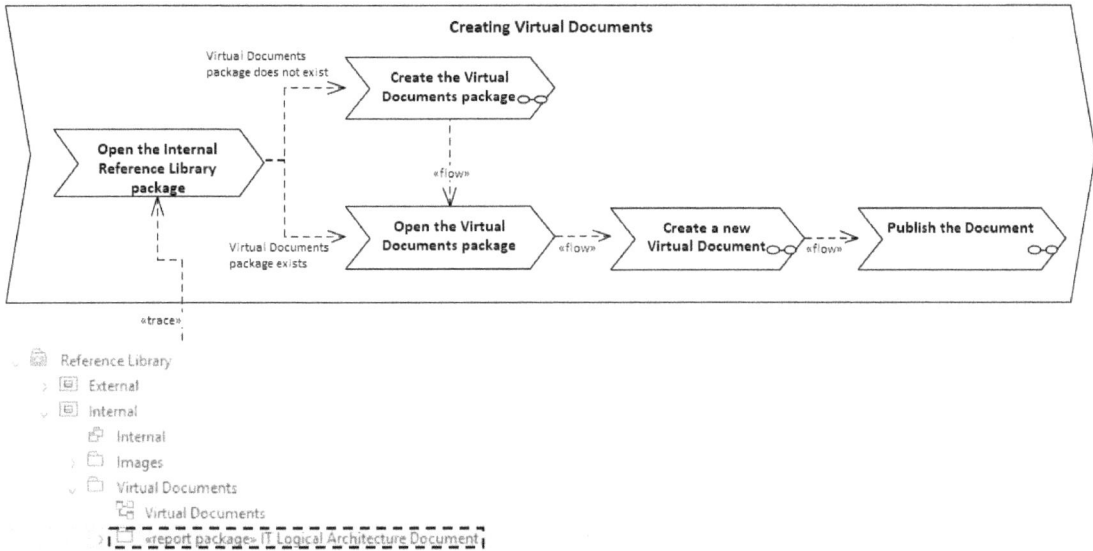

Figure 14.10: Creating Virtual Documents Process

The suggested location for the **Virtual Documents** package to be under **Reference Library | Internal** can be replaced by any location of your choice, and you can even give it any name you prefer. If the virtual documents package does not exist, *Figure 14.11* models the Process to create it. You only need to create this package once, so if you already have created it before, you can skip this sub Process:

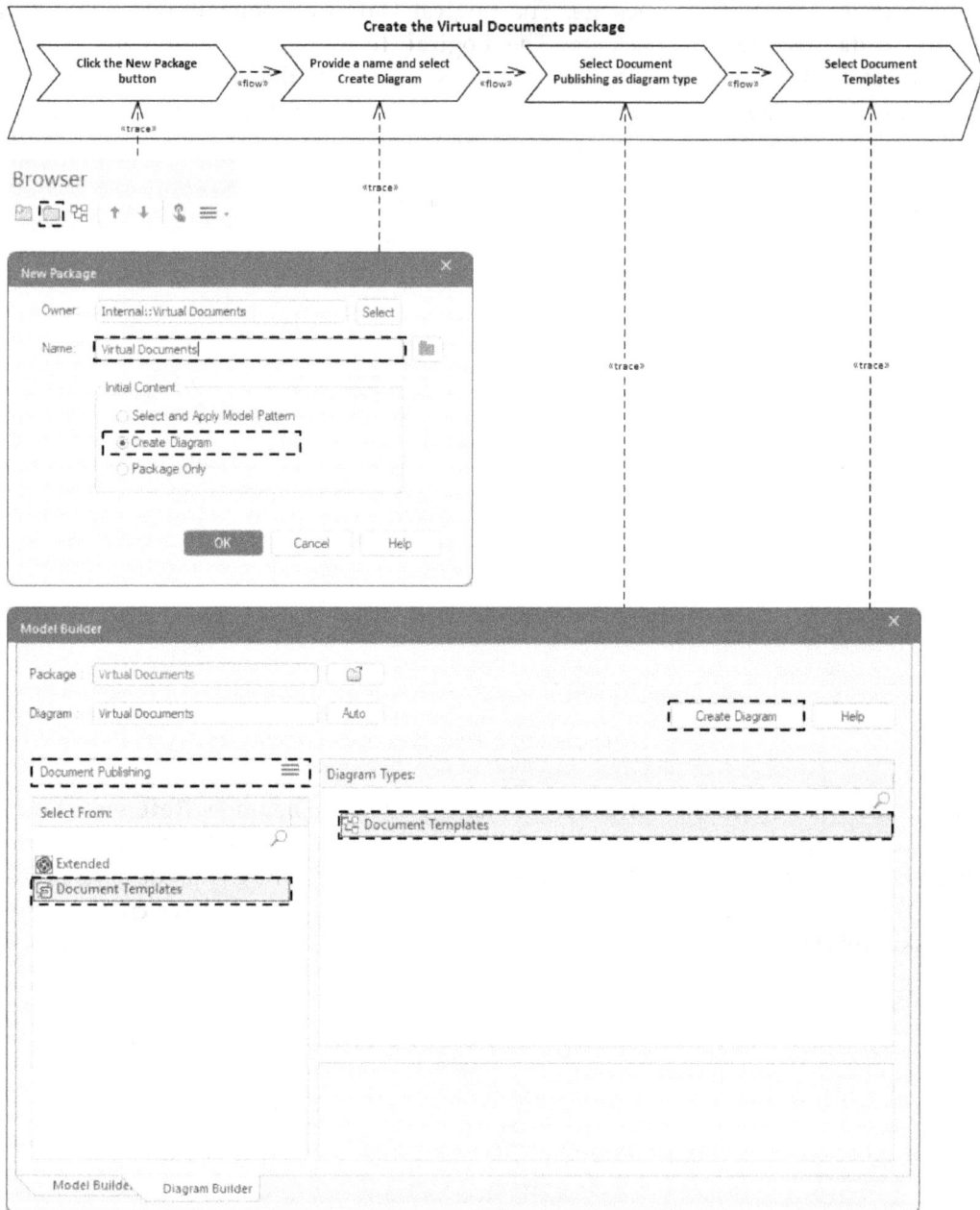

Figure 14.11: *Create the virtual documents package Process*

When you open the virtual documents package for the first time, an empty diagram will be opened. This is the diagram that will contain a list of all the virtual documents that we have in the repository. The toolbox that is associated with the diagram is a special toolbox that contains elements for creating virtual documents.

Since the document generator works at the package level, we must create a new **Report Package**, open it, and add a **Model Document** for each section in the virtual document template. To create a new virtual document, follow the Process in *Figure 14.12*:

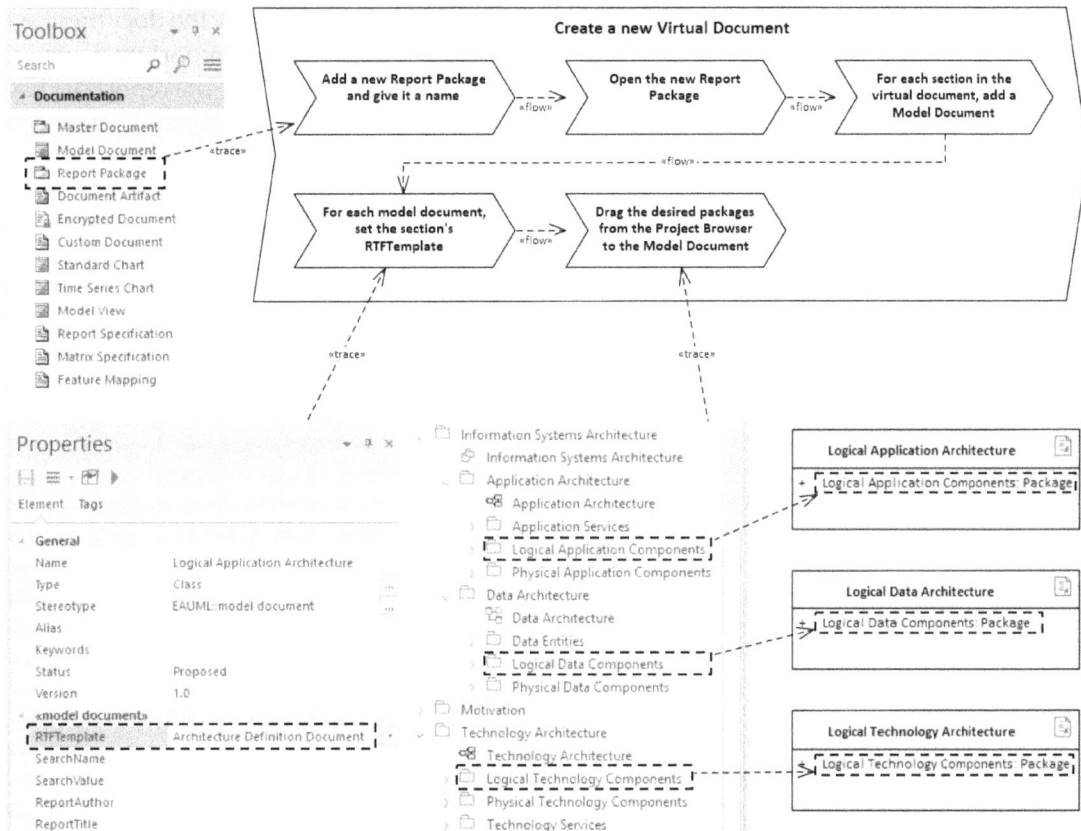

Figure 14.12: Create a new virtual document Process

In our IT logical architecture document example, we used three **Model Document** elements, one for each architecture layer. After that, from the **Project Browser**, we drag the package that has the content that we need, and we drop it on the model document element. Once we release the mouse, a new attribute will be created in the model document element, and the name of the attribute will be the same as the name of the source package.

We have the choice of either creating a new model document element for each section and adding a single source package to each model document or having a single model document and adding all the desired packages to it as attributes. In both cases, the attributes of the model documents will form the H1 heading level in the target document.

We prefer having a model document element for each package content because a virtual document can be composed of content from different architecture layers, and we may have a need to create each section using a different document template. We have the flexibility to do that by assigning a different document template type to each model document by selecting the desired template from the **RTFTemplate** property on the document model.

When you create all the needed document models in the virtual document, select the packages to include, and assign the different RTF templates to each document model, the document will be ready to be generated. *Figure 14.13* shows the steps for publishing the report package and generating the document. We need to set a few properties that are related to the report package element, such as the author's name, report title, report name, report version, and some other optional values. Set these values, select the report package element in the **Project Browser**, and launch the document generator the same way that we used to generate simple documents.

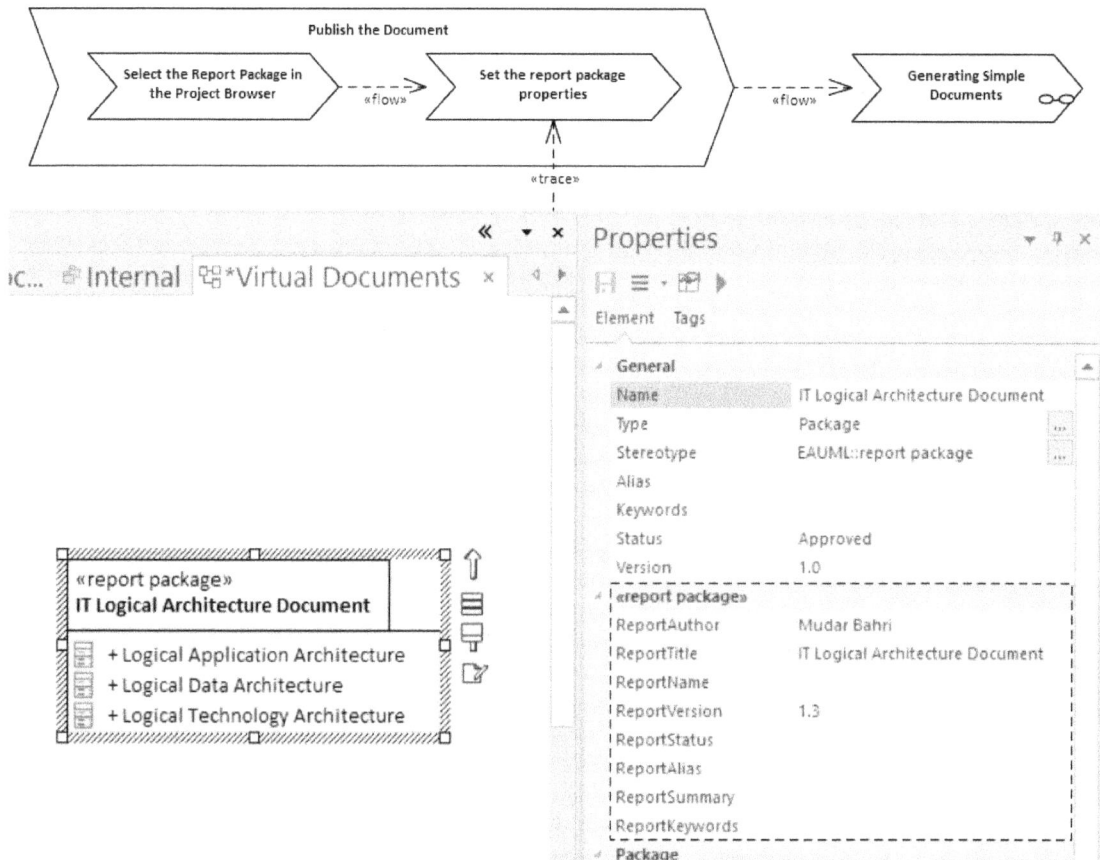

Figure 14.13: Publish the report package Process

Notice that because we are linking to **Generating Simple Documents**, which is the Process that we modeled in *Figure 14.4*, we placed the Process outside the boundary of **Publish the Document** Process because it is an external Process. In other words, *Figure 14.13* redirects the flow to *Figure 14.4*, which is another beautiful thing when having a repository.

Notice that the generated document may contain empty or unneeded sections, but unfortunately, the document generator is not perfect in that manner. You can read more about virtual documents and how to customize them in Sparx EA; however, unfortunately, a machine-generated document will never be like a human-written document. Nevertheless, you can always try to fine-tune your work. More information on virtual documents can be found at **https://sparxsystems.com/enterprise_architect_user_guide/17.1/model_publishing/ virtualdocuments.html.**

Generated documents are very helpful for sharing content with users who are not familiar with Sparx EA or do not have a license to use it. Although it has two disadvantages, the first is that documents do not provide navigation between diagrams, and the second is that large diagrams will be shrunk in size to fit the available space on a document page, which may limit their readability. Therefore, Sparx EA provides the ability to publish content from the repository as web content, and this will be our next topic to explore.

Publishing web content

Publishing web content is another functionality to convert EA content from Sparx EA into a format that can be accessed and consumed by users with no experience with the tool or who have no license to use it. One way is to use the built-in standard HTML report publisher, and the other way is to use *Prolaborate*. Prolaborate is a tool that is external to Sparx EA and requires a separate license. Using Prolaborate provides more flexibility in how to show and share the content; therefore, it is a good investment if you have a repository that is used on a large scale in the organization. However, it is a separate tool, hence it will not be covered in this book at all, but we highly recommend that you read about it due to its high value.

In *Figure 14.14*, we identified the two subfunctions that make up the **Publishing Web Content** Function, and **Using Prolaborate** is marked as part of the **To Be** state because it is currently not available, but it is in the plan to become available soon:

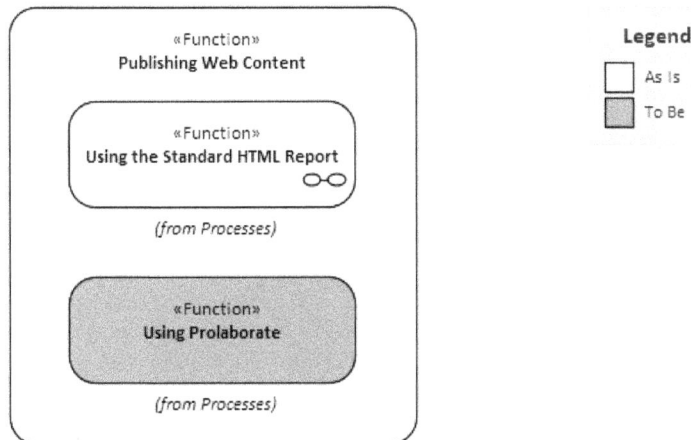

Figure 14.14: *Publishing Web Content Function*

Using the Standard HTML Report Function is realized by three Processes, as depicted in *Figure 14.15*:

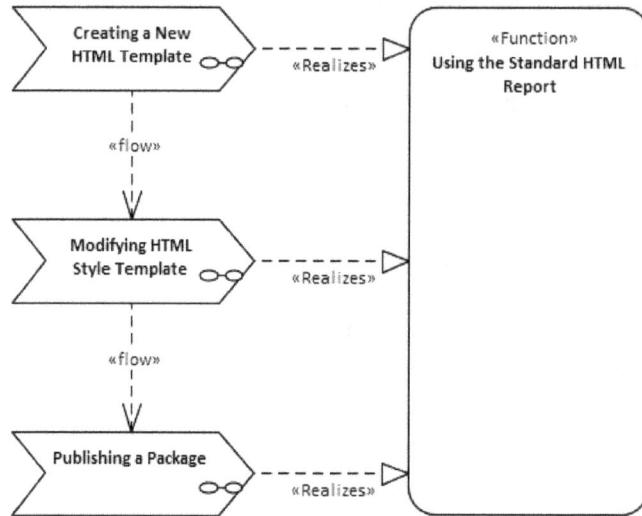

Figure 14.15: *Using the Standard HTML Report Process*

Each of the listed Processes will be detailed further in the following subsections, starting from the end with the **Publishing a Package** Process.

Publishing a package

Publishing packages using the standard HTML publisher works at the package level, like publishing documents, which we covered in the previous section. It works on regular packages and packages that contain virtual documents as well. We will start with one of the default templates that are built in Sparx EA, and once we understand how it works, we will learn how to create a new template and customize it.

The first step is to select the package to publish. Once the package is selected, press Shift+F8, provide a title and a destination folder, select the style, then click the **Generate** button. *Figure 14.16* models the Process:

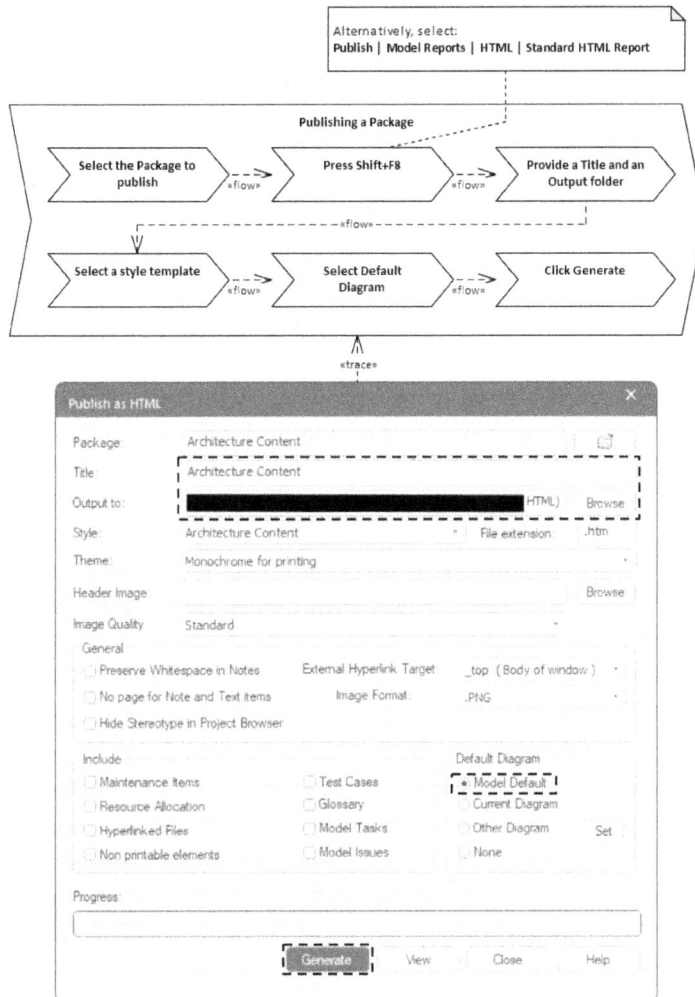

Alternatively, select:
Publish | Model Reports | HTML | Standard HTML Report

Publishing a Package

Select the Package to publish «flow» → Press Shift+F8 «flow» → Provide a Title and an Output folder

«flow»

Select a style template «flow» → Select Default Diagram «flow» → Click Generate

«trace»

Publish as HTML

Package	Architecture Content
Title	Architecture Content
Output to:	███████████████████ HTML) Browse
Style	Architecture Content File extension .htm
Theme	Monochrome for printing
Header Image	Browse
Image Quality	Standard

General
- Preserve Whitespace in Notes
- No page for Note and Text items
- Hide Stereotype in Project Browser

External Hyperlink Target _top (Body of window)
Image Format: .PNG

Include
- Maintenance Items
- Resource Allocation
- Hyperlinked Files
- Non printable elements

- Test Cases
- Glossary
- Model Tasks
- Model Issues

Default Diagram
- Model Default
- Current Diagram
- Other Diagram Set
- None

Progress:

Generate View Close Help

Figure 14.16: Publish the Package Process

Let us look at a few important things in the dialog box's fields. The output of the HTML generator is not a single file, but many HTML files, images, and folders nested inside folders. Therefore, when you provide a value in the **Output to** field, make sure that you provide a new folder, or else the HTML content will be mixed with other content in the target location. If you are using the HTML generator for the first time, the **Style** list will most probably be empty except for the **<default>** style, so select it, and we will learn how to create customized styles in the following subsection.

The **Theme** allows you to select the theme to use for the published content. It can be the same theme that is used in the repository, or it can be a different one. The **Header Image** field is to provide a path for an image to appear on the header of every page. By default, the logo of Sparx EA will appear in the page header; however, if you want a different image, such as the company's logo, to appear here, you must provide a path to the image. The image must be small, preferably less than 50 pixels in height, or else it will span beyond the header area to cover other parts of the page as well, as the publisher will not automatically resize it to fit.

The **Default Diagram** options tell the HTML generator which diagram will be set as the home diagram of the web content. You can select the Model Default option to open the default model diagram. Refer to the *Designing different views* section in *Chapter 13, Repository Management Processes*, to learn how to set a default model diagram. If you prefer the web content to start from a different diagram, select the **Other Diagram** option and select the desired diagram.

You can accept the default values for the other fields in the dialog and generate the report by clicking on the **Generate** button. Once you are prompted that the generation is complete, click **View** to view the content in the default web browser. Another way to view the content is to find the folder where the web content is generated and open the **Index.htm** file. *Figure 14.17* shows a sample from the published HTML content:

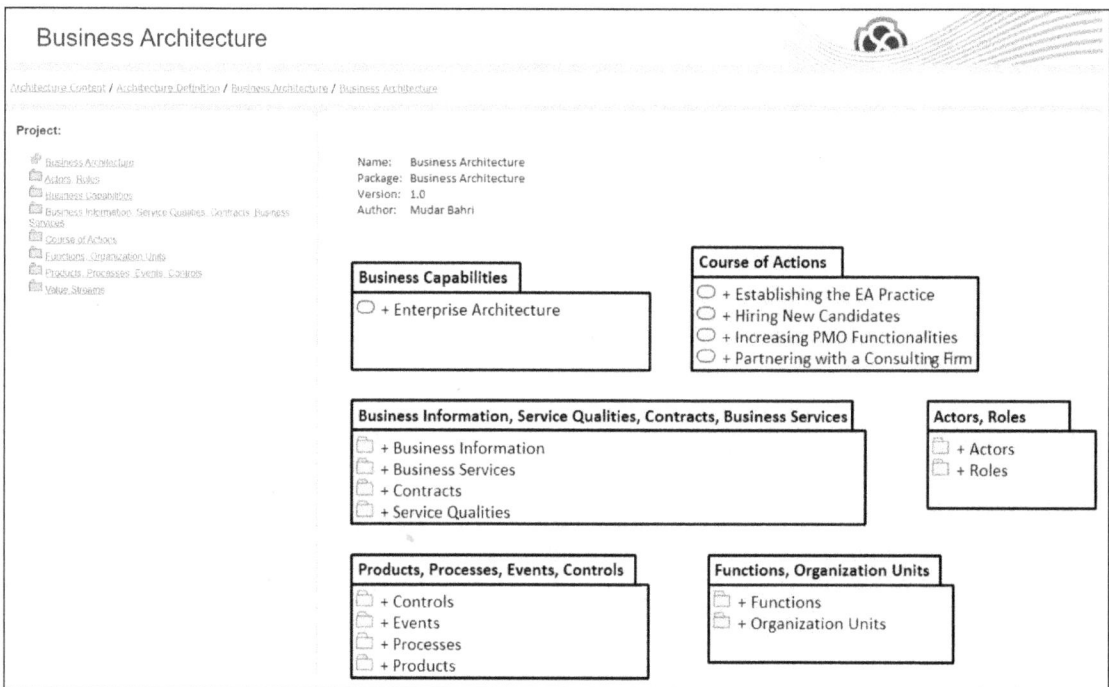

Figure 14.17: *Published HTML content*

An important rule to remember when selecting a package to publish: the HTML generator will generate only the diagrams that are contained within the selected package and its subpackages. This sounds obvious; however, the problem occurs when one diagram contains a link to another diagram that is out of the selected package. That second diagram will not be included in the published HTML content, and clicking on the link on the first diagram will open an empty page even though there is a diagram in the repository.

To avoid this problem, publishing the entire repository every time is the solution. However, with a large repository in a large organization, this will be a serious issue and a job that can only be run overnight or over the weekend to avoid slowing down or locking users. This approach will keep your HTML content out of synchronization as well. If this became a serious problem for you and for your users, the best solution is to use a specialized EA publishing tool that works with Sparx EA, such as Prolaborate; however, that is an investment in time, money, and people. The HTML publisher is an out-of-the-box solution that is included within your Sparx EA license, so you need to plan and decide based on your workplace circumstances and users' requirements.

As you can see, the page starts with a large title at the top, followed by navigation breadcrumbs, then there is the project navigation tree on the left, and the page content on the right. This content is closer to how the repository is structured in Sparx EA than the documents are. Navigate through the content and take notes of what needs to be changed or enhanced because the next subsection will explain how to customize the default style HTML template.

Creating a new HTML template

In some cases, what we get from the default HTML generator may not look the way you like it to appear to enterprise viewers. Luckily, Sparx EA provides a way to create new HTML templates and customize them as desired. The Process for creating a new template is modeled in *Figure 14.18*:

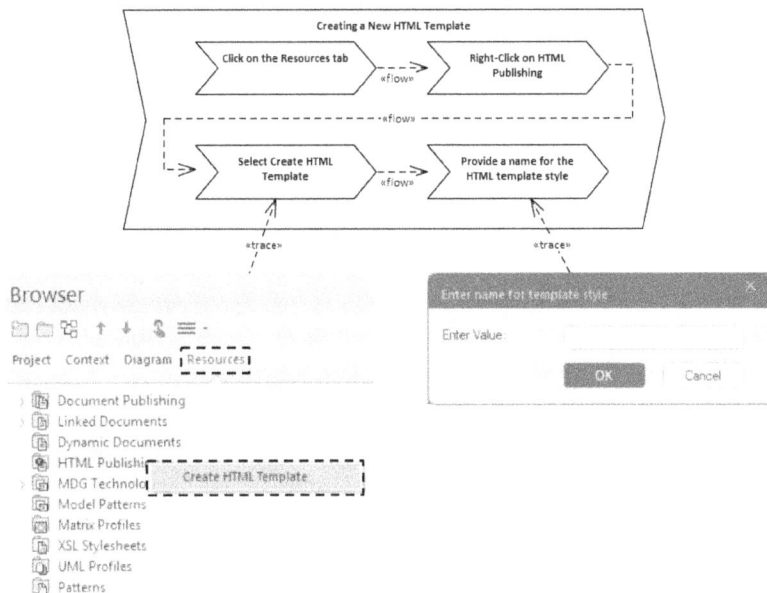

Figure 14.18: Create a new HTML Template Process

When you enter a name for the template and click **OK**, the HTML editor will open automatically to allow you to modify the HTML style template, so let us see how.

Modifying HTML style template

The ease or difficulty of understanding how the HTML editor works depends on your familiarity with HTML. If you have edited any HTML code before and have a basic understanding of stylesheets and the structure of the HTML tags, you will find the editor very easy to use and understand. If you have never used HTML before, then do not worry, there is nothing that you cannot learn. The good news is that the editor can restore the original code no matter how many changes are made to it, by clicking the **Get Default** button. *Figure 14.19* shows the Process for modifying an HTML template with a screenshot of the **HTML and CSS Style Editor**:

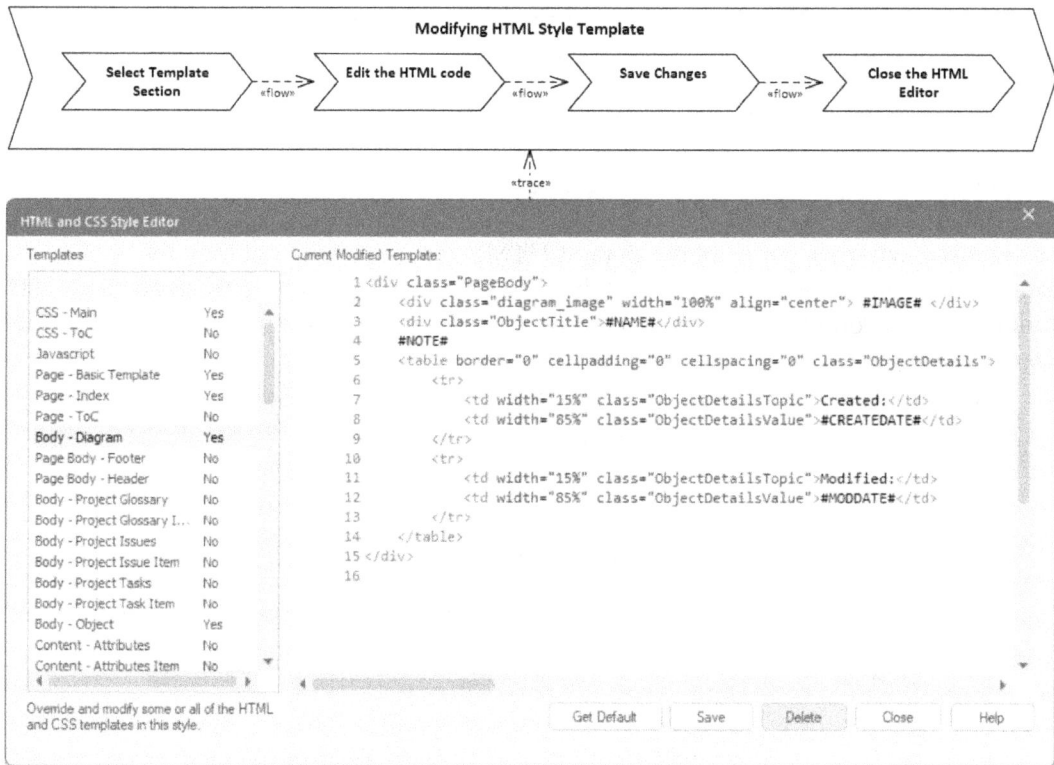

Figure 14.19: Modify HTML Style Template Process

On the left side of the dialog, there is a list of templates, one for each type of content. The **CSS – Main** section contains the general stylesheet that is applied to the entire published web content. The **Page – Basic Template** contains the tags that allow the customization of general page sections like the page title, the breadcrumbs section, and the project browser. The **Body – Diagram** section contains tags that allow the customization of the body of a page that contains a diagram. A modified section will show the word **Yes** next to its name, under the Modified column, so you can easily identify the sections that have been modified.

In the provided example, we modified the **Body – Diagram** section to a simpler view. We removed some of the sections that we do not need and reorganized some others. The text that appears between two hash symbols, such as `#NOTE#` is known as an **HTML Template Fragment**, and it indicates a dynamic field that will be replaced by a value after publishing the content. The `#NAME#` hash tag will show the diagram's name, `#IMAGE#` will show the diagram itself, and `#NOTE#` tag will be replaced with the value of the diagram's note.

The text that appears without the hash symbols is static text and will be displayed as it is. The interpretation of the HTML code that is in *Figure 14.19* is:

- Create a division and apply the `PageBody` style to it (can be found and modified in the **CSS – Main** stylesheet).

- Inside the `PageBody` division, create a new division, and use the `diagram_image` style to display the value of the `#IMAGE#` field, which is the diagram image itself.

- Under the image, create a new division, and use the `ObjectTitle` style to display the value of the `#NAME#` field, which contains the diagram name, followed by the static label **diagram**.

- Under the title, create a new division, use the `BODY` style to display the value of the `#NOTE#` field of the diagram.

- Under the note, create a table, use the `ObjectDetails` style.

- On the first row, show the static label `Created:` followed by the value of `#CREATEDATE#` field.

- On the second row, show the label `Modified:` followed by the value of `#MODDATE#` field.

Customizing templates is fun and makes the published web content more localized to your needs; however, it can also be time-consuming and takes a good investment of time and money, so you should always verify if customizations are really required or just good to have. The decision is, as always, up to you and to the needs and requirements of your enterprise. To read more about it, click the **Help** button in the HTML editor's dialog box, which will provide you with complete guidance on how to properly create an HTML style template, and here is the link to it if you are reading an online version of this book: **https://sparxsystems.com/ enterprise_architect_user_guide/17.1/model_publishing/webtemplate.html**.

Conclusion

We started this book with a very simple MDG that allowed us to build simple artifacts. We kept developing and advancing the MDG, which allowed us to build a collection of interconnected artifacts that form our Sparx EA repository. This chapter is the last in this book, and in this chapter, we learned how to publish the content that we built and will keep building in the EA repository.

The EA repository is the primary tangible product of the enterprise architecture office, so having more people using it and accessing its content is a sign of success and trust, which is a goal that must always be set.

Points to remember

- Publishing documents converts content from Sparx EA into a format that can be opened and read by a word Processor.

- Publishing web content converts content from Sparx EA into HTML content that can be accessed and viewed using a web browser.

- When publishing a document or HTML content, the package to be published must be the one selected in the Project Browser.

- F8 is a shortcut to launch the document publisher, and *Shift+F8* is a shortcut to launch the HTML publisher.

- Customizing templates requires investment in time and effort, so plan properly and get the right approval for doing this task, just like anything else you do in a project.

- You need to have a basic knowledge of HTML to properly build and customize HTML templates, but it is not difficult to learn at all.

Key terms

- **Virtual documents**: These are packages that virtually combine packages from different locations from the repository in one virtual place.

- **Publishing web content**: The Process that converts content from Sparx EA into HTML content that can be accessed and viewed using a web browser is called as publishing web content.

Join our Discord space

Join our Discord workspace for latest updates, offers, tech happenings around the world, new releases, and sessions with the authors:

https://discord.bpbonline.com

Index

www.ingramcontent.com/pod-product-compliance
Lightning Source LLC
Chambersburg PA
CBHW061759210326
41599CB00034B/6817